STUDENT PERSONNEL WORK
IN GENERAL EDUCATION

Student Personnel
Work in
General Education

A HUMANISTIC APPROACH

Edited by

HAROLD A. MOSES

CHARLES C THOMAS · PUBLISHER
Springfield · Illinois · U.S.A.

Published and Distributed Throughout the World by
CHARLES C THOMAS • PUBLISHER
Bannerstone House
301-327 East Lawrence Avenue, Springfield, Illinois, U.S.A.

©*1974, by* CHARLES C THOMAS • PUBLISHER
ISBN 0-398-03128-2
Library of Congress Catalog Card Number: 74 577

Printed in the United States of America
I-1

Library of Congress Cataloging in Publication Data

Moses, Harold A.
    Student personnel work in general education.

    1. Personnel service in education. I. Title.
LB1027.5.M67   371.2'02   74-577
ISBN 0-398-03128-2

To the memory of our dear
friend and colleague
Professor Wilfred L. Shoemaker

CONTRIBUTORS

Robert E. Boyd, Ph.D.: Director of Pupil Personnel, U46 School District, Elgin, Illinois.

John F. Eibl, Ed.D.: Associate Professor of Human Development and Counseling Psychology, Sangamon State University.

Henry R. Kaczkowski, Ph.D.: Associate Professor of Educational Psychology, University of Illinois at Urbana-Champaign.

Harold A. Moses, Ed.D.: Associate Professor of Educational Psychology, University of Illinois at Urbana-Champaign.

James J. Pancrazio, Ed.D.: Associate Professor of Human Development, and Counseling Psychology, Sangamon State University.

Cecil H. Patterson, Ph.D.: Professor of Educational Psychology, University of Illinois at Urbana-Champaign.

M. Jean Phillips, Ph.D.: Associate Professor of Educational Psychology, University of Illinois at Urbana-Champaign.

Joseph S. Zaccaria, Ed.D.: Professor of Educational Psychology, University of Illinois at Urbana-Champaign.

PREFACE

Education has traditionally been viewed as one of the major institutions for improving the standard of living in our society. Certainly, no one can dispute the fact that education has been successful in developing the technical expertise which in turn has produced the growing tide of material goods intended to improve our ever-increasing demand for a higher standard of living. Without a doubt, education has been successful in helping to raise our standard of living to the highest in the world.

By contrast, however, Americans have been largely unsuccessful in improving the quality of their lives. All around us are indicators such as mental illness and high divorce and crime rates, coupled with a nagging suspicion that somehow our enormously successful, technologically-oriented society is not a satisfied, happy, peaceful one.

Education has invested enormous resources in curriculum development and educational technology in order to increase the academic competence of students. As is the case in our culture at large, however, relatively few resources have been diverted toward the development of people as people. Student personnel work is the major effort in the school which focuses upon the personal needs of students. To date, the major emphasis in student personnel work has been that of providing a "constellation of services" to students. It is our belief (and there is considerable evidence to support this view) that the offering of sophisticated psychological services by highly trained experts such as counselors, psychologists, and social workers has drastically fallen short of the expected outcomes.

This is the case, we believe, because of an emphasis placed mistakenly upon the quality of the services provided rather than upon the goals and feelings of the students, the quality of the relationship between educational staff and students, and the relevance of the total educational process for the present and future lives of the staff and students. Thus, we offer an emerging point of view and an approach to student personnel work predicated upon such recent educational innovations as humanistic education, confluent education, open education, developmental guidance, differential staffing, systems therapy, and education for psychological maturity.

This book is intended for administrators, teachers, student personnel workers and other persons involved in or concerned about the growing alienation of staff and students from the ongoing educational process. The book emphasizes various aspects of student personnel work as it relates to the general educational process. It also describes a humanistic approach to human relations in the school. Student personnel work is presented as an integral aspect of a total educational process whose aim is that of facilitating the actualization of the latent potential in all members of the educational system.

CONTENTS

STUDENT PERSONNEL WORK
IN GENERAL EDUCATION

CHAPTER I

THE NATURE OF EDUCATION AND THE CONDITIONS FOR PERSONAL DEVELOPMENT

C. H. PATTERSON

The Nature of Education

EDUCATION HAS BEEN UNDER SEVERE and constant attack since the Russians launched the first space vehicle in 1957. The self-concept of America as the leader in science and technology was threatened, and the public education system became the scapegoat. Criticism has continued from many sources since then.

The first wave of the attack focused on the deficiencies in the academic curriculum. Demands were made for a more rigorous and a more scientifically oriented curriculum. "Soft subjects" and educational "frills" were ridiculed. The criticisms were not, of course, new. The same charges had been made only a few years earlier by both Bestor and Hutchins.[1] These critics were representative of the so-called "essentialist" philosophy of education which would limit the function of the school to the development of the intellect. From this point of view the personal and social development of the individual is not the business or responsibility of the school but should be left to the family and the church. The school is concerned with the mastery of the skills of reading, writing and arithmetic—the three R's—and the transmission of the accumulated knowledge of the human race. Subject matter is important, but emphasis is placed also on disciplined intellectual training, on developing the power to reason and to think.

[1]A. E. Bestor, *Educational Wastelands* (Urbana, University of Illinois Press, 1953). R. M. Hutchins, *The Conflict in Education in a Democratic Society* (New York, Harper & Row Publishers, Inc., 1953).

Recently, the criticisms of the school, while still insisting that the schools are not fostering the intellectual development or academic achievement of children, have focused on the psychological atmosphere of the school and the classroom.[2] These critics have questioned the appropriateness or relevance of goals and objectives of various aspects of the curriculum as well as methods of instruction. They have placed the blame for lack of achievement of students on the teachers as well as on poor physical facilities and equipment. Teacher attitudes toward disadvantaged students have been blamed for their lack of success. Teachers, it has been claimed, have expected little and have, therefore, gotten little. Blaming the teacher for all lack of achievement and academic progress in their students has been unfair; the attacks on the schools have often been less than constructive.

But some of these critics have gone beyond concern for academic achievement and pointing out what is wrong with the schools. They have suggested a different orientation to education, which is, as in the case of the early post-Sputnik critics, not entirely new. It is reminiscent of the "life-adjustment" education movement of the 1940s, which resisted the restriction of public education to the development of the intellect. It went beyond even the extension of education to preparation for making a living, through the development of vocational-technical curricula, to a concern with preparation for living. Such preparation would include attention to the social and emotional development of the student. Beyond interest in the mental and physical condition of the student, as it affects his intellectual and academic functioning, it was concerned with preparing the student for responsible citizenship.

In the opinion of some, even this is an undesirable restriction. It is overly concerned with the social, rather than the individual, implications of personal development. Before con-

[2]See, e.g. W. Glasser, *Schools Without Failure* (New York, Harper & Row Publishers, Inc., 1969); P. Goodman, *Compulsory Mis-education* (New York, Horizon Press Publishers, 1964); J. Holt, *How Children Fail* (New York, Pitman Publishing Corporation, 1964); J. Kozol, *Death at an Early Age* (Boston, Houghton Mifflin Co., 1967); G. Leonard, *Education and Ecstasy* (New York, Delacorte Press, 1968); C. E. Silberman, *The Crisis in the Classroom* (New York, Random House, Inc., 1970).

sidering the question of personal development as the responsibility of the school, let us turn briefly to a movement in education which has implications for the future of education in terms of its objectives and goals and which is related to the criticism of the essentialists.

The Development of a Technology of Education[3]

Education has been experiencing the beginnings of a technological revolution, the essence of which is the application to educational procedures of techniques developed from research in learning. Skinner has detailed this application in his book, "The Technology of Teaching." "Education," says Skinner, "must become more efficient."[4] The systematic application of knowledge about learning, particularly through programmed learning by use of teaching machines, can make learning efficient. Machines are necessary, says Skinner, because the teacher cannot effectively control the reinforcement contingencies for a class of children. "The simple fact is that, as a mere reinforcing mechanism, the teacher is out of date. . . . The contingencies of reinforcement which are most efficient in controlling the organism cannot be arranged through the personal mediation of the [teacher]. . . . Mechanical and electrical devices must be used. Personal arrangement and personal observation of the results are unthinkable."[5]

Advantages of Computer-assisted Instruction

Programmed learning through the use of teaching machines tied into computers (computer-assisted instruction, or CAI) is seen by many as the needed revolution in teaching. Its advantages have been widely proclaimed. They include the following:

1. The programming of subject matter leads to a concentration on a careful analysis of the essentials of the subjects which are to be taught and the reduction of the subject matter to the

[3]The following is based upon C. H. Patterson, "Pupil Personnel Services in the Automated School," *Personnel and Guidance Journal*, 48:101-110 (1969) and Chapter 21 in C. H. Patterson, *An Introduction to Counseling in the School* (New York, Harper & Row Publishers, Inc., 1971).

[4]B. F. Skinner, *The Technology of Teaching* (New York, Appleton-Century-Crofts, Inc., 1968), p. 29.

[5]Ibid., pp. 21-22.

basic terms, facts, concepts, laws, principles, etc. Then these must be arranged and presented in a logical, systematic, developmental order, with earlier steps leading to later stages and later material depending on earlier steps. The building of a program is not an easy matter, and the analysis of subject matter which is required is in itself a valuable process which could lead to improvement in education.

2. Programmed instruction provides *individualized* instruction, with each student being able to proceed at his own pace. "A program which is designed for the slowest student in the school system will probably not seriously delay the fast student, who will be free to progress at his own speed."[6] This individualizing of instruction, it is claimed, "will facilitate learning at a speed and depth that now seem impossible to achieve."[7] It is said that the use of computers will make the teaching machine responsive to the individual learning problems of students on the basis of data obtained and stored from use of the machines with many different students.

3. A major contribution of the principles of programmed instruction, according to Skinner, is the change of the whole atmosphere of the classroom. At present, according to Skinner, teaching is based upon the use of aversive controls.[8] Students are *punished* for *failure* to learn—no longer with corporal punishment, it is true—but verbally, with ridicule, scolding, sarcasm, criticism, detention, extra assignments, ostracism, etc. Even when rewards are used, the reward is the excusing of students from assignments. The student escapes by truancy, dropping out of school, inattention and daydreaming, or forgetting. Learning is unpleasant and is avoided by the student. Resentment toward the teacher and the school leads to defiiant behavior by the student, which leads to counterattack by the teachers, and escalates into an open, continual conflict. A vicious circle develops in which both teachers and students suffer psychologically.

In contrast to the methods of aversive control of behavior,

[6]*Ibid.,* p. 56.

[7]P. Suppes, "Plug-in instruction," *Saturday Review,* pp. 25-30 (July 23, 1966).

[8]*Op. cit.,* pp. 95-103.

programmed instruction utilizes positive reinforcement. Behavior which is desired is rewarded immediately following its occurrence. Programming begins with easy material, giving the student the experience of success as he makes the correct response, and continues by small gradations so that the experience of success can continue.

4. The new technology of teaching frees the classroom teacher from classroom routine. As printing freed the teacher from reading to students from manuscripts, so computer-assisted instruction will free the teacher from the routine of drill. The new technology is most useful in providing the drill and repeated practice necessary in such things as arithmetic skills. The teacher can devote time to preparing special lectures to be taped or filmed for repeated use, to small group discussions, to individual attention or troubleshooting with students having difficulty, or even, it is suggested by some, to counseling, though this term is not actually used in a professional sense. "The teacher," says Skinner, "may begin to function, not in lieu of a cheap machine, but through intellectual, cultural, and emotional contacts of that distinctive sort which testify to her status as a human being."[9]

The promise of the technology of education is appealing. The schools have been severely criticized for not doing a good job of teaching, for not developing the potentials of all students, for not stimulating or retaining their interest in learning, for not keeping them in school by providing an appropriate program or curriculum. Now we are told that technology can solve all these problems. Is it any wonder that there is optimism about its promises? Students will be able to learn faster and to learn more, and we need not accept any limits to the capacity of the human being to learn. Subject matter considered to be at the college level, it is suggested, can be learned by elementary school children.[10] We will even be able to teach subjects such as Russian by means of computers in schools where no one can speak or is trained in Russian.

[9]*Ibid.*, p. 27.

[10]P. Suppes, The Computer and Excellence," *Saturday Review*, pp. 46-50 (January 14, 1967).

Some Flaws in the Technology

The development of educational technology—or, in the words of a feature writer, the substitution of computers for the little red schoolhouse—would appear to be highly desirable. There are, however, some flaws in the picture which need to be recognized.[11]

1. While computer-assisted instruction is individualized, it is individualized only for the rate of progress. It is limited to a few standard programs which must be laboriously constructed. The computer does not adapt to individual problems; therefore, teachers are needed. However, it is conceivable that, not only will the number of programs increase greatly to adapt to individual needs, but that the computer can to some extent adapt to the student. Although Bushnell talks of the development of automated teaching systems modeled after the experienced teacher under student control,[12] the extent to which instruction can be individualized by machines is limited.[13] Further, writers confuse *individualization* with *personalization* of instruction and state or imply that machine instruction is personalized. This is clearly a misuse of the term, as instruction can be *personalized* only by a *person.*

2. As has been noted, computers are most useful in providing drill-and-practice systems. This is a serious limitation, since education is more than the development of computational skills, or reading skills, or writing skills. In fact, it may be argued that learning skills is not education at all, but only the preparation for education, the acquisition of the tools with which one attains an education. The importance of these tools thus is very great, and any increase in efficiency with which they can be acquired

[11]See the following for a more extensive review of some limitations and problems: R. S. Barrett, "The Computer Mentality," *Phi Delta Kappan,* 49:430-434 (1968); R. F. Bundy, "Computer-assisted Instruction—Where Are We?" *Phi Delta Kappan,* 49:424-429 (1968); D. D. Bushnell and D. W. Allen (Eds.), *The Computer in American Education* (New York, John Wiley & Sons, Inc., 1967); P. W. Jackson, *The Teacher and the Machine* (Pittsburgh, University of Pittsburgh Press, 1968); A. G. Oettinger, "The Myths of Educational Technology," *Saturday Review,* pp. 76-77 and 91 (May, 1968).

[12]D. D. Bushnell, "For each student a teacher," *Saturday review,* p. 30 (July 23, 1966).

[13]P. W. Jackson, *op. cit.,* pp. 39-43.

is welcome. However, while "training to minimal competence in well-defined skills is very important in a variety of military, industrial, and school settings, it is not the whole of what the education process should be."[14]

Thus, apparently computers are currently limited to tool subjects, but attention is being given to developing them to go beyond this level. Suppes projects two additional systems. In the tutorial system "it is possible . . . to approximate the relationship a tutor would have with a student."[15] This would approach individual instruction, but would still be limited to skill subjects, would require a very large number of programs, and would need teachers as troubleshooters. The other system, called a dialogue system, would make possible a real interaction between the student and the computer in terms of response to individual questions. Since the responses must be programmed, however, the questions must be anticipated and the computer must be programmed to recognize questions on the basis of cues or key words.

3. Although it is claimed that the student can learn more in less time with less effort by computer-assisted instruction,[16] this has not been adequately demonstrated. One must be careful about accepting the reports of subjects and even the objective results of experiments with computers. Since computer-assisted instruction places the student in a novel situation, he may be subject to the well-known Hawthorne effect, a possibility not taken into account by the researchers, perhaps because they themselves are influenced by the same effect.[17] It may well be that computer instruction is more efficient for skill subjects, but for subjects that do not need drill, fast learners may be slowed unless different programs are developed. While even the simplest program is long compared to books for the material covered, the program may be more efficient than books for imparting terms, definitions, concepts, etc. However, books may be, not only more

[14]A. G. Oettinger, *op. cit.*

[15]P. Suppes, "Plug-in Instruction," *op. cit.*

[16]B. F. Skinner, *op. cit.*, p. 54.

[17]R. F. Bundy, *op. cit.*

efficient, but necessary for advanced material, for literature, for theory, and for presenting the results of research. Computers are not likely to replace books, as feared by some publishing companies, as evidenced by their merging with electronics firms.

4. On the basis of their novelty, computers have a current appeal, but it is necessary to caution against acceptance of computer-assisted instruction as the panacea for everything that is wrong with schools and education. The basis for the operation of programmed instruction or computer-assisted instruction is, as has been noted earlier, the use of reinforcement as it functions in operant conditioning. Although the problem of effective reinforcers has not arisen so far, it certainly will. Skinner states that "the mere manipulation of the device will probably be reinforcing enough to keep the average pupil at work for a suitable period each day."[18] This apparently has been the case so far in the experimental use of computer-assisted instruction for short periods of time.

As the novelty of the machines wears off, however, it can be anticipated that other, external, reinforcers will be needed. And as the length of time at the computer increases, the difficulty of getting the student to the computer and keeping him there will increase. Skinner goes on to say that "if the material itself proves not to be sufficiently reinforcing, other reinforcers in the possession of the teacher or school may be made contingent upon the operation of the device or upon progress through a series of problems."[19] What these reinforcers will be has not been adequately considered. In experimental studies in operant conditioning in schools, jelly beans and M & M's® have been widely used. Aside from the expense involved in the widespread use of these reinforcers, there will be problems regarding their effects on students, such as parental complaints about the school spoiling the appetites of the fast students. There may also be problems regarding the ineffectiveness of such reinforcers when fast students take it easy after accumulating a surplus. Satiation is likely to occur, or perhaps the accumulation will be sold or bartered to

[18]*Op. cit.,* p. 24.
[19]*Ibid.,* pp. 24-25.

the slow students, who will then cease to work. Perhaps we will see a revival of the use of gold stars and other similar contrived reinforcers.

The problem of reinforcement on a long-term basis has not been solved. Intermittent reinforcement on a high ratio is a powerful method, as evidenced by the gambling machines at Las Vegas. But this method has not yet been used in computer-assisted instruction and presents some difficulties. If, however, it comes into use, it will become a dangerous temptation to overwork the student, since "when properly programmed" the student will not stop working until he is stopped.[20]

Thus the problem of motivation, which seems to have been so easily solved by computers, will return to plague us. The student who now creeps "like a snail unwillingly to school," will be creeping unwillingly to the computer. In order to benefit from computer-assisted instruction, the student must initiate contact with the computer. He must do something, and thus want to do something, or be made to do something. "A student, like any organism, must act before he can be reinforced. In a sense he must take the initiative."[21] There is also the problem of replacing contrived reinforcers by natural or self-reinforcers, a problem glossed over by Skinner and other enthusiasts for programmed instruction.

Skinner, in recognizing the need for the use of contrived contingencies of reinforcement, seems to be aware of this problem. Although he continues to talk about positive reinforcement and the willing attention and participation of the student, he implies, perhaps inadvertently, the need to resort to adversive control. He says, for example, in referring to the use of a teaching machine, "A child can be *made* to 'look at the sample' by *requiring* him to press the sample window at the top."[22] When the child is *forced* to interact with the machine, presumably the rewards of success gained by giving correct answers will keep him at it. However, this assumes that such success is rewarding,

[20]*Ibid.*, p. 167.
[21]*Ibid.*, p. 143.
[22]*Ibid.*, p. 78. Emphases added.

which may be true only if the student is curious, intrinsically interested in the subject matter, or has a desire to learn. Of course all children may, as has been suggested, have these characteristics before aversive treatment killed them.

5. A final characteristic of computerized instruction is that it is impersonal. It has been pointed out as an asset that no student can complain that the teacher does not like him. While the computer is fair and objective, it is not a teacher, not a person, and the interaction with the computer is not an interaction with a human. It may be true that a student does not have to be in contact with a person in order to learn, at least in order to learn what can be learned by means of computerized instruction. Nevertheless, the amount of contact the student has with a human environment is reduced by that amount of time which he spends with a computer. Possibly the computer can be programmed to simulate a human relationship or to be somewhat human, in that it reflects the humanness of the programmer. Thus computers can, when the student gives his number and first name, respond with his last name, or vice versa, and, by means of printed tape or perhaps by a recorded human voice, give the illusion of being a person. At any rate, it appears that such programming can lead the student to regard the machine as almost human. That this will be a substitute for relationships with human beings is questionable, however.

These are only a few of the many questions about computer-assisted instruction. Many of the problems are simply technical in nature and will soon be remedied or overcome. No doubt machines and programs will be perfected as a result of the tremendous amount of money and research being poured into the field. There seems to be no question but that we can look forward to the time, in twenty or thirty years, when computer-assisted instruction will be commonplace in our schools. However, I may be overoptimistic about the extensiveness of its use. Perhaps as a result of the "breakthrough complex," the proponents of technology underestimate the difficulties that are nontechnical in nature. High costs and implementation problems may slow the pace of adoption. Perhaps, as Jackson contends, changes resulting from educational technology will not be as dramatic or occur as rapidly as the headline-makers would have us believe.[23] However, as in every other sphere of our life, technology will undoubtedly eventually prevail. It has been contended that Americans are not highly creative in original scientific or philosophic discovery, but they have no peers, except perhaps now the Russians, in technology. It is claimed that education and educators are conservative and highly resistant to change, but the pressure is on for change, and the appeal of technology cannot be resisted. Acceptance may occur faster than we think and the adoption of technology will be slowed only by financial considerations. In experimental studies, students now spend from fifteen to twenty minutes a day at a computer, but Suppes estimates that in twenty or thirty years the child will be spending 30 to 40 percent of his time in school at a computer.[24] I believe this is a conservative estimate, particularly at the elementary school level. Even at higher levels the tremendous amount of information being created by the so-called information explosion will result in increasing pressures on the schools to cram more and more facts into children. Teaching *facts* is the forte of computerized instruction, as well as films, slides, recordings, and tapes, all of which are impersonal methods of instruction.

The Classroom as a Factory

The increasing use of technology in the schools has caused big business to express an interest in education. Since the production of the hardware has made education a potential big customer, many giant electronics firms, such as IBM, Xerox, RCA, Raython, and General Electric, are involved in education. Patrick Suppes, head of the Institute for Mathematical Studies in the Social Sciences at Stanford, is consultant to RCA's Instructional Systems Division and is only one of many such consultants. However, the goal of business is profits, not education, and the appeal of business to education is that of efficiency. "Mass education," it is said, "requires mass production methods."[25]

[23]*Op. cit.*, p. 1.
[24]P. Suppes, "Computer Technology and the Future of Education," *Phi Delta Kappan*, 49:420-423 (1968).
[25]W. H. Ferry, "Must We Rewrite the Constitution to Control Technology?" *Saturday Review*, pp. 50-54 (March 2, 1968).

Picture, then, the classroom of the future, with each student at a computer keyboard. You have seen pictures of this already. What does the picture remind you of? Right! A factory—a modern, clean, well-lighted factory, but a factory. The teacher is a foreman or supervisor, a troubleshooter. We read a lot about technology freeing the teacher to do other things—to humanize education, to develop personal relationships with students—but nowhere have I seen anything about when and how this is to be done. The technology of education leads to increasing attention to and concentration on the academic progress and development of the student. Wilbur H. Ferry, Vice President of the Fund for the Republic and staff member of its Center for the Study of Democratic Institutions, warns that there is danger of our schools being invaded by technology, or technication, as he calls it. For instance, an educational system can be thought of in terms like those of a factory. "Factories," he says, "are fine for producing things, but their record with people is terrible. . . . Technication, as Robert M. Hutchins observes, will 'dehumanize a process the aim of which is humanization.'" He believes that the rebellion at Berkeley was centered on "the indifference of multiversity's mechanism to the personal needs of the students," symbolized by the IBM cards the protesters wore.[26]

Skinner states that mechanical devices will not necessarily shorten the time that the teacher will be in contact with the pupil;[27] this seems difficult to believe. One questions whether the picture presented here is inevitable. With our present attitude toward technology, and with the combined acceptance and support by educators and big business executives, automation will, I believe, be widely accepted and carried to extremes. This has been the history of technology in Western civilization. Skinner admits that it may be unwisely used and may need to be contained or controlled.[28]

The Humanization of Education

The move toward teaching machines and computer-assisted instruction represents a major trend in education. In its concern

[26]*Op. cit.*, p. .
[27]*Op. cit.*, p. 27.
[28]*Op. cit.*, pp. 91, 260.

for academic or subject-matter learning, this trend continues the philosophy of essentialism. There is, however, another trend, which could be considered an extension of the life-adjustment philosophy. It goes beyond the concern for the student's psychological and emotional state simply for its relevance to cognitive learning. It goes beyond the concept of preparing people for making a living. It also avoids conceiving of life adjustment as conformity to society or a particular social system.

There is no clear designation for this approach, but it is characterized as a humanistic approach to education. It is concerned with the psychological or emotional atmosphere of the classroom and conceives of teaching as essentially a good human relationship. It goes beyond even this in not restricting its concern to cognitive learnings as a goal of education. It includes as goals the development of good attitudes and feelings; it is the education of the emotions, the fostering of adequate emotional development as a legitimate and desirable goal of education. It has been called by some *affective* education, involving more than the concern with affective techniques in education. Jackson points out that "our most pressing educational problem involves learning how to create and maintain a humane environment in our schools."[29]

The child, like the pigeon, may be led to work continuously "for long periods of time without coercion or threat, showing few signs of fatigue, nervousness, or other forms of escape."[30] The results of this over a period of time, however, can be decidedly harmful. The obvious conclusion is that we are going to have to be concerned about humanizing the education process to counteract the dehumanizing effects of the machine. The child will need respite from the machine and will need human contacts. Because the interaction of the students with each other will be restricted by machine instruction, interaction in groups will be even more important than it is now. Since the need for informal interaction will also be greater, more attention and time will have to be given to play and recreation.

It has been reiterated again and again, almost defensively,

[29]*Op. cit.,* p. 90.
[30]B. F. Skinner, *op. cit.,* p. 81.

that the machine will not replace the teacher, that it will *free* the teacher for other activities, though it is never clear what these activities are or when they are to be performed. As a matter of fact, the talk of business technicians sometimes makes no reference to a teacher, who appears superfluous to the learning process. It appears that the teacher could easily become, rather than a professional, a technician who tends machines and mediates between the machine and the student to see that they continue to interact productively; there will not be much time to do anything else. If, as has been suggested, there are fewer machines than students because of cost, the children will have to take turns and the teacher will not be available for those not at the machine. It would be interesting to speculate on the implications of this for teaching, for teachers, and for the teaching profession, but that is beyond our purpose. Jackson notes that "some authorities think that the teacher might become more, rather than less, burdened by clerical work."[31]

In spite of disclaimers, it appears that every effort is being made to have machines replace teachers. If this occurs and all courses are canned (programmed), the current complaints about standardization, about limiting of inquiry and questioning and about originality in teaching will seem trivial. Now the student can question the text or the teacher, can find flaws, can know more about something than the book or the teacher. Could this possibly exist in a program carefully created by experts and presented by a machine?

The Reaction Against Technology

Such a situation will not persist; it cannot persist. Even now we find some voices raised against the trend toward the spread of technology. We will recognize that education is more than skill training, more than the three R's, as basic as these are. Teaching machines can never provide an education; they can only foster the skills and provide the materials out of which an education may develop. The realization of this will, no doubt, prevent higher education from becoming highly mechanized. But

[31]*Op. cit.*, p. 51.

the picture painted earlier is likely to materialize in elementary, and to a great extent in secondary, education, where the inculcation of skills and the imparting of information are important.

There are those now who are concerned with the fundamental question of "the extent to which a mechanistic ideology should be allowed to permeate our view of the educational process."[32] Such voices are, however, weak and are not likely to be listened to until we experience some of the mixed blessings of technology. To raise such questions now almost amounts to heresy and lack of faith in American ingenuity; such objectors will be, and are, accused of blocking progress. The picture of the classroom as a factory may be overdone. There certainly will be periods for art and music and for some teacher-student and student-student interaction, of which even now there is often very little. The real danger of technology in education, however, lies in the fact that, while it may produce technically skilled individuals, it cannot produce free, reasoning, responsible individuals. Education, it has been said, is too important to be left to educators. Actually it has never been left to educators, since they have been controlled by the local school boards. "The use of the computer in education is too serious a business to be left to the computer mentality."[33]

The Fourth R—Human Relations

An important aspect of self-actualization is interpersonal relationships. One cannot be self-actualizing in a vacuum. Therefore, education must, as must all of society, become concerned with the development of men as citizens, as persons, as members of a community, and as members of the human race. "Where the actions of one can drastically affect the lives of others far distant, it will be crucially important that each person master the skill of feeling what others feel. This skill, more than new laws or new politics, will soon become crucial to the survival of the race."[34]

The emphasis on education of the future, then, will be upon

[32]P. W. Jackson, *op. cit.*, p. 1.
[33]R. S. Barrett, *op. cit.*
[34]G. B. Leonard, *op. cit.*, p. 127.

human relations. As Ashley Montagu has said: "Our educational institutions should be training us in the ability to love, not the three R's, or, at the college level, remedial reading, remedial writing, and remedial arithmetic."[35] Rather than human relations being of concern only to student personnel workers, it will be the focus of the curriculum. Machines and computers will have their place, and assistants, aides, or technicians will be employed to supervise the interaction of students with them. Teachers will then be concerned with the human relations aspects of the curriculum which cannot be taught or learned by machines. The teacher will be "a specialist in human behavior, whose assignment is to bring about extraordinarily complex changes in extraordinary complex material. . . . In exposition, discussion, and argumentation (written or spoken), in productive interchanges in the exploration of new areas, in ethical behavior, in the common enjoyment of literature, music, and art—here the teacher is important as a human being."[36] This is true, to some extent, at the present time, as Skinner notes, but in the coming age of educational technology, computerized instruction will crowd out or displace much of such teacher activity. When the excesses of such technology are recognized, the importance of the teacher as a person will be recognized.

Then teachers will no longer be concerned with much of what we now call subject matter; they will not need to be trained to teach the three R's. Subject matter will be presented by films, slides, recordings, audio and videotapes, etc. The teacher will no longer need to be an expert in subject matter because mechanical aids will enable him to teach more than he knows. The answer to the criticism that the teacher will feel inadequate in comparison to the experts presenting subject matter on tapes and films is that there will not be a problem if the teacher has other meaningful and satisfying functions. Teachers in special subject-matter areas, such as art and music at the elementary level and the liberal arts and sciences at the upper levels, will

[35]A. Montagu. From a speech given at the Conference of the International Institute for Euthenics, Allerton House, Monticello, Illinois (October 5, 1968).

[36]B. F. Skinner, *op. cit.,* pp. 2, 254.

teach through group discussion methods and will, of course, have to be prepared in the subject matter. The major preparation of teachers at the elementary level, however, will be in human relationships. The major subject matter of the curriculum will be the fourth R—relationships.

The Real Revolution in Education

The talk about a revolution in education refers to the rapid increase in technology which we have been outlining, but this is not really a revolution. It is simply the mechanization of current processes, the application of technology to achieve, more effectively or efficiently, it is claimed, the same goals, objectives and purposes—essentially the mastery of skills and subject matter.

A real revolution in education would consist of a change in goals and in content. I believe that such a revolution will come when we are satiated by the machine technology, when we realize, not only its inadequacies even for our present limited purposes, but also the undesirability of what might be considered its side effect—the dehumanization of man. In industry this effect has also occurred—it was pictured long ago in the Charlie Chaplin movie, "Modern Times." For a long time nothing could be done directly about this dehumanization. Attempts have been made to counteract it in industry by shortening working hours and by providing personnel services such as recreational facilities, restaurants and cafeterias, and fringe activities. It seems possible now that automation may free man from the machine as far as production of goods is concerned. Because of the very nature of the learning situation, in which the individual must be involved, however, it appears that this solution is not possible in education. We must change the whole focus and goal of the educational process.

It is probably true that we will always have to teach basic skills—the three R's—and the most efficient way may be to use computers. It will be recognized, however, that these basic skills are only a small part of education, actually only preparation for education. Although society's need for technicians will be reduced, there will still be a need for scientists. However, the

to selfish and self-centered behavior, but this is a misunderstanding of the nature of self-actualization. Since every individual lives in a society composed of other individuals, he can actualize himself only in interaction with others. Selfish, self-centered behavior would not lead to experiences which would be self-actualizing in nature. As Rogers states it, the self-actualizing person "will live with others in the maximum possible harmony, because of the rewarding character of reciprocal positive regard."[43] "We do not need to ask who will socialize him, for one of his own deepest needs is for affiliation and communication with others. As he becomes more fully himself, he will become more realistically socialized."[44] He is more mature, more socialized in terms of "the goal of social evolution," though he may not be conventional or socially adjusted in a conforming sense.

The Self-Actualizing Person

A major criticism to setting self-actualization as a goal is that it is too general and vague to be useful. The behaviorists ask for a specific, objective, or operational definition. It is necessary to give some consideration to defining or describing self-actualization so that the education criteria by which we can judge whether the objective is being achieved can be developed. While it is not possible at present to provide objective criteria and measures of them, it is in principle an attainable objective.

Some progress has been made in defining the characteristics of self-actualizing persons. Maslow has been the foremost contributor to this area.[45] Maslow adopted an accepted and sound

[43]C. R. Rogers, "A Theory of Therapy, Personality, and Interpersonal Relationships," in S. Koch, ed., *Psychology: A Study of Science. Study I. Conceptual and Systematic. Vol. 3. Formulations of the Person and the Social Context* (New York, McGraw-Hill Book Company, 1959), pp. 234-236.

[44]C. R. Rogers, "A Therapist's View of the Good Life: The Fully Functioning Person," in C. R. Rogers, *On Becoming a Person, op. cit.,* p. 194.

[45]A. H. Maslow, *Motivation and Personality,* rev. ed. (Harper & Row Publishers, Inc., 1970); A. H. Maslow, *Toward a Psychology of Being,* 2d ed. (New York, Van Nostrand Reinhold Company, 1968); A. H. Maslow, "Self-Actualizing People: A Study of Psychological Health," in C. E. Moustakas, ed., *The Self: Explorations in Personal Growth* (New York, Harper & Row, Publishers, Inc., 1956), pp. 160-194.

method in his attempt to study the nature of self-actualization. He obtained a criterion group of persons (living and dead) who were selected on the basis of a professional judgment that they were outstanding as self-actualizing persons, defined generally as people who made "the full use and exploitation of talents, capacities, potentialities, etc. Such people seem to be fulfilling themselves and to be doing the best that they are capable of doing. They are people who have developed or are developing the full stature of which they are capable."[46] These subjects were studied intensively to determine what characteristics they had in common, and those which differentiated them from ordinary or average people. Fourteen characteristics emerged.

1. MORE EFFICIENT PERCEPTION OF REALITY AND MORE COMFORTABLE RELATIONS WITH IT. This includes the detection of the phony and dishonest person, the accurate perception of what exists rather than the distortion of perception by one's needs. *Self-actualizing people are more aware of their environment,* both human and nonhuman. They are not afraid of the unknown and can tolerate the doubt, uncertainty and tentativeness accompanying the perception of the new and unfamiliar.

2. ACCEPTANCE OF SELF, OTHERS AND NATURE. Self-actualizing persons are not ashamed or guilty about their human nature, with its shortcomings, imperfections, frailties, and weaknesses; nor are they critical of these characteristics in others. *They respect and esteem themselves and others.* Moreover, *they are open, genuine, without pose or facade.* They are not, however, self-satisfied, but are concerned about discrepancies between what is and what might be or should be in themselves, others, and society.

3. SPONTANEITY. Self-actualizing persons are not hampered by convention, but they do not flout it. *They are not conformists;* neither are they anticonformist for the sake of being so. They are not externally motivated, or even goal directed; rather their

---

[46]A. H. Maslow, "Self-Actualizing People: A Study of Psychological Health," in C. E. Moustakas, ed., *The Self-Explorations in Personal Growth, op. cit.,* pp. 161-162.

motivation is the internal one of growth and development, the actualization of their selves and potentialities.

4. PROBLEM-CENTERING. Self-actualizing persons are not ego-centered, but focus on problems outside themselves. They are mission oriented, often on the basis of a *sense of responsibility, duty,* or obligation rather than of personal choice.

5. THE QUALITY OF DETACHMENT; THE NEED FOR PRIVACY. The self-actualizing *person enjoys solitude and privacy*. It is possible for him to remain unruffled and undisturbed by much which upsets others. He may even appear to others to be asocial.

6. AUTONOMY, INDEPENDENCE OF CULTURE AND ENVIRONMENT. Self-actualizing persons, though dependent on others for the satisfaction of the basic needs of love, safety, respect, and be-longingness, "are not dependent for their main satisfactions on the real world, or other people or culture or means-to-ends, or in general, on extrinsic satisfactions. *Rather they are dependent for their own development and continued growth upon their own potentialities and latent resources.*"[47]

7. CONTINUED FRESHNESS OF APPRECIATION. Self-actualizing persons repeatedly (though not continuously) *experience awe, pleasure, and wonder in their everyday world.*

8. THE "MYSTIC EXPERIENCE," THE "OCEANIC FEELING." In varying degrees and with varying frequencies, *self-actualizing persons have experiences of ecstasy, awe, and wonder*, with feelings of limitless horizons opening up, followed by the conviction that the experience was important and valuable and had a carry over into daily life.

9. GEMEINSCHAFTSGEFUHL. *Self-actualizing persons have a deep feeling of empathy, sympathy or compassion for human beings in general.* This feeling is in a sense unconditional, in that it exists along with the recognition of the existence of negative qualities in others which provoke occasional anger, impatience and disgust.

10. INTERPERSONAL RELATIONS. *Self-actualizing people have deep interpersonal relations with others.* They are selective, how-

[47] *Ibid.*, p. 176.

ever, and the circle of friends is small, usually consisting mainly of other self-actualizing persons. They attract others to them as admirers or disciples.

11. THE DEMOCRATIC CHARACTER STRUCTURE. *The self-actualizing person does not discriminate* on the basis of class, education, race or color. He is humble in his recognition of what he knows in comparison with what could be known and is ready to learn from anyone. He *respects everyone* as potential contributors to his knowledge, but also just because they are human beings.

12. MEANS AND ENDS. Self-actualizing persons are highly ethical. *They clearly distinguish between means and ends and subordinate means to ends.*

13. PHILOSOPHICAL, UNHOSTILE SENSE OF HUMOR. Although all the self-actualizing subjects studied by Maslow had a sense of humor, it was not of the ordinary type. Their sense of humor was the spontaneous, thoughtful type, intrinsic to the situation. Their humor did not involve hostility, superiority, or sarcasm.

14. CREATIVENESS. All Maslow's subjects were judged to be creative, each in his own way. The creativity involved here is not the special-talent creativeness. It is a creativeness potentially inherent in everyone, but usually suffocated by acculturation. It is *a fresh, naive, direct way of looking at things.*

These characteristics give a description of the kind of person who would not only be desirable in our society, but who would be functioning at a high level in terms of utilizing his potentials and experiencing personal satisfaction. Facilitating the development of such persons would, therefore, be the goal of the educational process.

Conditions for Facilitating Personal Development

If the school is to be responsible for facilitating the development of self-actualizing persons, it is necessary to consider the conditions under which such persons develop. It is apparent, from the characteristics of self-actualizing persons, that the inculcation of standard subject matter is not adequate. The mastery of certain academic skills may be necessary, but not sufficient for such an objective or outcome.

The field of counseling and psychotherapy has been concerned with the goals of counseling and psychotherapy. While on the surface there may appear to be little agreement, particularly in terms of immediate and specific goals, when one looks at the more general or ultimate goals, the kind of person who is projected as the result of successful counseling or psychotherapy is very similar to Maslow's description of the self-actualizing person.

The conditions of counseling or psychotherapy then may be viewed as the conditions for the development of self-actualizing persons. If these conditions are effective with so-called disturbed or "abnormal" persons, they should also be effective with average or "normal" persons. Recent research in counseling or psychotherapy has confirmed the existence of several conditions, although referred to by different terminology, which have been aspects of every major counseling or psychotherapy theory. The three basic conditions which have been identified are empathic understanding, respect, and genuineness.

1. EMPATHIC UNDERSTANDING. Empathic understanding means an understanding from an internal frame of reference; it is the understanding achieved by putting oneself in another's place in order to see him and the world as much as possible as he does. It is expressed perhaps as well as possible in Roger's definition, "an accurate, empathic understanding of the (other's) world as seen from the inside. To sense the (other's) private world as if it were your own, but without losing the 'as if' quality —this is empathy. . . ."[48] There seem to be no synonyms for empathic understanding. Unlike other languages, English does not have two words to designate the two kinds of understanding or knowing—knowing about, and the knowing which is empathy. Some American Indian languages apparently had this concept, indicated by the phrase "walk in his moccasins." The theme of the novel *To Kill a Mockingbird* is dependent on the concept of empathy. At one point the lawyer Atticus Finch, trying to help his children understand people's behavior, said: "if . . . you can learn a simple trick . . . you'll get along a lot better with all kinds of folks. You never really understand a person until you consider things from his point of view—until you climb into his skin

[48]C. R. Rogers, *On becoming a Person, op. cit.,* p. 284.

and walk around in it."[49] However, it is not simple, nor is it a trick.

2. RESPECT OR NONPOSSESSIVE WARMTH. The second condition is a deep respect for the student, an acceptance of him as a person of worth, as he is, without judgment or condemnation, criticism, ridicule, or depreciation. It is a respect which includes a warmth and liking for the student as a person, with all his faults, deficiencies, or undesirable or unacceptable behavior. It is a deep interest and concern for him and his development. It is the warmth of a parent who may still reject, or not accept, particular behaviors of the child. Thus one may accept and respect a person as a person, but still not agree with or condone all of his behaviors.

3. GENUINENESS. Genuineness is the congruence or integration of the therapist in the relationship. It means that within the relationship he is freely and deeply himself, with his actual experience accurately represented by his awareness of himself."[50] The therapist is not thinking or feeling one thing and saying another. He is open, honest, sincere. He is freely and deeply himself, without a facade, and he is not playing a role. He is, as the existentialists term it, authentic, or, to use Jourard's term, transparent.[51]

It has been demonstrated that these three conditions relate to positive outcomes in counseling or psychotherapy. They are complex, but future research may succeed in breaking them up into more specific components. No doubt other conditions are part of the total relationship which constitutes the condition for facilitating personal development.

It is important to note that the conditions which have been described above are also *characteristics of the self-actualizing person*. It thus appears that if one wishes to facilitate the development of self-actualizing persons, one must be a self-actualizing person. The conditions operate in a complex manner, but one aspect of the nature of the influence is called *modeling*. One

[49]Harper Lee, *To Kill a Mockingbird* (New York, Popular Library, 1962) p. 24.
[50]C. R. Rogers, "The Necessary and Sufficient Conditions of Therapeutic Personality Change," *Journal of Consulting Psychology*, 21:95-103 (1957).
[51]S. Jourard, *The transparent self* (New York, Van Nostrand Reinhold Company, 1964).

becomes like those with whom he associates or engages in close interpersonal relationships.

A relationship which consists of, or includes, conditions for developing self-actualizing persons is nonthreatening. It provides an atmosphere in which learning is facilitated with a minimum of anxiety and without the restrictions and inhibitions related to threat. It is well known that threat interferes with or disrupts learning, that the threatened person is overanxious, afraid, and constricted and he does not engage in the exploration which is necessary for problem solving. The result of this constriction is rigid, repetitive, stereotyped or compulsive behavior which is inadequate for solving problems or for learning.

A self-actualizing relationship is conducive to or facilitative of personal development. The person is free to change, to grow, because he is not threatened and does not have to focus on defending himself. The aspect of personal growth will be considered in the chapters on the counseling relationship.

Self-actualizing conditions are not new, nor would there appear to be anything revolutionary about them. Yet their consistent application in interpersonal relations might well be revolutionary. While they have been known for centuries and their effectiveness has been demonstrated by over 2,000 years of experience, experience is discounted by the provincialism of western science. A one-hour experiment in a laboratory, from which actually little, if any, generalization to everyday life may be possible, is given more weight than the thousands of years of experience of the human race.

If one considers the totality of the facilitative conditions—understanding, empathy, concern, liking, prizing, acceptance, respect, warmth, sincerity, openness, authenticity, transparency, intensity, intimacy, specificity—they add up to a concept which has long been recognized as basic to good human relationships. The Greeks had a word for it, *agape.* St. Paul called it love. His letter to the Corinthians (I Cor. 13: 4-8) might be rewritten in the language of these conditions. Love is the therapy for all disorders of the human mind and spirit and of disturbed interpersonal relationships. We do not need to wait for a breakthrough, for the discovery of new methods or techniques. Good human relationships provide the answer to all our social and psychological problems. A student (Caroline Pomodoro) stated the situation well: "No matter how great the strides of future advancement, it is highly unlikely that there ever will be discovered a synthetic substitute for social feeling. The experiencing of positive relationships is the prerequisite for healthy adjustment and growth." Bettelheim speaks of the "unique gratifying experience that only a genuine human relationship can offer." The condition for self-actualizing persons is love.[52]

The need for love, for good human relationships, is not new. Its importance for self-actualization is recognized in folklore and popular music, as witness the titles and lyrics of popular songs, "What the World Needs Now is Love, Sweet Love," and "You're Nobody Until Somebody Loves You."

Summary

Education has been under attack for many years for its failure to produce people who have mastered the fundamental educational skills (reading, writing and arithmetic) or who have not reached a level of academic achievement in other subject matter areas which parents and critics have felt is reasonable. These criticisms have led to focusing upon better and more efficient ways of teaching subject matter. Curriculum reform and the use of automated instruction has been seen by many to be the answer to this problem.

More recently another group of critics has become concerned with the lack of consideration for students as human beings. Their concern has gone beyond the earlier interest in the mental health or personal adjustment of the student as a condition for effective academic learning. While accepting the truth that academic learning is inhibited in classrooms where there is little, if any, interest in the student as an individual,[54] the new critics have become interested in personal development, in

[52]B. Bettelheim, *Love is Not Enough* (New York: Free Press, 1950), p. 28.

[54]See J. Coleman, *Equality of Educational Opportunity* (Washington, D.C., Department of Health, Education and Welfare, 1966), for evidence that academic achievement is related to elements in the student's personal adjustment such as self-concept, sense of control over one's fate, and interest in the school.

addition to or even apart from academic achievement, as a goal of education.

The function of the school, conceived as the fostering or facilitating of personal development, requires understanding the conditions necessary for the development of fully functioning or self-actualizing persons and providing these conditions in the operation of our schools—in the classroom, in administration, and in student services.

In this chapter, drawing upon experiences and research in the field of counseling and psychotherapy, the nature of the self-actualizing person and the basic conditions necessary to his development have been described. The implementation of these conditions in our schools will be considered in the next chapter.

The school must become involved in teaching, in addition to providing, the conditions of good or facilitative interpersonal relationships. It must be concerned with affective education, the development of adequate feelings, attitudes and human values. A necessary and basic aspect of affective education is the provision of the conditions which facilitate personal development and which incorporate the feelings, attitudes, and values which students should learn. Those who teach our children and who are involved in their education must be self-actualizing persons themselves; in providing the conditions for personal development, they are the models for the students. Although we have begun to recognize, through research and experience, that modeling is perhaps the most powerful and effective method of teaching and learning, it is desirable, if not necessary, to incorporate direct instruction in human relations into the curriculum. There are some suggested readings which deal with this aspect of education.

SUGGESTED READINGS

Borton, T., *Reach, Touch, Teach*. New York, McGraw-Hill, 1969.

Jones, R. M., *Fantasy and Feeling in Education*. New York, New York University Press, 1968. (Paperback edition by Harper & Row Publishers, Inc.)

Lyon, H. C., *Learning to Feel and Feeling to Learn — Humanistic Education for the Whole Man*. Columbus, Charles E. Merrill, 1971.

Rogers, C. R., *Freedom to Learn*. Columbus, Ohio, Charles E. Merrill Publishing Company, 1969.

CHAPTER II

THE ORGANIZATION OF PERSONNEL WORK IN THE SCHOOL

JOSEPH S. ZACCARIA

THE HOME, the church, and the school are the three major institutions charged with making contributions to the rearing of youth and the maintenance of our American way of life. There has been a lack of clarity with respect to the extent to which the role of education should reflect current societal goals and the degree to which it should create and implement societal change. Educators with varying philosophical, political, social, and economic motives have taken many different positions on this issue, but the mainstream of American education has tended to reflect rather than change current social norms. As a result the prime thrust in education has been the socialization of youth and the transmission of our culture. Five major themes have emerged in American education:

1. Character and moral development.
2. Mental discipline.
3. Literacy and information.
4. Vocational and other practical aims.
5. Civic or social aims.[1]

Woven throughout the above themes is the fundamental tenet that the school should be turning out a "product" prepared to make adequate economic, political, and social contributions to the American way of life. The educative process

---

[1] R. F. Butts, *A Cultural History of Western Education* (New York, McGraw-Hill Book Company, 1955).

has been largely derived from such philosophical positions as essentialism (learning important things) and perennialism (learning the old enduring truths). Until very recently the theme of education for individual development, psychological maturity, and good human relations has been given token recognition but has remained largely ignored. Historically, there have been three major periods with respect to the school's concern with the psychosocial (emotional) development of students. Up to the 1920's or 1930's, i.e. the traditional period, there was a virtual neglect of the psychosocial and human relations aspect of the curriculum except for occasional, accidental or incidental help given to students by concerned staff members in the school. Then, largely due to the growing influence of the mental health movement, a parallel concern occurred in education between traditional academic learning and learning in the psychosocial-human relations sphere, i.e. a neo-traditional period. From the 1960's to the present there has been a growing concern over the psychosocial-human relations aspect of education.

A Traditional View of Education and the Place of Personnel Work in the School

During the traditional period the school was essentially seen as a machine. It was viewed as a mechanical device built with given sets of specifications according to a blueprint for achieving its goals. A certain kind of efficiency was sought in which complex tasks, derived from the major goals, were attained by subdividing the general functions of operational units, e.g. departments, into smaller partial tasks (the division of labor). Through the specialization of jobs, the many sub-tasks of the school became rather easily learned and efficiently performed by staff members. Work tasks became arranged according to positions (jobs). Descriptions (job specifications) for each position were developed. Expectations (role behaviors) for each job category emerged and performance expectations (role and function) became standardized. People with appropriate skills were assigned to corresponding positions. Lastly, facilities, finances, and a chain of command energized the machine. The machine-like institution we know as the school, conceived in this way, functions smoothly if there is an operational communication system, a status system, and an effective system of authority and influence operating through appropriate rewards and punishments.

Traditionally, the operation of the school has been facilitated by grouping work positions according to functions. The instructional function is carried on by teachers. The learning function is carried on by students. The management function is performed by administrators who plan, organize, make decisions, influence, coordinate, and evaluate the operation of the school. This traditional view of the school as an efficient bureaucracy is that of Weber.[2] Implicit in this bureaucratic view of the school is a specific view of man which has been called Theory X by McGregor.[3] Most organizational members are seen as hedonistic, i.e. pleasure seeking. Because of the inherent displeasure in work by teachers and students, for example, they attempt to gain the most amount of economic and social rewards with the least amount of work for the school. Thus, the bulk of the people in the school are lazy, uncommitted, passive agents who prefer to be told what to do. They must be controlled by threats, coercion, reward, and punishments, or they simply will not contribute to the achievement of the school's goals. Most organizational members must be regulated by policies, rules, directives, syllabi, agenda, regulations, etc.

A few people, however, are self-motivated and self-controlled. They are the ones who should become the administrators who in effect control the large mass of untrustworthy and irresponsible workers. The major thrust of school life is directed toward controlling organizational members, purchasing their cooperation and effort, and providing adequate

[2]M. Weber, *The Theory of Social and Economic Organization* (Oxford, Oxford University Press, 1947).

[3]D. M. McGregor, *The Human Side of Enterprise* (New York, McGraw-Hill Book Company, 1960).

realization of the school's goals through the proper application of authority, power, and control. Feelings, attitudes, morale, etc. are at best only a secondary concern. There is no formal personnel function, *per se*. Satisfaction of organizational members becomes a concern of the school only if people are not producing efficiently, in which case jobs are redesigned, organizational structure is altered, organizational relationships are changed, or the incentive and control system of the school is reorganized. Thus, in the traditional conception of the school as a bureaucracy there is no formal personnel function. There are no formal personnel workers. School life becomes a dehumanizing experience, replaced by an environmental press for the efficient acquisition of largely academic knowledge through what has been called by Havighurst the "Theory of Restraint."[4]

A Neo-Traditional View of Education and the Place of Personnel Work in the School

During the neo-traditional period (1920-1960) the growing impact of the mental health movement resulted in a recognition of the interdependence of cognitive and noncognitive elements in the educative process. This point of view is exemplified most clearly in the writing of Roethlisberger and Dickson.[5] An organization such as a school must attend to two major problems. It must produce a product, i.e. educated graduates, and it must provide for the reasonable satisfaction and psychological functioning of organizational members. The efficient production of the organizational products is dealt with by the technological aspect of the organization. Thus, teachers and administrators are responsible for efficient academic learning. Human relations problems are dealt with by the personnel function. The primary goal of education is the furthering of rather traditional academic learnings, but there is a recognition of the

---

[4]R. J. Havighurst, *Human Development and Education* (New York, Longmans, Green, and Co., 1953. David McKay Co., Inc.)

[5]F. J. Roethlisberger and W. J. Dickson, *Management and the Worker* (Cambridge, Harvard University Press, 1939).

dynamic relationship of formal academic learning and personal concerns reflected in the human relations aspect of the school.

Personnel work in the broad context of the term becomes an important but secondary consideration in the operation of the school. It remains supplementary to the mainstream of the educative process. Personnel workers provide help to students in the form of eliminating problems (e.g. underachievement, vocational indecision, and problems related to discipline), offering services (e.g. vocational guidance, testing, group work), and providing remedial help (e.g. individual counseling). Instrumentalism (pragmatism) and life adjustment education have been two prominent philosophies underlying the neo-traditional approaches to education and personnel work.

The intent of these programs has been to offer some type of help to students to complement or supplement the primary organization-centeredness of the administration and the subject matter centeredness of the teachers. Operationally, however, the organizational and operational aspects of the school have tended to compartmentalize education, to separate teachers and personnel workers, to foster decision-making only by upper-level personnel who tend to be detached from the day-to-day activities of the school, to decrease the flexibility of the school, to magnify status differences, and to bind the vital growth producing energy of the school as a dynamic system. Nevertheless, operating from a variety of points of view, many different types of formal personnel programs have emerged as neo-traditional approaches to personnel work.

Neo-traditional student personnel programs have utilized numerous themes. In general the types of programs summarized below have tended to offer services to students, to aid in socializing students, to remove problem behaviors, and to prepare students to fit into rather conventional notions about the nature of a mature well-functioning adult society. Personnel programs have tended to operate under the rubric of the term "guidance" in which the personnel worker functioned as a generalist. Some of the major types of guidance programs are briefly outlined below:

1. Vocational Guidance: helps students to find an appropriate occupation.
2. Educational guidance: empasizes helping students to function more adequately in academic aspects of their development.
3. Character (moral) guidance: assists students to develop proper attitudes, values, standards, etc.
4. Social (civic) guidance: directs students toward better citizenship.
5. Remedial (crisis or problem-centered) guidance: attempts to remove problems in such areas as the classroom, the home, etc.
6. Classroom (homeroom) guidance: emphasizes the use of relatively untrained teachers as guidance personnel to help students.
7. Developmental guidance: tries to prevent problems from arising through a long-term program beginning in kindergarten and extending through the high school.
8. Economic guidance: seeks to make students wiser consumers.
9. Distribution/adjustment guidance: disperses students through appropriate curricula in the school and helps students to be more well-adjusted in the school setting.
10. Leisure (recreational) guidance: helps students to lead a better life by enjoying nonwork activities.
11. Health guidance: seeks to promote physical and mental health in students.
12. Religious guidance: attempts to provide students with a functional understanding of how to use religion in day-to-day living.

Neo-traditional programs have been organized according to many different patterns. Some of the more prevalent organizational patterns are summarized in Figure II-1. In Pattern A there are no personnel workers. Teachers function as personnel workers in an attempt to fuse the traditional instructional function and the personnel function. Personnel work occurs in the homeroom, in extracurricular activities, in the classroom, or in closely-related-to-classroom activities. In Pattern B there are no full-time personnel workers. On the other hand, some of the teachers (often with professional training in personnel work) are released part of the time from classroom activities to carry on personnel work. As shown in Pattern C, some small schools, for example, utilize teachers and a small number of personnel workers. There are no personnel administrators and personnel workers occupy the same general position as classroom teachers on the organizational chart of the school. Patterns D, E, and F represent three common organizations for medium-sized schools in which there is a student personnel administrator and a somewhat larger number of personnel workers than in small schools. In patterns D, E, and F the student personnel workers are in a line relationship to the principal and may have a variety of formal relationships with the major student personnel administrator who typically holds such titles as Director of Guidance, Director of Counseling, Coordinator of Psychological Services, etc. Patterns G and H are typical organizational patterns for larger school sys-

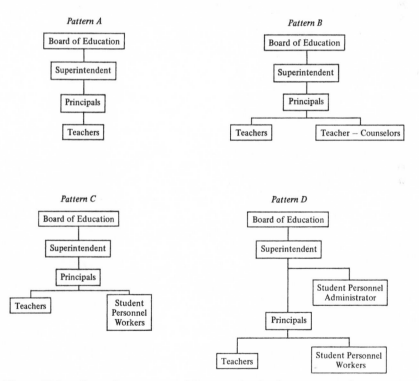

Figure II-1 — Some Organizational Patterns for Student Personnel Programs

tems. In Pattern G all student personnel workers are administratively responsible to the student personnel administrator. In many larger systems, on the other hand, guidance counselors (who work only in one school) are administratively responsible to their respective building principals as shown in Pattern H. Student personnel workers who function in a number of different

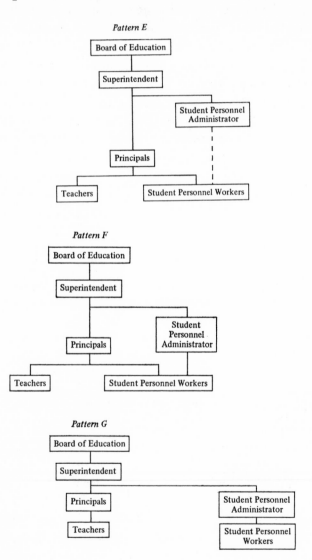

schools, e.g. school psychologists and school social workers, are in a line relationship to the major student personnel administrator. In large school systems the major student personnel administrator typically holds a title such as Assistant Superintendent of Student Personnel Work or Assistant of Pupil Personnel Services.

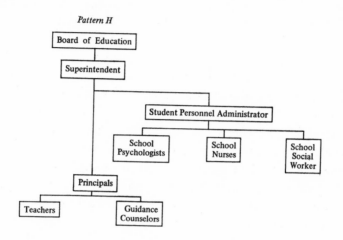

Pattern H

A Human Relations View of Education and the Place of Personnel Work in the School

Traditional views of education largely ignore the human relations aspect of the school. Neo-traditional views of education recognize the human relations dimension of the educative process but relegate it to an ancillary position in favor of a major thrust toward academic (intellectual) centered education. A restricted type of concern for people is shown in that persons are considered largely when their behavior causes problems in meeting organizational goals, when their maladjustment impedes their academic progress, or when a concerned staff member reaches out to help a student with a problem. A human relations centered view of education, on the other hand, places the person at the center of the educative process. The school is not primarily a therapeutic institution. Its function is to teach — to educate in the broadest context of the term. The word education comes from the latin verb *educo* which means to draw out. Thus, a human relations view of education envisions education as a process of facilitating, i.e. drawing out relevant learning. Students are not processed in a machinelike way as in the case of a manufacturing plant. Rather, it is in a climate of human caring, concern, and a genuine interest in students as people that meaningful education occurs.

There are several possible human relations points of view which could be utilized. The positions of Combs and Snygg,[6] Jourard,[7] Maslow,[8] and Rogers[9] (developed in Chapter I) are reflected in the theoretical perspective which McGregor[10] has called Theory Y and Havighurst[11] has called the Theory of Freedom.

According to this view, rather than being inherently lazy, man naturally seeks to expend physical and mental energy toward organizational goals if these goals are meaningful to the individual. Self-direction and self-control can be exercised toward organizational objectives without external rewards and punishments if the achieving of those rewards is related to ego-satisfaction and self-actualization needs. The ability to use a relatively high degree of imagination, ingenuity, and creativity to solve important problems in an organization such as a school is present in many organizational members, provided that the organizational climate is conducive to their getting involved in decision-making, implementing decisions, and subsequently evaluating the effectiveness of the course of action chosen. When organizational members show a lack of commitment, an avoidance of responsibility, a lack of ambition, and/or an emphasis on security, it is because

---

[6]A. W. Combs and D. Snygg, *Individual Behavior* (New York, Harper & Row Publishers, Inc., 1959).

[7]S. Jourard, *The Transparent Self* (New York, Van Nostrand Reinhold Company, 1964).

[8]A. H. Maslow, *Motivation and Personality* rev. ed. (New York, Harper & Row Publishers, Inc., 1970).

[9]C. R. Rogers, *On Becoming a Person* (Boston, Houghton Mifflin Co., 1961).

[10]D. M. McGregor, *op. cit.*

[11]R. J. Havighurst, *op. cit.*

they are threatened or they see organizational goals and/or processes irrelevant to their lives.

Much of the criticism of traditional and neo-traditional education with their correlative conceptions of student personnel work has focused upon the futility and irrelevance of education. Instead of socializing, restructuring, enculturating, adjusting, restricting, etc., human relations centered education seeks to facilitate and draw out the latent potential of all organizational members. The goal of human relations centered education is to foster the development of fully-functioning people, i.e. people who experience and behave in a more self-actualized way. Traditional academic subject matter is important but not as an end in itself. It becomes important only as it is interpreted, as it becomes meaningful, and it is utilized by individuals to become more fully functioning. Thus, a major effort of the school is directed to "conduct education in depth, to move toward something that is personally significant beyond the facade of facts, subject matter, logic, and reason . . . to encourage self-discovery."[12]

As noted above, neo-traditional approaches to student personnel work have used two basic strategies for attaining their goals. A classroom strategy located either in the home room, the academic classroom, or student (co-curricular) activities has sought to utilize relatively untrained teachers. A supplementary services strategy has employed a variety of approaches such as limited guidance services, psychological counseling, guidance generalist strategies, or the use of a wide range of highly trained specialists (pupil personnel services). A major limitation of these neo-traditional approaches is that ". . . in spite of the common goals of educators, cleavages have developed between personnel workers on the one hand and faculty members on the other. In a large number of institutions the faculty member, trained as a specialist in a particular subject matter area, has devoted himself to the classroom, to increased expertness in his field, to research,

[12]A. T. Jersild, "Education for Psychological Maturity," in P. H. Phenix, ed., *Philosophies of Education*, (New York, John Wiley & Sons, Inc., 1961). p. 46.

and to particular professional interests. In personnel work, developing specialism and concentration on particular skills have resulted in a multiplicity of 'services' to the student, with the experts focusing upon their unique tasks within a highly co-ordinated, hierarchical system. As a result, the environment has been segmented and fragmented, organized and compartmentalized so that the American student of today lives in a much divided world."[13]

Brunson has described the following divisive factors and their operation in both the general society and the educational system of our country: the background of our increasingly complex society; capitalism, with its emphasis on individualism; intellectualism; impersonalism; curriculur expansion and the growth of the elective system; increasing enrollments; increasing class size; the impact of institutional organization producing a separation of guidance from the rest of the system; variations in educational philosophy; variations in training for guidance functions; excessively heavy faculty loads; lack of recognition of faculty for functions other than teaching; inadequate facilities; specialization; administrative load for guidance personnel.[14] A major effort is directed toward maintaining a high level of integration within the student personnel program and between the student personnel staff, the school community, and the public community. "Integration is a continuous process directed toward the achieving of functional unity of the school with the objectives, functions, and activities of the administration, faculty, personnel staff, and students so interwoven, so interrelated, and so interacting as to form a complete whole. In such a process the focus is upon the whole student as he interacts with the total educational environment."[15]

Reed notes that "A reciprocal enterprise does not depend upon hierarchy of power and differentiation in the right of offi-

[13]M. A. Brunson, *Integrating Student Personnel Work with the Educational Program of the College Campus.* Unpublished doctoral dissertation, New York Teachers College, Columbia University, 1957, p. viii.

[14]*Ibid.*, pp. 8-32.

[15]*Ibid.*, p. 73.

cers. It requires instead a dissemination of joint responsibilities. Like the arc described by the pendulum these are spread over wide territory. Success in coordination depends not so much on unification as upon permeation. It includes all effort, whether this be professional, student, or lay contribution. It is not a task to be performed administratively but it is an integral element throughout the educational program."[16]

A student personnel program functions within a certain context. It has one or more major themes. It operates within a certain explicit or implicit framework. The neo-traditional student personnel programs function in such contexts as educational guidance, vocational guidance, crisis-centered (remedial) guidance, classroom guidance, etc. A human relations centered personnel program views the school as a social system. The major elements of that system are people. The focus of the program is people and helping people to become more fully functioning as persons rather than learners, instructors, administrators, and personnel workers. Human development is facilitated as individuals interact with each other and their environment. Operationally, human development results from the twin processes of maturation and learning. The general underlying theoretical context for a human relations centered student personnel program is summarized in Chapter I.

The term human relations is broad and complex. As used in this book it includes elements of humanistic psychology, phenomenology, existentialism, self-concept theory, as well as other theoretical perspectives. The major continuing theme of a human relations centered personnel program, however, is that of facilitating human development by creating a school environment within which individuals can become more fully functioning and self-actualized. Certain principles guide the general operation of the human relations centered school and its personnel program:

1. *The principle of free intelligence.* The life of an organization is enriched to the extent that each individual feels that his intelli-

[16]C. Reed, *a Functional Coordination of Personnel Services.* Unpublished report, Sixteenth Annual Meeting of American College Personnel Association, 1939.

gence counts, is respected, and utilized in the day-to-day activities of organizational life.

2. *The principle of participation.* Each member of an organization should be encouraged to take part and become involved in such processes as planning, policy making, implementing organizational change, program evaluation, etc.

3. *The principle of individuality.* Each person is a unique person whose individuality can be used as a major contributing factor in achieving a richness of organizational life and a successful realization of organizational goals.

4. *The principle of cooperation.* Human development is facilitated as individuals jointly share and work toward creating a healthy social condition in the organization wherein the particular strengths of each person are valued.[17]

Summarized in Table II-I are the goals of neo-traditional and human relations centered personnel programs. A major shortcoming of neo-traditional student personnel programs is that for the most part they have sought limited goals and have tended to view personnel work as a vehicle for fitting students into existing social structures. A human relations centered student personnel program such as the one described in this book, on the other hand, would help the individual to seek the appropriate balance, for him, between relating to societal expectations and meeting his own personal expectations.

A human relations centered personnel program could be organized in many ways. It could be organized, for example, according to any of the patterns summarized in Figure II-1 (See page 37). The organizational structure is perhaps less important than such matters as programatic goals, processes, and personnel. Nevertheless, the organizational structure which is congruent with programatic goals and processes greatly facilitates the operation of a personnel program. A major limitation of the

[17]H. G. Hullfish, *Democracy in the Administration of Higher Education* (New York, Harper & Row Publishers, Inc., 1950).

[18]J. Cribbin, "A Critique of the Philosophy of Modern Guidance," *Catholic Educational Review,* 53:73-91 (1955).

[19]D. E. Hamachek, *Encounters with the Self* (New York, Holt, Rinehart, & Winston, Inc., 1970).

TABLE II-I

GOALS OF NEO-TRADITIONAL AND HUMAN RELATIONS-CENTERED ATTEMPTS TO FACILITATE HUMAN DEVELOPMENT

GOALS OF NEO-TRADITIONAL STUDENT PERSONNEL PROGRAMS[18]	GOALS OF A HUMAN RELATIONS CENTERED STUDENT PERSONNEL PROGRAM[19]
1. To develop student initiative, responsibility, self-direction, and self-guidance,	1. To help the individual to move away from facades toward the type of person that he really is. (Genuiness)
2. To develop in the student the ability to choose his own goals wisely.	2. To assist the individual in moving away from "oughts." (Flexibility)
3 To know one's self, to know the school, and to be known by the school.	3. To facilitate the individual in moving toward meeting his own expectations rather than the expectations of other people. (Trust in one's own organism)
4. To anticipate and prevent crises from arising in the life of the student.	4. To promote the individual's attempting to become more self-directive. (Responsible independence)
5. To help the student to adjust satisfactorily to school and life.	5. To develop in each individual a healthy acceptance and respect for other people. (Nonpossessive warmth and respect)
6. To help the student to recognize, understand, meet and solve his problems.	6. To aid the individual to examine himself, to develop more self understanding, and to accept himself. (Self-understanding)
7. To assist the student in making wise choices, plans, and interpretations at critical points in his life.	7. To aid the individual in being more open to his experiences. (Openess)
8. To help the student acquire insights and techniques necessary to enable him to solve his own future problems.	8. To develop in the individual the ability to understand others with different backgrounds and experiences. (Empathy)
9. To assist teachers to teach more effectively.	
10. To help administrators to administer more efficiently by making a maximum contribution to the total school program.	
11. To develop citizens who will participate in and contribute to the democratic way of life.	
12. Miscellaneous objectives: assisting in the home, helping the community, building ethical character, fostering human relations and international understanding.	

major current organizational patterns is that they do not have built-in mechanisms for assuring maximum utilization of free intelligence, participation, individuality, and cooperation. Described below are two unique organizational patterns that could be utilized for an effective personnel program. Both patterns attempt to do two things. First they attempt to de-emphasize the traditional line and staff notions for, while line and staff organizational patterns have such advantages as being able to be easily charted, have clearly evident lines of communication and authority, have precisely defined areas of responsibility, and have simplified administrative decision making, there are many inherent limitations. A major limitation, for example is that the hierarchical organizational structure reflects and maintains authority, influence, involvement, commitment, etc. at the upper strata of the organization. Such an organization operates at odds with a human relations centered program because at best it forces the human relations centered program to become an ancillary part of the educative process. Such an organization encourages divisiveness in the school community. A more appropriate type of organizational structure would be based upon such perspectives as participative administration, circular administration, and organic administration wherein councils, boards, committees, etc. become utilized as primary vehicles for promoting involvment, for tapping into latent human potential, and for facilitating human development within the dynamics of organizational life. Also, individuals in the school should be challenged and free to cross traditional structural lines in order to promote internal cooperation, concern, and integration.

Shown in Figure II-2 is an attempt to restructure a basic line and staff organization and to facilitate maximum involvement and maximum contribution of all aspects of the school community. The major feature of the formal organizational chart is a triangular-shaped pattern wherein each apex of the triangle represents school principals and their respective school organizations. Central to the entire structure is a Human Relations Council. The council serves as liaison and advisory body to ad-

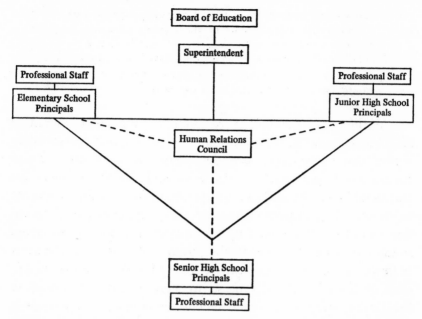

Figure II-2 — A Modified Line and Staff Pattern for a Human Relations Centered Personnel Program

ministrators, teachers, students, and personnel workers. Its major functions include liaison and advisory activities in such areas as staff relations, student-staff relations, interracial relations, school-community relations. In terms of the student personnel area, for example, the Human Relations Council could perform the following functions:

1. Act as a liaison between the student personnel program and various segments of the school community.
2. Assist in adopting, changing, and interpreting policies and practices in the student personnel program.
3. Study other student personnel programs and recommend adoption of practices considered appropriate for the local student personnel program.
4. Evaluate the specific practices of student personnel programs in individual schools within the school system and suggest the adoption of successful practices in other schools within the system, where appropriate.

5. Carry on an ongoing evaluation of student personnel work.
6. Transmit the achievements of the student personnel program to various segments of the school and the community.
7. Identify school personnel who could make a contribution to the student personnel program and submit the names of these people to appropriate student personnel staff members.[20]

Within each building there might be a parallel committee called a Human Relations Committee or a more operationally limited committee called a Student Personnel Committee. These committees might range in size from eight to fifteen members and should be composed of representatives from various segments of the school community. The exact size, composition, and operation would be determined by the unique situation of any given setting. In general, however, the purpose of these committees is to facilitate a continuing sensitivity to the human relations dimensions of the educational process, to serve as advisory groups to the various subgroups in the school community, and provide a valuable liaison function within the formal organization of the school.

Shown in Figure II-3 is a model based upon circular or organic administration. The structural representation takes the form of circles centering around mutual concerns. Each peripheral circle represents a different aspect of the school community. The central circle represents the area of concern. The intermeshing of the circles represents the intermeshing of ideas as involved segments of the school community cooperatively focus upon and contribute to the effective operation of the school. The circles vary in size from institution to institution and from concern to concern within a given institution reflecting the extent of participation and interaction among administrators, teachers, personnel workers, and students. Obviously, the applicability of organic administration is limited to specific aspects of the operation of the school in general and the student personnel program. In some appropriate instances, therefore, shared concern could

[20]R. N. Hatch and B. Stefflre. *The Administration of Guidance Services*, 2nd ed. (Englewood Cliffs, Prentice-Hall Inc., 1965). pp. 84-85.

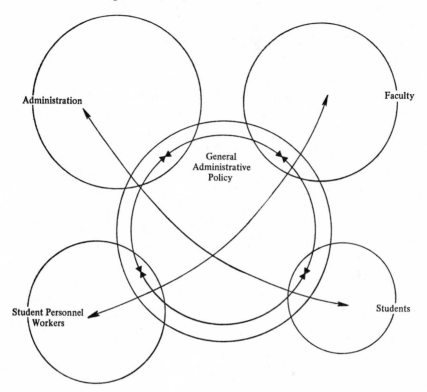

Figure II-3 — An Organic (circular) Pattern for Organizational Decision Making

result in shared decision making. On the other hand, general consultation on all matters through council or committee action is excessively time-consuming, expensive, and generally inappropriate. Where it is appropriate, the intermeshing of ideas might begin with a student group, move to a committee composed of representatives of teachers, administrators, student personnel workers, and students. The idea might then flow outward to administrators who might add their inputs and send the communication back to the committee again. The committee might send the idea to a special faculty group who might send it back to the committee. From there the idea might go back to the administrators who should bring about some change in policy, structure, or process. This open communication pattern is reflected in the arrangement of arrows on Figure II-3. Certainly, such a process takes time. It is not as fast as unilateral administrative decision-making. It does, however, facilitate better and more open communication. More importantly it facilitates better human relations by meaningful involvement in and contribution to the solutions of mutual matters of concern.

Thus, the student personnel function organized as a human relations centered program could be organized as a comprehensive, person-centered, integrative, well-coordinated program. Ideally, the human relations approach to student personnel work would involve the total staff of the school, the students, parents, and community people. Personnel work becomes closely related with instruction, the total curriculum, the cocurriculum, and various aspects of the community. It requires a great deal of technical skill on the part of the school staff as well as a continuing effort to maintain an effective cooperative effort and a good working relationship. Ideally, it also requires a great deal of school-community cooperation. Operationally, the program could be implemented through providing specific services to students such as an inventory service (appraisal and record keeping), an information service (educational, occupational, and personal-social), a counseling service (individual and group counseling), a placement service (occupational, post-high school education, part-time employment), and evaluation service (follow-up and research services). On the other hand, the implementation of student personnel work could be carried out by emphasizing professional guidance activities *per se*, e.g. individual counseling, group work (group guidance and group counseling), testing, classroom consultation, etc. The program could also be implemented by emphasizing the major general personnel functions such as individual work with students, group work with students, individual and group work with staff, individual and group work with parents, working with the community, assembling data about students, providing information about opportunities. Obviously, there is a great deal of overlap among the above strategies. While any one or combination of these strategies could be employed by a human relations centered student personnel program, the major emphasis and the prime focus of the program would be the individual and the providing of interpersonal and environmental conditions which facilitate the individual becoming a more fully-functioning, self-actualized person. Described below are the principles which when followed facilitate a flexible, constantly evolving, coordinated, person-centered student personnel program.

1. *The Principle of Reciprocal Activity.* Integration is achievement in proportion to the degree and manner in which the parts have freedom and opportunity to interact with each other and with the whole. The parts must be so mutually relating and interpenetrating that the activity of each part reciprocally affects the activity of each of the other parts and, in turn, changes and is changed by the whole. The process is never completed because of the chain of reaction constantly in operation.

2. *The Principle of Responsible Participation.* Where opportunity is provided for all members of the school community to participate in the functional whole, integration is fostered. Such participation is more than verbal agreement or approval; it is active and responsible contribution. It is a part of the process from its very beginnings. It satisfies human need in that it is accompanied by feelings of belongingness and self-esteem. Since men value that which they bring into being, they will appreciate the total enterprise to which they have contributed their beliefs, decisions, and energies.

3. *The Principle of Shared Concern.* If integration is to be achieved, concern for the total situation must pervade each member of the whole. Mutual concern is a dynamic quality which cements the relationships of men; furthermore, it evokes the free expression of their ideas and blends their efforts in a common loyalty.

4. *The Principle of Mutual Respect.* Integration is possible where there is mutual respect among members of an organization. Respect for all members is imbedded in the conviction that each individual is a person of dignity and worth, that he differs from all others in interests and abilities, and that his contributions are both unique and worthy of consideration. The differences should be used to enhance the quality of the process.

5. *The Principle of Communication.* If the maximum contribution

of each individual is to be evoked, if men are to relate to each other in shared enterprises, individuals must be free and able to communicate with one another, regardless of position in a social system. Communication is essential to interaction. Only as men are able to speak with others, to make themselves understood, and to listen to and understand what others are saying, can they unite in spontaneous give-and-take, merge their purposes, and form an integrated society.

6. *The Principle of Cooperation.* A sense of we-ness, of working cooperatively with rather than competing against others, is necessary if integration is to be developed. This accrues in an environment conducive to implementation of the principles of reciprocal activity, responsible participation, shared concern, mutual respect, and communication. Cooperation brings together in creative collaboration those of similar and dissimilar backgrounds, abilities, and skills. It frees individuals to rise to their highest levels as individuals and as members of society as they work together toward mutually accepted goals.[21]

Summary

The personnel function in education has grown from a neglected, ancillary, and accidental part of the educative process to become an integral part of the total program of most school systems. Although there are critics of the current operation of some of the personnel programs, there is rather widespread acceptance of the need for the personnel function in today's schools. Because of differing philosophies, facilities, financial conditions, community factors, etc. personnel programs in schools have taken a variety of forms. As compared with the traditional views of education which tended to reject the student personnel function, the mainstream of contemporary personnel work may be characterized as neo-traditional. To the major continuing emphasis of formal academic instruction has been added a set of strategies whereby various approaches to personnel work are being utilized to help students with various types of problems. Although the personnel function has been a recognized aspect of the total educative process, it remains supplementary, secondary, isolated, fragmented, and peripheral to the central aca-

[21]M. A. Brunson, *op. cit.,* pp. 65-89.

demic thrust of education. The major current foci of student personnel work continue to be adjustment, problem elimination, compensatory assistance, vocational help, etc. within relatively limited conceptions of the nature of help required by students.

In recent years, the growing criticism of education and educative process has been paralleled by a reevaluation of traditional and neo-traditional approaches to personnel work. Some critics have suggested revamping the organizational structure or the theoretical contexts of contemporary programs. In the area of vocational guidance, and related areas, for example, theorists have suggested existentialism[22,23] behaviorism,[24,25,26,27] cognitive dissonance theory,[28,29] chain theory,[30] and environmental press theory[31,32,33] as new frameworks. Other critics have suggested different target groups for student personnel programs.

[22]E. L. Johnson, "Existentialism: Self Theory, and the Existential Self," *Personnel and Guidance Journal*, 46:53-58 (1967).

[23]J. S. Zaccaria, "Some Aspects of Developmental Guidance Within an Existential Context, *Personnel and Guidance Journal*, 48:440-445 (1969).

[24]J. D. Krumboltz and C. E. Thoresen, "The Effect of Behavioral Counseling in Group and Individual Settings on Information-seeking Behavior," *Journal of Counseling Psychology*, 11:324-333 (1964).

[25]J. D. Krumboltz and W. W. Schroeder, "Promoting Career Information Through Reinforcement," *Personnel and Guidance Journal*, 44:19-26 (1965).

[26]A. W. Miller, "Learning Theory and Vocational Decisions," *Personnel and Guidance Journal*, 47:18-23 (1968).

[27]R. P. O'Hara, "A Theoretical Foundation for the Use of Occupational Information," *Personnel and Guidance Journal*, 46:636-640 (1968).

[28]T. L. Hilton, "Career Decision-making," *Journal of Counseling Psychology*, 9:291-298 (1967).

[29]D. B. Hershenson and R. M. Roth, "A Decisional Process Model of Vocational Development," *Journal of Counseling Psychology*, 13:368-370 (1966).

[30]P. R. Lohnes, "Markov Models for Human Development Research," *Journal of Counseling Psychology*, 12:332-337 (1965).

[31]A. W. Asten. "Effects of Different College Environments on the Vocational Choices of High Aptitude Students," *Journel of Counseling Psychology*, 12:28-39, (1965).

[32]D. H. Ford and H. B. Urban, "College Dropouts and Social Strategies," *Educational Record*, 46:77-92 (1965).

[33]E. L. Herr, "Differential Perceptions of 'Environmental Press' by High School Students," *Personnel and Guidance Journal*, 43:678-686 (1965).

The major effort of contemporary personnel programs has been directed toward such student groups as the college bound students, the vocationally undecided students, and students exhibiting discipline problems or other maladjustments interfering with the smooth operation of the school. Innovative programs have sought to provide help for such neglected segments of the school as the mentally retarded, the physically handicapped, the alienated, drug users, girls, the disadvantaged and other minority groups.

New procedures include computer-assisted counseling, programmed counseling, computer-based occupational information systems, multimedia educational and occupational systems, bibliotherapy, gaming, simulation, and the use of para-professional staff. Suggested programmatic emphases include such processes as family therapy and various team-oriented approaches. The role and function innovations have included a wide range of changes such as the personnel worker as a curriculum consultant, classroom consultant, human engineer, social engineer, environmental engineer, liaison officer, advocate, legal adviser, ombudsman, trouble-shooter, change agent, etc. One of the most far-reaching changes in personnel work is that of including a greater emphasis on group work in existing programs including group guidance techniques, group counseling, T-groups, basic encounter groups, motivation groups, actualization groups, etc.

Each of the innovations mentioned above, however, represents either a modest restructuring of old procedures, a drastic mechanization, or the application of sophisticated technology to make older procedures faster, more efficient or more applicable on a wider scale. None of the above innovations emphasizes the total individual, his view of life, and the conditions which facilitate his becoming a more fully-functioning self-actualized person. The major shortcoming of the above approaches to student personnel work is that in their quests for a certain kind of therapeutic efficiency they have tended to neglect the area of human relations as a goal of education and as a process for attaining that goal. An overemphasis on technology, organizational structure, and techniques has contributed to the problems to which the personnel function addresses itself. Many students feel the same way about humanness and the personnel function in schools as they do about Christianity or Jesus and the Church. One student summed it up this way: "I dig Christ but the Church turns me off!" The essence of humanness, i.e. good interpersonal and intrapersonal relations, together with the conditions which facilitate humanness, i.e. emphatic understanding, respect, and genuiness constitute the foundation upon which a human relations approach to personnel work attempts to facilitate human development. Such a student personnel program involves staff resources, facilities, and personnel practices within the context of a formal and an informal organizational structure. The following chapters describe the various aspects of a human relations approach to facilitating human development in the school.

CHAPTER III

FACILITATING PERSONAL DEVELOPMENT THROUGH COUNSELING

C. H. PATTERSON

COUNSELING IS A TERM widely used and almost as widely abused. Many people call themselves counselors. Clergymen claim to be counselors, doctors do counseling, teachers are counselors. We have financial or loan counselors, investment counselors, legal counselors, travel counselors, beauty counselors and mortuary counselors, and others. Everyone seems to want to be called a counselor. Almost everyone who gives information to or talks with others as part of his job considers himself a counselor.

It is obvious that counseling means many different things to different people. It is therefore necessary to clarify what counseling is in a professional sense. Difficulties arise in clarification since there are almost as many definitions as there are authors of texts on counseling. We may begin with a simple definition which indicates what is common to all more extensive definitions. The essence of counseling is that it is a human relationship, a special kind of relationship, the nature of which will be considered in this chapter. Because there are so many misconceptions about what counseling is, it is necessary to consider what counseling is not. First, a definition by exclusion, by designating what a thing or a concept is not, is useful. Let us consider some actions taken by teachers and administrators, often considered to be counseling, which are not counseling in the professional sense of the term.

WHAT COUNSELING IS NOT

Despite what the lay concept of counseling may be, counseling is not, first of all, simply the giving of information (though information is sometimes given in counseling), nor is it the giving of advice, suggestions, and recommendations. Professional advice is not counseling, and professional consultation with people in the fields of law, medicine, and engineering is not a counseling relationship. The giving of advice should be so labeled and recognized and not camouflaged as counseling.

Counseling is not influencing attitudes, beliefs, or behavior by means of persuading, leading, or convincing, no matter how indirectly, subtly, or painlessly. It is not the process of getting someone to think or behave in ways which we want him to or think it is best for him to think or behave. Let us recognize the process of persuasion for what it is and not mistake it for counseling; counseling is not brainwashing. Counseling is not the influencing of behavior by admonishing, warning, threatening, or coercing without the use of physical force, or coercion; discipline is not counseling. Counseling is not the selection and assignment of individuals for various jobs or activities; personnel work is not counseling, even though the same tests may be used in both. Finally, interviewing is not synonymous with counseling. Interviewing is involved in the relationships listed above, as well as in other noncounseling situations. The intake interview, to gather information about an applicant or client or to orient him, may be a prelude to counseling, but it is not counseling.

Although it seems elementary to point out that these activities are not counseling, all of them are being done under the name of counseling. In many schools, counseling is seen as a way to do something to a student, to get him to do what he should do, what we think he should do, or what we think is good for him to do. Counseling is seen as a group of techniques or devices utilized to manipulate or influence the student to accept the counselor's goals or objectives. Thus we hear about counseling the student into or out of a vocational field or objective, of counseling him to accept this or that goal or objective, or of counseling him toward this or that choice or decision. These activities are not counseling and one misuses the term in calling them counseling. Counseling is not something you do to or practice on a student or client.

GENERAL CHARACTERISTICS OF COUNSELING

What, then, is counseling? Isn't it concerned with influencing and changing behavior? Certainly it is. If it weren't, there would be little point to counseling. Counselors are interested in changing the client's behavior; but counseling is a particular kind of influencing with particular methods and goals. First of all, counseling is concerned with voluntary behavior change, that which the client wants and for which he seeks the help of the counselor.

Second, the purpose of counseling is to provide the conditions which facilitate such voluntary change. These conditions respect the right of the individual to make his own choices. He is treated as an independent, responsible individual capable of making his own choices under appropriate conditions.

Third, as in any sphere of life, there are limits which are imposed on the individual. The client is not permitted to attack the counselor physically or to tear up his office. The counselor does not do personal favors for the client, help the client obtain special privileges through his influence, or prevent the client from suffering the consequences of his actions.

While a common aspect of counseling is the interview, not all interviewing as we have seen is counseling. There are those who feel we can do away with the interview. The application of conditioning in the changing of behavior is having a revival, and conditioning is being used in the interview to condition the verbal behavior of clients. This approach is called behavioral counseling, and it is suggested by some that the interview is not necessary for changing behavior by conditioning, so that counseling can be done without interviewing. But there seems to be a confusion here between behavior change and counseling or therapy. Not all behavior change is counseling, and while conditioning is a method of behavior change it is not counseling. Thus, while not all interviewing is counseling, counseling always involves interviewing.

The same might be said of another common aspect of counseling—listening. All counselors listen to their clients, at least some of the time, but not all listening is counseling. Many people listen to others at times but the counselor listens in a special kind of way.

The counselor understands his client, but others understand people. Although the counselor usually understands better and in a different way, we cannot say that understanding alone makes counseling different from other relationships.

Counseling is conducted in privacy and is confidential, but so are the private and confidential interviews between doctors and lawyers and their clients and between the priest and parishioner in the confessional.

None of these characteristics, by themselves, constitutes counseling or differentiates it from all other interviews or interpersonal relationships. Counseling involves an interview, held in privacy, in which the counselor listens and attempts to understand the client, the counselee, and in which it is understood that what the client says will be held in confidence. A change in the client's behavior, in the way or ways he himself chooses, is within limits expected. This seems to be an acceptable definition of counseling, but is it adequate? It is not if it does not distinguish counseling from other relationships. Even the presence of all these factors does not differentiate counseling from other kinds of relationships. What is there then about counseling which is different?

Two other characteristics are necessary for a counseling relationship. First, one participant (the client) has a problem, but not one which he could take to a lawyer, doctor or engineer; the client of a *counselor* has a *psychological* problem. Second, the counselor is skilled in working with clients who have psychological problems, which obviously requires specialized training or preparation in psychology, beyond that which the usual person has and differing from that which most other professional people have.

Counseling, then, is unique in that it is a relationship between a client with a psychological problem and a counselor who is trained to help clients with such problems. This relationship shares many characteristics with other relationships, as those between other professional persons and their clients. It also has the characteristics of all good human relationships, which include acceptance of and respect for others, understanding, mutual confidence and trust, genuineness, sincerity, openness, honesty and integrity.

THE GOALS OF COUNSELING

Before considering the specific nature of the counseling relationship, goals of counseling, neglected until recently, must be discussed. Mahrer opens his book on the goals of psychotherapy with the statement that "the literature on psychotherapy has little to offer on the goals of psychotherapy—their identification, significance, and organization. On this point clinicians, researchers, and theoreticians have been curiously inarticulate."[1]

Goals have been implicit, if not explicit, in all of the major theories or approaches to counseling or psychotherapy. Individual counselors or psychotherapists are often able to define the goals of their counseling efforts. Confusion arises, however, because goals of different counselors and psychotherapists appear to differ widely. They may be talking about different levels of goals, sometimes about specific, sometimes about general goals, or about immediate or longterm goals. Perhaps the confusion can be eliminated if we think about the three levels of goals.

ULTIMATE GOALS. Ultimate goals are broad and general in nature and involve long-term outcomes. In establishing ultimate goals we are concerned with what kind of persons we want to be and what people should be like. We are raising the question of the goals of life and living, of a society and, in a more limited area, of both formal and informal education. In Chapter I we considered the goal of education and proposed that it should be the facilitation of the personal development of students or the development of self-actualizing persons. This is the ultimate goal of counseling or psychotherapy. Counseling or psychotherapy attempts to assist persons who have special or particular problems in becoming self-actualizing.

The concept of self-actualization thus provides a single, common, or universal need or goal, not only of counseling or psychotherapy and of all helping relationships, but of life. Counseling

[1]A. R. Mahrer, ed., *The Goals of Psychotherapy* (New York, Appleton-Century-Crofts, Inc., 1967).

is thus consistent with life, its goal is a part of everyday living and inherent in it. Many writers in counseling and psychotherapy accept some form of self-actualization as the goal of counseling or psychotherapy.[2] May, for example, states that "the goal of therapy is to help the patient actualize his potentialities."[3]

MEDIATE GOALS. Mediate goals, specific steps toward the general goal, are the subgoals which appear to be the major concern and focus of the behaviorists. In some cases, some of these goals vary among individuals. Thus, there are apparently two kinds of mediate goals, the subgoals that are general and those that have individual variance.

Many of the goals discussed by counselors or psychotherapists are subgoals in the context of self-actualization. They include reduction of symptomatology, reduction of psychological pain and suffering including anxiety, reduction of hostility, increasing of pleasure, elimination of unadaptive habits, acquisition of adaptive habits, understanding of one's self and one's needs, and obtaining a job or finding a satisfying one.

Mediate goals allow for individual differences. Maslow points out that, since self-actualization is the actualization of a self and since no two selves are alike, individuals actualize themselves in different ways.[4] The different ways in which individuals actualize themselves or their differing potentials are represented in the different subgoals—or mediate goals—of counseling. Thus, individuals with different talents or abilities are able to develop their specific potentials. Improvement in academic performance might be a goal for some but others might actualize themselves by developing ability or talent other than academic potential. Graduation from high school or college might be a goal for some but not for others. Marriage might be an appropriate goal for

---

[2]A. R. Mahrer, *op. cit.*; A. H. Maslow, "Self-actualization and Beyond," in J.F.T. Bugental, ed., *Challenges of Humanistic Psychology* (New York, McGraw-Hill Book Company, 1967), pp. 279-286; C. R. Rogers, *On Becoming a Person* (Boston, Houghton Mifflin Co., 1961).

[3]R. May, *Psychology and the Human Dilemma* (New York, Van Nostrand Reinhold Company, 1967), p. 109.

[4]A. H. Maslow, *Toward a Psychology of Being* (New York, Van Nostrand Reinhold Company, 1962), p. 196.

some clients but not for others; and separation or divorce might be the appropriate goal for some married clients.

In addition to recognizing a basic common goal and different individual goals, the concept of ultimate and mediate goals has another value. The goal of self-actualization constitutes a criterion for subgoals or for individual mediate goals. The behaviorists, in their concern for concrete, objective, specific goals sometimes appear to have no criterion for the acceptance of goals other than these characteristics. But it is the meaning to the individual client of the specific goals for self-actualization which determines their acceptability.

THE IMMEDIATE GOAL. The immediate goal of counseling is to set in motion and continue a process which will lead to the mediate goals and to the ultimate goal. The counseling process has been described in various ways, and no review of these descriptions will be attempted here. A number of theoretical approaches to the counseling process are discussed by C. H. Patterson.[5]

The mediating goals of the counseling process mentioned by Parloff are: to make the unconscious conscious, to recall the repressed, to decondition, countercondition, strengthen or weaken the superego, to develop and analyse the transference neurosis, to promote increased insight, and to increase self-acceptance.[6] The great amount of research on the counseling process and on counseling outcomes gives little evidence that the mediating goals listed by Parloff relate to outcomes. There is some evidence, on the other hand, that insight does not necessarily lead to behavior change or is not necessary for change in behavior to occur.[7]

An aspect of the counseling process which appears to be universal, that is present regardless of the counselor's theoretical approach, is client exploration of himself, intrapersonal exploration. The concept of *self-exploration* includes many of the mediat-

[5]C. H. Patterson, *Theories of Counseling and Psychotherapy.* 2nd ed. (New York, Harper & Row Publishers, Inc., 1973).

[6]M. B. Parloff, "Goals in Psychotherapy: Mediating and Ultimate," in A. R. Mahrer, *op. cit.,* pp. 5-19.

[7]N. Hobbs, "Sources of Gain in Psychotherapy," *American Psychologist,* 17:18-34 (1962).

ing goals, such as developing awareness of unconscious (or pre-conscious) material, mentioned by Parloff.

Rogers, in describing how therapy is experienced by the client, discusses the experience of exploration.[8] Truax and Carkhuff develop the concept of self-exploration to include the client's activity in "attempting to understand and define his own beliefs, values, motives and actions." Truax has developed a Scale of Depth of Self-Exploration which defines degrees of the process so that interview materials can be rated.[9]

Self-exploration consists of several stages. Before an individual can engage in intrapersonal exploration he must be able to reveal or expose himself; thus the first step is self-disclosure. Self-exploration, perhaps revealing first negative, followed by more positive, aspects of the self, can then occur. The later stages lead to increasing self-awareness, which makes possible the development of the characteristics of the fully-functioning person described by Rogers: an increasing openness to experience, increasingly existential living, and an increasing trust in one's organism.[10] These, in turn, make possible and are underlying aspects of self-actualization. In May's terms, self-awareness makes possible self-directed individual development.[11]

THE CONDITIONS

What are the conditions which set in motion and continue the process of self-exploration? They are the same as those described in Chapter I which facilitate self-actualization, since self-exploration is a means toward self-actualization; they will be considered as they apply specifically to the counseling process. First, a word about the general assumptions and atmosphere of the counseling relationship. In the counseling relationship an atmosphere is created in which the individual is able to take re-

[8]C. R. Rogers, *Client-centered Therapy* (Boston, Houghton Mifflin Co., 1951), pp. 72-75.

[9]C. B. Truax and R. R. Carkhuff, *Toward Effective Psychotherapy* (Chicago, Aldine Publishing Company, 1966), pp. 189 and 195-208.

[10]C. R. Rogers, *On Becoming a Person* (Boston, Houghton Mifflin Co., 1961), pp. 187-192.

[11]R. May, *op. cit.,* p. 68.

sponsibility for himself, to begin to develop or restore the self-esteem which is necessary for his functioning as a healthy, responsible, independent human being, able to make adequate decisions and resolve problems.

This therapeutic atmosphere is created when the counselor offers or provides certain conditions to the client. These conditions, expressions of the counselor's philosophy toward other people, are more dependent on the counselor's attitudes and feelings than on his techniques. The three basic beliefs, assumptions, or attitudes are:

1. Each individual is in himself a person of worth.
2. Each individual is capable of assuming responsibility for himself and can and will, under appropriate conditions, become a responsible, independent, self-actualizing person.
3. Each individual has the right to self-direction, to make his own decisions, to choose or select his own methods or means of achieving self-actualization.

There are at least three essential conditions necessary to create an atmosphere in which the individual can take responsibility for himself and his development into a self-actualizing person:

1. *Respect or nonpossessive warmth.* This is similar to Rogers' unconditional positive regard: "To the extent that the therapist finds himself experiencing a warm acceptance of each aspect of the client's experience as being a part of the client, he is experiencing unconditional positive regard."[12] Warmth which includes acceptance, interest, concern, prizing, respect, liking, is nonjudgmental, a valuing without conditions. It is the acceptance of and nonjudging of a client as a person, but not necessarily of his behavior. Truax and Carkhuff in defining their Tentative Scale for the Measurement of Nonpossessive Warmth, say that "it involves a nonpossessive caring for him (the client) as a separate person, and thus, a willingness to share equally his joys and aspirations or his depressions and failures. It involves valuing

[12]C. R. Rogers, "The Necessary and Sufficient Conditions of Therapeutic Personality Change," *Journal of Consulting Psychology,* 21:95-103 (1957).

the patient as a person, separate from any evaluation of his behavior or his thoughts."[13]

2. *Empathy or empathic understanding.* A second major characteristic of the atmosphere or conditions conducive to client progress is the counselor's understanding and his ability to communicate this understanding to the client. The kind of understanding most effective in counseling is not knowledge of or about the client, nor does it consist of the results of tests, the data in the client's record, or the records of extensive case studies, no matter how voluminous or complete. Most effective is an empathic understanding, an understanding which has no trace of evaluation or judgment and which does not categorize or label in terms of problem or areas or complex or presumed etiological or causal conditions. The counselor who is empathetic has a "feeling with" his client, enters his client's internal, rather than external, frame of reference, and sees the world, insofar as possible, through his client's eyes: he attempts to put himself in his client's place. He realizes that if he is to really understand his client's feelings, attitudes, and behavior, he must see things as his client does. Everyone behaves in response to the world as he perceives it, not necessarily as it exists in "reality."

3. *Therapeutic genuineness.* The third major condition of a good counseling relationship is genuineness. The counselor must be real, honest, freely and deeply himself. He does not play a role; there is no such thing as a counselor role, assumed when the client enters the counseling office. He places no facade between himself and the client. There is no conflict between what he thinks and feels and what he says. While the counselor must not blurt out all his negative feelings or hostility, since this would not help his client, he does not present a false friendship or liking.

Genuineness appears to be misinterpreted by some as an "anything-goes" policy. "Genuineness must not be confused, as is so often done, with free license for the therapist to do what he will in therapy, especially to express hostility."[14] There is a dif-

[13]C. B. Truax and R. R. Carkhuff, *op. cit.*, p. 58.

[14]R. R. Carkhuff and B. G. Berenson, *Beyond Counseling and Therapy* (New York, Holt, Rinehart & Winston, Inc., 1967), p. 29.

ference, as Carkhuff and Berenson point out, between a construct of genuineness and the construct of facilitative or therapeutic genuineness, since a genuine person can be destructive. It is unlikely, for example, that a highly authoritarian person, no matter how genuine he is, would be therapeutic.

Genuineness does not mean that the therapist discloses himself extensively or completely to the client. Truax and Carkhuff, in their definition of the Tentative Scale for the Measurement of Therapist Genuineness or Self-congruence, note that "being himself . . . does not mean that the therapist must disclose his total self, but only that whatever he does show is a real aspect of himself, not a response growing out of defensiveness or a merely 'professional' response that has been learned and repeated."[15] Complete self-disclosure is the client's function in self-exploration, and, while the therapist often gains from the therapeutic encounter, therapy is for the client, not the therapist. "While it appears of critical importance to avoid the conscious or unconscious facade of 'playing the therapeutic role', the necessity for the therapist's expressing himself fully at all times is not supported. . . . However, there exists some tentative evidence indicating the effectiveness in some situations of therapist self-disclosure . . . in which the therapist (with discriminations concerning the client's interests and concerns) freely volunteers his personal ideas, attitudes and experiences which reveal him, to a client, as a unique individual."[16]

These three conditions, respect, empathy, and genuineness, often called the core conditions (or the "central therapeutic ingredients"[17]) appear to be well-established, both theoretically and experimentally. All have been demonstrated to be related both to client self-exploration and to various outcome criteria in counseling. There are no doubt other conditions which contribute to a facilitative counseling relationship. Carkhuff and Berenson mention therapist spontaneity, confidence, openness, flexibility, commitment, and the intensity of the therapeutic contact.[18] Truax

[15] *Op. cit.,* p. 69.
[16] R. R. Carkhuff and B. G. Berenson, *op. cit.,* pp. 29-30.
[17] C. B. Truax and R. R. Carkhuff, *op. cit.*
[18] *Op. cit.,* pp. 4, 30.

and Carkhuff view intensity and intimacy of the therapeutic contact as theoretically a separate aspect of the process.[19] A tentative scale to measure intensity and intimacy yielded a significant relationship with client self-disclosure and outcome but also with the three core conditions.

One condition, probably not closely related to the three core conditions and therefore constituting a fourth condition, is concreteness or specificity. Concreteness means dealing with specific feelings, experiences, and behavior and is the opposite of generality and abstraction or vagueness and ambiguity. Carkhuff and Berenson suggest that concreteness serves at least three important functions: it keeps the therapist's response close to the client's feelings and experiences; it fosters accurateness of understanding of the therapist, allowing for early client corrections of misunderstanding; and it encourages the client to attend to specific problem areas.[20]

Concreteness and specificity appear to be the opposite of interpretations, which are mainly generalizations, abstractions, higher level labeling, or inclusion of a specific experience under a higher level classification. Such interpretation is often not useful. Interpretations that are threatening by nature or that are abstractions, generalizations, or simple labeling tend to cut off the client's self-exploration. For example, a therapist might suggest that a client, who has explored his relationship with his parents, has an Oedipus complex. Although the client might feel that his problem has been solved and that he has insight, his behavior will probably change very little. No doubt he will see no point in further discussion or in engaging in further self-exploration. Ratings on a tentative scale to measure concreteness have shown concreteness to be related to client self-exploration and outcomes.[21]

Respect, empathy, genuineness and concreteness provide an atmosphere and a relationship which does not threaten and in which the client can engage in self-exploration. As Truax and

[19]*Op. cit.*, pp. 289-290.

[20]R. R. Carkhuff and B. G. Berenson, *op. cit.*, p. 30.

[21]C. B. Truax and R. R. Carkhuff, "Concreteness: A Neglected Variable in Research in Psychotherapy," *Journal of Clinical Psychology*, 20:264-267 (1964).

Carkhuff express it, the conditions operate through four channels, which constitute a hierarchy of immediate goals in counseling or psychotherapy. First in priority is the reinforcement of approach responses to human relating, which leads to self-disclosure. Second is reinforcement of self-exploration, which includes the identification of sources of anxiety. Third is the elimination of specific anxieties or fears, and fourth is the reinforcement of positive self-concepts and self-valuations.[22]

It is worth noting that there is a reciprocal relationship between the conditions of a good human relationship and the resulting effects on the recipient of the conditions (Truax and Carkhuff call it the principle of reciprocal affect.)[23] The recipient of the conditions begins to manifest the conditions in his own behavior. *The conditions are aspects of self-actualization.* Self-actualizing people facilitate self-actualization in others. The facilitative conditions are also the goal of the process—*the conditions and criterion for counseling are the same.* Furthermore, the client, in becoming a self-actualizing person, becomes therapeutic for others by providing the conditions for their self-actualization.

The core conditions, as they are now known, are general and complex. It may be possible to break them down into more specific conditions, as a general factor may be broken up into group and specific factors. There may be other core conditions in successful therapy, which will become apparent as the present conditions are better isolated, defined, and measured.

The counseling relationship characterized by these conditions is absent of threat. Although it may be a negative way of looking at counseling and mental health, the concept of threat appears to be extremely important. Threat to the self and the self-concept is apparently the basis for personality disturbances or poor mental health. The basic need of the individual is to preserve and enhance the self; all other needs or drives may be subsumed under this. Frustration of or threat to the satisfaction of this basic need results in a lowered evaluation of the self; a loss of self-esteem is the core of personality disturbance.

[22]*Op. cit.*, pp. 151-152.
[23]*Op. cit.*, p. 151.

The influence of threat on behavior has been demonstrated. Threat can cause the individual's perception to become so narrow that he literally does not see many aspects of the situation. Literally paralyzed with fear, he may withdraw, to the point of freezing, under extreme threat. Under less extreme threat, he may become defensive or aggressive; it may be that behavior once considered naturally and instinctively aggressive is always a reaction to threat, a universal reaction because threat in some form is universal. Thus, while threat or frustration may lead to reactions other than aggressiveness, aggressiveness is always a result of threat or frustration. Another defense against threat, in addition to not recognizing or seeing it, withdrawal, or aggression, is self-deception to avoid loss of or to restore self-esteem.

We are aware of the results of pressure or threat in everyday life. The individual is unable to perform effectively or efficiently or learn easily; he persists in ineffective attempts at problem-solving rather than in fruitful exploration. We know that we create resistance in those whom we attempt to change by pressure or threat, from the child who becomes more insistent on doing what he wants to do to the girl who insists on marrying the clearly unsuitable boy to whom her parents object.

Changes in attitudes and behavior, self-actualization, development of independence and responsibility—in short, mental health or adequate personality development—occur only under conditions in which serious threat to the self and the self-concept is absent. Since the goal of counseling is the preservation or restoration of good mental health or self-esteem, and the fostering of self-actualization, it follows that the counseling situation must be characterized by an absence of threat. Respect for, interest in, and acceptance of the client as a person, absence of evaluative attitudes, and understanding from his point of view, all contribute to an atmosphere devoid of threat.

IMPLEMENTING THE CONDITIONS IN COUNSELING

Formal Characteristics of Counseling. One may ask, if counseling is nothing more than the practicing of good human relationships, why it is so difficult to become a counselor? Why shouldn't everyone be a counselor? To some extent, everyone who practices good human relationships is a counselor, sometimes, with some people. Certain characteristics of counseling, however, set it aside as a specific kind of relationship.

In the first place, the principles of good human relationships, though many are known, are not obvious, necessarily natural, nor easily practiced. If they were, our society would be much more advanced and much happier with less mental disorder or disturbance than it is at present. Understanding the nature of good human relationships must be learned.

Second, to practice these principles requires training and experience. The ability to apply the principles is related to the psychological characteristics or mental health of the individual applying them. It is not a matter of information or knowledge; it is a matter of attitudes.

Third, the implementation of these principles in a counseling relationship differs somewhat from their practice in everyday relationships, because the counseling relationship is a special kind of relationship. It is a formal relationship between two persons who may, perhaps preferably, have no other relationship. Its sole purpose is to improve or restore the mental health, adjustment, or functioning of one of the participants. The counselor consciously and purposefully practices the principles of good human relations for the benefit of the counselee.

Fourth, the relationship is usually established between a trained individual and another individual in need of assistance, because he is disturbed, unhappy, or in conflict over an unresolved problem, or because he is dissatisfied with himself or lacks self-esteem. While the principles of good human relationships in general are applied to maintain good mental health among normal, average individuals, they are applied in counseling to restore or improve the mental health of disturbed persons.

Fifth, the relationship is established at the request of the disturbed individual, is continued at his wish, and is characterized by certain conditions, which are privacy, confidentiality, set time limits, and regularity of appointments.

Sixth, the counseling relationship, even though formal and

limited in time (seldom more than an hour a day, more often only an hour a week), is a closer, more intense, and deeper relationship than any ordinary social relationship, because of its purpose and the application of the principles of good human relations in their purest form, divested of the formalities of the usual social relationships.

COUNSELOR ACTIVITIES. We have emphasized that the attitudes of the counselor should form an atmosphere in which the client can achieve a feeling of security and self-esteem. But what does the counselor do? How does he act? What does he say? How does he express the proper attitudes? How does he understand the client and convey this understanding to him? While the attitudes of the counselor are of first importance, their implementation must also be considered. Their expression in a therapeutic manner is not usually natural or automatic. While their expression must become natural, so that the counselor may be genuinely himself and not play a role, he must be his *counseling* and *therapeutic* self, not his social or teaching self.

The objectives of the counselor are to show his genuine interest in the client, to show that he accepts the client as someone worthy of respect and esteem, and to understand the client and communicate this understanding to him. How can the counselor do this and, at the same time, allow the client to be responsible for himself, for his behavior, for his decisions, and for his communications with his counselor from the beginning of the counseling process?

The techniques by which this can be accomplished appear simple and yet are often difficult to practice. The first basic activity of the counselor is *to listen*, often difficult to learn, because people tend to think of what they want to say instead of really listening to others. This preparing to have one's say is not the kind of listening needed in counseling. Listening in counseling is an active attention to and interest in what the client is saying or trying to say without letting personal reactions or associations interfere. The client is given freedom to express himself in his own way without interruption, questioning, probing or judgments. The counselor is not a Sergeant Friday trying to get at "the facts," nor is he concerned with obtaining a complete life history that he can record and file away; he is concerned with trying to see things as the client sees them and with helping the client express his attitudes, his feelings, his concerns, and his perceptions of himself and of the world.

Listening with respect and interest shows that the counselor thinks that the client is worth listening to and that he has something important to say and it is the first step in making the client take responsibility for himself. The client who asks the counselor what he wants to know, who asks what the counselor wants him to talk about, or who suggests that the counselor ask him some questions is expressing his dependency and his lack of responsibility and self-esteem. For this client, the counselor points out that the client may decide what he wants to talk about, that the counselor is interested in whatever he has to say, and that the counseling time is his to use to discuss his concerns.

Listening of this kind is the basis for empathic understanding and is the way by which the counselor is able to learn how the client sees things and to perceive from the point of view of the client. Listening and understanding are the basis of or perhaps constitute empathy, the ability to place oneself in the place of, to take the role of, and to think and feel as, another.

While listening is perhaps the most important way, there are other ways of expressing interest in and respect for the client. *Simple acceptance responses,* such as "Yes," "I see," "Uh huh," or "Mm . . . Mmmm," are useful and may represent the second major class of techniques used by the counselor. They indicate to the client that the counselor understands him and is following what he has to say. At times, the simple statement, "I understand," may be all that is necessary. Simple restatement of the client's statements, usually called reflection of content, indicates to some extent to the client that the counselor understands.

Perhaps the most appropriate way of communicating understanding is by *reflection* and *clarification* of the client's feelings and attitudes, which are the significant facts in counseling. Reflection is the attempt to understand from the client's point of view and to communicate that understanding. The ability to reflect and clarify the feelings and attitudes of the client requires genuine understanding based on empathy. It requires skill to focus on attitudes and feelings, which are the significant facts of counseling, rather than on the content or the objective facts expressed by the client. This skill must be acquired through training, experience, and supervised practice in counseling.

It is important that the counselor not pretend to understand when he does not. If he is not able to follow the client, which may happen when the client is confused himself, he should say so. He may say, "I don't follow you," "I don't understand," or "I'm not sure I know what you're saying." If the counselor has some idea, but is not sure, of what the client is expressing, he may say, "Is this what you are saying . . . ?" or "Let me see if I follow you. Are you saying . . . ?" etc. It is not necessary, indeed it is impossible, for the counselor to understand completely all that the client says or feels. He may misunderstand and show this in his reflections; but the client will correct him if a nonthreatening atmosphere is maintained. As long as the client feels that the counselor is trying to understand him, and shows some evidence of doing so, apparently progress can occur.

The simple methods described above, applied by a skilled, understanding counselor appear to be effective in helping clients and seem to constitute the necessary and sufficient conditions for therapeutic personality change. It is apparently not necessary for the counselor to question, probe, interpret, give advice, etc., techniques that are inconsistent with the assumptions and goals of counseling and which may be threatening to the client. Support, persuasion, and advice may prevent the client's assuming responsibility for himself and for solving his problems.

No techniques for achieving rapport have been prescribed because such techniques are neither necessary nor desirable and are usually the result of the counselor's rather than the client's need. Counseling is not and should not be begun as a social relationship or a social conversation. If the client has come to the counselor voluntarily, or if he has been referred and has come involuntarily, he has not come to discuss the weather or the pending football or basketball game. The counseling interview should be started simply and directly, recognizing what the client came for. "What's on your mind?" "What would you like to talk about?" or "Where would you like to start?" is usually all that is necessary to begin the counseling session.

Rapport is not achieved by artificial techniques or social devices, but develops and exists where the counselor is genuinely interested in the client and his problems. The expression of the attitudes described above are sufficient for the establishment of rapport.

It must be emphasized again that counseling is not a matter of techniques, even those suggested above. Counseling is a relationship in which the attitudes of the counselor are expressed, genuinely and spontaneously, not laboriously or self-consciously. It would perhaps be better to abandon the word *technique*, since it has connotations of being a deliberate, conscious, artful device for achieving a goal and even of manipulating a situation. The expression of the attitudes of the counselor in the counseling situation is not a matter of techniques in this sense but a matter of making known to the client his respect, interest, and understanding in simple, genuine, spontaneous, natural ways.

THE CLIENT'S ACTIVITY. We have discussed the conditions of counseling which must be provided by the counselor and have indicated that these conditions, when presented and communicated to (or perceived by) the client, lead to such outcomes in the client as appropriate (for him) decisions, increased independence, responsibility, increased self-esteem, or more self-actualizing behavior. But what is the client's contribution to the process? What does he do in the counseling relationship?

The ideal counseling conditions, which minimize threat, permit the client to engage in the process of self-exploration, to examine himself and his situation and to recognize aspects of which he was unaware or not clearly aware. Self-exploration is a complex process that begins with self-disclosure. In the safety of the counseling relationship, where the client realizes he is not being judged or evaluated, he is able to disclose perhaps for the first time in any relationship, his innermost, often most negative, self. He is able to recognize, if not accept, aspects of his self-concept which he had been unable to recognize before. He develops a more complete, realistic picture of himself. With this disclosure of himself, he is able to explore himself in relation to others and his situation. His thinking is more complete and more accurate, because it includes elements and aspects which were not present before. In addition to his negative and undesirable aspects he comes to recognize his positive and desirable aspects. As a result of his self-exploration, he develops more self-awareness and becomes more open to himself and to his experiences. He becomes aware of his potentialities and possibilities, of the self that he could be.

SUMMARY

To summarize then, we can say that counseling is a relationship. It is a relationship between a client, who has a psychological problem, and a counselor, who by preparation and experience is able to help the client resolve this problem. It is not simply an immediate, temporary, specific problem, but one in the broad sense of what kind of life the client wants. Since counseling is a relationship, it is not a matter of techniques. Counseling is not so much what a counselor does as what he is, not so much what he can do for the client in terms of goods and services as what he can give of himself. It is not restricted to tangible, concrete, limited outcomes, such as good vocational choices, other decisions, or placement in employment, but is concerned with whether the client has maintained or improved his self-esteem, his self-respect, his independence, his status as a human being—in short, whether he has become a more self-actualizing person. This is the goal of all counseling, whether educational, vocational, rehabilitative, marital, or therapeutic. Such an outcome is achieved, not by techniques or the giving of material things, but only as a result of a good human relationship.

SUGGESTED READINGS

Patterson, C. H., *Relationship Counseling and Psychotherapy*, New York, Harper & Row Publishers, Inc., 1974.

Patterson, C. H., *Theories of Counseling and Psychotherapy.* New York, Harper & Row Publishers, Inc. 2nd ed., 1973.

Rogers, C. R., *Client-centered Therapy.* Boston, Houghton Mifflin Co., 1951.

Rogers, C. R., *On becoming a Person.* Boston, Houghton Mifflin, 1961.

CHAPTER IV

FACILITATING PERSONAL GROWTH THROUGH GROUP PROCESSES

JOHN F. EIBL AND JAMES J. PANCRAZIO

> *I am less interested in inducing any particular change than I am in fostering and nourishing the condition under which constructive change may occur.*[1]

HUMAN BEINGS have often been referred to as social animals. Biologists and other scientists point out that most living organisms are interdependent upon one another for survival. Cooperation among members of the same species is common in nature and the collective behavior of human beings is the key to individual and societal survival. Human beings are collective members of groups from birth until death. Group membership varies culturally, but there are many characteristics of groups that are basic and quite similar across cultures. These characteristics can be broadly identified as the group process of human growth and development.

Individual human growth and development has been studied more vigorously than has group human growth and development. National media coverage of the impact and effects of group process approaches has forced behavioral scientists to engage in group process research. The purpose of this chapter is to focus upon characteristics of groups in general and specific group process approaches to facilitate human growth and

[1]J. W. Gardner, *No Easy Victories* (New York, Harper & Row Publishers, Inc., 1968) p. 51.

development. The discussion of characteristics of groups in general points out major commonalities of facilitative groups. A specific section dealing with an historical perspective is not included. The reader is referred to several texts which deal with the heritage of group process approaches, such as Corsini,[2] Moreno, *et al.*,[3] and Gazda.[4] While an historical perspective is not included some background leading up to the development of particular group approaches are presented. Different group process approaches are identified and defined to help differentiate among approaches. Recent research findings and questionable assumptions which point to major professional issues within the broad group area will be discussed. Ethical considerations are discussed to alert the reader to the lack of widely accepted and adhered to ethics in group process approaches. Finally, a brief discussion concerning change and possible directions for change is presented.

GROUPS IN GENERAL

Toward a Definition

Social scientists have attempted, via multiple definitions, to specify what constitutes a group. Consensus among social scientists as to a single definition is as rare as agreement among politicians of widely divergent political persuasions. While a single agreed-upon definition of group is presently unavailable, a generally accepted definition is presented in the context of this chapter.

Bass defines group as a collection of individuals whose existence as collection is rewarding to the individuals. Group is defined in terms of collective need and motivation.[5] Steiner

---

[2]R. J. Corsini, *Methods of Group Psychotherapy* Chicago, William James Press, 1957).

[3]J. L. Moreno, *The International Handbook of Group Psychotherapy* (New York, Philosophical Library, Inc., 1966).

[4]G. M. Gazda, *Basic Approaches to Group Psychotherapy and Group Counseling* (Springfield, Illinois, Charles C Thomas, 1968).

[5]B. M. Bass, *Leadership, Psychology and Organizational Behavior* (New York, Harper & Row Publishers, Inc., 1960), p. 39.

approaches group from a task orientation when he asserts that a group is a collection of individuals who have joined to create, produce, or otherwise develop an answer to a problem, a product, or other task orientation. He states, "to say that a group consists of a set of mutually responsive individuals is to provide only a minimal definition of this phenomenon . . ."[6] Sherif bases his definition of group upon empirical data collected over a period of six years.

> A "group" was defined as a social unit consisting of a number of individuals whose interactions at a given time have the following measureable properties: (1) more or less definite and interdependent status and role relationships among the individuals and (2) a set of values, standards or norms peculiar to them regulating their behavior, at least in matters of consequence to the group, such as its existence and perpetuation.[7]

A group may be defined as a collection of uniquely different individuals who interact with one another for a purpose; the needs and perceptions of each individual, the group norms and individual values, and the establishment of communication patterns have an impact upon the establishment and continuation of any one particular group.

Content and Process

Within any group, two concepts that many individuals have difficulty in differentiating between are *content* and *process*. Content refers to the *what* the group is focusing upon, the topic of discussion, the cognitive content within the group. When the President of the United States makes a speech, most people focus upon the content of his speech, the *what* of his particular topic. Content is relatively easy to identify within the context of any group.

Process, which occurs at the same time within a group, is

[6]I. D. Steiner, *Group Process and Productivity* (New York, Academic Press, Inc., 1972).

[7]M. Sherif, "Experiments in Group Conflict," *Scientific American,* pp. 54-58 (1956).

a much more difficult concept to identify, even for some professionals. Process is essentially *how* the group deals with the content or topic within the group context. Steiner defines process as including "all those intrapersonal and interpersonal actions by which people transform their resources into a product, and all those nonproductive actions that are prompted by frustration, competing motivations, or inadequate understanding."[8]

Anyone who wishes to understand groups as an effective part of his professional competence must learn to distinguish content and process, but more specifically must be able to 'tune-in' to the process of the group. Content is *what* and process is *how*.

Group Norms

Every group has norms, "rules of conduct." Norms specify acceptable behavior within the context of any particular group. Norms are not established within a group for every conceivable interaction, rather norms are established for significant interactions or decisions that have specific meanings for that group. For example, a code of ethical behavior may be established by a professional group and its members are expected to behave in accordance with those ethics. When an individual deviates from the established group norm, sanctions are brought to bear upon that individual, e.g., Socrates. Norms and conformity have often been equated but, contrary to the popular notion of conformity for the sake of conformity, most social scientists seem to point to conformity as agreement with the majority only for the sake of agreement.[9] To aid the professional in his work with a group, the norms that have been established must be identifiable.

Group Climate

"The tension was so thick, you could've cut it with a knife," is a generalized statement which describes the climate of a par-

---

[8]*Op. cit.*, p. 63.

[9]M. E. Shaw, *Group Dynamics: The Psychology of Small Group Behavior* (New York, McGraw-Hill Book Company, 1971), p. 248.

ticular group. Since our focus here is upon facilitative groups, climate is defined as the emotional tone of the group. Dimensional bipolar concepts such as tense/relaxed, fast/slow and angry/ harmonious are closely associated with group climate. Concepts which contribute to group climate and eventually may become group norms are (1) mutual trust, (2) recognition that the venture is a joint exploration, (3) individuals within the group who are willing to listen, and (4) group behavior that makes it easier for any one individual to take risks, i.e. talking, trying out new behavior, etc.

Group Communication

Communication in any context is complex and usually interactional in nature. Impressions are sent and received in any effort toward accurate communication. Communication, in a group context is used essentially to maintain the group while attempting to complete a common purpose. Individual needs and motivations must be taken into account when the communication process is being observed within a group.

The following circular process of social interaction, illustrates the nature of communication among group members. (P. 81)

Phases of Group Development

Social scientists have identified varied stages or phases of group development. Gazda points to four rather definite phases of group development. His phases are (1) Exploratory, (2) Transition, (3) Action and (4) Termination.[10] Bennis and Shepard identify two major phases with five basic subphases present in any group as it develops. The summary chart (P. 82) identifies the two major phases along with the subphases.[11]

Blocker in his summary of the Trow, *et al.* research includes a number of basic propositions that are important to those who wish to work with groups. His summary includes:

[10]G. M. Gazda, *Group Counseling: A Developmental Approach* (Boston, Allyn & Bacon, Inc., 1971). pp. 31-35.

[11]W. G. Bennis and H. A. Shepard, "A Theory of Group Development," *Human Relations*, 9:415-457 (1956).

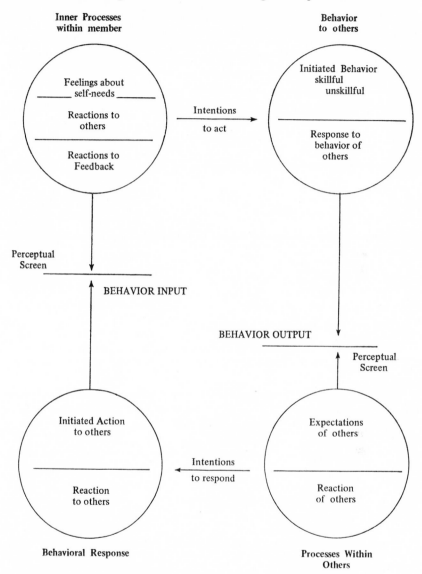

Figure IV-1 — Circular Process of Social Interaction

1. The attitudes of individuals have their anchorages in groups. It may be easier to change the attitudes of individuals in the group by changing the group climate than by attempting to address intervention directly to the individual.
2. All groups demand a certain degree of conformity from members.

Figure IV-2 BENNIS AND SHEPARD'S PHASES OF GROUP
DEVELOPMENT, SUMMARY CHART

Phase	Sub-Phase	Identification/Brief Definition
I		DEPENDENCE: Struggle, leadership definition, Common Goal
	I	*Dependence*: search for common goal
	II	*Counterdependence*: Leadership Struggle, Process
	III	*Resolution*: Task orientation, group unity
II		INTERDEPENDENCE: Concern with individual members, task
	IV	*Enchantment*: Cohesiveness of group
	V	*Disenchantment*: Effective interpersonal relations
	VI	*Consenual Validation*: termination, task completion

The closer and more cohesive the group, the more power it has over the behavior of members.

3. When decisions are made by a group, the commitment of members is much greater than when the decision is arbitrarily imposed from outside the group.

4. Highly cohesive groups can overcome greater difficulties and frustrations in pursuit of group goals than can less cohesive groups.

5. Group cohesiveness is largely a function of the degree to which members feel the group is meeting their needs.

6. People tend to become more effective leaders when they are acting as group members in a training situation than if they are acting as individuals in an audience situation.

7. The amount of verbal interaction among members is a function of group factors.

8. Cooperation and communication is greatest in groups where goals are mutually defined, accepted and understood.

9. The group climate or style of group life can have an important impact on the personalities of members. The behavior of members may differ greatly from one group climate to another.[12]

In summary, there are five basic questions that a professional must ask in working with or observing a group: (1) What is (are) the reason(s) for the group meeting? (2) What is the effectiveness of the group leader/facilitator? (3) How has

[12]D. H. Blocker, *Developmental Counseling* (New York, Ronald Press Company, 1966), pp. 171-172.

the group been organized? (4) What is the group climate? and finally, (5) What are the established norms for the group?

GROUP PROCESS APPROACHES: IDENTIFICATION

Individuals and professionals alike have made choices and judgments about the group movement and group process approaches in general, based upon limited information. Some professionals have noted four basic characteristic attitudes about group process approaches: (1) Total resistance, (2) Indifference, (3) Curiosity, and (4) Intense Interest. The purpose of this section is to identify, define, and delineate among general types of group process approaches. Figure IV-3 below may help the reader to understand the levels of group process approaches. Three general types of groups are identified. The first two types, group guidance and group counseling, are general types of group process approaches. The third type, encounter groups, is specific and each approach is identified and discussed. Organizational development is not included in the Figure IV-3 because the authors feel that this is distinctly unique and significantly different from the other general types that a brief discussion is presented in this section.

Group Guidance

Guidance, especially in an educational environment, plays

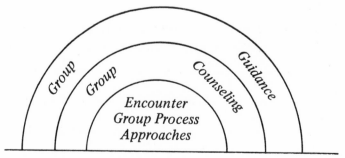

Figure IV-3 — Spectrum of Group Process Approaches

a role with each person. Glanz and Hayes state that, "Psychotherapy may be only for a few, but guidance is for all."[13]

As previously stated in this chapter, the guidance movement has had much to do with the development and expansion of group process approaches. Initially, group counseling had not clearly been delineated in the literature. Bennet defines group guidance in a rather general manner: ". . . group guidance refers to any phase of a guidance program carried on with groups of individuals rather than between counselor and counselee or clinician in the face-to-face situation."[14]

Lifton defines group guidance in contrast to group therapy, when he states: ". . . group therapy in an educational setting is here considered to be operating in any group where the emphasis is upon providing group members with opportunities to explore their own feelings and attitudes *rather than upon imparting information.*"[15]

In his re-edited and retitled text, Lifton does not attempt to specifically define group guidance, even in contrasting it to group counseling. He does, however, imply a similar definition when he refers to group guidance orientation programs and other vehicles for mass dissemination of information. Lifton criticizes society for its attempt to answer a common problem by starting a group in the area. He clarifies his position by stating "Although a major role of orientation (group guidance) is to provide information, it falls on deaf ears if the hearers have not been helped first to perceive the need for the information and then to face the anxieties the new situation may provoke.[16]

Glanz and Hayes define group guidance as a term used historically to describe many types of guidance activities carried

---

[13]E. C. Glanz and R. W. Hayes, *Groups in Guidance* (Boston, Allyn & Bacon, Inc., 1967).

[14]M. E. Bennet, *Guidance in Groups* (New York, McGraw-Hill Book Company, 1955), p. 3.

[15]W. Lifton, *Working with Groups: Group Process and Individual Growth* (New York, John Wiley & Sons, Inc., 1966), p. 14.

[16]*Ibid.*, p. 250.

on within a classroom setting.[17] Their definition, together with Lifton's implications of what group guidance isn't, and Bennet's definition point to a general definition: group guidance may be viewed as a planned orientation, registrational process of a group of individuals with a common need for information and has as its primary function the imparting of information to the group, e.g., need for general career knowledge, general test interpretations, etc.

This group process approach may be used to impart needed information and has as its content educational, vocational, personal, and social kinds of information that is not usually found in other settings. Through the providing of accurate information, individual concerns which could occur may be prevented.

The goals for each group guidance session are determined by the particular needs that each session is designed to meet. Leadership institutes, management training seminars, effectiveness training and other like-titled group activities fall under the general classification of group guidance activities.[18]

Group Counseling

Professionals have been struggling with various definitions of group counseling and have used group guidance, group counseling, multiple counseling, conjoint family therapy, and other terminology. Group counseling is more than adequately defined as a:

> . . . dynamic, interpersonal process focusing on conscious thought and behavior and involving the therapy functions of permissiveness, orientation to reality, catharsis, and mutual trust, caring, understanding, acceptance, and support. The therapy functions are created and nurtured in a small group through the sharing of personal concerns with one's peers and the counselor(s). The group participants (counselees) are basically normal individuals with various concerns which are not debilitating to the extent of requiring extensive personality change. The group participants (counselees) may utilize the group interaction to increase understanding and acceptance

[17]*Op. cit.*, p. 274.
[18]J. H. Kirby, "Group Guidance," *Personnel and Guidance Journal*, 49:593-598 (1971).

of value and goals and to learn or unlearn certain attitudes and behaviors.[19]

Mahler, in a review of the major concerns of group counseling, states that in group counseling the major concerns that individuals bring up center on the socialization process. The main questions that they ask are: How do I maintain a close relationship with my family? Who am I, anyway? How do people really see me? What are my abilities and talents and where can I use them? Do men's and women's world views differ?[20] Mahler continues and defines group counseling as:

> ... the process of using group interaction to facilitate deeper self-understanding and self-acceptance. There is a need for a climate of mutual respect and acceptance, so that individuals can loosen their defenses sufficiently to explore both the meaning of behavior and new ways of behaving. The concerns and problems encountered are centered in the developmental tasks of each member rather than on pathological blocks and distortions of reality.[20]

Muro and Freeman[22] discuss group counseling and state that the primary focus of group counseling is upon student reactions to test scores, occupational information and life experiences. The professional working with a group of students in an attempt to attach personal meaning to college exploration is performing a group counseling function.

Group counseling at whatever age level can provide a powerful range of specifically tailored physical and social environments to assist a wide variety of clients, clients experiencing concerns of (a) deficient decision-making skills, (b) ineffective academic skills, (c) inappropriate social skills, and (d) excessive fears and

---

[19]G. M. Gazda, J. Duncan, and E. Meadows, "Group Counseling and Group Procedures Report of a Survey," *Counselor Education and Supervision,* 6:305-310 (1967).

[20]C. A. Mahler, "Group Counseling," *Personnel and Guidance Journal,* 49:601-608 (1971).

[21]C. A. Mahler, *Group Counseling in The Schools* (Boston, Houghton Mifflin Co., 1969), p. 11.

[22]J. J. Muro and S. L. Freeman, eds. *Readings in Group Counseling* (Scranton, Pa., International Textbook Co., 1968), pp. 46-47.

anxieties, according to Thoresen. He stresses that group counseling is not "therapy," but a process of looking at the concerns of individuals and the specific processes of change. Professionals, states Thoresen, need to show that group counseling makes a desirable difference in the specific actions of participants.[23]

Group counseling, as indicated by Thoresen and others, has multi-use potential in a variety of settings. Gazda points to current practices by student personnel professionals that include among others, speeches by experts on drugs and drug effects, vocational awareness and opportunities, academic skill enhancement, and human relations training.[24]

Encounter Group Process Approaches

T-Groups, sensitivity groups, "Bob and Carol, Ted and Alice," marathon groups, human potential groups, nude encounters, encounter tape groups, growth groups, Esalen Institute, and many other popularized labels have been attached to general encounter process approaches. Encounter groups, in general, commonly refer to intensive small group experiences in which the emphasis is upon personal growth through expanding awareness, exploration of intrapsychic as well as interpersonal issues, and release of dysfunctional inhibitions.[25] The purpose of this subsection is to identify, define, and attempt a delineation of the myriad of encounter group process approaches. The encounter group process approaches that are identified (in alphabetical order) are:

Gestalt groups
Marathon groups
NTL Model Groups
Psychoanalytic Groups

[23] C. Thoresen, "Comment," *Personnel and Guidance Journal*, 49:608-609 (April, 1972).

[24] *Op. cit.*, pp. 172-173.

[25] W. B. Eddy and B. Lubin, "Laboratory Training and Encounter Groups," in R. C. Diedrich and H. A. Dye, eds., *Group Procedures: Purposes, Processes, and Outcomes* (New York, Houghton Mifflin Co., 1972).

Psychodrama Groups
Transactional Analysis Groups

These six approaches identified here tend to represent the major movements within this group process classification. Offshoot, or hybrid, encounter approaches which the reader may wish to gather additional information and understanding of would include: Synanon Game Groups, Human Potential Groups, Primal Scream Groups, Human Relations Groups, OASIS Groups, YMCA Groups, Family Groups and others.

Gestalt Group Process Approach

Frederick Perls is considered the founder of Gestalt therapy in the United States. *Gestalt,* in a general translation, means the forming of an organized meaningful whole. Sager and Kaplan define "gestalt" as a theoretical construct which postulates that awareness of a need or wish leads to the formation of a perceptual and cognitive field which contains elements necessary for the gratification of the need. They continue with an illustration to clarify their definition of "gestalt":

> Once a particular need (or wish) has been fulfilled, its gestalt is destroyed and another gestalt is permitted to emerge. To illustrate, obtaining a drink of water destroys the drinker's thirst gestalt, with its memories and images of the kitchen, water tap, the shelf where the glasses are kept, etc. and a new gestalt, subserving the wish to socialize for example, or to finish work, achieves prominence.[26]

The aim of gestalt therapy is to help become whole, to help the person become aware of, admit to, reclaim, and integrate his fragmented parts. Integration helps a person make the transition from dependency to self-sufficiency; from authoritarian outer support to authentic inner support.[27] According to Perls, a person who refuses to integrate his fragmented personality, his awareness of only parts of himself, is a neurotic.[28]

[26]C. J. Sager and H. S. Kaplan, *Progress in Group and Family Therapy* (New York, Brunner/Mazel, Inc., 1972), p. 76.
[27]F. Perls, *Gestalt Therapy Verbatim* (Lafayette, Calif., Real People Press, 1969).
[28]F. Perls, *In and Out of the Garbage Pail* (Lafayette, Calif., Real People Press, 1969).·

To illustrate that most individuals are fragmented, Perls uses a chair technique; (1) a "hot seat," the chair for the participant who chooses to "work" and (2) an empty chair facing the "working" participant. While a participant is "working," the other participants become essentially observers, and the group leader "works" with the participant on the "hot seat." Role playing is the prime focus of Gestalt groups. Unlike psychodrama, other group participants do not actively role play, but the "working" participant plays all the roles; another person "sitting" in the empty chair is imagined by the "working" participant.

It is the aim of this approach to enable each "working" participant to consciously experience previously avoided thoughts, feelings, and sensations and to finish his "unfinished business," and thereby promote impulse control, autonomy, integration, and growth. (Gestalt group leaders) . . . . contend that the mere conscious experiencing of these excluded aspects of the personality will, in itself, result in conflict resolution and attainment of . . . . (integration).[29]

Dreams are also of importance to this group process approach. Dreams are integrated, *not* interpreted through the role playing process. As Perls states,

> . . . all the different parts of the dream are fragments of our personalities. Since our aim is to make every one of us a wholesome person, which means a unified person without conflicts, what we have to do is put the different fragments of the dream together. We have to *reown* these projected, fragmented parts of our personality, and *reown* the hidden potential that appears in the dream.[30]

Emotional, affective awareness, and cognitive knowledge awareness are goals of Gestalt groups. The methodology is, in itself, a highly potent emotional group method which leads to increased affective and cognitive self-understanding.

Marathon Group Process Approach

Historically, the marathon group process is a relatively new

[29]C. J. Sager and H. S. Kaplan, *op. cit.,* pp. 76-77.
[30]*Op. cit.,* p. 67.

approach to facilitate human growth. Bach, Stoller, and Gibb are names associated with early pioneering efforts in the Group Marathon. The participants in the group marathon do not sleep and do not leave the group except to freshen up. This intensive approach is intended to motivate participants to interact truthfully, authentically, openly, and transparently. The participants are urged to communicate at a feeling or "gut" level, to be completely honest and authentic in whatever they say. Marathons may run from twenty-four to seventy-two hours with or without short rest breaks which serve as a method of processing the total experience, thus allowing participants to become more aware of self.

Jack and Lorraine Gibb have developed an offshoot marathon group approach which they call Emergence Therapy. Through TORI (Trust, Openness, Realization, and Independence) individual and group growth are fostered. "Growth is accelerated in high-trust relationships and is inhibited in defensive or high-fear relationships. In the process of growth, each person develops an implicit life style and life theory which are consonant with the particular balance of defensive and growth needs of the person.[31]" Demos expresses the belief that more and more individuals in an ever depersonalized society are having considerable difficulty breaking the barrier of anonymity.[32] He continues. "A syndrome of psychological problems seems to be developing, which is characterized by apathy, depression, lack of affective reaction and concommitant identify crises . . . which is unhealthy." He states that through the group marathon approach, these barriers may be eliminated.[33]

The marathon group process approach through its intensive, compacted processing offers a method for quickly creating the norms previously mentioned for facilitative group growth. The main criticism for this particular group process is that it does too

[31]J. Gibb and L. Gibb. "Emergence Therapy," in G. M. Gazda, ed., *Innovations to Group Psychotherapy*, (Springfield, Illinois, Charles C Thomas, Publishers, 1968), pp. 96-129.

[32]G. Demos. "Problems of Integrating the College Student to the College Campus," *Journal of the American College Health Association*, pp. 291-294 (April, 1967).

[33]*Ibid.*, p. 294.

much, too soon, too quickly. Adherents to this approach point to the growth change that can occur within this short span of time.

National Training Laboratory Model (T(for Training) Group, Sensitivity)

> The laboratory method had its beginning in the wedding of social action and scientific inquiry. Since its inception in 1947, laboratory training has exerted an important influence on developments within a number of fields, including education, religion, community development, and volunteer and professional agencies.[34]

National Training Laboratories, Institute for Applied Behavioral Science, grew out of the initial 1946 group process approach in New England. Lewin, Lippitt, and Bradford were among the founders of NTL, the first professional organization concerned with personal growth and organizational development in the United States. Lubin and Eddy summarize the rationale and method of the laboratory approach through a series of underlying assumptions:

1. Participants have been culturally conditioned to inhibit the expression of the emotional aspects of their communications, thus reducing interpersonal effectiveness.

2. The laboratory method legitimizes feeling and facilitates experiencing, expressing, and examining emotional aspects of communication.

3. Participants, however well they may function interpersonally, have developed resistances against attending to certain classes of cues about the effect of their behavior on others. Thus, their potential for learning newer, more functional behaviors is inhibited.

4. Even though participants might have opportunities in everyday life situation to receive such information as mentioned above, it is extremely difficult for them to feel free enough to practice new behavior because of the real or imagined high risk involved.

5. It is unlikely that participants have had the opportunity to ex-

---

[34]B. Lubin and W. B. Eddy. "The Laboratory Training Model: Rationale, Method and Some Thoughts," *International Journal of Group Psychotherapy*, 20:305-339 (July, 1970).

amine dimensions of their "home" group at work and their own performance in relation to the working group dimensions.

6. While participants may have considerable cognitive knowledge about "principles" of leadership, communication, group dynamics, etc., they may not be able, for a variety of reasons, to translate the knowledge into action. The experience-based laboratory approach may help them to operationalize their knowledge into action.[35]

Through the laboratory design of looking at communication modes, leadership styles, group roles, and group process, the participants learn about the group process, receive feedback, and try out new behaviors. Schein and Bennis describe the attitudinal changes that often occur in laboratory training, in three developmental phases (after Kurt Lewin): (1) unfreezing, (2) changing, and (3) refreezing. Table IV-I illustrates the design focus, individual and organizational relevance, and experiences throughout a basic T-Group. Different T-Groups have different foci, i.e. conflict resolution, personal growth and training in laboratory education, and organizational development.[36]

Psychoanalytically Oriented Group Process Approaches

Traditional Freudian and neo-Freudian psychoanalytic approaches tended to initially reject the group as a treatment milieu.[37] Burrow was the first to apply psychoanalytic methods to a group of persons who sought the resolution of deeper internal conflicts.[38] Wolf, *et al.*, state that

the focus of the psychoanalytically oriented group process approach is on an understanding of the unconscious processes and motivation, the significance of resistance, transference, and dreams, the importance of historical determination in current behavior, the necessity for working out and working through psychodynamic and psychopathological mechanisms.[39]

[35]*Ibid*, p. 326.

[36]*Ibid*.

[37]F. Alexander and L. S. Saul. "Three Criminal Types as Seen by the Psychoanalyst," *Psychoanalytic Review*, 2:24 (1937).

[38]A. Wolf, *et al.*, in C. J. Sager and H. S. Kaplan, *op. cit.*, p. 48.

[39]*Ibid*, p. 48-49.

TABLE IV-I BASIC LABORATORIES IN HUMAN INTERACTION

DESIGN FOCUS	INDIVIDUAL AND ORGANIZATIONAL RELEVANCE	EXPERIENCES
PERSONAL AND INTERPERSONAL	more openness and honesty in dealing with self and others/reduced defensiveness and game-type behavior/increased ability to learn from one's own behavior/expanded awareness to growth potential/increased awareness of racially conditioned feelings and attitudes	T-Groups Nonverbal Painting Improvisation and fantasy Body movement
	improved communication with others/development of new ways of working with others/locating feelings that block satisfactory and effective relationships, and bringing these out for examination/working for creative resolution to conflict	Interpersonal confrontation Racial confrontation
INTERGROUP	effects on your behavior when your group is working with another group/looking at your loyalties in multigroup operations/diagnosing intragroup problems brought on by intergroup work/examining the effect of different racial mixtures	T-groups Competitive and collaborative exercises Observation of groups
	examining intergroup consultation, cooperation, and competition (corresponds to interdepartmental relationships in a firm)/how changes can be made between groups/looking at payoffs for collaboration and competition/conceptualizing and confronting conflict, including that generated by racial differences	Conflict models Multiple loyalty simulations Construction of conceptual models
GROUP	increasing ability to act in different ways in a group and to live with different types of group climate, including that in which race is a problem/getting feedback on your group style and work methods/using your own feelings to help understand group process/feeling freer in groups	T-groups Role analysis Cluster and large groups Team building Consultation
	understanding stages of group life and development/leadership/membership in groups (such as departments, task forces, teams, classes)/learning why some problems get "solved" over and over, and why some decisions don't stick/constructive methods for dealing with problem members/experimenting with different methods for handling racially generated problems	Helping relationships Construction of conceptual models Group problem-solving exercises

The fundamental difference between psychoanalytic group approaches and all other approaches may be identified as working with unconscious material, or the exploration of intrapsychic processes.

Similar techniques, such as free association and dream interpretation, are used by therapists whether in individual or group situations. Wolf summarizes psychoanalysis in groups by stating the following:

> Pressures toward group conformity are on the increase today to the point where many fear the individual, with his problems, hopes and aspirations, will be overwhelmed. Experience in psychoanalysis in groups has shown that in successful treatment each patient interacts with other members of the group, at the same time he analytically confronts his own conflicts and disturbances, the pressures exerted by his neurosis and by the group and authority are lessened. As this process continues, each individual increases his independence, his capacity for positive fulfillment, his sense of personal responsibility, and his ability to make more reasonable, more humanized, and more courageous adaptations. These changes in character and behavior attend his own real needs and the appropriate needs of group members and meaningful individuals in his life outside the group.[40]

Psychodrama Group Process Approach

Joseph Moreno was one of the first psychotherapists to recommend the use of activity as a means of creating a therapeutic climate in a group setting.[41] Role-playing is the primary focal point of this approach. Moreno defines role as:

> the actual and tangible form the individual assumes in the specific moment he reacts to a specific situation in which other persons or objects are involved. The symbolic representation of this functioning form is perceived by the individual and others. The form is created by past experiences and the cultural patterns of the society in which the individual lives, and may be satisfied by the specific type of his

---

[40]A. Wolf, "Psychoanalysis in Groups," in G. M. Gazda, ed., *Basic Approaches to Group Psychotherapy and Group Counseling,* (Springfield, Illinois, Charles C Thomas, Publishers, 1968), pp. 80-109.

[41]J. L. Moreno, *Psychodrama: The Principle of Spontaneity,* Vol. 1 (New York, Beacon House, Inc., 1946).

productivity. Every role is a fusion of private and collective elements. Every role has two sides, a private and a collective side.[42]

There are four principles which characterize the therapeutic process in psychodrama. They are: (1) Therapeutic interaction—the interactive skills of each individual are productively employed; (2) Spontaneity—free and unhindered participation of group members; (3) Catharsis: individual, group and action; and finally; (4) Confrontation with reality or reality testing. In psychodrama, an experimental climate is established through role-playing. Participants are faced with the task of improvising roles and creating those roles on the spur of the moment. Moreno states that through role-playing the 'true' self of the individual emerges; the self emerges from the portrayal of various roles.[43]

Psychodrama may be defined as the group approach which explores the truth through *dramatic* methods. Moreno and Kipper point to five basic instruments which are necessary to psychodrama (Drama as used here is defined as action or a thing done.): (1) The Stage—a space which is an extension of life beyond and including the reality range; (2) The Participant—the playwright, the focal patient; (3) The Director—producer, therapist, and analyst; (4) Staff of Auxiliary Egos—actors, therapeutic agents and social investigators; (5) The Audience—'becomes' the participant, participates in the stage action.[44]

Through a series of techniques, the participant increases his self-awareness, "rehearses" new behaviors and begins to understand his own behavior in psychodrama. The sharing of the total responsibility of all participants throughout the 'drama,' clarifies to each participant the role and their real selves in relation to the outside world.

Transactional Analysis Group Process Approach

In the life of every individual the dramatic life events, the roles that are learned, rehearsed, and acted out, are originally determined by

---

[42]J. L. Moreno and D. A. Kipper, "Group Psychodrama and Community-Centered Counseling," in G. M. Gazda, *op. cit.,* 1968, pp. 27-79.

[43]*Ibid,* pp. 42-43.

[44]*Ibid,* pp. 56-59.

a script, life drama a person may be unaware of but feels compelled to live by. An individual plays out his script within the context of the society in which he lives and which has its own dramatic patterns. As Shakespeare said, all the world is a stage. Culture follows scripts; families follow scripts; individuals follow scripts. Each individual's life is a unique drama which can include elements of both family and cultural scripts. The interplay of these scripts affects the drama of each person's life and thereby unfolds the history of a people.[45]

Originally developed as a method of psychotherapy by Eric Berne, Transactional Analysis (TA) has developed into a general group process approach. Developed from Berne's observations of clients who were eager to learn, change, and understand their behaviors, TA attempts to clear the way to expression of genuine affect rather than encouraging mere dramatic incidents based on external motivation.[46]

He observed that individuals have various "selves" and that these "selves" transacted with others in different ways and these transactions can be interpreted and analyzed, hence, the name Transactional Analysis.

TA tends to be among the more rational approaches to group process in that it is: ". . . based upon the assumption that any individual can learn to trust himself, think for himself, make his own decisions, and express his feelings."[47] TA is essentially a cognitive group process approach in that cognitive processes, intellect, are a prime focal point. An important goal of TA is to establish the most open and authentic communication possible between the affective (feelings) and the intellectual (cognitive) components of the personality.[48] Berne states that within each individual are three transactional persons: 1) the parent, 2) the adult, and 3) the child. For a more complete exposition of this three-in-one concept, see *I'm O.K., You're O.K.*, by Thomas Harris. The group facilitator's function

[45]D. Jongeward and M. James, *Winning with People* (Reading, Mass., Addison-Wesley, 1973).

[46]E. Berne, *Principles of Group Treatment* (New York, Oxford University Press, 1966), p. 216.

[47]M. James and D. Jongeward, *Born to Win* (Reading, Mass., Addison-Wesley, 1971), p. 12.

[48]E. Berne, *op. cit.*, p. 216.

within the group is to observe, analyze, and interpret in TA terminology the group participant's behavior in each transactional state. Through this structural analysis of a participant's script, the participant can come to a better understanding of who he is and why he behaves in any one particular manner.

Organizational Development

Organizational Development (OD) as a broadly based group process approach has its origin essentially in the business and industrial field. Argyris[49] cites the properties of organizations from which OD derives its basis:

1. Organizations are ongoing systems with a past, present, and future.
2. Organizations draw from the environment in order to maintain their steady state.
3. Organizations have been created in order to accomplish something that was too difficult and complex for an individual or a few individuals to accomplish.
4. An organization, being a human creation, represents a universe of discourse which is value-laden rather than value-free.[50]

McGregor[51] in his synthesis of Maslow's hierarchy of needs into bipolar theoretical assumptions about leadership and management, focuses upon the need of any individual to understand his personal assumptions about human nature and groups in general. McGregor's Theory X and Theory Y are summarized below:

The *Theory* X Manager, Dean of Students, or College President holds that:

1. Management is responsible for organizing the elements of productive enterprise—money, materials, people—in the interest of economic ends.
2. With respect to people, this is a process of directing their efforts,

---

[49]C. Argyris, *Intervention Theory and Method: A Behavioral Science View* (Reading, Mass., Addison-Wesley, 1970).

[50]*Ibid.*, pp. 279-280.

[51]D. McGregor, "The Human Side of Enterprise," *Adventures in Thought and Action Proceeding of the Fifth Anniversary Convocation of the School of Management* (Cambridge, Mass., M.I.T. Technology Press, April 9, 1957).

motivating them, controlling their actions, modifying their behavior to fit the needs of the organization.
3. Without this active intervention by management, people would be passive even resistant to organizational needs.
4. The average man is indolent—he works as little as possible.
5. He lacks ambition, dislikes responsibility, prefers to be led.
6. He is inherently self-centered, indifferent to organizational needs.
7. He is by nature resistant to change.
8. He is gullible, not very bright, the ready dupe of the charlatan and the demagogue.

On the other hand, the *Theory* Y Manager, Dean of Students or College President holds that:

1. Management is responsible for organizing the elements of productive enterprise—money, materials, people—in the interest of economic ends.
2. People are *not* by nature passive or resistant to organizational needs. They have become so as a result of experience in organizations.
3. The motivation, the potential for development, the capacity for assuming responsibility, the readiness to direct behavior toward organizational goals are all present in people. Management does not put them there. It is a responsibility of management to make it possible for people to recognize these human characteristics for themselves.
4. The essential task of management is to arrange organizational conditions and methods of operation so that people can acheive their own goals *best* by directing *their own* efforts toward organizational objectives.[52]

The OD Specialist strives, through a specified design, to help an organization develop its goals and objectives, usually a group process approach. Fordyce identifies nine goals that an OD specialist works toward in working with an organization:

1. To create an open, problem-solving climate throughout the organization.
2. To supplement the authority associated with the role or status with the authority of knowledge and competence.
3. To locate decision-making and problem-solving responsibilities as close to the information sources as possible.

[52]The Conference Board, Inc., *Behavioral Science: Concept and Management Application* (The Conference Board, Inc., 1969), pp. 11-16).

4. To build trust among individuals and groups throughout the organization.
5. To make competition more relevant to work goals and to maximize collaborative efforts.
6. To develop a reward system which recognizes both the achievement of the organization's overall goals and organizational development.
7. To increase the sense of 'ownership' of organizational objectives throughout the work force.
8. To help managers to manage according to objectives which are relevant rather than according to 'past practices' or according to objectives which do not make sense to one's area of responsibility.
9. To increase self-control and self-direction for people within an organization.[53]

The techniques employed in OD vary widely, depending upon the particular needs of any one organization or person within the organization. Leadership training, management seminars, and simulation training are usual group methodologies which have proven to be effective with specific client populations. A minimum of flexibility is built into these "packaged-programmed materials" which might introduce the above generalized objectives.

Beckhard discusses the more involved OD consultant's group process methodology and states that the consultant's strategies and underlying assumptions are a part of a developmental process. The consultant follows a planned sequence of intervention. New behaviors are taught to and learned by the client system. The OD consultant's primary goal is to . . . . "help the client collect appropriate and correct information about feelings in the situation and then help create a training or learning situation in which those concerned could, in a supportive climate, look at this information and work jointly on ways of dealing with it."[54]

The ultimate goal for any OD Consultant or Specialist is to help the client system develop strategies for dealing with itself

[53]J. Fordyce, "What is O.D.?" *News and Reports*, Washington, D.C., NTL Institute for Applied Behavioral Science, 2, No. 3 June, 1968.

[54]R. Beckhard, "Helping a Group with Planned Change," *Journal of Social Issues*, 15. No. 2, 1959, 13-19.

and its environment. The group process continuum moves from an initial highly dependent phase to a highly independent phase when the OD consultant's services are no longer needed, i.e. the client system is capable of developing and instituting its own changes.

The following points are presented to increase reader understanding of Organizational Development:

1. It is important to remember that OD is *not* a specific group process approach, e.g. sensitivity training. Many businesses use little or no sensitivity training in their organizational development work. Other companies include T-Groups, but only as one of the many available strategies and in most instances to achieve work-related goals.

2. OD is *not* giving advice. There are so-called professionals who are usually called public relations consultants who advise organizations. OD consultants, on the other hand, do not give advice, rather they attempt to teach process skills that enable client systems to make their own decisions and work to develop their own answers.

3. OD does *not* concentrate on changing individuals, but on changing the climate or culture of an entire organization.

When the above points are taken into consideration, OD will continue to produce essentially positive results. The organization will tend to be healthier for those who work for the organization and the benefits for each individual within the organization will also be healthier.

RESEARCH ON GROUP PROCESS APPROACHES

Within the last few years, the importance and use of group process approaches, including sensitivity training, basic encounter, group counseling, and group therapy, have been emphasized. Rogers has referred to the intensive group experience as "the most significant social invention of this century."[55] Kagan has stated the belief that "a counseling (or encounter group) conducted by a competent counselor (or facilitator) is the most potent current

[55]C. R. Rogers, *Interpersonal Relationships: U.S.A. 2000,* (mimeo) Symposium paper, Esalen Institute, January 10, 1968, p. 1.

[56]N. Kagan, "Issues in Encounter," *The Counseling Psychologist,* 2:43 (1970).

learning experience in psychology or education."[56] Lakin, who has discussed ethical issues concerning sensitivity training, has noted that it is a "powerful form of experiential learning," and adds that it is "an obviously significant and often helpful growth in American psychology."[57]

Such statements represent significant and highly positive endorsements of the importance and potential value of group counseling or encounter. It should be noted though, that Lakin also points out that sensitivity training may be "abused or subverted into an instrument of unwarranted influence and ill-considered, even, harmful practices."[58] It should also be noted that in Kagan's statement, concerning the potency of group counseling or encounter groups the words "conducted by a qualified counselor" are included. Apparently, group experiences can be important, meaningful, valuable, effective, and therapeutic. On the other hand, it is also apparent that not all group experiences are effective.

Enthusiasm concerning the value of group experiences has often been extreme for both many leaders and for many participants. Often, though not always, the sources of enthusiasm appears to be rather superficial, such as focusing on the expression of hostility *per se*, ("it was really tough in there"), the experiencing of anxiety ("my hands were sweaty"), or the ability to tolerate silence ("I could hardly stand it, but I didn't break!"). Likewise, enthusiastic reports have often focused upon the expression of affection and warmth, including both verbalizations of "liking" or "loving" or nonverbal expressions of touching or embracing.

No doubt these kinds of experiences may be new, novel, or meaningful for some persons, and they may be phenomena or events that act as means toward ends, but frequently, they seem to be treated as "ends" in and of themselves. It is very questionable that effectiveness of a group experience can be equated with the expression of hostility or the ability to tolerate silence, though

[57]M. Lakin, "Some Ethical Issues in Sensitivity Training," *American Psychologist,* 24:923 (1969).

[58]*Ibid.,* p. 928.

any of these may represent aspects of a process that develops and occurs as the individuals in the group move toward growth.

In some instances, the assumption that aspects of group process equals effectiveness is made, not only by participants, but also by leaders. At times, it appears that the leader who is concerned about his own effectiveness as a facilitator or counselor may clutch at superficial aspects or highly intense emotional experiences as a proof to himself that he is being effective or that his group is "moving." Statements that a group session was "good" sometimes appear to be based on such events as two people embracing, someone breaking down and crying, or two people yelling angrily at each other. These kinds of things may occur in groups. To equate them with effectiveness, however, appears to be open to question. The counselor who equates such aspects with effectiveness may, with or without awareness, provoke and reinforce such behaviors in order to feel that he is effective.

Reports, whether or not they are enthusiastic, need to be considered, but they hardly constitute research data. Reports, anecdotes, or first-person accounts may be useful in generating hypotheses for investigation, but research investigations are necessary.

Statements concerning the effectiveness of group experiences vary. Mahler states that "the past research efforts in group counseling have had generally inconclusive results."[59] In terms of group psychotherapy, Goldstein, Sechrest, and Heller point out that practice is based upon literature "consisting overwhelmingly of anecdoted, case history, and related impressionistic reports."[60] Similarly, Burton indicates that evidence for the effectiveness of encounter is "simply testimonials."[61] The problem with testimonials is that they also provide evidence for astrology, witch doctor's cures, and homemade medicines (some of which may be

[59]C. A. Mahler, "Group Counseling," *Personnel and Guidance Journal,* 49:607 (1971).

[60]A. Goldstein, L. B. Sechrest, and K. Heller, *Psychotherapy and the Psychology of Behavior Change* (New York, John Wiley & Sons, Inc., 1966), p. 319.

[61]A. Burton, "Encounter, Existence, and Psychotherapy," in Arthur Burton, ed., *Encounter,* (San Francisco, Jossey-Bass, Inc., Publishers, 1970) p. 23.

10 to 14 percent alcohol which might account for their enabling the user to "feel better"). Testimonials may provide hypotheses for further testing but are not "hard data." Before the picture of group process research appears too bleak or dismal it should again be pointed out that reactions do vary to some extent.

On the other hand, for example, Rogers has stated that, though "the research on group experiences is not a masterpiece of precision," he notes that some changes in self-concept, attitudes, and behavior have been found and that "a reasonable number of these changes persist over time."[62] Furthermore, he points out that some research of "high quality" is available."[63] In reviewing a large number of studies on group therapy, Bednar and Lawlis reported that group therapy contributes to improved self-adjustment and to improved environmental adjustment in the hospital setting.[64] They further state that "the evidence is sufficiently clear to indicate the potential value of group therapy, irrespective of the treatment population, in any program involved with institutional living."[65] The potential value of group therapy is pointed out, but Bednar and Lawlis also note that group psychotherapy research lacks sophistication. They state the following:

> Few areas of psychology are characterized by as diffuse experimentation as group psychotherapy. This may be partly the result of a practical interest in specific areas, but mainly it represents the elementary status of group psychotherapy as a scientific discipline. Most of the literature is not experimental in nature, but rather descriptive of therapists' experience or recommendations.[66]

A second review by Gazda[67] of 145 group counseling re-

[62]C. R. Rogers, "The Group of Age," *Psychology Today,* 3:58 (1969).
[63]C. R. Rogers, *Carl Rogers On Encounter Groups* (New York, Harper & Row Publishers, Inc., 1970), p. 49.
[64]R. Bednar and G. Lawlis, "Empirical Research in Group Psychotherapy," in Allen E. Bergin and Sol L. Garfield, *Handbook of Psychotherapy and Behavior Change: An Empirical Analysis,* (New York, John Wiley & Sons, Inc., 1971), p. 818.
[65]*Ibid.,* p. 821.
[66]*Ibid.,* p. 833.
[67]G. M. Gazda, *Group Counseling: A Developmental Approach,* (Boston, Allyn & Bacon, Inc., 1971), p. 194-215.

search studies from 1938-1970 yielded somewhat similar conclusions. There is evidence of some positive growth or change in terms of group counseling, but his "basic conclusion is that group counseling is still inconclusive."[68] He points out that there are many weaknesses in group counseling research[69] and that "many of the studies reporting positive change through group counseling intervention were anecdoted or descriptive reports in which no control groups were used."[70] In somewhat more than one half of the studies positive change was reported, but "the majority of positive changes were reported through descriptive means." He states the following:

> ... about 50 percent of the studies utilizing GPA and/or academic achievement showed significant increases or improvement versus an equal number which showed no significant improvement. Self-concept improvement and related self-variable changes were reported in approximately 20 percent of the studies. Other significant improvement was reported as decreased anxiety, improved family and peer relations, improved relationships with authority figures, improvement in work attitudes, improved behavior in school, improved school attendance, increased acceptance of others, increase in educational and occupational-seeking behavior, improved sociometric choices, and improvement in reading.[71]

Again, the literature appears to indicate the potential value of group experiences, but the evidence is hardly conclusive. Undoubtedly, more research is needed, and the research needs to become more sophisticated.

One particular recent study by Lieberman, Yalom, and Miles needs to be examined. In this study, 209 undergraduate students were assigned by stratified random sampling to eighteen groups, ranging from sensitivity training, Gestalt, and psychoanalytic to synanon, marathon, transactional analysis, and leaderless group approaches. The control group consisted of sixty-nine subjects. All group leaders were highly experienced, and the groups met for about thirty hours. Outcome data consisted of seventy-three

68*Ibid.*, p. 209.
69*Ibid.*, p. 212.
70*Ibid.*, p. 213.
71*Ibid.*, p. 206.

indices including attitudes toward encounter, self-rating, inter-personal values, interpersonal behavior, perceptions of significant others, friendship patterns, self-system, self-image, self-ideal dis-crepancy, and coping styles.[72]

Lieberman, Yalom, and Miles state that at the end of the group experience "61 percent of students reported that the group had changed them in a positive direction." Also, it was reported that at termination participants' self-ratings significantly differed from those of controls on a number of behaviors, clustering in the areas of increased understanding of inner feelings and in-creased sensitivity to others." It is noted that it is not uncommon for encounter group participants to be enthusiastic about their experience at termination, but they point out that six months later the ratio of high to low evaluations by students in their study was reduced from 4.7 to 1 to 2.3 to 1.[73] It was also found that "the most powerful change discriminators between experi-mental and controls were found in the self-system area."[74] Major differences were not revealed between experimentals and con-trols on many of the change measures, "nor was there any evi-dence of major change in how the person related to significant others outside the group."[75] Lieberman, Yalom, and Miles state:

> There can be no question that the encounter experience was mean-ingful to those who participated, but the impact of the experience seems to have been internal and not readily apparent to those in the participants' social network. At this stage of analysis, the impact of the group experience seems best understood as influencing a shift in participants' value attitude system, a shift which is accompanied by efforts to redirect behavior in forms consonant with encounter group values.[76]

A final note, though a discouraging one, must also be pointed out concerning this study. Lieberman, Yalom, and Miles report

[72]M. Lieberman, I. Yalom, and M. Miles, "Impact on Participants," in L. Solomon and B. Berzon, eds., *New Perspectives on Encounter Groups*, (San Francisco, Jossey-Bass, Inc., Publishers, 1972), pp. 119-134. See Also M. Lieberman, I. Yalom, and M. Miles, *Encounter Groups: First Facts*, (New York, Basic Books, Inc., 1973).

[73]*Ibid.*, p. 129.

[74]*Ibid.*, p. 130.

[75]*Ibid.*, p. 131.

[76]*Ibid.*, p. 131.

"that four to eight months after the group experience, 9.4 percent of the participants who completed the experience . . . showed evidence of negative outcome."[77] An individual who suffered enduring psychological harm as a result of the experience (evident six to eight months after the end of the group), was defined as a casualty or negative outcome. The researchers further note that they feel that their casualty rate figures are conservative. Just as surprising and alarming was the finding that the most accurate predictor of casualties was not leader rating, but rather peer judgment; it was, however, also pointed out that most of those identified as casualties "could not have been identified easily during the life of the group."[78] It should also be noted that leaders characterized by aggressive stimulation and relatively high charisma conducted groups with high casualty rates.[79]

The few selected findings of the study by Lieberman, Yalom, and Miles reported above hardly does justice to the vast fund of information presented in their work. Readers are strongly encouraged to intensely examine the preceding references. A statement from their most recent book states the following:

> Based both on the number of individuals who experienced benefit from the groups and on the comparison of the different areas in participants and their controls, it was concluded that overall, encounter groups show a modest positive impact, an impact much less than has been portrayed by their supporters and an impact significantly lower than participants view of their own change would lead one to assume.
>
> To a considerable extent, the modesty of the gain can be attributed to the wide differences among the various groups studied. Some groups were highly productive learning environments, others were innocuous, providing a certain degree of pleasurable stimulation but little learning as measured here. Still others were on balance destructive, leaving more of their participants psychologically harmed than psychologically benefited.[80]

[77]*Ibid.*, pp. 131-132.

[78]*Ibid.*, p. 133.

[79]M. Lieberman. "Behavior and Impact of Leaders," in L. Solomon and B. Berzon, eds., *New Perspectives on Encounter Groups,* (San Francisco, Jossey-Bass, Inc., Publishers, 1972), p. 162.

[80]M. Lieberman, I. Yalom, M. Miles, *Encounter Groups: First Facts,* (New York, Basic Books, Inc., 1973), p. 130.

In summary, concerning the effectiveness of group experience as determined by research, certain points seem to stand out. *First,* much of the data reported tended to be descriptive and anecdotal, rather than experimental. *Second,* there is a need for improvement and sophistication in research. *Third,* enthusiastic reports or positive evaluation by participants at the end of a group experience need to be viewed with some caution since it appears that the degree of positiveness tends to decrease to some extent over time. *Fourth,* people can be hurt in groups, and the percentage of negative effects is probably greater than what has usually been expected. *Fifth,* and finally, there is some evidence, though apparently modest, that group experience can be effective. Perhaps, the evidence available indicates primarily the *potential* value of group experience. It is very apparent that more research is needed in this most complex area.

The research raises questions for both group leaders and participants concerning the validity of their assumptions regarding group approaches and their experiences in group experiences.

It appears that some of the assumptions made concerning group process, in general, are open to question.* Ten such assumptions, which are either implied or verbalized by leaders and/or participants, will be examined. The focus is upon group process approaches or methods in general, rather than any specific approach or method. One reason for this general focus is that descriptions of two experiences, both labeled as sensitivity training, may differ greatly. It also appears that what occurs under the label "group counseling" in two different groups may be similar or different. Encounter for one writer or practitioner may not be the same as encounter for another. Therefore, it is difficult to deal with assumptions in terms of "group counseling" or "encounter." Rather, the focus is upon those assumptions in group process in general or those made by some leaders and

*The discussion of assumptions is a revision and an extension of a paper by Pancrazio entitled, "A Group Experience—For What?" which was published in *The Journal of the Student Personnel Association for Teacher Education,* 2:52-55 (1970).

participants which appear to be open to question. To question an assumption does not necessarily mean that it is false, though it may be. Questioning indicates that certainty may not be as great at this time as would be desirable, in particular where empirical data related to effectiveness is lacking or inconclusive.

It is not suggested that all group leaders or counselors make these assumptions, that the assumptions relate to any one type of group activity, or that the value of all group process methods is questioned. It is rather an attempt to present and discuss questionable assumptions which appear to be in need of consideration and examination.

First, *the expression of hostility and/or affection per se can be equated with effectiveness.* Hostility or affection may be expressed in groups. No doubt, it is often necessary to work through hostilities or anxieties in order for movement or growth to occur, but these are not goals or ends.

Frequently, there seems to be a premium placed on the expression of negative feelings. Coulson points out that an encounter group is *not* defined as "where one vents his emotions." He states that feelings and emotions are not the same. Feelings are defined as things "which are hard to say"; one often becomes emotional in saying them.[81] An encounter group, he adds, is not always emotional, but it is always feelingful. Apparently, many participants expect or perceive a group as a place to "vent their emotions." Lakin points out that "the motivation of many present participants is cathartic rather than intellectual, . . . seeking an emotional experience rather than understanding."[82] If persons (participants or leaders) expect a focus on expression of negative (or positive) feelings, the likelihood that this will occur probably increases. If a leader evaluates progress on the basis of such aspects, he may, as previously stated, provoke their occurrence and maintain them.

Second, *group process consists of a series of techniques.* To

[81]W. Coulson, "Inside A Basic Encounter Group," *The Counseling Psychologist,* 2:16 (1970).

[82]*Op. cit.,* p. 924.

assume that affective techniques or exercises are essential to group effectiveness is questionable. Techniques to increase awareness or sensitivity may be of value when used appropriately and effectively. Not all leaders of group process approaches use techniques. Techniques abound! They are easily accessible. On the surface, many appear to be simple and easy to administer. This is most likely deceptive. Techniques in the hands of an uninformed and inadequately prepared leader (or counselor) may do more harm than good. For some, though not all, techniques appear to serve as a crutch. For others, they seem to be utilized as an attempt to speed up group process. For a few leaders, there appears to be an equating of group counseling with merely participation in a series of techniques, which are exciting, novel, or fun. Experiencing the techniques may become an end, rather than a means toward understanding self and others, improving communications, or understanding processes or dynamics occurring in a group. Counseling, in any form, is *not,* simply a set of techniques.

Third, *the effectiveness of techniques, including nonverbal exercises, has been demonstrated through research.* Gazda, Duncan, and Sission state that there is little research evidence, concerning nonverbal techniques, to "validate their use or to tell us when they may be most appropriately employed."[83] Most available information concerning the use of techniques appears to be generally descriptions of the technique and results of its use based upon the observations and experience of a particular person who used it. Research data are rare, or nonexistent.

Fourth, *experience is of value in and of itself.* Mahler states the following:

> Some group workers, particularly the encounter type, assume that learning derives from experience. These leaders often feel that catharsis and exhilarating responses will lead to changed behavior. Transfer of learning experiments have produced too much evidence that change of behavior is not easy enough to leave it to chance.[84]

[83]G. M. Gazda, J. A. Duncan, and P. J. Sisson, "Professional Issues in Group Work," *Personnel and Guidance Journal,* 49:642 (1971).
[84]*Op. cit.*, p. 602.

According to Burton, encounter "overstresses the direct experience."[85] It appears that the experience *per se* is not as important as what one gains from achieving goals whether they be self-acceptance, acceptance, and understanding of others, improved interpersonal skills, improved academic skills, weight loss, or highly specific behavior changes. It would appear that participation in group experiences should result in personal learnings that can be related to living outside the group. Apparently, experiences do not automatically lead to such results. Ohlsen notes a tendency of some participants to "return repeatedly to groups for peak experiences rather than to learn to apply in daily living what they learned in groups."[86] Burton states that some people "go to encounter groups like some go to Arthur Murray clubs."[87] Joining groups as "the thing to do" or developing dependency on the group would hardly be a positive outcome. Lakin states that "participants are often dramatically affected by training," and both trainer and the group in some instances "are mutually reluctant to end the group."[88]

Fifth, *everyone needs and can benefit from a group experience*. To the extent that the counselor or leader is facilitative, clients or participants tend to benefit, but not all relationships with counselors or leaders are facilitative.

Mahler states that there is a "too frequent naive view that the mere placing of individuals in a group will be good for them."[89] Also, Golembiewski and Blumberg state that "not everyone can learn in a T-Group, of course."[90] Seashore, in discussing research on sensitivity training, points out that "everyone does not benefit equally." Burton states that encounter "is not in-

[85]*Op. cit.*, p. 18.

[86]M. M. Ohlsen, "Reactions to Coulson's Paper," *The Counseling Psychologist,* 2:39 (1970).

[87]*Op. cit.*, p. 23.

[88]*Op. cit.*, p. 927.

[89]*Op. cit.*, p. 601.

[90]R. T. Golembiewski and A. Blumberg, eds., *Sensitivity Training and the Laboratory Approach: Readings about Concepts and Applications,* (Itasca, Illinois, F. E. Peacock Publishers, Inc., 1970), p. 13.

tended for the impoverished or the racially deprived but for the middle class."[91] Probably not all would agree with his point.

The assumption of need and benefit for all is open to question, but appears often to be held (or even stated) by those who are most deeply enthusiastic about their own group experience(s). On occasion, tremendously enthusiastic advocates sincerely, and with good intensions, want others to gain as they feel they have from their experiences. Ironically, such "good intentions" result frequently in a pushing or subtle pressuring of others to "group" whenever or wherever the enthusiast finds himself with two or more people. The "pushing" may occur even when the verbal or nonverbal cues being sent out by those being "pushed" indicate a lack of interest, annoyance, or even anger that someone else is implying that they need what is being offered and will be provided with it whether or not invited or requested to do so.

Sixth, *all feedback is good*. Feedback may be harmful, as well as helpful. Lakin sees the goal of feedback as providing honest, constructive reactions.[92] Honesty for the sake of honesty may not always be constructive. Confrontation for the sake of confrontation, likewise, may not lead to constructive results.

It appears that in some groups a premium is placed on the expression of negative feelings. In others, where the norm of the group is on excessive support and reassurance, a premium may be placed on expressing affection, "being nice," or avoiding negative reactions or conflict. This type of experience may also be ineffective.

It is not enough to have open, honest communication; hopefully, the communication will be constructive, rather than destructive, and positive, as well as negative. At least two dimensions of feedback might be considered: (1) positive, negative, and (2) constructive, destructive. Negative feedback can be honest as well as constructive.

An atmosphere in which *only* negative or hostile feedback occurs seems no more desirable than one where *only* positive or affectional feedback is allowed. Lakin states: "In some groups that

[91]*Op. cit.*, p. 8.
[92]*Op. cit.*

emphasize emotional expressiveness, some trainers purposefully elicit aggressive and/or affectionate behaviors by modeling them and then inviting imitation."[93]

The leader obviously needs to know himself. If he has needs to express his own hostility, a group whose norm is aggressive reactions may be an avenue, though an inappropriate one, for him. The leader who cannot deal with his own feelings of hostility, who is easily threatened by conflict, or who needs to be "loved by everyone in the group," may manipulate the group by modeling and reinforcing only positive or affectional reactions.

Seventh, *a group will protect and defend its weaker members.* Goodstein states that this may be true in some cases, but not all: ". . . this is not necessarily the norm which develops in all groups. Much depends upon the personal styles of the individual group members, including the trainer, the particular history of the group, and how the group norms were developed."[94]
Groups for which the assumption is met may be those in which the leader is an experienced facilitator who models understanding, acceptance, sensitivity, and constructive honesty, all of which undoubtedly would influence the development of such a norm.

Ohlsen states that "consideration also must be given to the antitherapeutic effect of norms."[95] Pressures to conform may be intense. Individuals may be coerced. For example, a point of enthusiasm sometimes voiced is that an individual in a group has begun to change his behavior to be more similar to other group members (i.e. a priest removes his Roman collar or a quiet member may begin to talk). It may be in either instance that the individual chooses to do this because he feels comfortable enough in the group to change or to risk. On the other hand, he may be conforming to group standards through pressure (for which he may now in some groups be highly reinforced and no longer ignored or rejected). Hopefully, the leader or counselor is sensitive to such possibilities and can deal with them in ways which

[93]*Ibid.,* p. 925.

[94]L. D. Goodstein, "Some Issues Involved in Intensive Group Experience," *The Counseling Psychologist,* 2:52 (1970).

[95]M. M. Ohlsen, *Group Counseling,* (New York, Holt, Rinehart & Winston, Inc., 1970), p. 94.

protect the right and freedom of the individual to be different and to make his own choices, rather than be coerced.

Eighth, *anyone can lead a group.* Preparation, training, and experience of those who provide group experiences vary widely, from those who have read a book or two, to those who have participated in a weekend marathon, or to those who have completed practicum supervision in group counseling. Concerns of professionals are great. There is evidence reported by Carkhuff and Berenson[96] that suggests that all human interactions can have facilitative or deteriorative effects. Burton states: "The fact that encounter is potentially so pregnant does not alter the fact that in practice it leaves much to be desired. Like all new growth movements it attracts the opportunist, the promotor, the self-styled healer, the charismatic would be saint, the sick and the sadistic."[97]

Ninth, *people can't be hurt in groups.* As previously discussed in this chapter, the percentage of negative outcomes or psychological casualties was nearly 10 percent. Also, Eddy and Lubin state that about 10 percent or less of those who participate in T-groups report negative feelings about their experiences, that research of negative effects of encounter is "almost totally nonexistent," and that for about .2 to .5 percent of participants in laboratory training in general there are harmful effects.[98] Seashore also states, concerning T-groups, that less than one percent is the rate of incidence of serious stress and mental disturbance, and that in nearly all cases those persons had a history of prior disturbance.[99] Eddy and Lubin state that "laboratory training should *not* be viewed as a benign and foolproof method."[100] Burton points out that encounter "has not yet gotten around to specifying its dangers, and it ignores those who have been hurt by it and even suicided."[101]

[96]R. R. Carkhuff and B. G. Berenson, *Beyond Counseling and Therapy,* (New York, Holt, Rinehart & Winston, Inc., 1967).

[97]*Op. cit.,* pp. 22-23.

[98]W. B. Eddy and B. Lubin, "Laboratory Training and Encounter Groups," *Personnel and Guidance Journal,* 49:630-633 (1971).

[99]*Op. cit.*

[100]*Op. cit.,* p. 633.

[101]*Op. cit.,* p. 23.

Tenth, *the effectiveness of group experiences has been clearly demonstrated through research.* In view of the previously discussed research, it is obvious that this assumption as stated is highly questionable. At best, the research evidence suggests the potential value of group experiences.

These assumptions need to be examined and questioned by those counselors and leaders who offer group experiences. Those who equate the expression of hostility with effectiveness, who provide simply a series of techniques, or who believe that no one can be hurt in a group might further examine their beliefs. Those who lack preparation or training might "look before they leap."

Group process methods have much potential. More needs to be known, and more will be learned through future research. Any attempt to help others may be facilitative. But, less than facilitative, or even harmful, effects can also occur. It is not enough to want to help. The need *is to help as effectively as possible.* It appears that the competencies of counselor or leader of group experiences are crucial.

ETHICAL CONSIDERATIONS

The ethical lag within group process approaches is analogous to the development of the automobile in the United States. The advent of the creation of the automobile heralded a fantastic technological explosion with regard to transportation. What our technological forefathers neglected was the cumulative effect that automobile emissions would have upon our environment resulting in the imposition of safety and emission standards on the automobile industry. The development of a code of ethical standards within the area of group process approaches, training, and practice lag almost as far behind the explosion of group process practices as the emissions standards have lagged behind the development of the automobile.

Participant Ethics

Peters[102] discusses the types of adaptation that group mem-

102D. Peters, *Transfer of Group Experience Learnings to Real World Situations.* Mimeographed paper, Basic Human Relations Laboratory, Lake Arrowhead, Calif., 1968).

bers generally make with regard to their (experiences) group process. His analogy to social travel holds much for participants in various approaches to think about and for professionals to consider. Peters described the *Tourist Reaction* as resistence toward group involvement, the over-reality testing of every novel/ new experience within the group, rating the experiences within the group as too impractical, visionary or queer to be taken seriously. The *Expatriate Reaction,* on the other extreme, is a total real-world membership rejection and has three identifiable sub modes: (1) The Easy Convert Reaction—the new experiences of the group were totally accepted, because it was the thing to do within the group experience, (2) The Missionary Reaction— the reaction is to gather ammunition to fight the real world and carry the gospel of the Group to unbelievers in the real world, and (3) The Mystic Reaction—it was a terrific experience for me, but I can't say how or why." One added sub mode, omitted by Peters, but added by the authors is the *"Gung Ho"* Reaction—a combination of the Easy Convert, The Missionary, and the Mystic, this individual not only becomes the self-proclaimed group expert and goes forth to save the world and its inhabitants, but is convinced that he is "qualified" to lead/facilitate any group for any purpose.

Peters' third major adaptation is the *Learner-Critic Reaction.* This reaction embodies a middle-of-the-road approach to viewing a group experience. Peters introduces a series of questions that encompass the *sine qua non* that individuals who participate in any group are responsible to ask themselves. These questions are the focus of ethical participant behavior in whatever the group process approach.

What Learning Can be Transferred To Other Situations?

1. We can transfer only what we can both feel at a *gut* level and understand at an intellectual level; we do need cognitive handles, concepts, and sound generalizations.
2. We can transfer only to those situations where we see a linkage or similarity to the Group Experience. (We are not saying that good groups should run like T-Groups or the Group Experience; we are saying that all groups contain many elements which we see in the Group Experience).

3. We can transfer only in terms of some "action model," some decisions about how we are going to behave in future situations to take advantage of what we have learned.

    a. Consciously attempt to obtain feedback messages and to use them in modifying our own behavior.

    b. Practice skills of leadership—membership and participant observer based on sound diagnosis of what the group needs.

4. We can transfer only what we can genuinely integrate into our personality; as long as we are too self-conscious or uncomfortable with new behaviors we will have a hard time transferring them to new situations.

Ultimately each of us must sort out the many things learned, put them into perspective, and make intelligent choice based on his values of what changes in himself to make.

What Are Some of the Basic Questions or Areas of Choice?

In a sense, what we have been playing out in the group has been some of the drama of real life around questions, such as:

1. What is my relationship to other important persons like? How deep? How healthy? What are our hidden feelings? What is our interpersonal contract?

2. What is the relation of a person to the group? How do I maintain individuality and integrity in the midst of pressures to conform? How do I acquire membership? How much of an organization man must I be? How do I work out this concern in the group and what does it teach me about my job?

3. What is my relation to authority? How do I deal with my feelings about authority, bosses, and leadership? How can I lead without guilt, or failure, or domination of others? What is the relation of freedom to boundary in this group for me—and what do I do about this on the job? In my home?

4. How do I participate in the process of organization? How do groups organize for action? What is my responsibility in this process? How much formal organization is necessary? How does participation with others get a job done?

5. How do I get data about the important decisions of management? What kinds of data are important? How can I get valid data? Are feelings facts? How does data get fed into groups, staffs, planning teams, etc.? How much data do we need in order to act? How do I help a group reach a consensus? What kinds of behavior do I have to learn in order to work with others in setting goals, in managing by objectives?

6. How do we learn? How do we grow and develop? How do I achieve integrety of self and a feeling of self worth? How do I continue to learn from my experiences as a person?[103]

Peters summarizes his discussion of ethical participant behavior in the following manner: "These concerns are not simple concerns. There are no simple answers! Anyone who looks for the gimmick, the 'answer,' the Holy Grail, is doomed to end up in a snipe hunt. The person finds his answer in a continual improvement of his own spontaneous competence, in continual working through and continual reestablishing his tentative answers to the concerns mentioned above."[104]

Participant Screening and Selection

The screening and selection of participants in the group process approaches described in this chapter are not uniform. Ohlsen among others makes a rather strong recommendation that participants in any group be carefully screened prior to group entrance.[105] The notion explicated is that the participants are protected and the group is assured of "success," with a built in screening mechanism. On the other hand, Rogers states that:

. . . . participants are largely self-selected, though preference is given to those who are already dealing with significant groups. By and large, the summer partcipants hold positions of influence in American institutional life, numbering among them college deans, elementary school administrators, college presidents, a large cadre of classroom teachers, psychologists, counselors, members of industry, some college students and chaplains, and ministers of a variety of denominations.[106]

The NTL (National Training Laboratories) Institute has developed program standards with regard to admission to group participation. Participants in all NTL programs should meet the following criteria:

[103]*Ibid.*, pp. 3-4.

[104]*Ibid.*, p. 4.

[105]M. M. Ohlsen, *Group Counseling*, (New York: Holt, Rinehart & Winston, Inc., 1970).

[106]C. R. Rogers, *Carl Rogers on Encounter Groups*, (New York, Harper & Row Publishers, Inc., 1970), p. 152.

1. Participation in the program should be voluntary.
2. No person should use the program(s) as a substitute for psycho-therapy. Anyone currently undergoing treatment for emotional difficulties or in psychotherapy is requested to discuss the advisa-ability of program attendance with the person directing his treatment.
3. Each participant should have a genuine desire to learn about himself and about interpersonal relations, small group behavior, and organization dynamics.
4. Applicants are advised that during the many years of NTL activities, an extremely small percentage of participants have experienced stress reactions in varying degrees. There is no effective means of predicting such a reaction or screening out or otherwise identifying those predisposed to such a reaction based on their prior medical history or present emotional problems identified or otherwise. Should any applicant be concerned about entering a stress situation, he is advised not to participate in the program.[107]

While the NTL Institute criteria for participant self-selection is an initial attempt at careful selection criteria, there are no valid assurances that anyone who applies to an NTL program actually meets the above criteria. On some of the more recent application forms distributed by the NTL Institute, each applicant is asked to sign a statement that he has read the admission criteria and understands and subscribes to the criteria.

Facilitator Training

Few professionals at the present time are extensively trained in various leadership modes of various group process approaches. The "Gung Ho" Reaction, which was previously described, in-dicates the enthusiasm that many participants have when re-turning to their home environments. These self-avowed "experts" call themselves leaders, facilitators, and practice their new semi-learned skills upon an unsuspecting audience, with potentially frightening results. The major concept lacking with most self-avowed "experts" and even some practicing professionals is the concept of built-in support network which may be used to refer

[107]*Application Information,* National Training Laboratories Institute for Behavioral Science (1972).

some individuals following an unsatisfactory or harmful group experience.

Gazda summarized illustrative unethical practices/behaviors reported in a 1969 study of such practices as follows:

1. A university professor who teaches introductory counseling courses was conducting encounter groups which students in these courses were required to attend. Several became upset, but they felt they had no recourse.
2. An unqualified student was reported to be leading fee-paid encounter groups.
3. A group leader was reported to be encouraging the use of drugs by participants.
4. Nude encounter groups with sexual experimentation were held for beginning teachers in a particular school system.
5. Under the pretense of a group marathon, a group leader permitted participants to be inflicted with abuse which created a situation resulting in psychotic decompensation for a participant.
6. A philosophy professor was reported to have attended a weekend group at Esalon Institute and upon returning initiated his classes in nude bathings and baptismal-type rites in a campus stream.
7. A medical doctor (a general practitioner) untrained in group work was reported to be serving as a psychologist-hypnotist doing family therapy.
8. An untrained probation officer claimed to be doing "Group psychotherapy."[108]

Again, the NTL Institute has been the professional organization which stresses training, program standards, and ethical behavior. During its initial development, an individual could become a trainer/facilitator via an apprentice program. In 1969, the Board of Directors of the NTL Institute clarified the criteria for trainer qualifications:

1. NTL Institute endorses the Ethical Standards of Psychologists of the American Psychological Association and urges its members to guide their conduct accordingly.
2. In relationships with individual clients and client groups, persons representing NTL Institute are expected to discuss candidly and fully the goals risks, limitations, and anticipated outcomes of any program under consideration.
3. NTL Institute trainers and consultants are expected to endorse

[108]*Op. cit.*, 1971, pp. 220-221.

the purposes and values and adhere to the standards presented in this paper.

4. NTL Institute trainers and consultants are expected to have mastered the following skills:

Ability to conduct a small group and to provide individual consultation using the theory and techniques of laboratory method.

Ability to articulate theory and to direct a variety of learning experiences for small and large groups and for organizations.

Ability to recognize their own behavior styles and personal needs and to deal with them productively in the performance of their professional roles.

Ability to recognize symptoms of serious psychological stress and to make responsible decisions when such problems arise.

5. NTL Institute trainers and consultants are expected to have a strong theoretical foundation. This ordinarily implies graduate work in a behavioral science discipline or equivalent experience in the field.

6. NTL Institute trainers and consultants are expected to complete the following training experiences:

Participation in at least one NTL Institute basic Human Relations laboratory.

Supervised co-training with senior staff members.

Participation on laboratory staff with experienced trainers in programs for a variety of client groups.

Participation in an NTL Institute or university program specifically designed to train trainers. (This sequence of activities usually requires a minimum of two years to complete.)

7. NTL Institute trainers and consultants are expected to continually evaluate their own work, to seek individual growth experiences, and to contribute to the evaluation and development of the art and science of training and consultation.

NOTE: Basic human relations laboratories, executive development programs, and similar beginning level programs are designed to help participants be more effective in personal and job roles, not to become trainers. *No capabilities as a T-group trainer or consultant should be assumed as a result of participation in one or more basic laboratories or other short term experiences.*[109]

Many group facilitators utilize fantasy and nonverbal tech-

[109]*Standards for the Use of Laboratory Method in NTL Institute Programs,* National Training Laboratories Institute (Washington, D.C., 1969) pp. 10-11.

niques to heighten participant awareness of self and others. These methods, while a focus of at least two group process approaches, are extremely controversial. The Midwest Group for Human Resources, now an affiliate of the NTL Institute, included criteria for the use of fantasy and nonverbal techniques in its "Laboratory Training Standards and Trainer Qualifications."

> Considerable misunderstanding and concern have been engendered by the use of nonverbal exercises and those involving fantasy and physical contact. The following criteria should be applied when the use of such an activity is considered: a) it should be an integrated element of the design of a laboratory program—it should relate to the other planned activities and not be an isolated element; b) it should clearly be related to laboratory learning goals, and not be done solely to heighten affective response; c) the goals and meaning of the exercise should be fully explained to participants and adequate time should be allowed to talk through the impact of the experience; d) trainers who use such methods should have prior experience and instruction in their use; e) care should be taken that participants be allowed to choose whether or not to participate in such activities without group or trainer pressures for conformity.[110]

Until the major national professional organizations concerned with standards for training, facilitator qualifications, and ethical facilitator behavior can form a "National Consortium for Group Process Ethical Standards," the public will be wide open to unprofessional and unethical behavior of those who proport to be group "experts."

Warnings

Shostrum indicates seven considerations that anyone should think about before plunging headlong into any group process experience. His *caveat emptor* is summarized here with additional comments.

1. *NEVER RESPOND TO A NEWSPAPER AD.* GROUPS RUN BY TRAINED PROFESSIONALS, OR HONESTLY SUPERVISED BY THEM, ARE FORBIDDEN BY ETHICAL CONSIDERATIONS TO ADVERTISE DIRECTLY. If you should

[110]Board of Directors, *Laboratory Training Standards and Trainer Qualifications,* mimeographed, (Kansas City). Midwest Group for Human Resources.

receive a brochure describing an upcoming group experience, question the source, whether received from another individual, a professional, or in the mail.

2. *NEVER PARTICIPATE IN A GROUP OF FEWER THAN A HALF-DOZEN MEMBERS.* THE NECESSARY AND VALUABLE CANDOR GENERATED BY AN EFFECTIVE GROUP CANNOT BE DISSIPATED AND SHARED IN TOO SMALL A GROUP AND SCAPEGOATING OR PURELY VICIOUS GANGING-UP CAN DEVELOP.

3. *NEVER, JOIN, or force anyone else to join, AN ENCOUNTER GROUP ON IMPULSE*—AS A BINGE, FLING OR SURRENDER TO THE UNPLANNED. ANY IMPORTANT CRISIS IN YOUR LIFE or your organization's life, HAS BEEN A LONG TIME IN PREPARATION AND DESERVES REFLECTION.

4. *NEVER PARTICIPATE IN A GROUP ENCOUNTER WITH CLOSE ASSOCIATES,* PERSONS WITH WHOM YOU HAVE PROFESSIONAL OR COMPETITIVE SOCIAL RELATIONS. Make sure the group facilitator states that all communication within the group is to be confidential. If not, stand up and leave!

5. *NEVER BE OVERLY IMPRESSED BY BEAUTIFUL OR OTHERWISE CLASS-SIGNALED SURROUNDINGS OR PARTICIPANTS.* Effective encounter groups may be held in any setting; the setting is relatively unimportant.

6. *NEVER STAY WITH A GROUP THAT HAS A BEHAVIORAL AX TO GRIND*—Any group that forces you to fit their 'mold' is unhealthy, ... AND IT HAS NOTHING TO DO WITH YOUR SELF, YOUR SWEETEST GOALS OR YOUR FULLEST LIFE AS A SELF-KNOWING, SELF-INTEGRATING HUMAN BEING.

7. *NEVER PARTICIPATE IN A GROUP THAT LACKS FORMAL CONNECTION WITH A PROFESSIONAL ON WHOM YOU CAN CHECK.* ANY REPUTABLE PROFESSIONAL HAS A VITAL STAKE IN ANY GROUP HE RUNS OR IN ANY GROUP WHOSE LEADER HE HAS TRAINED AND CONTINUES TO ADVISE AND CONSULT. Do not make any assumptions about the leader or the group, no matter how much financial investment you have in the group; you are not worth "x" amount of dollars. If the answer(s) you receive seem unreasonable to you, stand up and leave the group! You have nothing to lose except yourself![111]

[111]E. Shostrum, "Group Therapy: Let the Buyer Beware," *Psychology Today,* Vol. 2, No. 12:17-40 (1969). Quoted material in Italicized caps and caps. Authors' comments in lower case.

These are general guidelines for ethical behavior and should apply to both the participant and the group facilitator. For more specific ethical standards, the reader is referred to professional behavior models developed by organizations such as the American Guidance and Personnel Association, the American Psychological Association, the NTL Institute for Applied Behavioral Science and the American Group Psychotherapy Association. Shostrum aptly concludes his article with the following comment: "Encounter groups in all their forms are far too valuable, and the demand for such groups is far too clamorous and desperate for us to let ignorance, psycho-social greed or false prophecy tarnish them."[112]

Despite all the warnings and ethical situations discussed in this section, the authors have extremely positive feelings and attitudes toward group process approaches to facilitate personal human development. It is hoped that the intelligent reader will *not* make a generalized judgment of group process approaches based upon limited information and, thus, condemn all approaches. The use of groups, whatever the environmental setting, has yet undiscovered potentials for personal and societal growth.

SUMMARY

No society can invite change for the sake of change. It must court the kinds of change that will enrich and strengthen it rather than the kinds that will fragment and destroy it.[113]

So it is with individuals who are afraid to look at themselves, who decide not to make changes or to look at themselves and others in new and different ways. Any individual or organization that doesn't look at change and make some decisions about directions of change is bound to become stagnant, moribund, and eventually extinct. Group process approaches are attempts to understand and implement change in an ever more complex society, through individuals and organizations.

As Rogers says:

[112]*Ibid.*
[113]J. W. Gardner, *op. cit.*, p. 48.

... the whole movement toward intensive group experience in all its forms has profound significance for both today and tomorrow. Those who may have thought of the encounter group as a fad or phenomenon affecting only a few people temporarily would do well to reconsider. In the troubled future that lies ahead of us, the trend toward the intensive group experience is related to deep and significant issues having to do with change. These changes may occur in persons, in institutions, in our urban and cultural alienation, in racial tensions, in our international frictions, in our philosophies, our values, our image of man himself. It is a profoundly significant movement, and the course of its future will, for better or for worse, have a profound impact on all of us.[114]

[114]C. R. Rogers, *op. cit.*, pp. 167-168.

CHAPTER V

PSYCHOLOGICAL EDUCATION AND HUMAN RELATIONS TRAINING

James J. Pancrazio

INTRODUCTION

THE COUNSELOR, or the psychologist-counselor, is frequently the center of the student personnel program. More than this, however, in the approach to education taken in this book, he becomes, as the staff member most specifically trained in human development and human relations, the center of the total educational program. As the school moves from a subject matter orientation to a personal development orientation, the counselor becomes an active participant, as well as a consultant, in the educative process.

A number of books on affective education have been directed toward teachers. Their approaches focus upon the integration of the affective and cognitive in learning. This area will be reviewed, but the major purpose of this chapter is to examine the role of the counselor as a specialist in human relations and psychological education. In developing this examination, the following will be considered:

1. Discussion and description of various approaches to psychological education and affective learning.
2. Comparison and contrast of approaches.
3. Research data concerning effectiveness of approaches.
4. Criticism of approaches.

The importance and necessity of a movement within education from a strictly subject-matter to personal-development orientation calls for a concern for and focusing upon the affective realm—the emotional and feeling aspects of learning. The primary (and apparently often the only) concern in education, from kindergarten through graduate school, has been on knowledge, subject matter content, or the cognitive realm. As Weinstein and Fantini have stated

> "the discrepancy between the behavior of individuals in society and what they have learned, or at least what the schools purport to teach, suggests the need for examination of education's chosen channel for changing or affecting behavior. Traditionally, this channel has been subject matter *per se*—the courses offered, the curriculum taught, the academic disciplines . . . . Rarely is curriculum designed to help the student deal in personal problems of human conduct."[1]

Even though knowledge is important, it is apparent that knowledge *per se* does not necessarily affect one's attitudes or behavior. It is quite possible, for example, to know about aggression, yet not be able to understand and deal effectively with one's aggressive feelings; to know about prejudice, yet discriminate against others; to know about the attitudes and values of Willy Loman in *Death of a Salesman,* yet be unaware of one's own attitudes and values.

The personal meaning of subject matter to the learner or how the learner feels about what he learns has generally been ignored in education. Both the cognitive and affective are important in human learning and experience. As Brown points out, "there is no intellectual learning without some sort of feeling, and there are no feelings without the mind's being somewhat involved."[2] It seems that educators have been unaware of or have ignored this relationship between cognition and affect.

Our educational system has been most concerned with cognitive content. As Weinstein and Fantini state it, we have assumed that "by mastering cognitive content, the individual learns to behave appropriately as a citizen in an open society." They have questioned the assumption that "extrinsic subject mat-

[1]G. Weinstein and M. D. Fantini, *Toward Humanistic Education: A Curriculum of Affect* (New York, Praeger Publishers, 1970), p. 7.

[2]G. I. Brown, *Human Teaching for Human Learning* (New York, Viking Press, Inc., 1971), p. 4.

ter alone can lead to humanitarian behavior—that is, whether the cognitive man is necessarily the humanitarian man."[3]

Not only has affect been ignored as it relates to cognitive learning, but special programs or curricula dealing with psychological growth have been rare. Ivey and Weinstein have stated that attention to a curriculum related to psychological growth "in which children explore themselves and their relations with others" has been in general lacking.[4] Apparently, this area has been omitted not only for children, but also for adolescents and college-age adults. McCandless notes that the public schools have tended to neglect teaching human relations. He writes that "matters concerning human relations and social responsibility are not taught fully or adequately in . . . elementary and secondary schools (and probably not in colleges)," even though several experiments emphasizing preventive and creative mental health "have yielded encouraging though tentative results."[5]

A growing concern and emphasis regarding the relevance of learning for human welfare has been apparent. Not only have a number of approaches been developed for integrating the cognitive and affective in learning, such as psychological education, affective education, confluent education, and human relations training, but there also appears to be greater concern for the responsibility of psychology to society. Miller urges the practice of psychology by nonpsychologists, where "psychology" is based on scientifically valid principles.[6] He pointed out that "when the ideas are sufficiently concrete and explicit, the scientific foundations of psychology can be grasped by sixth-grade children."[7] Stollak and Guerney state that the psychologist "can and should teach specific types of interpersonal skills to those *who want to*

---

[3]*Op. cit.*, p. 31.

[4]A. E. Ivey and G. Weinstein, "The Counselor as Specialist in Psychological Education," *Personnel and Guidance Journal,* 49:99 (1970).

[5]B. R. McCandless, *Children: Behavior and Development* (New York, Holt, Rinehart, & Winston, Inc., 1967), p. 510.

[6]G. A. Miller, "On Turning Psychology Over to the Unwashed," *Psychology Today,* 3:53-54, 66-74 (1969).

[7]*Ibid.*, p. 72.

learn those skills."[8] They cite programs in existence which focus on such skills as coping with frustration and aggressive feelings and improving parent-child relationships.[9]

In discussing the social responsibility of psychology, Patterson offers a number of suggestions, including the following: "But we now know, on the basis of considerable research . . . the basic conditions of good interpersonal relationships. . . . If we know some of the principles of such relationships then it behooves us to teach them to everyone in our society."[10]

Research data reported by Carkhuff and Berenson[11] concerning facilitative or helping relationships are sobering to say the least. In a number of studies of various helpers, including such groups as the general public, college freshmen, lay helpers, and professional counselors, it was found that on the average, these groups *did not meet even minimal* facilitative levels in helping another person. When their data are considered, it is not surprising that our society is viewed as psychologically non-nourishing. Another important finding reported by Carkhuff and Berenson is that all human processes may have constructive or destructive effects. It is important to note that *all* human process may be helpful or harmful. Carkhuff and Berenson point out that to a large extent whether or not a process is facilitative or retarding is related to the extent to which the core dimensions or conditions of empathic understanding, nonpossessive warmth, genuineness, and concreteness of expression are present.

In terms of helping others, the importance of the core dimensions is not limited to counseling. As pointed out by Patterson, "these conditions are the conditions for all good interper-

[8]G. E. Stollack and L. Guerney, "A Format for a New Mode of Psychological Practice: or How to Escape a Zombie," *The Counseling Psychologist,* 2:99 (1970).

[9]*Ibid.,* p. 100.

[10]C. H. Patterson, "The Social Responsibility of Psychology," *The Counseling Psychologist,* 1:100 (1969).

[11]R. R. Carkhuff and B. G. Berenson, *Beyond Counseling and Therapy* (New York, Holt, Rinehart, & Winston, Inc.), 1967.

sonal relationships."[12] They are relevant for people in general in many areas of helping: teaching, parent-child relationships, and counseling. As Truax and Carkhuff point out, "the person . . . who is able to communicate warmth, genuineness, and accurate empathy is more effective in interpersonal relationships no matter what the goal of the interaction. . . ."[13]

Much progress has been made in providing more effective training programs and in assisting both lay and professionals in more effective helping.[14] Various programs in affective education, human relations, and psychological education have also been developed.

APPROACHES

There is no one single term or label that encompasses all the approaches to integrating the cognitive and the affective. Some approaches focus on developing interpersonal skills while others emphasize the importance of the relationship between teacher (or trainer) and learners. Some focus upon integrating the cognitive and affective in the standard curriculum, while still others deal with psychological education as a separate curriculum or course of study.

According to Weinstein and Fantini, "at least 350 major approaches to dealing with psychological growth and some 3,000 affective exercises and techniques have been identified."[15] Lyon describes a number of approaches, varying from Weinstein's curriculum of concerns and Rudman's learning theater to Simon's classroom exercises and experiences focusing upon values.[16] In this chapter, six approaches, that appeared to be representative

---

[12]C. H. Patterson, A Model for Counseling and Other Facilitative Relationships," in William H. Van Hoose and John J. Pietrofesa, eds., *Counseling and Guidance in the Twentieth Century* (Boston, Houghton Mifflin Co., 1970), p. 174.

[13]C. B. Traux and R. R. Carkhuff, *Toward Effective Counseling and Psychotherapy* (Chicago, Aldine Publishing Company, 1967), p. 116-117.

[14]C. B. Traux and R. R. Carkhuff, *Toward Effective Counseling and Psychotherapy* (Chicago, Aldine Publishing Company, 1967).

[15]G. Weinstein and M. Fantini, *op. cit.*, p. 220.

[16]H. C. Lyon, *Learning to Feel—Feeling to Learn* Columbus, Charles E. Merrill Publishing Company, 1971), pp. 66-117.

of the numerous approaches available, have been selected for consideration. The reader is encouraged to examine in greater depth, the descriptions which are presented as introductions to the approaches.

Carl Rogers: Experiential Learning

Rogers[17] is particularly concerned with significant or experiential learning, which he defines as containing the following elements: (1) it has a quality of personal involvement of the learner, including his feelings and cognitions; (2) learning is self-initiated; (3) it is pervasive; (4) it is evaluated by the learner; (5) its essence is meaning. It appears to be important to note that both feelings and cognitions are listed. Frequently, there seems to be a stereotype of Rogers' view of counseling and teaching as merely the reflection of feeling only.

Also presented by Rogers is the following list of principles or hypotheses for self-initiated, significant learning:

1. Human beings have a natural potentiality for learning.
2. Significant learning takes place when the subject matter is perceived by the student as having relevance for his own purposes.
3. Learning which involves a change in self-organization—in the perception of oneself—is threatening and tends to be resisted.
4. Those learnings which are threatening to the self are more easily perceived and assimilated when external threats are at a minimum.
5. When threat to the self is low, experience can be perceived in differentiated fashion and learning can proceed.
6. Much significant learning is acquired through doing.
7. Learning is facilitated when the student participates responsibly in the learning process.
8. Self-initiated learning which involves the whole person of the learner—feelings as well as intellect—is the most lasting and pervasive.
9. Independence, creativity and self-reliance are all faciliated when self-criticism and self-evaluation are basic and evaluation by others is of secondary importance.
10. The most socially useful learning in the modern world is the

[17]C. R. Rogers, *Freedom to Learn* (Columbus, Charles E. Merrill Publishing Company, 1969), p. 5.

learning of the process of learning, a continuous openness to experience and incorporation into oneself of the process of change.[18]

It appears that from Rogers' viewpoint the teacher's role is more one of a nonthreatening facilitator of learning, rather than that of a "teacher" in the traditional sense, i.e. a giver of knowledge, a presenter of "wisdom," a knower "who passes out knowledge to the "unknowing." Confidence in the ability of people to learn is stated clearly in the hypothesis that there is a *natural* potentiality for learning.

Rogers further states that the facilitation of significant learning is based upon attitudinal qualities existing in the relationship between learner and facilitator, rather than the usual characteristics of teaching:

... the initiation of such learning rests not upon the teaching skills of the leader, not upon his scholarly knowledge of the field, not upon his curriculum planning, not upon his use of audio-visual aids, not upon the programmed learning he utilizes, not upon his lectures and presentations, not upon an abundance of books, though each of these might at one time or another be utilized as an important resource. No, the facilitation of significant learning rests upon certain attitudinal qualities which exist in the personal relationship between the facilitator and the learner. [19]

The relationship variables included by Rogers are (1) realness or genuineness; (2) prizing; accepting, trusting, caring for (nonpossessively) the learner; and (3) empathic understanding.[20]

It may be threatening to some (or many) leaders or teachers to consider the possibility that the relationship between the learner and facilitator is more, or as, important to learning than his lectures, materials, or audio-visual aids. We have been taught in an educational system which has emphasized the cognitive and we, too, may teach in the way we have been taught. Modeling, or imitation, can and does occur. Possibly, more importantly,

[18]*Ibid.,* pp. 157-163.
[19]*Ibid.,* pp. 105-106.
[20]*Ibid.,* pp. 106-112.

a "good" lecture embellished with audio-visual aids may help us to maintain our self-esteem as "good teachers."

Concerning teaching, Rogers points out that trust is *"the important ingredient which the facilitator provides."*[21] He further stated, concerning the facilitator:

> He may also be sensitively empathic. He will, I hope, participate with his own feelings (owned as *his* feeling, not projected on the other person) . . . . But underlying all of these behaviors is the trust he feels in the capacity of the group to develop the human potential which exists in this group and its separate members. This trust is something which cannot be faked. It is not a technique. . . .[22]

"Trusting" is not an empty verbal statement, a gimmick, or a technique to manipulate learners. Teachers differ in the degree to which they trust or have confidence in a learner or group of learners. It appears that the facilitator needs to be aware of his real feelings concerning his confidence or trust in learners. Honesty with self and others, however, is to be preferred to an attempt through techniques to leap to total trust when the teacher does not actually have complete confidence. Experience may lead to increased trust and confidence.

Rogers presents the following guidelines for facilitation:

1. The facilitator has much to do with setting the initial mood or climate of the group or class experience.
2. The facilitator helps to elicit and clarify the purpose of the individuals in the class as well as the more general purposes of the group.
3. He relies upon the desire of each student to implement those purposes which have meaning for him as the motivational source behind significant learning.
4. He endeavors to organize and make easily available the widest range of resources for learning.
5. He regards himself as a flexible source to be utilized by the group.
6. In responding to expressions in the classroom group, he accepts both the intellectual content and the emotionalized attitudes endeavoring to give each aspect the approximate degree of emphasis which it has for the individual or the group.
7. As the acceptant classroom climate becomes established, the

[21]*Ibid.*, p. 75.
[22]*Ibid.*

facilitator is able increasingly to become a participant learner, a member of the group, expressing his views as those of one individual only.

8. He takes the initiative in sharing himself with the group—his feelings as well as his thoughts—in ways which do not demand nor impose, but represent simply a sharing which students may take or leave.

9. Throughout the classroom experience, he remains alert to the expressions indicative of deep or strong feelings.

10. In his functioning as a facilitator of learning, the leader endeavors to recognize and accept his own limitations.[23]

In examining the guidelines, it seems apparent that Rogers' views of the facilitator do not fit the inappropriate, stereotyped misnomer—"nondirective." The term "nondirective" applied to Rogers' theory is and has been highly questionable. In this writer's experience, those who use the term as a label for Rogers' theory appear to be persons who do not understand the theory or whose experience with the theory has been limited to a few secondary sources. In the guidelines, Rogers points out that the facilitator has much to do with setting the climate, elicits and clarifies purposes, makes resources available, accepts content and feelings, becomes a participant learner, and shares himself with the group. The facilitator is hardly passive or "nondirective." He is an active participant in learning.

It seems also important to note that both the cognitive and affective are considered. The facilitator accepts both intellectual content and emotionalized attitudes, shares his feelings and thoughts, and remains alert to feelings. Also, attention is given to resources for learning.

Robert R. Carkhuff: Training and Treatment

Training programs developed by Carkhuff and his associates have focused on interpersonal skills. In this approach to training, an emphasis is placed upon "didactic and modeling sources of learning in shaping effective trainee responses. . . ."[24] Studies

[23]*Ibid.*, pp. 164-166.

[24]R. R. Carkhuff, "Training as a Preferred Mode of Treatment," *Journal of Counseling Psychology*, 18:124 (1971).

by Carkhuff and his co-workers, related to the teaching of inter-personal relationships with such diverse populations as college students, parents of emotionally disturbed children, biracial groups, and groups from different generations, have provided methods of training and have been demonstrated to be effective. Effective training programs focus upon facilitative and action-oriented dimensions and upon procedures for discrimination and communicative training. The dimensions include empathic under-standing, respect and warmth, exploration of specific feelings and content, genuineness, self-disclosure, confrontation, and im-mediacy.[25]

Carkhuff states that helping processes in general may have constructive or deteriorative effects. Constructive consequences to a large extent are functions of the facilitative and action-ori-ented dimensions. Training, as well as other interpersonal pro-cesses, may have positive or negative effects. He notes that training and treatment programs "built systematically around facilitative and action-oriented core conditions have been most effective while those that have not been so constructed have been least effective."[26]

Carkhuff discusses training as a mode of treatment. One ap-proach involves training significant others, who are involved with the cilent (such as parents of emotionally disturbed chil-dren), in the skills necessary to affect the client's functioning. Research indicates that training significant others in relationship conditions has positive effects on the development of both the client and the significant other. A second approach involves training the client directly, which Carkhuff states is the most direct and effective mode, in skills necessary for effective func-tioning. Training is thus seen as a mode of treatment. According to Carkhuff, training as a mode of treatment is a function of "an effective helping relationship plus an effective helping pro-gram."[27]

[25]R. R. Carkhuff, *Helping and Human Relations: A Primer for Professional and Lay Helpers,* Vols. I and II (New York, Holt, Rinehart & Winston, Inc.), I: 148 (1969).

[26]*Ibid.,* Vol. II, p. 14.

[27]*Op. cit.,* p. 128.

Carkhuff states that "traditional training and treatment programs in the helping professions have not established their effectiveness in terms of translation to helpee benefits."[28] A number of assumptions, propositions, corollaries, and conclusions regarding helping processes and training programs are presented by Carkhuff. Some of these related to training are presented below:

1. Helping processes and their training programs all are instances of interpersonal learning or relearning processes.
2. All interpersonal processes may have constructive or deteriorative consequences.
3. Training in the helping professions may be for better or for worse.
4. All effective interpersonal processes share a common core of conditions conducive to facilitative human experiences.
5. Trainees in training programs in the helping professions that offer high levels of the core, facilitative, and action-oriented conditions improve while those in programs that offer low levels of those conditions deteriorate.
6. Those treatment and training programs that are built systematically around the core, facilitative, and action-oriented dimensions are most effective in translating their efforts to helpee benefits.
7. The helper's effectiveness may largely be accounted for independent of his orientation and technique by assessing the level of core conditions he offers.
8. Both professional and nonprofessional persons can be brought to function at levels of core conditions that effect positive gains in others.[29]

Any approach to psychological education, affective learning or human relations training involves a relationship between teacher, counselor, or trainer and learners. Since all interpersonal processes may have constructive or deteriorative effects, the importance of the core dimensions in all approaches to psychological education needs to be considered, regardless of the affective techniques or exercises, methods, or curricular content used by the teacher or trainer. The contributions of Carkhuff and his associates in terms of the conditions, training approaches, and research findings are relevant to helping processes in general.

[28]*Op. cit.* Vol. II, p. 3.
[29]*Ibid.*, pp. 3-14.

George I. Brown: Confluent Education

Brown defines confluent education as the "integration or flowing together of the affective and cognitive elements in individual and group learning. . . ."[30] This approach focuses upon adapting "approaches in the affective domain to school curriculum,"[31] rather than isolating affective learning from the regular curriculum.

Brown presents various affective techniques, unit outlines in secondary school social science and English, and reports of teachers who utilized confluent education in their classes. The background for this approach was a pilot project which was aimed at (1) assembling various approaches to affective learning and (2) examining the appropriateness of approaches for classroom use.

About forty techniques are presented, including aggression exercises, trust walk, mirroring, Gestalt projection game, group fantasy, and Gestalt responsibility technique.[32] Five unit outlines are presented, including such units as: "Courage, Non-Courage and Being Human," and "What is Man?"[33]
A unit by Aaron Hillman[34] on listening, hearing, and understanding, using *Death of a Salesman* as a text for tenth-grade English "slow learners," includes general objectives, text and supplementary materials, activities, affective exercises, and summation. Objectives include the following:

1. to gain an understanding of the play.
2. to gain further understanding of human beings and situations.
3. to see ourselves in the lives of others.
4. to further skills in communication and critical thinking.
5. to further skills in the use of language through verbal and nonverbal means.

[30]*Op. cit.*, p. 3.
[31]*Ibid.*, p. 19.
[32]*Ibid.*, pp. 27-51.
[33]*Ibid.*, pp. 55-59.
[34]*Ibid.*, pp. 72-79.

The objectives are stated in a general sense rather than as specific behavioral objectives. Objectives for all of the other units presented also tend to be stated in general, rather than specific, terms. The objectives above appear to emphasize both cognitive and affective aims.

Daily activities include daily diary, discussion, reading, writing, classwork (projects and affective training exercises), homework, and miscellaneous (individual guest). Questions and problems included in the daily activities related to the play include such questions as the following:

1. What is it you would like to do but "can't"?
2. Are you self-directed or other-directed?

Problems for discussion include the following:

1. Fathers live through sons.
2. Many people talk; few hear.

Homework activities vary from seeing and reporting on an analogous play to reporting on Eugene O'Neill's life or observing others to determine whether or not they are listening and hearing. Miscellaneous activities include preparation of a story and visiting a mental-health clinic. Various affective exercises are also presented in the unit outline, including "Touch Conversation," "Experiencing the Resources of Communication," painting dialogue, "Evoking the Other with Listening" and interpersonal mirroring.

Evaluation of confluent education has been subjective. Extremely little statistical data are presented. Evaluation consists primarily of teacher observations and reactions, along with student reactions. Brown states that there is a need for empirical research to determine "when, where, how, and with whom confluent education has effect."[35]

Whereas Rogers and Carkhuff emphasize the importance of relationship variables in teaching and other helping processes, in Brown's confluent education there is very little direct discussion of the teacher's qualities in terms of the core dimensions. Even so, the importance of the relationship between students

[35]*Ibid.*, 5. p. 255.

and teachers seems to this writer to be implied. For example, the following two statements were made by a girl and a boy, speaking of their teacher who utilized the confluent education approach:

> For me, it's not just the teacher-student bit. It's not all those field trips he took us on, but it's what he did for me as a person. . . . I'm a better person because of him! I mean, I can tell him anything and he listens and he understands. . . .

> Ya know, that guy really understands us kids. Ya know, he knows when to let up and let us goof off and yet he knows how to get us to work. I mean we'd really work for him, but he always seemed to know how we were feeling. . . .[36]

Such statements raise a number of questions:
1. Are affective techniques and excercises the important variables in confluent education?
2. Are relationship qualities of the teacher the important variables?
3. Is it the interaction of techniques and teacher—student relationship that is important?
4. Are the techniques necessary if the teacher establishes effective relationships with students?
5. If a teacher relates ineffectively, is the use of techniques sufficient?

Gerald Weinstein and Mario Fantini: Curriculum of Affect

This approach to psychological education focuses upon behavioral objectives and behavioral change. It is an outgrowth of the Elementary School Teaching Project, which began as an attempt to improve education of the disadvantaged, but resulted "in the formulation of a new approach to the education of all children."[37]

This new approach focuses upon the feelings and concerns of the learner. Cognitive knowledge alone is not enough. Weinstein and Fantini state:

> The chances of affecting behavior will be greater if the learner's feelings and concerns are recognized and made to direct the cognition

[36] *Ibid.*, pp. 203-204.
[37] G. Weinstein and M. Fantini, *Op. cit.*, pp. 3-4.

that logically should follow and if congition is used to help the learner cope with his concerns. . . . We believe that the affective realm contains instrinsic motivation and, consequently, may have greater impact on behavior and on realizing human potential. We regard cognition and affect as complementary, not contradictory, forces.[38]

The importance of the affective base of instructional content and methods is emphasized, regardless of the background of students or whether or not content and procedures are traditional or newly developed.

Weinstein and Fantini state that their general hypothesis is that relevance connects the affective and cognitive. They discuss the following causes of irrelevance in education.

1. Failure to match teaching procedures to children's learning styles.
2. The use of material that is outside or poorly related to the learner's knowledge of his physical realm of experience.
3. The use of teaching materials and methods that ignore the learner's feelings.
4. The use of teaching content that ignores the concerns of the learners.[39]

In terms of student concerns, Weinstein and Fantini include concern about self-image, concern about disconnectedness ("A wish to establish a connection with others or with society at large, to know where one fits in the scheme of things"), and concern about control over one's life.[40]

Analysis indicated that "fundamental concerns of poor children were shared by children from more privileged families—in fact by all people, adults and children."[41]

The model does not suggest changing concern directly or immediately, but rather attempting to change behavior in relation to the way a child deals with his concerns. The teacher begins with a diagnosis of the learner's concerns and de-

[38]*Ibid.*, pp. 31-32.
[39]*Ibid.*, pp. 21-22.
[40]*Ibid.*, p. 39.
[41]*Ibid.*, p. 10.

termination of behavioral changes toward which teaching procedures should be aimed. An example[42] of positive change in self-concept is given below:

STARTING POINT	DESIRED OUTCOME
Statements and behavior that indicate acceptance of inferiority. For example: "We're dumb." "You have to be stupid or crazy to be in this class."	Statements and behavior that indicate a sense of pride in certain aspects of uniqueness. For example:

I AM SPECIAL

My eyes are special
My hair is special
I feel special
I was made special
I was born special.

Jerry R.

As stated by Weinstein and Fantini, the teacher must differentiate between the student's "verbalized knowledge of the objective" and an expression of his own feelings. The poem, "I Am Special," by Jerry R., a fifth-grader, was judged by both the teacher and field staff to be a "genuine outcome based on real feelings."[43]

Specific curriculum content can be developed around generalizations, ideas, principles and concepts, which are cognitive organizers or organizing ideas, related to the learner's concerns. Examples are as follows:

1. Man learns to judge his own worth on the basis of certain cultural factors that may or may not be reasonable and accurate.
2. To know who you are it is necessary to be aware of how you are defining yourself (a) in terms of your own society and culture, (b) in terms of wide groups and values, (c) in terms of your own individual criteria.[44]

According to Weinstein and Fantini, content vehicles include conventional subject areas (or units within the areas); other subject disciplines (psychology, sociology, anthropology, etc.); media; classroom situation (incidents, problems, etc.); experiences outside school; children themselves. Learning skills are

[42]*Ibid.*, p. 45.
[43]*Ibid.*, p. 45.
[44]*Ibid.*, pp. 47-49

basic skills (reading, writing, speaking, computation), skills in learning to learn (analyzing a problem, trying out alternatives, evaluating results, etc.), and self and other awareness skills.[45]

Two other aspects of the model are teaching procedures and evaluation. Weinstein and Fantini state that teaching procedures should be selected on the basis of matching procedures with student learning styles and selecting procedures with the greatest "effective *affective* results."[46] They add that "whatever the procedures selected, teachers should develop interaction systems that support the learner emotionally and strengthen his feelings of selfworth."[47] Evaluation should be continuous; the following typical questions are suggested:

1. Has the children's behavior changed?
2. Were the content vehicles the best that could have been employed?
3. Were the cognitive skills and teacher procedures the most effective for achieving the affective goals?[48]

Examples of units (providing information about the learners, concerns, behavioral outcomes, organizers, content vehicles and teaching procedures, learning skills, and evaluation) for identity education are presented.[49] Also included are sample lessons, diagnostic techniques, curricular materials, and games.

It appears that this model is more systematically presented than Brown's confluent education approach. Also, emphasis is given to behavioral outcomes, rather than objectives stated in general terms. However, the importance of the relationship qualities of the teacher does not appear to be adequately recognized.

Ralph Mosher and Norman Sprinthall: Psychological Education to Promote Individual and Human Development

This approach to psychological education at the Harvard

[45]*Ibid.*, pp. 52-54.
[46]*Ibid.*, p. 56.
[47]*Ibid.*, p. 57.
[48]*Ibid.*, p. 58.
[49]*Ibid.*, pp. 66-121.

Graduate School of Education resulted in a tentative curriculum, described "most simply as a course in individual and human development to be taught to high school seniors or juniors."[50] The Harvard group produced the curriculum and participated as observers and teachers in four sections of an elective psychology class at the high school level which was taught by two high school teachers.

Some of the assumptions underlying psychological education, according to Mosher and Sprinthall, are as follows:

1. Belief in the value of self-knowledge and of the examined life.
2. There may be developmental stages or a sequence in personal psychological growth.
3. Formal schooling has little direct intentional effect on this process.
4. Psychological or emotional processes (e.g. to perceive people correctly and efficiently, to express feelings) can be taught . . . such processes can contribute not only to the individual's self-understanding and emotional development but they can also generalize to his understanding of, and ability to relate to, other people.[51]

Mosher and Sprinthall point out that teachers are already psychological educators, whether or not they are aware of it. Students experience powerful psychological education in the schools today. The values, attitudes, and self-concepts of students are affected by school experience, not always, obviously, in positive ways. Psychological development is affected. For example, Mosher and Sprinthall state:

> In addition to teaching mathematics, they (teachers) often teach children that adults have power, that children are impotent, irresponsible, and should be intellectually and personally dependent. A value for achievement, competitiveness (or cheating), and a belief that self-worth is tied to academic achievement are further examples.

[50]R. L. Mosher and N. A. Sprinthall, "Psychological Education in Secondary Schools: A Program to Promote Individual and Human Development," *American Psychologist,* 25:917 (1970). *See also* "Psychological Education: A Means to Promote Personal Development During Adolescence," *Counseling Psychologist,* 2:3-82 (1971).

[51]*Ibid.,* p. 915.

This is a harsh critique of the school, but our evidence suggests that this hidden curriculum is typically more inimical and psychologically crippling than it is positive and developmental. That these effects of schooling are largely unrecognized (and presumably unintended) is hardly an extenuating factor.[52]

The core of the course, taken by all students, is cognitive, presenting material from psychology related to understanding individual and human development. The material is focused upon early childhood, adolescence (both black and white) in this culture, and adulthood. Issues which could be examined include (1) the nature of authentic relations with parents, peer minority groups, (2) personal history, (3) competence and the future, and (4) authority relationships and personal values. For the first trial, the focus was on personal history:

Who was I as a child?

Who am I now?

Who am I becoming?[53]

Mosher and Sprinthall state that "the most ambitious and much more difficult part of the course to define involves *personalizing* the general intellectual learning . . . to affect the student's understanding of himself. . . ."[54] Affective objectives of the course included the following from the list of thirteen:

1. to enable the individual to listen to people—to their ideas and to their feelings.
2. to enable the individual to accurately perceive people—to judge people correctly and efficiently.
3. to enable the individual to understand himself.
4. to enable the individual to express feelings of his own.
5. to enable the individual to formulate a set of personal meanings—a personal philosophy.[55]

Each student, in addition to the core, also chooses one laboratory activity to study in depth which constitutes two-thirds to three-fourths of the course. Laboratory activities vary from film making and teaching to volunteer work and counseling.

[52]*Ibid.*, pp. 915-916.
[53]*Ibid.*, p. 917.
[54]*Ibid.*, pp. 917-918.
[55]*Ibid.*, p. 918.

Teaching Mental Hygiene in the Schools

Another approach to psychological education, which over-laps with preceding methods, is the teaching of mental health in the schools. It will be discussed separately since a number of different writers have utilized this approach. According to Kaplan, the teaching of mental health has been approached in three ways: (1) separate courses in mental hygiene; (2) informal or incidental instruction arising from needs, interests, and problems of children; and (3) mental hygiene units in established courses.[56] An example of classroom materials in the form of a textbook for students in grades seven, eight, or nine, related to psychological education by Pancrazio,[57] emphasizes such topics as the nature of psychological health, nature of perception, communication, self-perception and behavior, acceptance of self and others, individual differences, cultural pressures, prejudice and stereotypes, decision-making and problem-solving, sexuality, and values. Each unit consists of an opening situation in dialogue form, basic content, questions for discussion, case studies, suggested activities, and role-playing situations. The primary orienta-of the material is phenomenological, stressing perception and its relationship to behavior.

A program which emphasized incorporating psychological concepts into the curriculum was the Preventive Psychiatry Project where curriculum materials and stories were developed which emphasize "psychological problem solving" and which "attempt to teach the child to look for causes of behavior."[58] According to Ojemann, data indicate the following:

> . . . it is possible to incorporate. . . psychological concepts through-out the school curriculum and the teaching of these concepts can be effective. It also appears that the extension of the child's under-standing and appreciation of the dynamics of behavior is accom-panied by significant changes in such dimensions as manifest anxiety,

[56]L. Kaplan, *Education and Mental Health* (New York, Harper & Row Publishers, 1971), p. 365.

[57]J. J. Pancrazio, *It's Your Life: Movement Toward Greater Psychological Health,* (Chicago, Benefic Press, 1972).

[58]B. McCandless, *op. cit.,* p. 565.

tendency to immediate arbitrary punitiveness, antidemocratic tendencies, conception of the teacher, and tolerance for ambiguity.[59]

Another illustration of a special program was described by Bessell[60] as a twenty-minute guided group experience for children. This program focused upon developing an awareness of motives determining personal behavior, increasing self-confidence, and understanding causes and effects in interpersonal relationships. A kindergarten curriculum included such areas as awareness of self and others; positive feelings, thoughts, and behavior; and awareness of positive and negative feelings, thoughts, and behavior. Subjective reports from teachers using the program indicate that "discipline problems are reduced markedly and that children show increased personal involvement, . . . more self-confidence, higher motivation. . . ."

A final illustration is from Faust[61] who suggests the introduction of "feelings classes," which focus upon developing the following:

1. an awareness that feeling exists.
2. an awareness that all people possess, at times, all kinds of feelings.
3. an awareness that feelings are not bad, naughty, or immoral.
4. an introduction of socially approved methods of expressing feelings.

Numerous approaches and methods thus exist. The approaches described in the preceding pages are by no means exhaustive. Approaches to psychological or affective education vary.

---

[59]R. H. Ojemann, "Incorporating Psychological Concepts in the School Curriculum," in H. F. Clarizio, ed., *Mental Health and the Educative Process: Selected Readings* (New York, Rand McNally & Co., 1969), p. 367.

[60]H. Bessell, "The content is the Medium: The Confidence is the Message," *Psychology Today*, 61, 1968, 1, 32-35, 61.

[61]V. Faust, *The Counselor-Consultant in the Elementary School*, (Boston, Houghton Mifflin Co.), 1968.

Comparison and Contrast: Similarities or Common Elements and Differences

Even though approaches differ, there appear to be a number of common elements which run through most, if not all, of them:

1. The various approaches emphasize the integration of the cognitive and affective. The importance of the cognitive is not ignored. The approaches are not affect-oriented only.
2. There appears to be an emphasis upon techniques. Numerous techniques are presented, explained, and illustrated. It appears that empirical evidence concerning the effectiveness of affective techniques and exercises in general is lacking. Descriptions and illustrations of the use of techniques are based on personal experience and observations of those who use the techniques.
3. There seems to be an emphasis on experiencing by the learner, rather than upon the learner being told or lectured to.
4. There appears to be an emphasis upon the "here and now," the present moment, on current feelings and concerns.
5. There appears to be an emphasis upon the use of group process, methods, techniques, or discussion.
6. There appears to be a focus on aims, goals, or objectives which are related to personal and interpersonal functioning, such as self-concept, relations with others, self-direction or independence. It appears that cognitive knowledge is seen as important in terms of its relationship to self, others, and the environment. Knowledge for the sake of knowledge is not viewed as sufficient for change.
7. It appears that psychological education is not equated with counseling or therapy, group counseling or T-group. Though the effects of psychological education may be therapeutic to the learner, the psychological educator is not labeled in general as a therapist.
8. It seems that often psychological education approaches were developed and continued by utilizing a team of specialists working together.
9. Evaluations of the effectiveness of approaches, at this time, tend to be subjective in nature.
10. The approaches appear in general to be value-based. It seems that psychological educators have tended to be willing to base their efforts on philosophies or philosophical statements related to what ought to be. For example, assumptions concerning the importance of self-knowledge or identity seem to be clearly accepted.

Differences between the approaches are also apparent. Some of these appear to be the following:

1. Some approaches seem to emphasize the importance of the relationship between the psychological educator and learner more than others.
2. Approaches appear to differ in their emphasis on specific versus general goals or objectives and the extent to which they are systematically developed.
3. Approaches appear to differ in their emphasis on skill building versus understandings.
4. Approaches seem to differ in terms of their integration into the curriculum: psychological education as a separate discipline, as separate courses, as units within courses, as informal or incidental instruction.
5. Approaches appear to differ in emphasis upon the importance of affective exercises and techniques. Rogers and Carkhuff, for example, appear to place little, if any, emphasis on affective techniques.
6. Approaches appear to differ in terms of the populations with which projects have been conducted: elementary, secondary, college, parents, etc.
7. There appear to be differences in the emphasis given to training of those who utilize psychological or affective education approaches.
8. Even though the approaches in general lack empirical research evidence, research by Carkhuff on training methods and effectiveness stands out as exceptional. Also, some research has been conducted concerning approaches to teaching mental health.

RESEARCH AND EVALUATION

According to Lyon, humanistic education "is a movement, rather than a discipline." He adds that "there is little research to prove, disprove, or improve the efficiency of its techniques." Even though the convictions of teachers and students tend to be highly positive, he notes that "sophisticated evaluation efforts of humanistic education projects are rare."[62]

While Lyon's comments appear to be valid for the vast majority of the approaches examined, there are some encouraging signs. First, research by Carkhuff and his co-workers is most

[62]H. Lyon, *op. cit.*, p. 288.

impressive.[63] Second, McCandless indicated that some preventive mental health programs indicated "encouraging though tentative results."[64] Third, Ojemann reported positive results on a number of dimensions.[65] Fourth, Mosher, Sprinthall, *et. al.* found a statistically significant increase in empathy and immediacy ratings of high school students after training.[66] Fifth, Lyon reports on an experimental humanistic high school program in which the experimental group showed significantly greater improvement on such variables as reading achievement, problem-solving ability, and level of ego maturity after one semester.[67] Sixth, Kaplan, commenting upon studies of the teaching of mental health in the schools, stated:

> These studies and others show, in general, that mental health instruction in the classroom improves the behavior of children. There is less tension in school living and greater orderliness and comfort in the classroom. Children learn to cooperate with one another and to respect the rights and opinions of others. Very often accompanying these changes in attitude and behavior is a marked improvement in academic achievement.[68]

Kaplan also reports other changes such as greater teacher confidence in ability to deal with classroom problems, greater teacher support in relations with children, greater teacher self-understanding, and change in parents attitudes toward child-rearing and in involvement and support of the school. Such changes as improvement of children's behavior in the classroom and greater teacher confidence in dealing with problems no doubt would probably benefit the teacher by making his job easier and more pleasant, as well as improving morale. Benefits to the teacher need to be considered also.

It is pointed out by Kaplan that findings lack longitudinal

---

[63]R. R. Carkhuff, *op cit.*

[64]B. McCandless, *op. cit.*, p. 560.

[65]R. H. Ojemann, *op. cit.*, pp. 360-368.

[66]R. Mosher, Sprinthall, *et. al.*, "Psychological Education: A Means to Promote Personal Development During Adolescence," *Counseling Psychologist*, 2:30, (1971).

[67]H. Lyon, *op. cit.*, pp. 268-282.

[68]L. Kaplan, *op. cit.*, pp. 367-368.

verification and are fragmentary; he also states: "These studies are not sufficiently comprehensive or conclusive to justify extensive claims regarding the results to be expected from education for mental health, but many workers in the field feel that they are sufficiently indicative to warrant the attention of educators."[69]

Even though research findings are not conclusive in terms of the approaches in general, it appears that there is some research that indicates the potential of psychological education. The need for further research is apparent.

CRITICISMS

One of the criticisms of psychological education approaches in general, as previously stated, is the lack of and need for empirical research. Other criticisms include the following:

1. There appears to be some indications of "faddishness," related to accessibility of affective techniques and procedures. Weinstein and Fantini state: . . . ethical issues, appropriateness, requisite competencies of teachers, and above all, objectives of these procedures are being overlooked or ignored by novice educators.[70]

2. The integration of the cognitive and affective, though desirable, is seldom practiced and the movement is undisciplined and unorganized, consisting of "highly individualistic innovaters."[71]

3. Affective techniques, exercises, and games abound to the extent that the resulting impression, though not intended, appears to be "affective education equals techniques." The insecure, uncertain, or rigid, novice psychological educator has thousands of crutches available to "lean on." This is not meant to imply that techniques should not be presented, but rather that limitations, cautions, and the necessity of training for their use might be more highly emphasized than has seemed to be the case.

4. The importance of the relationship between psychological educator and learners has not, in general, been emphasized. Are techniques effective with anyone and everyone? Are they effective only when an effective relationship (including empathy, genuineness, etc.) exists? Are techniques necessary? These and similar questions might be explored in future research.

[69]*Ibid.*, p. 368.
[70]G. Weinstein and M. Fantini, *op. cit.*, p. 219.
[71]H. Lyon, *op. cit.*, p. 66.

5. Psychological education courses may be (and have usually been) didactic and moralistic.[72] Teaching that involves students in giving the "right" answers, passing tests, simply gathering knowledge about affect, or being "told" would hardly be an illustration of integrating the cognitive and affective, nor would moralizations about ideas, verbalizations, or feelings of students. Psychological education, it appears, cannot be equated with conformity to particular values (i.e. those of the psychological educator) though an exploration and examination of alternative values systems might be relevant. It would appear to be important for the psychological educator to be aware of his own values.

6. In examining the approaches in general, it appears that little attention is given to the selection and preparation of psychological educators. Can anyone be a psychological educator? What qualities are necessary? Is training or preparation necessary, and what types of training are necessary or effective? Again research is needed. Likely candidates for psychological education include teachers, as well as counselors. It seems logical to assume that if the affective realm has been ignored in education by teachers that change is necessary. *How do formerly cognitive-oriented teachers become oriented toward integrating the cognitive and affective?* Enthusiasm, desire, and good intentions do not appear to be sufficient. Research indicates that teaching tends to be primarily telling, with students generally passive and dependent.[73]

The last criticism warrants further discussion, in terms of teacher classroom behavior and relationships with students. That teaching may not always be representative of an ideal relationship is apparent in view of various studies of teacher behavior in the classroom. Perkins, for example, found in a study of seventy-two fifth-grade students and their teachers over a five-month period that praise was used by teachers only one percent of the time.[74] Hughes in a study of forty-one elementary teachers found that the "teaching acts most frequently used were those of control." Control meant not only discipline, but also goal

[72]L. Kaplan, *op. cit.,* p. 364.

[73]R. Mosher and M. Sprinthall, *op. cit.,* p. 913.

[74]H. V. Perkins, "A Procedure for Assessing the Classroom Behavior of Students and Teachers," in Ronald T. Hyman, ed., *Teaching: Vantage Points for Study* (New York, J. B. Lippincott Company, 1968), p. 285-294.

setting, naming the content and holding children to a specific answer and working process.[75] Amidon and Hunter raised the following questions: "Why do researchers engaged in classroom observation find that teachers are so controlling, restrictive, and inhibiting? Why is it that teachers tend to do most of the talking (about 70% in the average classroom, according to Flanders)?"[76] Such studies appear to indicate that often teacher behavior is controlling, inhibiting, or tending toward the negative, rather than positive.

It is important that safe, nonthreatening relationships be offered to students. These relationships must be marked by empathy, warmth, and genuineness. As Hyman stated concerning his study of the description of concepts of the ideal teacher-student relationship, ". . . the ideal therapist-patient relationship and the ideal teacher-student relationship are but special cases of an ideal person-person relationship." His findings emphasized "the importance of good communication, of eliminating to some degree the superior-subordinate relations, and of responding warmly to the students."[77]

Concerning the teacher as a helper or as a facilitator, it appears that such qualities as warmth, empathy, and genuineness are important in the atmosphere of the classroom for the best student achievement. A number of studies reported by Truax and Carkhuff focus upon the teacher in the classroom.[78] For example, Truax and Tatum found that the degree of warmth and empathy of the teacher was related to positive changes in both the performance and social adjustment of preschool children.[79] Aspy found that third-grade teachers who were warm, empathic, and genuine "were able to produce greater behavior change in

[75]M. M. Hughes, "What is Teaching: One Viewpoint," in Ronald T. Hyman, ed., *Teaching: Vantage Points for Study* (New York, J. B. Lippincott Company, 1968), p. 275.

[76]E. Amidon and E. Hunter, *Improving Teaching: An Analysis of Classroom Verbal Interaction* (New York, Holt, Rinehart & Winston, Inc., 1966), p. 2.

[77]R. T. Hyman, "The Concept of an Ideal Teacher-student Relationship: A Comparison and Critique," in Ronald T. Hyman, ed., *Teaching:Vantage Points for Study* (New York, J. B. Lippincott Company, 1968), pp. 183-184.

[78]Truax, C. and Carkhuff, R., *op. cit.*

[79]*Ibid.,* p. 115.

terms of reading achievement than those less warm, empathic, and genuine."[80] Apparently, regardless of the goal of the interaction, the core dimensions are an important part of effectiveness.

In any human process, whether teaching, parent-child relationships, or counseling, the recipient of the conditions of empathy, warmth, and genuineness appears to gain beyond achieving particular goals such as academic achievement. When a person receives empathy, warmth, and genuineness, he (the recipient) becomes more empathic, warm, and genuine. Patterson states the following: "The recipient of the conditions begins to manifest the conditions in his own behavior. The conditions are aspects of self-actualization. Self-actualizing people facilitate self-actualization in others . . . the client, in becoming a self-actualizing person, becomes therapeutic for others by providing the conditions for their self-actualization."[81] Providing the conditions of a good relationship, as a teacher or as a counselor, it appears, would not only assist students in achieving goals, but also in becoming more therapeutic toward others.

It appears, then, that one approach toward preparing psychological educators is training in the core dimensions. Not only does there appear to be a relationship between the dimensions and the goals of teaching, but also those who receive the conditions appear to tend to become more therapeutic in their relationships with others.

Another approach to preparation of psychological educators is the behavioral approach to human relations of Ivey and Rollin.[82] Performance curricula in more than thirty human relations areas, such as relaxation, listening, and empathy, have been developed. In this approach, a specific area of human relations is identified. The steps in the process include the following:

1. Skills of the area are learned.
2. Skills are taught to another person.
3. Alternative ways to teach or demonstrate skills to others are generated.

[80]*Ibid.,* p. 116.
[81]C. H. Patterson, *op. cit.,* p. 181.
[82]H. Lyon, *op. cit.,* p. 148-215.

4. Alternatives are acted upon.

Ivey and Weinstein, in discussing teacher training, point out that after the trainee demonstrates the behavior, teaches it to someone else, and uses it in daily life, "we work with him on developing ways in which he could use the same behavior to facilitate child growth."[83]

Some approaches to the preparation of psychological educators do exist, and very likely, other approaches will be developed. Training or preparation is no doubt important. Research on teacher behavior tends to indicate the need for change if psychological education approaches are to focus upon concerns and feelings of learners, as well as cognitive gains. In general, teachers have not tended to focus upon feelings of students.

Also, "facts," knowledge—cognitive aspects—in psychological education appear to be important in terms of the personal meanings, perceptions, and relevance to the learner. Information must be personalized by the learner. Accuracy or validity of the information in and of itself is not sufficient. For example, the writings of great authors may be potentially valuable vehicles for psychological education, but reading, learning about, or memorizing details from Shakespeare's plays (primarily to pass a test) do not automatically translate to an understanding of human nature, regardless of the number of lesson plans that state this as an objective. To the extent that learners have opportunities to think about, question, discuss, express their feelings and thoughts, and relate or personalize the content to themselves and their relationships to others and to their world in the "here and now," it might be meaningful.

The importance of openness and freedom of expression, including expression of negative as well as positive feelings, must be emphasized. As Weinstein and Fantini state: "It is not enough for the teacher to determine curriculum on the basis of his awareness of children's feelings of powerlessness or weak self-image. He must also identify and work with the manner in which groups of children express the concerns, even with their irrational and de-

[83]*Op. cit.*, p. 101.

structive ways of dealing with concerns. He must encourage constructive techniques. . . ."[84]

Training approaches might make contributions to psychological education in terms of assisting teachers at all levels of education to deal more effectively with feelings, to develop further competencies in helping learners to personalize information, and in providing a more open and free atmosphere for the expression of thoughts and feelings.

Many of the preceding references obviously were related to classroom teaching. It is rather unlikely that teachers, who generally have been taught (or prepared) on a primarily cognitive basis (or who have been teaching on a primarily cognitive basis), can "leap" into approaches which emphasize integrating the cognitive and the affective. Dealing effectively with emotions, feelings, attitudes, or values appears to be, in general, "foreign" to most teachers. Nonetheless, psychological or affective education approaches emphasize feelings as well as knowledge. It seems apparent, therefore, that some part of preparation and training (pre-service or in-service) focuses upon affect and the integration of the cognitive and affective. It seems to be apparent, in view of studies of teacher behavior in the classroom, that the emotional and feeling aspects of learning are not effectively dealt with automatically or "inherently" as a part of the teaching process. Preparation or training are no doubt necessary.

The Role of the Counselor in Psychological Education

Ivey and Weinstein suggest that the counselor "review several alternatives for psychological education and utilize the ideas that impress him as most fruitful for his settings."[85] There are obviously many approaches from which to draw. It is assumed that the role of the counselor includes, not only individual and group counseling with students, but also functioning as a psychological educator or human relations specialist. The counselor's role and functions in terms of psychological education will be dependent upon his qualifications, training, and

[84]*Op. cit.,* p. 46.
[85]*Op. cit.,* p. 106.

experience. Also, since the counselor would likely be involved in working with teachers and other personnel, the quality of his relationships with others is very important. Such possibilities as working as a team member with teachers, providing in-service training in psychological education, or serving as a consultant to teachers call for effective relating.

Consultation with teachers, concerning such items as teacher behavior or classroom atmosphere, assumes invitation by the teacher, rather than imposition by the counselor or an administrator. The development of a relationship, characterized by such qualities as acceptance, understanding, and a lack of threat, appears to be a necessary first step. Also, counselors and teachers need to work together, rather than oppose each other. Both need to recognize that they have contributions to make to students and that they both are concerned about helping students. Acceptance, empathy, and genuineness are not the exclusive realm of the counselor.

Concerning the role of the counselor in psychological education a number of possibilities can be considered:

1. Developing psychological education programs related to student concerns and needs.
2. Working with teachers and other personnel in the development, preparation, and presentation of psychological education curricular materials and/or procedures.
3. Providing psychological education programs and experiences to teachers and parents.
4. Providing in-service training to teachers in psychological education, seminars related to psychological education, or group process theory, research, methods and approaches.
5. Providing training to teachers and other personnel in the core dimensions.
6. Consulting with teachers concerning classroom atmosphere and teacher behavior, utilizing observational analysis systems.

In implementing these possibilities, the training of the counselor is basic. Training teachers in the core dimensions and utilizing observation systems, for example, implies not only knowledge of, but also experience with and preparation to use these in consulting or training.

Implications for Counselor Preparation

Two implications for counselor preparation in terms of the counselor's role in psychological education need to be examined. First, it appears that the counselor who functions as a specialist in psychological education would need and benefit from experiences during his preparation which relate to classroom learning, teacher preparation (in particular, supervision and analysis of teacher behavior), curriculum development, and behavioral objectives as they relate to teaching. For example, several readings concerning various systems for analyzing teaching and the social-emotional climate of the classroom are presented by Hyman[86] including those of Flanders (social), Withall (emotional), and Galloway (nonverbal). Another approach to observation and classroom consultation might focus upon such core dimensions as empathy, nonpossessive warmth, and genuineness in the classroom. Supervised experiences in teacher supervision and consultation in psychological education might also be considered. Supervised experience in group process may be necessary.

There is a need to explore the extent to which typical counselor education programs need revision to prepare counselors to serve as human relations specialists. The orientation of some courses or experiences may need to change, or some experiences or courses may need to be replaced. The importance of knowledge and experience with the core dimensions and psychological education approaches, along with supervised experience in training and consulting, is obvious.

Second, the suggestions presented in this chapter focus upon a team approach in which counselors work cooperatively with teachers. Both are (or should be) concerned about helping individuals in their total development, not only in academic achievement. Both offer skills and competencies necessary for individual development. Many approaches are available for experimentation which include the talents and abilities of both teachers and counselors. They can work together, each offering his or her skills and competencies; they can work as a team, rather

[86]R. T. Hyman, *Teaching: Vantage Points for Study* (New York, J. B. Lippincott Company, 1968).

than separately, without one acting or feeling that he or she is superior to the other. It may be advisable for teachers and counselors to participate together in a group experience (in which the facilitator is not a staff member) in order to increase their acceptance and understanding of each other in order to work as a team more effectively.

A FINAL NOTE

Education has been primarily cognitive. The affective realm has generally been ignored. It is questionable that an impact on many societal problems can be made by an emphasis on knowledge *per se*. Numerous approaches to integrating the cognitive and affective have been developed.

In this chapter, six approaches were examined and similarities and differences among approaches were presented. Research data and criticisms of psychological education in general were also discussed. Implications for the role of the counselor and implications for counselor preparation were considered.

There is a need for psychological education or human relations training. As Leonard suggests: "The order in the future will certainly call for a more sensitive citizen, one who is attuned to his own feelings and the feelings of others, one who has learned a new sense of community and openness with all the other individuals of his social organism."[87]
Professional organizations are exhibiting more concern in this area. For example, the American Personnel and Guidance Association devoted a recent issue of *The Personnel and Guidance Journal* to psychological education. The interested reader is referred to this publication.[88]

Both counselors and teachers have a concern, a responsibility, and a contribution in terms of human relations training, psychological education, and the helping process. There is a need for a society in which individuals provide and are provided with greater human nourishment. Psychological education approaches offer a beginning.

[87]G. P. Leonard, "The Future of Power," *Look*, 34:40.
[88]*The Personnel and Guidance Journal*, 5:581-592 (1973).

CHAPTER VI

FACILITATING PERSONAL DEVELOPMENT IN THE CLASSROOM

C. H. PATTERSON

IN CHAPTER I we indicated that the goal of education is the development of self-actualizing persons and described three of the basic conditions for producing self-actualizing persons or for facilitating personal development. The major concern of this book is with the facilitation of personal development outside the classroom. However, since students spend most of their time in the classroom what goes on in the classroom should not be inconsistent with what goes on outside. Furthermore, the conditions which facilitate personal development in general are also the basic conditions for all learning, including classroom learning. Therefore, it is necessary that we consider the application and implementation of the conditions for personal learning and personal development in the classroom by the teacher. The two major aspects of this process are first, the person of the teacher, and second, how the teacher behaves or functions to provide the facilitative conditions.

THE HUMANISTIC TEACHER

It will be recalled that in Chapter I we described the characteristics of self-actualizing persons and that this description included the facilitating conditions. There it was stated that if one wishes to facilitate the development of self-actualizing persons, one must be a self-actualizing person oneself. The two

[1]A more extensive treatment of this topic will be found in the author's book entitled *Humanistic Education* (Englewood Cliffs, N.J., Prentice-Hall, Inc., 1973).

important facts about teaching or instruction which become apparent are that: First, good teaching is not a matter of subject matter, knowledge, or methods, but of who the teacher is and second, teaching is a relationship, and the nature of this relationship becomes an important matter for consideration.

Rogers states it clearly as follows:

"We know . . . that the facilitation of . . . learning rests not upon the teaching skills of the leader, not upon his curricular planning, not upon his use of audio-visual aids, not upon the programmed learning he utilizes, not upon his lectures and presentations, not upon an abundance of books, though each of these might at one time or another be utilized as an important resource. No, the facilitation of significant learning rests upon certain attitudinal qualities which exist in the personal relationship between the facilitator and the learner."[2]

AUTHENTICITY OR GENUINENESS. One of the basic attitudinal qualities or characteristics of a facilitative teacher is genuineness or authenticity. Too many teachers play a role, one that originates in their preparation for teaching and in their early experiences in teaching. Unprepared for relating to students, they retreat behind a facade, their concept of the teacher role. They are confirmed in this role by other teachers, by their supervisors, and by the demands and expectations of administrators. The fear of having disciplinary problems and of a noisy classroom leads teachers to develop a routine and a method of teaching whose purpose is to ensure control. To be themselves or to be open and warm in their relations with their students is to risk being taken advantage of and to lose control. Thus teachers develop into the stereotype of a teacher—an authoritarian, immobile, unfeeling, cold, impersonal, hardly human being.

If teaching is to be a genuine human relationship, it is no place for role playing. The teacher is a human being, a real person and should not try to be something other than he naturally is. The humanistic teacher is genuine and real, not a facade or the stereotype of a teacher.

A teacher who trys to be something he is not is under

[2]C. R. Rogers, *Freedom to learn* (Columbus, Ohio, Charles E. Merrill Publishing Company, 1969), pp. 105-106.

constant tension and anxiety. Moreover, his phoniness will be detected by students, even though they may conceal this recognition, and the teaching relationship is affected. A teacher who pretends to be something he is not creates feelings of uneasiness and tension in students who see beneath his pretensions. They begin to "test" him to see where he really stands, so they can know where they stand. A teacher who is trying to play a role is unsure of himself, vacilitating, hesitating, inconsistent, and invites "discipline problems."

It happens, of course, that a teacher who assumes the role of a controlling, dominating autocrat of the classroom becomes such a person in reality. To some people, especially administrators, such a teacher is successful and is presented as a model to beginning teachers. The classroom is quiet, the students appear to be working and studying, and there seem to be no disciplinary problems. But such an authoritarian environment is not conducive to learning, to the self-initiated change which is real learning. An authoritarian environment is not an atmosphere for the development of self-actualizing persons. The autocrat, even though genuine, is not a good teacher. Thus, when we speak of genuineness, we need to think of it as facilitative, or therapeutic, genuineness.

The genuine teacher, then, is not preoccupied with techniques or methods, which distract from a good personal relationship. "Authenticity frees the helper to devote his full attention to the problems at hand. His behavior can be smoothly congruent and *en rapport* with students."[3] The behavior of the authentic teacher is not highly self-conscious, but spontaneous, intuitive, based on a feeling that it is the thing to do. The teacher trusts himself.

The authentic teacher is not always free from so-called negative feelings and behavior. He may become impatient, irritated, even angry. When he has these feelings—when they are strong or persistent, not simply momentary and fleeting—he

[3]A. W. Combs, D. L. Avilla, and W. W. Purkey, *Helping Relationships: Basic Concepts for the Helping Professions* (Boston, Allyn & Bacon, Inc., 1971), p. 292.

doesn't attempt to hide or suppress them. He doesn't feel one thing and say something else. (It isn't likely that he would be successful in concealing his real feelings from students completely or consistently.) But he recognizes and accepts his feelings as his own and accepts responsibility for his own behavior. He doesn't project his feelings on his students and blame them for his feelings and behavior. He may say "I'm irritated," "I'm angry," "I'm disturbed," not "You irritate me," "You make me angry," "You disturb me."

Moreover, he can express his negative feelings about a student's work without condemning the student. "He can dislike a student product without implying that it is objectively good or bad or that the student is good or bad. He is simply expressing a feeling for the product, a feeling which exists within himself. Thus he is a person to his students, not a faceless embodiment of a curricular requirement nor a sterile tube through which knowledge is passed from one generation to the next."[4] In any expression of feeling the teacher accepts responsibility for it as his behavior. If he is irritated or angry, he makes it clear that it is with the child's behavior and not with the child himself.

This is not to encourage teachers to express every feeling of anger nor to imply that a highly volatile and emotional teacher is a good one. The damaging effects of anger directed at children is clear.[5] They may disobey, fight with each other, and do less studying. Realness or genuineness is important, but not as an excuse for cruelty nor as an excuse for continuing to employ a cruel, sadistic, or disturbed teacher. The perceptive teacher, sensitive to his own feelings and the beginnings of a situation, can often avoid an outburst of anger by voicing his incipient anger, "All right, kids, cool it before I blow my stack."[6]

A student of the writer recognizes the desirability of the teacher becoming aware of her feelings and doing something about them before they reach the explosive stage. She reports her experience in student teaching:

[4]C. R. Rogers, *op. cit.*, p. 106.

[5]H. M. Greenberg. *Teaching with feeling* (Toronto, Macmillan Company, 1969).

[6]*Ibid.*, p. 65.

Last semester I went through a traumatic and distressing time in connection with my student teaching. I had been given advice by teachers in how to conduct a good classroom: I was told not to smile too much, to establish my authority at the outset, and never to show my emotions, because the students would then know they could "get my goat." For six weeks I labored to follow this advice because it came from supposed experts. One day I became so angry at the noise in the classroom that I burst out in an emotional attack upon the students, screaming at them for their terrible behavior. The students were startled; they felt that I had been unfair. If I had been more real in this situation I would have been able to tell the students that I got annoyed at this noise much earlier, and we could have worked out some sort of compromise on the noise level. This realness could have avoided my personal attack on them as bad persons. It could also have helped me to avoid my tremendous feelings of guilt, for, even though my cooperating teacher felt that the students got what they deserved, I knew that I had been most unfair. In the future, when in the teaching situation, I will try my personal best to be real, to express my feelings as they occur truly in my awareness. If I am real, my students will be able to relate to me as I am — a human being with feelings and ideas, not an authority figure who issues mandates from above. They will realize that I am being my whole 'self,' and that I can and do make mistakes; furthermore, when I make mistakes, I will be able to admit them. It is only human to make mistakes, but very few teachers are accustomed to letting their students know that they are less than infallible. In my opinion, students would feel more at ease with a teacher who is able to admit errors and who relinquishes his role of all-knowing authority. The teacher would also become a learner in the eyes of the student if he were able to admit that his ideas are not always absolutely correct.

A. S. Neill has said: *"It doesn't matter what you do to a child if your attitude toward that child is right."*[7] This of course does not mean that the teacher should take out all his negative feelings on children. Clearly, we are talking about feelings which are a result of the behavior of the children themselves and not feelings originating from a disturbed personality. There is no place, as noted above, for the emotionally disturbed teacher in the classroom.

Being real is difficult for many, if not most, people in our society, which is so impersonal, competitive, and evaluative. Teachers particularly find it difficult because of the fears en-

[7]A. S. Neill, *Summerhill* (New York, Hart Publishing Company, 1960), p. 144.

gendered by the expectations as represented by the myths of the "good teacher." As a student put it, "I cannot become real just by verbalizing this wish; it is not an easy thing to become, because so much of my experience has conditioned me to put up appropriate fronts for the different roles I should play in society, according to normative standards."

Rogers notes that:

"Only slowly can we learn to be truly real. For, first of all, one must be close to one's feelings, capable of being aware of them. Then, one must be willing to take the risk of sharing them as they are, inside, not disguising them as judgments, or attributing them to other people.[8]

The attitude of the teacher toward children is basic and is the second major condition for learning and self-actualization in students.

RESPECT FOR THE CHILD AS A PERSON. The humanistic teacher respects each child as a person of worth in his own right, as a unique human being, and accepts each child as he is, for what he is. This attitude makes no demand that the child be different to be accepted; it is unconditional. It is not an impersonal respect, but a real liking, and what Rogers has called a "prizing" of another—of his feelings, his opinions, his person.[9]

It involves a caring for another, a feeling of warmth toward him, but it is a nonpossessive caring and warmth, which recognizes his integrity as an individual. Such an attitude is inconsistent with controlling, directing, or guiding another in the way you think he should go or manipulating him by subtle means.

Acceptance of another does not require that the other be perfect, that he always agree with us, or that his behavior be acceptable or good or right. There is acceptance of mistakes and errors, imperfections, changes in mood and motivation, etc. that are aspects of being human. But there is also a confidence in the basic goodness of each person, of his capacity to grow and to develop, and to actualize his potentials when given the opportunity in a facilitating environment.

Acceptance of a child as he is does not mean being satisfied

[8]C. R. Rogers, *op. cit.*, p. 114.
[9]*Ibid.*, p. 109.

to let the child remain as he is. It is not inconsistent with having expectations for change and development. If you like and care for another you want him to be what he is capable of being, his best self, but you do not withhold your caring or liking to control his behavior. That is, your acceptance, respect, and liking are not conditional on his meeting your specific expectations.

It appears that you cannot help another, by teaching or in any other personal relationship, unless you like him. Yet there are children whom a teacher just cannot like. If a teacher cannot develop a minimal liking for a particular child, it would be desirable then to place him with another teacher who could feel some liking for him.

Respecting your students engenders self-respect in them and leads to a feeling of self-confidence and competence reflected in their performance.

EMPATHIC UNDERSTANDING. The third condition for real learning, and the third characteristic of the effective teacher, is empathic understanding. As indicated in the chapter on individual counseling, this is a special kind of understanding. It is not the knowledge obtained from the student's file or cumulative record nor the information passed on from one teacher to the next. It is not the understanding obtained from reports of social workers or psychologists, or from the usual case study of a child.

Empathic understanding requires that the teacher put himself in the place of the student, and become tuned in to his perceptions and feelings about what is happening. "It is the completely unbiased attitude of seeing what an experience means to the child, not how it fits into or relates to other experiences, not what causes it, why it exists, or for what purpose. It is an attempt to know attitudes and concepts, beliefs and values of the child as they are perceived by him alone."[9]

Information and "facts" obtained from various sources interfere with empathic understanding because they present an external point of view and prevent the teacher from taking the student's internal frame of reference. Comments and observa-

[9]C. Moustakas, *The Authentic Teacher: Sensitivity and Awareness in the Classroom* (Cambridge, Mass., Howard A. Doyle, 1966), p. 30.

tions of others are not "facts," but represent their own perceptions, which are usually evaluative and judgmental.

Empathic understanding is rare in our society with its evaluative orientation. It is rare in teachers who are evaluators. Rogers
writes that it is "almost unheard of in the classroom. One could
listen to thousands of ordinary classroom interactions without
coming across one instance of clearly communicated, sensitively
accurate, empathic understanding." He continues: "If any teacher
set himself the task of endeavoring to make one nonevaluative,
acceptant, empathic response per day to a student's demonstrated
or verbalized feeling, I believe he would discover the potency of
this currently almost nonexistent kind of understanding."[10]

The three basic conditions, genuineness, respect and empathy, are the essence of love and are nonthreatening. Self-
initiated learning, which involves exploration, not simply memori-
zation, can occur only in a nonthreatening environment.

It is clear that the teacher, while an imperfect human being,
must be a self-actualizing person. Only self-actualizing persons
can foster self-actualization in others. Teaching is a demanding
occupation and in one respect more difficult than psychotherapy.
It demands the same characteristics as psychotherapy in its practitioners, but it is more difficult to provide the conditions for
personal growth and development to thirty unique and often
disturbed children for five or six hours a day than to provide
these conditions to four or five clients or patients in individual
interviews. The humanistic teacher, while not a therapist in the
conventional sense of the term, is therapeutic. Indeed, if children
were exposed to humanistic teachers (and, prior to entering
school, to humanistic parents), few children would need formal
counseling or psychotherapy.

IMPLEMENTING THE CONDITIONS IN THE CLASSROOM

It is not enough to tell teachers to be more genuine, more
respecting and warm, more empathic. They ask, "But how do I
act, just what do I do?" Although it may seem peculiar that we
must consider how one functions as a human being, in our so-

[10]*Op. cit.,* p. 112.

ciety it appears to be necessary. While it is not sufficient that teachers simply behave in certain ways, it is helpful for teachers to know some ways to implement or practice the conditions for facilitating learning and personal development.

LISTENING. Listening, considered the first requirement of a counselor, is also the first requirement of a humanistic teacher. A frequent complaint of students is that teachers don't listen to them. Studies show that classroom teachers talk approximately 75 percent of the time; when they are talking they are unable to listen.

Real learning is personal, and often accompanied by feelings and emotions, since it involves change in the student. In order to express his real feelings, the child must feel that he is free to do so and that he won't be evaluated, criticized, or condemned for having negative feelings. If he is to express any ideas or thoughts, he must feel that they will be accepted as worthwhile. The teacher must therefore convey genuine interest, concern, and respect for the child by his willingness and ability to listen empathically. The teacher expresses respect by listening. The teacher who says to a student, "Never mind what you think about that, Jimmy. What does the book say?" is not willing to listen to or respect the student.[11]

RESPONDING. Listening alone is helpful and can make another feel respected and understood, but it is often desirable and necessary to communicate understanding. To effectively communicate empathic understanding, the listener's responses must remain in the internal frame of reference and must not be evaluative or judgmental.

Understanding responses may be nonverbal, such as a nod of the head, or simple verbal responses, such as "yes," "I see," "I understand," "Mm Hmm." A simple restatement indicates that you have heard and understand. Complete understanding is not possible or necessary; it is often enough to try to understand. Pretending to understand when one does not is of course not useful or helpful. Questions help you understand more clearly what is being said.

[11]A. W. Combs, D. L. Avila, & W. W. Purkey, *op. cit.*, p. 95.

Beyond the initial response, to indicate understanding need not indicate agreement. Disagreements, or confrontations, can be fruitful, only if both parties understand each other.

SETTING LIMITS. All social situations are characterized by limits of acceptable behavior. Progressive education was mistakenly believed to place no limits on behavior. In counseling or psychotherapy there are few, if any, limits on verbalization but there are limits on other behavior.

In the classroom there must be limits, but, hopefully, wider on verbalization than on behavior. The problem of limits, that of discipline, is one of the most difficult a teacher faces. Limits that are too restrictive and unreasonable generate tension and interfere with learning but no limits result in chaos. Neill's *Summerhill,* contrary to some people's impression, has limits. Limits are necessary to protect individuals from the unfair impositions of others and to provide a structure for the development of relationships.

The teacher must define reasonable limits and then adhere to them consistently. If limits are vaguely defined, students seek to determine what they are, test them; this is the source of most disciplinary problems in the classroom. The problems described by Herndon, Kohl, and Kozol, essentially those of defining limits,[12] are perhaps extreme examples because of the nature of the schools in which they worked.

Limits are determined to some extent by what the teacher can be comfortable with. If the teacher can be comfortable only with narrow limits, not conducive to learning nor reasonable to impose on active, living children, the teacher will need to learn to be comfortable with more reasonable limits. Too often strict limits represent fear of losing control.

It has long been claimed that the goal of discipline is to develop self-discipline in students, a goal seldom made possible in the system because students are feared and distrusted. However, where students have been involved in setting or are per-

---

[12]J. Herndon. *The Way It Spozed To Be* (New York, Simon & Schuster, Inc., 1965), Herbert Kohl, *36 Children* (New York, American Library, 1967), Jonathon Kozol, *Death at An Early Age* (New York, Bantam Books, 1968).

mitted to determine limits, as in Summerhill and some of the open or free schools, there have been few discipline problems.

One of the most frequent complaints of students about teachers concerns the inconsistency with which limits are enforced. An articulate eighth grade boy being counseled by one of the writer's students expressed it as follows:

Student: "It just seems to me that since the teachers and the principal are the people who are in authority, well, they kind of have to take care of everybody else, it seems like they ought to be a little more careful about what they say and things like that."

Counselor: "You feel that the teachers and principals are not very careful about the way they use their power?" (Student: "Mmh mmh") "And that they seem to sort of . . ."

Student: "A lot of times they'll—well, just for a little thing —if they're in a bad mood they'll take and—well not many times—I know it has happened to some people—take and send somebody out into the hall, when they didn't do anything—and sometimes, you know, it's what they're leading up to—they maybe hadn't done anything all day, and then just for a little thing they'll fly off the handle and get real mad and—it just doesn't seem fair that they should take it out on this one person. They should call each person down as he does something instead of waiting until . . ."

Counselor: "Uh huh."

Student: "Finally taking it out on one person."

Counselor: "It's sort of cornering one person in the class?"

Student: "Uh uh."

Counselor: "That usually causes most of the problems."

Student: "I think that the schools ought to give the kids so much leeway and then enforce it strictly instead of saying you don't have any leeway and then when they go ahead and do something they don't enforce it very strictly and . . . sort of like you give them an inch and they'll take a mile. I think they ought to stop you as soon as you get as far as you should go and after a while the kids would learn, but the way it is they let them go on and on until they decide they don't like it then they take it out on one person and . . ."

Counselor: "You feel then that the rules are not defined . . . Is this what you're saying that if you go beyond a certain point . . ."

Student: "They should, well, say they give you so much room . . . things you can do in the room—each teacher usually sets that up herself—and I think as soon as you've gone that far . . . if you're doing anything you're not supposed to I think they should call you down for it . . . maybe give you a warning—you know—one time—and then the next time you do it they send you out in the hall or down to the principal's office if you do it again. But the way it is they just let certain people go on past that and then after a while somebody else saw them do it and they didn't get into any trouble so they do the same thing and they'll get called down for it. And I think they should call everybody down for the same things. Because quite often one person does—maybe the teacher likes this person just a little bit more than another person . . . and this other person does something and gets sent out in the hall but this person does it and she just says 'now don't do that' . . ."

THE POWER OF EXPECTATIONS. The importance of expectations in behavior has long been recognized in the saying "Give a dog a bad name and he will live up to it." It is the theme of Shaw's *Pygmalion*, in which the flower girl becomes a lady when she is expected to be a lady and is treated like one. The influence of expectations has been referred to as the self-fulfilling prophecy since Robert Merton used this term.[13]

Teachers have beliefs and attitudes about individual children and groups of children that create expectations which influence the behavior of the children. Teachers' expectations are a powerful factor in the actual performance of children in school. Robert Rosenthal and Lenore Jacobson conducted a study of the expectations of classroom teachers. In the spring they administered a test of general ability to all the students in grades K through six of a school. The teachers were told that the test could predict which of the children would be expected to show a spurt in academic achievement. The following September each teacher was given a list purporting to contain the names of these children, but in fact, contained names selected at random. After retesting the children the next January and May, the authors concluded that those children whose names appeared on the lists gained more, on the average, than the other children.[14] Unfortunately, the results are poorly reported and have been questioned statistically. However, there has been a mass of literature including research with animals supporting the effects of expectations. In one study two groups of psychology students were given rats to be tested for performance in running mazes. One group was told that their rats were maze-bright, while the other was told that theirs were maze-dull; the rats were in fact, from the same litters. The results reported by the students, however, were as expected—the students who thought that their rats were brighter reported better performance.

The way in which expectations alter behavior is not clear. A student of the writer in one of the most detailed studies of

[13]R. K. Merton, "The Self-fulfilling Prophecy," *The Antioch Review* (Summer, 1948). Reprinted in R. K. Merton, *Social Theory and Social Structure,* rev. ed. (New York, Macmillan-Free Press, 1957).

[14]R. Rosenthal & L. Jacobson, *Pygmalion in the Classroom* (New York, Holt, Rinehart & Winston, 1968).

expectations, was able to identify few observable behaviors related to the expectancy effect. It appears that the behaviors are very complex and may vary with the sex of the experimenter and of the subject. Awareness of the phenomenon of the expectancy effect may lead to an attempt to counteract an unfavorable effect leading to a "reverse effect."[15] The modes of influence are subtle yet effective, particularly over a period of time.

It is well known that expectations are transferred from teacher to teacher by the communication of stereotypes. A seventh grade boy who was a client of a counseling student of the writer expressed it as follows:

Student: "It wouldn't have been so bad if it was like in the lower grades, you know, primary grades, where we had only *one teacher*. Now you've got four teachers, and *Mrs. Thompson*, she just can't stand me, and then they go down and sit together at the lunch table and she tells all about the things I do, and I have a funny feeling she exaggerates just a little bit. And then the other teachers hear about it and they're on edge and everytime I breathe too deeply they get down on me too and it's like having the whole school down on you."

Counselor: "Things you do aren't quite as bad as what the teachers seem to . . ."

Student: "Uh uh."

Teachers pass on expectations from year to year. The student above went on to say:

Student: "You walk into a new class, you know, the teacher has never had you and she doesn't know all your names yet. You look up and she's all big

---

[15]N. Yarom, "Temporal Localization and Communication of Experimenter Expectancy Effect with 10-11 Year Old Children." Unpublished doctoral dissertation, University of Illinois, Urbana-Champaign, 1971.

smiles and everything, you know, and goes down the line asking everybody their names, and you say *Ronald James*—and she falls through the floor or something."

Counselor: "It gets that bad."

Silberman states it clearly and simply: "The teacher who assumes that her students cannot learn is likely to discover that she has a class of children who are indeed unable to learn; yet another teacher, working with the same class but without the same expectation, may discover that she has a class of interested learners. The same obtains with respect to behavior; the teacher who assumes that her students will be disruptive is likely to have a disruptive class on her hands."[16]

The humanistic teacher who respects each student as a unique human being and believes that each one has more potential than is evident, conveys his attitude in his treatment of the student. High expectations can be expressed in the maintenance of high standards. However, standards must not be too high or unrealistic and must be adapted to the individual student.

What students *can* do is often surprising. Borton notes incidents of children surpassing their own expectations in art and drama. One self-conscious girl of seventeen, after participating in a creating experience, became almost ecstatic. "Over and over, bouncing on the grass, she said, 'I did it. I did it!' "[17] In another instance, Borton was surprised by the creation of "Fred, the one kid in the class whom I considered a dolt." His poorly written paper, which "graded as a conventional essay . . . was a disaster," when respaced on the page with the spelling corrected became striking blank verse. Borton writes: "I still cannot explain how Fred did it. He never came close to repeating that high performance though he often tried."[18] The atmosphere created by Borton, combined with the interest of the student, ignited a brief spark or flame of expression.

[16]C. E. Silberman, *Crisis in the classroom* (New York, Rondom House, Inc., 1970), p. 83.
[17]T. Borton, *Reach, touch, and teach,* New York: McGraw-Hill, 1970, p. 33.
[18]*Ibid.,* pp. 18-19.

Although it is not possible to identify just how expectations are communicated (except in extreme situations), it is possible for the teacher to become aware of his expectations and thus to anticipate the direction of his influence on students.

The teacher who is concerned about his students, who respects them, who recognizes the great unused potentials which they possess, expects much—even "demands" much. Love expects the best. The expectations others have of us act as a challenge to us to do our best, to be our best. The fact is that you cannot care deeply for someone without expecting, even demanding, that he do and be the best of which he is capable.

The Self as Instrument. Interpersonal relations are not a matter of techniques. Humanistic teaching, therefore, cannot be reduced to a bag of tricks or techniques. This is the error of those writers whose educational backgrounds have imprinted on them the importance of methods. In the effort to be objective, concrete, specific, and practical they have focused on developing lists of activities, procedures, projects, devices, etc., for teachers to use. These are often not much more than tricks or gimmicks to initiate and give content to an interaction. To some extent, perhaps, this is necessary for teachers who have been so content-oriented, so lesson plan-dependent, that they are unable to enter a relationship spontaneously, without an agenda. To the extent that they are, and continue to be, dependent on such crutches they will be prevented from becoming free to enter and establish a spontaneous relationship.

It is true that some writers (e.g. Brown[19]) present evidence to support the effectiveness of such an approach. But they fail to realize that the success is probably more dependent upon the effectiveness of the teachers as persons—their interest, concern, enthusiasm—than upon the methods or techniques per se.

You cannot really tell someone how to express his caring or his love. Each of us must find his own way of doing it—his own style of implementing his attitudes and beliefs, his own way of giving himself. In a basic sense your self is the instrument of

[19]G. I. Brown, *Human Teaching for Human Learning: An Introduction to Confluent Education* (New York, Viking Press, Inc., 1971).

teaching, as of all human relationships, and you must learn to use yourself as an instrument for facilitating the development of others. You can be assisted in doing this but you must *do* it yourself.

RECEPTIVENESS OF THE STUDENT. An important aspect of any human relationship must be noted; failure to recognize and be aware of it has caused many teachers to suffer feelings of guilt and inadequacy or to feel that they have failed a student. Understanding, respect or warmth, and genuineness offered by the teacher, must also be received—or perceived and accepted—by the student. Young children are usually open and receptive, but some young children and perhaps many older children are not. Their experiences have closed them up, sometimes so tight that they are unaware of or insensitive to warmth and genuineness. The experiences of some have led to distrust and suspiciousness; resentment and resistance of others prevent their recognizing or accepting the genuine interest and concern of the teacher. These children have been mistreated—deceived, mistrusted, let down, treated as inadequate, etc.

The teacher can only offer himself, and try repeatedly to break through walls of suspicion, distrust, resistance, hostility and insensitivity. The theme of many of the books concerned with humanistic teaching, by Dennison, Herndon, Kohl and Kozol, is the attempt to break through to such students. When the attempt is successful the results sometimes appear to be miraculous. When the attempt is not successful, as too often happens, it is not always the fault of the teacher. It takes two to establish a good relationship. Mutual trust is necessary.

The books by Dennison, Herndon, Kohl, and Kozol contain illustrations of students who were difficult, and sometimes impossible to reach. Borton presents an instance from his experience:

> "Bob—a senior in my slow section. On my first day of teaching he took the seat directly in front of my desk and interrupted my introductory remarks by asking, 'you new?' When I nodded my head, he grinned, 'we got your number.' From then on he made my life miserable, always quitting just before I got to the breaking point. A month later he was suspended by some other teacher, a month after that he was jailed. At about the same time I learned that he

had started out as a freshman in the best academic class, and had been moved down one track each year as various teachers retaliated for his wisecracks."[20]

Such children might be reached by humanistic teaching in the early grades; later may be too late. Usually, when psychotherapy is recommended and even attempted, these students do not accept it and it is often not successful.

SUMMARY

This chapter has been concerned with the facilitation of personal development in the classroom, which can occur only under the influence of a humanistic teacher. The nature of the humanistic teacher's characteristics, genuineness or authenticity, respect and warmth, and empathic understanding, as expressed in the classroom teaching situation, was described.

While these characteristics are basically attitudes, they must be expressed and implemented by the teacher in his classroom behavior. Methods or means of implementing these characteristics or conditions, such as listening, responding, and setting limits and expectations, were considered.

Throughout, it was emphasized that teaching is a relationship in which these characteristics are manifested, not a matter of methods or techniques to be applied automatically. A total relationship is a unique, individual thing, and each teacher has or develops his own style of teaching and of relating to his students.

[20]T. Borton, *op. cit.*, p. 153.

CHAPTER VII

APPRAISAL TECHNIQUES AND PERSONAL DEVELOPMENT IN EDUCATIONAL SETTINGS

M. JEAN PHILLIPS

The Individual and the School

"ONCE UPON A TIME, the animals decided they must do something heroic to meet the problems of a 'new world,' so they organized a school. They adopted an activity curriculum consisting of running, climbing, swimming, and flying; and to make it easier to administer, all the animals took all the subjects.

The duck was excellent in swimming, better in fact than his instructor and made passing grades in flying, but he was very poor in running. Since he was slow in running, he had to stay after school and also drop swimming to practice running. This kept up until his webbed feet were badly worn and he was only average in swimming. But average was acceptable in school, so nobody worried about that except the duck.

The rabbit started at the top of the class in running but had a nervous breakdown because of so much make-up work in swimming.

The squirrel was excellent in climbing until he developed frustration in the flying class where his teacher made him start from the ground up instead of from the tree-top down. He also developed muscle cramps from overexertion and then got 'C' in climbing and 'D' in running.

The eagle was a problem child and was disciplined severely. In the climbing class he beat all the others to the top of the tree, but insisted on using his own way to get there.

At the end of the year, an abnormal eel that could swim exceedingly well, and also run, climb, and fly a little had the highest average and was valedictorian.

The prairie dogs stayed out of school and fought the tax levy because the administration would not add digging and burrowing to the curriculum. They apprenticed their child to a badger and later joined the groundhogs and gophers to start a successful private school.[1]"

Education, in its broadest sense, has been defined as "the deliberate, planful, conscious, and directed processes whereby people 'learn' their culture and learn to participate in it effectively."[2] All too frequently, literal implementation of this definition results in acculturated but unhappy ducks, psychotic rabbits, frustrated but conforming squirrels, defiant and embittered eagles, acclaimed mediocrities, and recalcitrant taxpayers.

Education in America is predicated upon two fundamental beliefs: a) that a free public school assuring equal educational opportunities to all children is essential for the achievement of a truly democratic society; and b) that every individual in our society has the right — if not the obligation — to maximize himself to the fullest extent of his potentialities. These twin tenets of universality and individuality may be compatible philosophically. In practice, however, the unique qualities of the individual — his attributes, needs, personal goals and idiosyncratic values — are subsumed under the rubric of "the greatest good for the greatest number."

In the social system of the school we must, of necessity, treat students as though they are more alike than they actually are. We cannot take all individual differences into account, nor should we try to. Rather our function may be to serve as role models, to help children learn to use information about themselves to resolve conflicts which inevitably arise between society and the individual. Weitz has pointed out that society establishes the

[1]G. H. Reavis, *Fable of the Animal School* (Primary source unknown).
[2]R. F. Butts, *A Cultural History of Western Education* (New York, John Wiley & Sons, Inc., 1964), p. 2.

values to be transmitted by the teacher; the individual interprets these values in idiosyncratic ways.[3] Society controls instructional methods and dictates curricula; the individual selects his methods of response and sets the pace for his learning. Society determines the goals of instruction and evaluates the degree to which these goals are achieved; the individual determines the relevance of the school's objectives according to his needs and incorporates (or rejects) the evaluations into his concept of self.

The instructional and administrative staff within a school system serve primarily as representatives of the larger society; personnel services specialists function on behalf of the learner at the point where the needs of the individual merge and conflict with the values of society.[4] It is precisely at this point that the recognition of individual differences assumes paramount importance.

WHY STUDY STUDENTS?

"Schools use appraisal techniques to promote individualized instruction."[5] . . . "The primary purpose of pupil appraisal is improved self-understanding on the part of each pupil."[6] Each of these statements is commendably child oriented, but closer examination reveals subtle differences between institutional intent and the personnel point of view.

The implication of the first declaration is that the school's basic duty is to know the child as an individual in order to gear learning experiences to his or her unique potential. The learner is passive; evaluation is external, and instruction (treatment) is adjusted to fit the needs of the child as perceived by parents, teachers, personnel specialists, and others. The latter statement suggests the child is helped to discover forces within himself and

[3]H. Weitz, *Behavior Change Through Guidance* (New York: John Wiley & Sons, Inc., 1964), p. 63.

[4]*Ibid.*, p. 4.

[5]L. J. Karmel, *Measurement and Evaluation in the Schools* (London, The Mac Millan Company, Collier-Macmillan Ltd., 1970), p. 4.

[6]G. A. Saltzman and H. J. Peters, eds., *Pupil Personnel Services* (Itasca, Illinois, F. E. Peacock Publishers, 1967), p. 285.

his environment which foster or impede growth. The learner is active; he understands the purpose of appraisal and participates in the evaluation and decision-making processes which follow.

Whether information is gathered to help the instructional and personnel staff understand the child or the child to understand himself, certain questions need to be asked. What can he do? What has he done? What does he want to do? What are his mental, physical, social, and emotional assets and limitations? What biological and environmental factors are contributing to his success or failure? As the child progresses up the educational ladder, data gatherers precede and follow him attempting to find answers to these questions.

All too frequently, information is collected assiduously, transcribed dutifully onto cumulative folders, and sealed in the vault behind the principal's office. Obviously, to be of maximum benefit, data must be obtained for valid reasons and must be utilized. The problem then becomes one of processing, of determining the value of the information to the learner and to the helper. An informational bit is relevant if it: a) helps to identify an area which markedly affects school performance; and b) indicates the need for differential treatment on the part of teachers and/or personnel specialists.[7]

Areas for study which may enhance or interfere with school performance include home and environmental conditions, previous educational experiences, health, abilities and aptitudes, interests, leisure time activities, social and emotional adjustments, immediate and ultimate goals, and work experience. After environmental influences and personal characteristics which contribute to the student's behavior in school are identified, treatment modalities may take the form of reinforcement of strengths and special attention to correction of faulty learnings, placement in special classes, remediation, counseling, consultation with parents, referral to resources or agencies within the community, etc.

[7]C. P. Froehlich and K. B. Hoyt, *Guidance Testing*, 3rd ed. Chicago, Science Research Associates, 1959), p. 1.

There are only two valid reasons why instructional staff and personnel specialists should be concerned with the study of students: 1) to understand students in order to render individualized assistance; and 2) to help students learn to use information about themselves in order to solve problems along the way to self-actualization.

Personnel specialists, particularly counselors, psychologists, and social workers, tend to enter a student's life space during periods of crisis or of conflict, or when he is judged to be heading toward difficulty by parents or teachers. Their function is to help the student to assess his resources and to use the information to resolve or alleviate a problem situation *and others like it as they arise*. Every attempt at conflict resolution should be viewed as a learning experience. In order to learn how to generalize the problem solving approach to similar situations, the student must have access to all available information about himself and must be fully cognizant of each step taken by himself and by the helper.

APPRAISAL FUNCTIONS OF PERSONNEL SPECIALISTS

From the first compulsory school attendance law enacted in 1852 to the economic opportunities and civil rights legislation of the present, state and federal programs have influenced the roles and functions of personnel workers. Historically, the disciplines grouped under the umbrella of personnel services were drawn into the school setting, not for the benefit of the individual, but for reasons of economic and social necessity.[8]

Background: Social-cultural Influences

"Truant officers" and "visiting teachers" were first employed to insure compliance with compulsory attendance laws in order to secure maximum beneficial benefits for the school district.[9] With incipient attendance coordinators and school social workers keeping children in school, the need arose to identify those who

---

[8]B. E. Shear, "Pupil Personnel Services: History and Growth," *Theory into Practice*, Vol. 4, No. 4:133-139 (October, 1965).

[9]*Ibid.*, p. 134.

should not be in school. Consequently, the responsibility of the first school health officers was to control the spread of contagious diseases by keeping the sick from infecting the well while psychologists were engaged to screen out the mentally and emotionally unfit.[10] The first guidance functions were conducted by a "vocational counselor" whose duties were concerned with helping secondary school youth choose and prepare for suitable occupations.[11]

As noninstructional, supportive personnel were added one-by-one to the educational milieu, their roles and functions were defined and delimited within the prevailing social context. Appraisal was an essential activity of each of the budding personnel services. The result of appraisal was frequently punishment or manipulation of the child or adolescent under investigation. Thus a child moving through a school system in the 1920's might find his daily attendance checked and absences investigated by a truant officer; his vaccination schedules, vision, hearing, and growth rates checked periodically by a school nurse; his socioeconomic background and family life investigated by the visiting teacher; his intellectual and emotional stability evaluated by a psychologist; and his academic achievements and interests nurtured to fit the job market by the vocational counselor. The maturing child was fragmented, the significant influences bearing upon him chopped up and rationed out like hardtack in a liferaft . . . and each bite jealously protected.

Educational innovations of yesterday become the traditions of today and change is effected slowly. Today the attendance coordinator has replaced the truant officer of 1920, the school social worker has succeeded the visiting teacher, and the adjective "vocational" no longer precedes the title of counselor. But today, despite the increased professionalization of each of the specialities, we find the activities performed by the first practitioners codified in official school policy statements and many

10J. K. Fisher, "Changing Concepts of Pupil Personnel Services," in G. A. Saltzman and H. J. Peters, eds., *op. cit.*, p. 26.

11C. H. Miller, *Foundations of Guidance* (New York, Harper & Brothers, 1961), p.5.

personnel workers function as they did in the twenties and thirties.

Current Practices

Personnel specialists, encouraged by their respective professional organizations, have broadened their operational framework to extend services to all children and youth at every educational level on a developmental — rather than on a remedial or crisis-oriented basis — and are reaching out into the community to effect social change. Appraisal, once the *sine qua non* of adjunctive services, has been de-emphasized (hopefully) and placed in context as a tool to be used constructively to support counseling, consulting, and follow-up acitivities.

The following excerpt from *Guidelines for Ohio Schools* illustrates recommended primary appraisal functions of the major personnel services:

CHILD ACCOUNTING PERSONNEL — to coordinate a program of student accounting services employing data processing procedures to provide all basic and essential data on each child of school age residing within the school district.

PUPIL APPRAISAL SERVICES — to coordinate a school-wide testing program, and to interpret the results of the testing program to appropriate personnel throughout the school and community.

SCHOOL COUNSELOR — to provide individual counseling services to students on matters pertaining to educational, vocational, and personal-social concerns.

SCHOOL HEALTH PERSONNEL — to develop and coordinate an identification, referral, and follow-up program for students with health problems.

SCHOOL PSYCHOLOGISTS — to conduct psycho-educational evaluation of students referred because of learning and behavior problems and to use the results in consultation with students, parents, teachers, administrators, and other professional workers in the school system and community.

SCHOOL SOCIAL WORKERS — to provide casework and referral services to students and families; to assist the student with attendance, social and emotional problems affecting adjustment and progress.[12]

[12]The Committee on Pupil Services, "Organization of the Pupil Services Program," *The Organization of Pupil Services,* Guidelines for Ohio Schools, 1964, in G. A. Saltzman and H. J. Peters, eds., op. cit., pp. 55-60.

Official statements like the one above help to define areas of responsibility and to delineate duties. (The separation of pupil appraisal services as an identifiable unit apart from the counselor and the teaching staff is noteworthy.) In practice, however, a great deal of role confusion and overlapping of functions occurs, particularly among school psychologists, school social workers, and counselors. Arbuckle, pleading for "ecumenicalization" among the three professions, has pointed out:

> When we check the literature of each camp looking for 'functions' the similarity is startling. On the other hand, it is somewhat distressing, but not unexpected, to note that the literature of each camp practically ignores the existence of the others . . . all three groups view themselves as working in the same milieu, namely the school and its immediate environment, and with the same basic population—the children, and those who most immediately affect them — teachers, parents, and the community. To varying degrees, all three see their functions as involvement in counseling, appraisal, and consultation, with children, teachers, parents, other school personnel, and various members of the community.[13]

Role and Function Confusion

A review of relevant literature indicates little confusion about the *process* of appraisal — who gathers what types of information, where, and when. Everyone concerned seems to agree social workers should prepare case histories and conduct home visitations, psychologists administer individual tests and projective measures and prepare diagnostic work-ups for special class placements, counselors (if the system lacks a designated appraisal specialist) administer group tests of achievement and aptitudes.

Role confusion and duplication of effort occur at the point most crucial to the individual student being studied, when the results of appraisal are evaluated and decisions are made. Fisher has reported a desire among psychologists and social workers for more involvement by personnel specialists and less admini-

[13]D. S. Arbuckle, counselor, social worker, psychologist "Lets Ecumenicalize," *Personnel and Guidance Journal*, p. 534 (February, 1967).

strative control in placement decisions and conferences with parents about behavioral problems of their children.[14]

Weiland surveyed the duties of 353 counselors, psychologists, and social workers and discovered these functions were duplicated by all three specializations: parental interviews concerning students' problems, consultation with teachers to identify causes of academic failures and to secure other types of information about students, counseling students with personal-social adjustment problems, and participation in staff conferences about students. In addition, social workers seemed to serve as referral agents and consultants to teachers to about the same extent as psychologists, while psychologists and counselors shared consultations with teachers and the identification of students with problems in common.[15]

Greater utliization of case conferences combined with an approach which is "group-centered"[16] rather than team-centered would alleviate the problem of needless or even harmful duplication of effort, *particularly when the student for whom decisions are made is a member of the group!*

APPRAISAL METHODS

Information about students may be obtained either *systematically,* in the sense that the same material is collected from many or all students; or *differentially,* to provide information needed by the individual for a specific purpose. Data sources may be *external* to the student being studied or *internal* stemming from self-perceptions. The individual has little or no control over the results aquired from external sources such as standardized tests, health records, cumulative folders, observational reports from

14J. K. Fisher, "Changing Concepts of Pupil Personnel Services," *Journal of the International Association of Pupil Personnel Workers* (June, 1966.)

15R. G. Wieland, *A Comparative Study of the Duties Performed Regularly by School Counselors, School Psychologists, and School Social Workers Working Together in Selected School Systems.* Unpublished doctoral dissertation, The Florida State University, 1966, Order No. 66-9092.

16C. H. Patterson, *An Introduction to Counseling in the School* (New York, Harper & Row Publishers, Inc., 1971), pp. 285-303.

parents, teachers, and peers, and case studies. On the other hand, he or she may exert a great deal of control over internal sources of appraisal. The value of information obtained from autobiographies, projective devices, diagnostic interviews, or counseling sessions, depends upon the quality of the relationship established between the student and the personnel specialist.

Information obtained systematically and externally is useful for describing the school population in demographic terms and for establishing broad educational outcomes. Like government census data, it helps to create a frame within which to view the individual. Personnel workers use results gathered systematically but apply them in terms of their meaning for the individual student. Techniques, or instruments, which tap perceptions of self should always be administered on an individual basis, for a specific purpose, and only by a qualified professional trained in their use.

Appraisal competencies of personnel workers

Although the extent to which data gathering methods are used will vary among the specialties, every personnel worker should acquire a basic understanding of test and measurement principles and should have at least a reading knowledge of statistical concepts and terms. In addition, the personnel specialist should have intensive training in the administration of instruments, or other appraisal techniques, unique to his discipline. After the specialist has learned thoroughly the "tools of the trade," he should have a closely supervised practicum experience in the use and interpretation of the results.

It is frequently in this last area that professional preparation is weakest. Most graduate programs emphasize measurement theory, test administration, and the characteristics of specific appraisal techniques but fail to provide courses in the utilization of results in the treatment or counseling process.[17]

[17]L. Goldman, *Using Tests in Counseling*, 2nd ed. (New York, Appleton-Century-Crofts, Inc., 1971), p. 6.

Standardized tests

Standardized testing is big business in the elementary and secondary schools of the nation. Approximately one million tests per day are administered in American schools.[18] Standardized test results provide a means for comparing performance levels of students within a school system or with groups of students in a larger population. A coordinated, system-wide testing program in harmony with the educational goals of the system is essential to sound institutional decision making. The results also provide a rich source of data for personnel specialists who deal with students on an individual basis.

Educational development (achievement) tests

School achievement may be assessed by standardized batteries which measure skills and content mastery over several grade levels or by separate achievement tests which cover content in specific curricular areas. Since the major function of the school is to help children learn, achievement batteries, such as those presented in Table VII-I,[19] have more relevancy to school staff members than any other type of instrument. Achievement measures, particularly when administered in the fall, assist curriculum planners to identify strengths and weaknesses at various grade levels and help the classroom teacher to plan specific learning experiences for individual students. Administrators use comparative local and normative data to measure the effectiveness of the school instructional program and to interpret the needs of the school to the board of education and to the community.

Standardized achievement results help parents understand the academic strengths and weaknesses of their children, both in comparison with other children of the same age and grade level and relative to the individual child. On an individual basis, results may pinpoint a particular misunderstanding or a logical

[18]H. B. Lyman, *Test Scores and What They Mean,* 2nd ed. (Englewood Cliffs, N.J., Prentice-Hall, Inc., 1971), p. 64.

[19]A. Anastasi, *Psychological Testing,* 3rd ed. (Toronto, Macmillan Company, 1968), p. 396.

TABLE VII-I REPRESENTATIVE GENERAL ACHIEVEMENT BATTERIES

BATTERY	1	2	3	4	5	6	7	8	9	10	11	12	13	14
*Adult Basic Learning Examination (ABLE)	Measures *adult* achievement in basic learnings. (Grade equivalents, 1 through 12)													
California Achievement Tests	x	x	x	x	x	x	x	x	x	x	x	x	x	x
Iowa Tests of Basic Skills (ITBS)		x	x	x	x	x	x	x						
Iowa Tests of Educational Development (ITED)									x	x	x	x		
*Fundamental Achievement Series	Taps competences acquired in the course of ordinary daily living; basic literacy to eighth-grade level.													
Metropolitan Achievement Test	x	x	x	x	x	x	x	x	x	x	x	x		
SRA Achievement Series	x	x	x	x	x	x	x	x	x					
Sequential Tests of Educational Progress (STEP)				x	x	x	x	x	x	x	x	x	x	x
Stanford Achievement Test	x	x	x	x	x	x	x	x	x	x	x	x		
Tests of Academic Promise (TAP)										x	x	x	x	

*Suggested for use with adults/educationally disadvantaged from A. Anastasi, *Psychological Testing,* 3rd ed. (Toronto, MacMillan Company, 1968), p. 396.

thought process with an illogical outcome.[20] Achievement scores, maintained cumulatively over several years, provide a record of academic growth which can be used to predict future performance. Changes in the overall growth pattern may reveal students under emotional stress who should be referred to a counselor.

Achievment test results are used in most schools for all the purposes cited above. Ironically, test results are frequently withheld from the child or adolescent who took the test. *This does not mean the actual scores should be communicated to the student nor should an interpretation be forced upon a reluctant examinee.* Most students, however, are interested in the results; particularly if they understand why a test is administered in the first place.

Definite benefits accrue when test results are communicated

[20]R. H. Bauernfeind, *Building a School Testing Program* (Boston, Houghton Mifflin Co., 1963), p. 136.

to the examinee, even in the elementary school level. Lyman has concluded:

> . . . Many will disagree, but I believe that some basic interpretation could be done effectively with children as young as ten years of age. The teacher might discuss the general nature of the tests with the class as a group. This could be followed up by an individual confer- ence with each pupil, perhaps focusing attention mainly on areas of highest and lowest achievement and a statement about his achieve- ment relative to his ability (without saying much about his intelli- gence level itself). Such interpretations would need to be handled carefully but could help youngsters in their search for an under- standing of themselves.[21]

Mental ability (intelligence) tests

Intelligence is a hypothetical ·construct inferred from in- telligence test scores which are a joint product of many factors — inherent capacity influenced by quality of education, experi- ential background, test adequacy, examiner competency, moti- vation, and the emotional and physical states of the examinee. For most purposes, group paper-and-pencil intelligence tests may be considered tests of general scholastic aptitude and are used to predict school achievement.[22]

The representative group mental ability tests listed in Table VII-II indicate the variety of instruments purporting to measure "intelligence," "scholastic aptitude," "general ability," "primary mental abilities," "mental maturity," "college ability," etc. With the exception of the *Concept Mastery Test* and the *Miller Analogies Test* which are used to assess the superior adult level, the instruments shown in Table VII-II are examples of multi- level batteries with each level covering a two-to-three year or grade span.

Despite the fact that group mental ability tests are avail- able for use in grades K through three, they yield IQ scores which are dangerously unreliable at this level when behavior

[21]*Op cit.*, p. 158.
[22]H. B. Lyman, *op. cit.*, p. 11.

TABLE VII-II REPRESENTATIVE GROUP MENTAL ABILITY TESTS

Academic Ability Test	Miller Analogies Test
Analysis of Learning Potential (ALP)	Otis-Lennon Mental Ability Test
California Test of Mental Maturity (CTMM)	Pintner General Ability Test - Revised
Concept Mastery Test	Revised Beta Examination
Cooperative School and College Ability Tests (SCAT)	SRA Short Test of Educational Ability (STEA)
Henmon-Nelson Tests of Mental Ability	SRA Tests of Educational Ability (TEA)
Kuhlmann-Anderson Intelligence Tests	Terman-McNemar Test of Mental Ability
Lorge-Thorndike Intelligence Tests	Tests of General Ability (TOGA)

patterns are being acquired.[23] In cases where assessment of intellectual functioning is needed, the primary grade child should be referred to a psychological examiner skilled in the administration, use, and interpretation of the Stanford-Binet and the Wechsler scales.

Findley[24] suggests group tests of listening comprehension and of reading readiness may be useful in kindergarten and the primary grades "if we are concerned with measuring potential that is not yet translated into immediately useful scholastic competence [p. 194]."

Traditionally, every-pupil group tests yielding "IQ" scores are administered at one or two points between grades four and ten. Because of widespread misinterpretation and confusion — if not outright abuse — of mental ability scores, increasing numbers of measurement specialists and educational leaders are recommending the abandonment of group "IQ tests" in favor of more diversified use of achievement test results and referral of individual students to psychological specialists for appraisal of behavioral or learning disorders.[25]

[23]L. J. Cronbach, *Essentials of Psychological Testing* 2nd ed., New York, Harper & Brothers, (1969), p. 223.
[24]W. G. Findley, "The Complete Testing Program," *Theory Into Practice,* Vol. 2, No. 4: pp. 192-198 (October, 1963).
[25]R. H. Bauernfeind, *op. cit.,* p. 185.

For most students at the intermediate grade level, where the stability and validity of achievement scores are greatest, future academic performance can best be predicted from current and past achievement records. There should be little need for additional group testing when a broadly based achievement test is used which reflects the curricular practices and educational objectives of a given school system.

Potential — the capacity to acquire proficiency with training is measured effectively at the junior and senior high school levels by a good multiple aptitude battery. The most commonly used aptitude batteries are shown in Table VII-III. The *Differential Aptitude Test Battery* (DAT), for example, yields eight scores: Verbal Reasoning, Numerical Ability, Abstract Reasoning, Clerical Speed and Accuracy, Mechanical Reasoning, Space Relations, Language Usage I — Spelling, and Language Usage II — Grammar. Results of an aptitude battery, particularly when combined with achievement and interest measures, provide assistance to a student planning his high school curriculum and beginning the process of vocational exploration. College entrance examinations, such as the *Scholastic Aptitude Test* (SAT) and the *American College Tests* (ACT) are also considered measures of potential since their results are used as predictors of academic success in college.

TABLE VII-III MULTIPLE APTITUDE BATTERIES

Academic Promise Tests (APT)	General Aptitude Test Battery (GATB)
Differential Aptitude Tests (DAT)	Guilford-Zimmerman Aptitude Survey
Employee Aptitude Survey (EAS)	Multiple Aptitude Tests
Flanagan Aptitude Classification Tests (FACT)	SRA Primary Mental Abilities, Revised

Measurement experts are in agreement that programs of every pupil "intelligence" testing at specified grade levels are widely abused and misunderstood, frequently inefficient because of duplication with broad-based achievement testing, and, thereby, uneconomical. However, the wise patient does not destroy the thermometer when it registers the presence of a fever. It behooves the personnel specialist to become thoroughly familiar with standardized tests in general use; to learn their assets and limitations, and to acquire proficiency in their interpretation.

Interest inventories

Two of the most important determiners of success in any field of endeavor are aptitude and interest. Aptitude refers to the amount of ability a person possesses to carry out the demands made by a job (or a course of study) and to his potential to undertake successively the training for it: interest refers to the extent to which a person likes or dislikes what he is doing.

Interest inventories may be of assistance to help the individual compare his high and low areas of tested interests, but these inventories should only be administered by qualified counselors or psychologists and the results communicated within the atmosphere of a counseling session. Interest measures with which the personnel specialist should become familiar are listed in Table VII-IV.

Interests and abilities do not always go hand in hand but they should never be considered independently of one another. A high school senior, for example, may share many of the tested

TABLE VII-IV INTEREST AND ATTITUDE
SURVEYS AND INVENTORIES

Gordon Occupational Check List	Minnesota Teacher Attitude Inventory
Guilford-Zimmerman Interest Inventory	Minnesota Vocational Interest Inventory
Holland Vocational Preference Inventory	Occupational Interest Inventory (Lee-Thorpe)
Kuder General Interest Survey	Pictorial Study of Values
Kuder Occupational Interest Survey	Strong Vocational Interest Blank (SVIB)
Kuder Preference Record — Personal	Study of Values (Allport, Vernon, Lindzey)
Kuder Preference Record — Vocational	Survey of Study Habits and Attitudes (Brown-Holtzman)

interests of physicians, may be strongly motivated to become a physician himself, but lacks the ability to survive eight or more years of academic training. By discussing his feelings about his talents, abilities, and measured interests, the student may arrive at some tentative decisions regarding his post-high school future.

Personality inventories

Psychologists probably spend as much time and energy trying to measure personality characteristics as educators spend trying to cope with personal-social misbehaviors. Part of the difficulty in developing an objective paper-and-pencil personality measure lies in semantics. Allport and Odbert have estimated the English language contains at least 17,953 words which describe behavioral "traits."[26] Even if a perfectly reliable and statistically valid instrument could be devised consisting of a reasonable number of universally agreed upon trait descriptions, discrepancies would exist between what subjects thought they did and their observable behavior.

There is no substitute for systematic observations reported by sensitive and responsible classroom teachers in the assessment and evaluation of personal-social behaviors in the school setting.[27] The teacher can be, and should be, a major—if not the central—participant in the evaluation of group dynamics and of interpersonal relationships within the classroom, homeroom, or other school-associated groups of students.[28] The implication is clear. If we are to help children and youth gain insight into their own personality dynamics, the establishment and maintenance of close working relations between personnel specialists and instructional staff is mandatory.

It should be evident from the foregoing discussion that there is no place for the *routine* assessment of personal-social adjust-

[26]G. W. Allport and H. S. Odbert, "Trait Names: Psycholexical Study," *Psychological Monographs,* 47:171 (1936).

[27]R. H. Bauerfeind, *op. cit.,* p. 248.

[28]J. R. Gerberich, H. A. Greene, and A. N. Jorgensen, *Measurement and Evaluation in the Modern School* (New York, David McKay Company, Inc., 1962), p. 149.

ment in the school setting. Personality inventories and projective measures should be administered solely on an individual basis by a fully qualified professional for diagnostic or therapeutic reasons only. Haas has expressed his concern in the following manner.

> All psychological tests are designed to be used by experts only. Unfortunately they are used too often by people who are simply not trained to understand the weaknesses and special problems inherent in all examinations and who are thus likely to draw false conclusions. Scoring most tests and assigning such labels as 'domineering,' 'agresive,' and 'anxious' to certain types of scores is a simple clerical job. The simplicity of this task is misleading, however. The scoring and diagnostic categories of most tests cannot be accepted at face value. In addition, the meaning of any single test must always be derived administered to the subject and the subject's own background. . . . On occasion, in qualified hands, personality testing is worthwhile. Too often, however, partially informed or even totally untrained people reach all sorts of unjust and bizarre conclusions on the basis of what they have read in the test manual or otherwise believe the test 'proves.'[29]

A review of Buros' *Seventh Mental Measurements Yearbook* reveals that most of the nonprojective personality instruments purportedly for use with children are of little practical value, even to the skilled psychologist.[30] With all their limitations, however, the administration and interpretation of personality measures may be beneficial or informative for the high school or college age student. For this reason, the school counselor and the school psychologist should be thoroughly familiar with the personality inventories in common use (Table VII-V).

It sometimes happens that the mere act of responding to a personality inventory will aid the student to pinpoint a problem area or a characteristic mode of behavior which he might find profitable to examine in detail with the counselor. For those individuals who are unable or unwilling to talk about themselves, a discussion of the inventory results may serve as an entree to

[29]K. Haas, *Understanding Ourselves and Others* (Englewood Cliffs, Prentice-Hall, Inc., 1965), p. 127.

[30]O. K. Buros, ed., *The Seventh Mental Measurements Yearbook* (Highland Park, New Jersey, Gryphon Press, 1972).

TABLE VII-V SELF-REPORT PERSONALITY INVENTORIES

Adjective Check List (ACL)	IPAT Children's Personality Questionnaire
A-S Reaction Study	Jr.-Sr. High School Personality Questionnaire
Adjustment Inventory (Bell)	Minnesota Counseling Inventory
California Psychological Inventory (CPI)	Minnesota Multiphasic Personality Inventory (MMPI)
California Q-set (CQ-set)	Money Problem Check List
California Test of Personality	Myers-Briggs Type Indicator
Edwards Personal Preference Schedule (EPPS)	Personal Orientation Inventory
Eysenck Personality Inventory	Personality Inventory (Bernreuter)
Gordon Personal Inventory	Rotter Incomplete Sentences Blank
Gordon Personal Profile	STS Youth Inventory
Guilford-Zimmerman Temperament Survey	Sixteen Personality Factor Questionnaire
	Tennessee Self Concept Scale

counseling. Exploration of personal feelings, concerns, motivations, and behaviors is legitimated for them since the stated purpose of the interview is to discuss personally oriented "test" findings. For others, the process of personality assessment may serve as a communication bridge between the individual counselee and the personnel worker. Frequently a student is able and willing—even eager—to discuss personal problems with a counselor but is unable to communicate in terms the counselor can understand. The discussion of results may focus the attention of both the counselee and the counselor upon an aspect of the counselee's problems in such a manner that the counselor is able to "hear" what the student may have been trying to tell him all along.

To be really useful, the selection and interpretation of *any* psychometric measure requires skillful counseling in addition to emotional involvement of both student and counselor. Test information must be related to other aspects of the individual's experience: self-esteem (or lack of it), aptitudes and achievements, the inevitable conflicts between family and peer-group values, as well as the student's life-style and life script. Without such opportunity to integrate information about himself, psychometric evaluation represents exploitation of the student, as well as an unwarrented intrusion upon his personal privacy.

SELF-ESTEEM

From the personnel services point of view, positive self-concept development is the raison d'etre for appraisal functions within the educational setting. All too frequently however, the fact that feelings of positive or negative self-esteem are entwined intricately with appraisal is ignored, especially by some personnel workers who, enamored of numerical results, lose touch with the human element.

Interest in the measurement of self-esteem reflects the influence of phenomenological psychology which focuses on the way events are *perceived* by the individual and on his subsequent efforts to integrate perceptions in order to maintain and/or enhance the phenomenological self.[31] Self-esteem has been defined by Coopersmith (1967) as the

> evaluation which the individual makes and customarily maintains with regard to himself: it expresses an attitude of approval or disapproval and indicates the extent to which the individual believes himself to be capable, significant, successful, and worthy. In short, self-esteem is a personal judgment of worthiness that is expressed in the attitudes the individual holds toward himself. It is a subjective experience which the individual conveys to others by verbal reports and other overt expressive behavior.[32]

Coopersmith, obtaining both subjective evaluations of self-esteem from a population of fifth-grade boys as well as behavioral ratings from school personnel, identified five groups for extensive study:

GROUPS	DESCRIPTION
1. High self-esteem High behavioral ratings	Personally effective, poised, competent, capable of independent and creative actions, low anxiety level, socially skilled, direct, incisive, good social relationships, gravitate to positions of influence and authority

[31]D. Snygg and A. W. Combs, *Individual Behavior: A Perceptual Approach to Behavior*, rev. ed. (New York, Harper & Row, Publishers, 1959).

[32]S. Coopersmith, *The Antecedents of Self-esteem* (San Francisco, W. H. Freeman and Co., Publishers, 1967), p. 5.

2. Medium self-esteem Medium behavioral ratings	"Typical" child, stable, moderate capacities and achievements, relatively well accepted, good defenses, strong value orientation, tend toward dependency, uncertain of personal worth, unsure of performance in relation to others
3. Low self-esteem Low behavioral ratings	Socially and academically unsuccessful, feel inferior, high anxiety levels, feel powerless, isolated, unlovable, incapable of self-expression, tend to withdraw, overtly passive and compliant
4. High self-esteem Low behavioral ratings	Defensive, maintain favorable self-regard despite low ratings by teachers, limited acceptance by peers, relatively poor academic performance
5. Low self-esteem High behavioral ratings	Low self-evaluation in the face of marked academic and social success, high anxiety levels, highly motivated, idealistic

The similarity is striking between the groups described by Coopersmith and the four basic positions of the transactional analysist:[33] (ie Groups 1 and 2—"I'm O.K., you're O.K." and "I'm (mostly) O.K., you're (mostly) O.K."; Group 3—"I'm not O.K., you're not O.K."; Group 4—"I'm O.K., you're not O.K."; and Group 5—"I'm not O.K., you're O.K.")

The first three groups reveal effects of the interlocking relationship between self-perception, overt behavior, and the perceptions of significant others. For a majority of children, self-appraisal has become self-fulfilling by middle childhood. In this sense, the children in each of the first three groups are "congruent" within their school environment. For Group 3, however, congruence is devastating. Clearly, counselors, teachers psychologists, and school social workers must be able to identify the low-

[33]E. Berne, *What Do You Say After You Say Hello? The Psychology of Human Destiny* (New York, Grove Press, Inc., 1973), p. 84.

esteem youngster in order to intervene productively in the "I'm not O.K." reinforcement process inherent in many educational settings.

Extreme divergence between self-evaluation and external behavior occurs in slightly less than 10 percent of the population—Coopersmith screened 1,748 children in order to locate sufficient numbers of the high esteem-low behavior ratings and the low esteem-high behavior ratings group, the latter being particularly rare.[34] Nevertheless, this unhappy and/or anxious minority merits utmost concern. Effective self-concept work requires training, skill, sensitivity, courage, emotional involvement, and commitment on the part of the personnel specialist and teaching staff if deeply ingrained self-other attitudes are to be altered or modified.

Wylie's scholarly review of self-concept research indicates that most studies have dealt with high-and-low-esteem disparity within groups or with real-and-ideal-self discrepancies within the individual.[35] Coopersmith has provided a major contribution by demonstrating the importance of understanding the majority who score within the middle ranges on self-esteem measures.

> Their generalized value orientation, their greater dependency, and their intermediate and hence ambiguous position of worth suggest that there may be particular, distinguishing characteristics associated with medium self-esteem. *Rather than being a mere pivotal, intermediate part of the range of self-esteem, the middle portion may well reflect the consequences of uncertain self-appraisal.*[36]

Counseling serves a useful purpose by providing a setting where the often neglected "average" child or adolescent may clarify self-perception through the self-evaluative process.

APPRAISAL OF SELF-ESTEEM

A variety of techniques have been devised to study subjective and objective manifestations of self-perception. Among the methods most frequently used are direct observation in natural or contrived situations, the diagnostic interview, and psychometric evaluations. It is essential to remember the devices have no value

---

[34]*Op. cit.,* p .14.
[35]R. Wylie, *The Self-concept* (Lincoln, Neb., University of Nebraska Press, 1961).
[36]*Op. cit.,* p. 249. (Emphasis by author).

in themselves. They serve only as a means of identifying and describing problem behaviors or debilitating self-perceptions.

Direct Behavior Observation

Behavioral observations are time-consuming and difficult to summarize; however, the results may be worth the effort. In addition to providing useful information, the observational process helps sensitize school personnel, particularly teachers, to interpersonal dynamics within the classroom as well as to unique and specific response patterns of individual students.

It is generally judicious to provide observers with a check list, rating scale, or a description of specific behaviors to record. To be of maximum value, behavioral observations should have these characteristics:

1. Must be made in a systematic manner.
2. Must be made by several persons whose presence is a natural part of the school setting.
3. Conditions under which each observation was made must be specified.
4. Report of the observations must be prepared in such a way as to separate the record of the behavior performed from any evaluation of it.[37]

The interested reader is referred to Wright (1960) for an extensive review of observational methods ranging from comprehensive, long-term techniques such as the diary method, to a series of short, highly controlled time samplings.[38] A useful modification of the customary observational check list is the *critical incident technique* in which the observer is requested to record specific instances of the behavior under scrutiny. For example, a classroom teacher may be asked to maintain detailed notes over a two-week period describing withdrawal behaviors of a particular child.

[37]H. Weitz, *op. cit.,* p. 90.

[38]H. F. Wright, "Observational Child Study," in P. E. Mussen, ed., *Handbook of Research Methods in Child Development* (New York, John Wiley & Sons, Inc., 1960), Ch. 3.

The Cumulative Record

A student's cumulative record represents a summary of observations over time. Identification data (age, sex, family structure, birth order), physical data (height, weight, vision, hearing, health history, attendance records), social data (extra-curricular activities, work records, socio-economic level), and the record of academic performance all provide diagnostic information which may be helpful to personnel specialists. Since academic performance, relative to the peer group, is a major antecedent of self-esteem,[39] sudden shifts or a progressive decline may be of particular significance.

Peer Ratings

Peer ratings, once highly touted as potentially valuable measures have fallen into disrepute during the past decade. However, sociometric nominations have generally proved to be one of the most dependable of rating techniques.[40,41,42] Sociometric nominations are obtained by asking each individual to indicate one or more class members with whom he would choose to play, study, eat lunch, etc., or peers may be asked to name the person who is most liked, most creative, least known, best sport, or any other designated characteristic.

There is some evidence from Peace Corps studies that peer ratings are among the better, if not the best, predictors of overseas performance, and there is indication that Duncan's reputation test of personality integration seems to have value when used in a setting, such as a college campus, where peers have regular opportunities to observe one another's behavior.[43]

[39]S. Coopersmith, *op. cit.*, p. 243.

[40]E. P. Hollander, "Validity of Peer Nominations in Predicting a Distant Performance Criterion," *Journal of Applied Psychology*, 49:434-438 (1965).

[41]H. P. Reynolds, "Efficacy of Sociometric Ratings in Predicting Leadership Success," *Psychological Reports*, 19:35-40 (1966).

[42]D. W. Fiske and J. A. Cox, "The Consistency of Ratings by Peers," *Journal of Applied Psychology*, 44:11-17 (1960).

[43]A. E. Bergin, "The Evaluation of Therapeutic Outcomes, in A. E. Bergin and L. L. Garfield eds., *Handbook of Psychotherapy and Behavior Change* (New York, John Wiley & Sons, Inc., 1971), p. 263.

Despite their limitations, peer ratings are useful in two respects: 1) peers are in a position to be better judges of interpersonal relationships within a group structure than are outside observers; and 2) an individual's behavior, whether adaptive or maladaptive, is reinforced by peer opinions reflected by peer actions. Whether peer opinions are right or wrong is not the issue. The personnel specialist desiring to intervene in the process of maladaptive learning must recognize the power of self-fulfilling reinforcers present within the peer group structure.

Observer Use of Self-report Instruments

Any self-report instrument may be used by observers to describe another individual. *The Adjective Check List, The Leary Interpersonal Check List,* various modifications of the *Semantic Differential,* and an assortment of Q-sort techniques are especially adaptable for this purpose. It is frequently desirable to obtain a self-report on the *Adjective Chcek List,* for example, as well as an observer's ACL report on the same individual, thereby acquiring both an internal and an external evaluation.

The Diagnostic Interview

The interview plays an important role in providing suggestions for areas warranting further exploration. Interviews may range in form from the highly structured orally administered questionnaire, through the guided interview covering predetermined areas, to the totally unstructured interview in which the interviewee is encouraged to explore thoughts and emotions at a deeply therapeutic level. The latter is characterized by the interviewer's efforts to understand from the student's verbal symbolism and nonverbal behavior how the student perceives his situation.

Data collection and relationship counseling are not necessarily antithetical. Information gathering, behavioral observations, problem exploration, problem identification, even tentative decision-making may occur within a climate of mutual understanding and shared endeavor.

Interviews serve three functions for the counselor, school psychologist, or school social worker. First, they provide a setting for direct observation of behavior manifested during the interview itself; speech patterns, language usage, reaction to an authority figure, physical coordination, poise, and mannerisms can be noted. Secondly, the interview affords opportunity to explore the student's world from his perceptual position. What does it mean to him to be the eldest in a family of seven? How does he feel about being fired from his job at the car wash? What happens inside when his mother curses him? A student-centered approach to the collection of life history information frequently serves as an entree to counseling—the third function of the diagnostic interview.

Psychometric measures

In a sense, all self-report inventories are measures of self-concept to the extent that test-defensiveness, faking, test-anxiety, response set, etc., reflect attitudes toward self. Many psychologists regard test-taking attitudes as the major source of variance in personality measures.[44]

Self-esteem or self-acceptance measures are widely used to measure psychotherapy outcomes.[44,45] Several of the relatively more reliable and valid measures of self-concept are: Dymond's *Q Adjustment Score*,[46] Van der Veen's *Family Concept Q Sort*,[47] Gergen and Morse's *Self-Consistency Score*,[48] and various adaptations of Kelly's *Role Construct Repertory Test*[49] (Rep Test).
These instruments and many of the self-reports listed in Table VII-V may be repeated by the same individual from different

[44]A. Anastasi, *op. cit.*, p. 532.

[44]J. M. Butler, "Self-acceptance as a Measure of Outcome of Psychotherapy," *British Journal of Social Psychiatry*, 1:51-62 (1966).

[45]C. B. Truax and R. R. Carkhuff, *Toward Effective Counseling and Psychotherapy: Training and Practice* (Chicago, Aldine Press, 1967).

[46]R. F. Dymond, "Adjustment Changes over Therapy from Self-sorts," in C. R. Rogers and R. F. Dymond, eds., *Psychotherapy and Personality Change,* Chicago: University of Chicago Press, 1954, pp. 76-89.

[47]F. Van der Veen, "The Parent's Concept of the Family Unit and Child Adjustment," *Journal of Counseling Psychology*, 12:196-200 (1965).

[48]K. J. Gergen and S. J. Morse, "Self-consistency: Measurement and Validation," *Proceedings of the 75th Annual Convention of the American Psychological Association*, 2:207-208 (1967).

[49]J. A. Loevinger, "A Theory of Test Response, in A. Anastasi ed., *Testing Problems in Perspective.* Washington, American Council on Education, 1966, pp. 545-556.

points of reference; i.e. as he is (real self), as he would like to be (ideal self), as people see him (social self), or from the subject's perception of how he is seen by spouse, parent, employer, or other significant persons.

According to self-theory, the goal of the maturational process is a fully differentiated concept of self, wherein the individual is fully—and realistically—aware of himself and accepts himself as he is. Few persons reach this goal. Many, if not most, remain at a lower level; maintaining a relatively comfortable psychological balance between self-awareness and a conventional acquiescence to societal values.

Loevinger has suggested that a curvilinear, rather than a linear, relationship exists between personality inventory results and levels of self-conceptualization.[49] Since personality inventory scores are based on normative data, "adjustment" is defined by the scores of the majority of persons who function at a stereotypical lower level. Her hypothesis may account for the findings that college seniors seem to have poorer adjustment scores than freshmen,[50] that some patients seem to deteriorate as a result of therapy when personality tests are used as criterion measures,[51] and that real and ideal-self disparity increases with age, IQ, and cognitive differentiation.[52]

The most consistent finding in research on self-image is the positive relationship typically found between self-ideal disparity and anxiety.[53,54,55,56] The key determinant would appear to be not

[50] N. Sanford, ed., "Personality Development During the College Years," *Journal of Social Issues,* 12:3-70 (1956).

[51] A. E. Bergin and S. L. Garfield, *Op. cit.,* 217-270.

[52] P. Katz and E. Zigler, "Self-image Disparity: A Developmental Approach, in I. J. Gordon, ed., *Readings in Research in Developmental Psychology* (Glenview, Ill., Scott, Foresman & Company, 1971), pp. 341-351.

[53] C. R. Rogers and R. F. Dymond, *Psychotherapy and Personality Change* (Chicago, University of Chicago Press, 1954).

[54] P. Bruce, "Relationship of Self-acceptance to Other Variables with Sixth-grade Children Oriented in Self-understanding," *Journal of Educational Psychology,* 49:229-238 (1959).

[55] S. A. Coopersmith, "A Method for Determining Types of Self-esteem," *Journal of Educational Psychology,* 59:87-94 (1959).

[56] L. P. Lipsitt, "A Self-concept Scale for Children and Its Relationship to the Children's Form of the Manifest Anxiety Scale," *Child Development,* 29:463-472 (1958).

the presence or absence of anxiety but rather the individual's ability to cope with anxiety in particular situations. Self-image congruence, as manifested in test results, may signify increased mental health and a reduction of maladaptive anxiety for some individuals. In the case of the fully functioning individual, psychometrically derived self-image disparity may be an index of maturation rather than an indication of maladjustment.

SUMMARY

Personnel services specialists function on behalf of the learner at the point where the needs of the individual merge and occasionally conflict with society. Appraisal activities by personnel specialists serve a valid purpose to the extent results are utilized on a developmental basis to assist the student in acquiring self-knowledge. Role confusion and duplication of effort exist among school psychologists, counselors, and school social workers despite the fact that specific appraisal duties have become differentiated over time. Greater utilization of case conferences and a group-centered approach is recommended. The personnel specialist's use of the principle tools of appraisal—standardized tests, behavioral observations, and the diagnostic interview—is not antithetical to the counseling relationship providing the core conditions essential to effective interpersonal communication are maintained.

CHAPTER VIII

EDUCATIONAL AND VOCATIONAL DEVELOPMENT, PLACEMENT, AND FOLLOW-UP SERVICES

HENRY KACZKOWSKI

THE FUNCTION OF WORK in American life has undergone change. Technological progress has not only affected the conditions of work, but the distribution of the workers into the various areas of employment. Approximately a hundred years ago, 75 percent of employed persons worked on farms. Currently, less than 5 percent of workers are so employed. Increased productivity also has affected man's philosophical orientation towards work. Work is no longer viewed as means for providing for the basic needs of life but a way of finding identification in society. Wrenn suggests that in America, a man's occupation is a key source of self-identity. " 'Who is he' most often means 'what does he do - what is his job?' "[1]

Although technological progress has improved the quality of man's life, it has also generated new problems. What was scarce has now become abundant. One of the means of resolving the farm surplus is to limit the acreage a farmer could plant. Some view this solution as highly unsatisfactory when a large segment of the world is hungry and suffers from malnutrition. Great economic growth has not prevented unemployment, since automation has greatly reduced the need for semi-skilled and unskilled workers. It has also led to under-employment of the talented. The majority of the current work force is employed in distributive and service occupations rather than in production.

[1] C. G. Wrenn, "Human Values and Work in American Life," in H. Borow, ed., *Man in the World of Work* (Boston, Houghton Mifflin Co., 1964), p. 24.

According to Venn the implication of this trend is "that education becomes a link between the individual and work, or to put it another way, the link between an individual and his place in society."[2] This relationship between level of employment and education has a psychological impact on today's youth. Paul Goodman states "there are not enough worthy jobs in our economy for the average adolescents to grow toward."[3] Wrenn has made the following observation on this point: "The nature of employed work in our society has changed and its power to give satisfaction to the worker has diminished; the sooner we accept this fact, the sooner we can develop a comprehensive set of solutions."[4]

Work, that is the right to work, has become a public issue; however, the meaning of work has not. Social theorists are divided on the issue. One faction suggests that through automation workers will be released from brute labor and be free to pursue leisure-time activities in which they can find self-identity. The other faction believes that through reorganization of working conditions (i.e. decentralization of facilities and worker participation in decision making) workers could obtain a greater sense of dignity. From a historical perspective, the current concerns over the value of work seem strange. Ancient societies did not analyze the meaning of work; for them, work and existence were identical. Wrenn in reviewing the historical antecedents of the meaning of work concluded that the concept of work has been affected by social and religious factors.[5] From feudal times, the "common man" could only obtain dignity through what he produced. St. Thomas Aquinas, Luther, and Calvin added a moral quality to work. "Work is good, unemployment is bad, unwillingness to work is perversity and sin."[6]

[2]G. Venn, "Needed: A New Relationship Between Education and Work," in H. J. Peters and J. C. Hansen, eds., *Vocational Guidance and Career Development* (New York, MacMillan Company, 1966), p. 32.

[3]P. Goodman, "Youth in Organized Society," *Commentary*, 95-107 (1960).

[4]C. G. Wrenn, *op. cit.*, p. 35.

[5]C. G. Wrenn, *op. cit.*, p. 25.

[6]R. L. Quey, "Toward a Definition of Work," *Personnel and Guidance Journal*, 47:223-227 (1968).

Although there is no doubt that Puritan traditions set the tone for the American attitude toward work, sociologists suggest that the belief that work is a virtue has been modified. The American belief in work was modified by the philosophy of experimentalism.[7]

> Work became valued because of its tangible (realistic) products. . . . What counted was value assigned to work in terms of what society seemed to hold important. Work values became associated with occupation and occupation with the changing perceptions of the significance of any perception.

Social approval could be obtained by producing those items that supported the social order.

Definition of Work

Wrenn defines work as an . . . "activity calling for the expenditure of effort toward some definite achievement or outcome. Paid or not, hard or easy, it is always effort toward a specific end."[8] Work as an intentional activity is given support by:

> Work is a purposeful mental and physical human activity which deliberately points beyond the present by creating economic products or values to be consumed in the future. In contrast random activity is without purpose and may be a spasmodic or indiscriminate response to any chance stimulus or event.[9]

If work is an intentional activity that promises some type of satisfaction in the future, then an economy of effort is required to undertake the task. That is to say, random activity in the performance of the task must be minimized. The efficiency with which the task is accomplished (i.e. goal is reached) is predicated on training and specialization. Through training, the worker learns appropriate methods of work and way of avoiding errors, and criteria for evaluating his performance. Specialization limits the range of tasks that a given worker can perform efficiently. Consequently, the degree of satisfaction a worker can obtain from his work may be limited. In one sense, the function of

[7]C. G. Wrenn, *op. cit.,* p. 29.
[8]C. G. Wrenn, *op. cit.,* p. 27.
[9]R. L. Quey, *op. cit.,* p. 223.

guidance could be to help a student to select the "right work" so that he can maximize his personal satisfaction from what he is doing.

Significance of Work

The changing conditions of work and the changing composition of the labor force have affected the degree of personal investment a worker has in his job. Since many jobs require specialization, many workers do not have an opportunity to see the relationship between their efforts and the final product. Work specialization, when it is unchecked and carried to its extreme, narrows and finally depersonalizes man. It requires man to conform to machine logic and pacing and the impersonal demands of systems and organizations.[10] Under an increasing system of automation can a worker find self-identity in his job?

Havighurst suggests that most jobs can be divided into two types.[11] The first type consists of ego-involving jobs.

> A job in this category is the organized force in a person's life. He lives for it, and life would be empty without it. He does not count his working hours. . . . . Satisfaction comes from challenging new experience, feeling of being creative, feeling of service to people, and satisfaction of being in a prestigeful occupation.

The second type are society maintaining jobs. Occupations of this type are generally those in which there is a fixed number of hours and pay is by the hour. Although the occupation may require a great deal of skill, it seldom demands the continuous thought that leads a man to worry about it or plan for it when he is actually not working. . . . The satisfactions derived from this kind of work are likely to be those of association with friends on the job, the money earned, and a pleasant or at least tolerable routine for passing the time. Havighurst believes that the proportion of ego involvement jobs is increasing. He does point out that "middle-class people tend to have ego-involving jobs while working-

[10] R. L. Quey, *op. cit.,* p. 224.

[11] R. J. Havighurst, "Youth in Exploration and Man Emergent," in H. Borow, ed., *Man in the World of Work* (Boston, Houghton Mifflin Co., 1964), p. 226.

class people tend to have society-maintaining jobs."[12] One of the functions of the guidance program would be to point out how any type of job could be ego-involving and that all types of worthwhile jobs help to maintain society.

One of the problems in reviewing the factors that affect the significance of work is that most studies do not "analyze job satisfaction in relation to satisfactions derived from other life areas."[13] Wilensky, in reviewing the studies on job satisfaction and life satisfaction, concludes that it is folly to assume that these two concepts are identical. He cites studies that indicate that the level of job satisfaction is directly related to the skill level of the job: relatively low-skilled workers are not necessarily job-oriented and tend to obtain satisfaction in life from sources other than their employment. Wilensky's remarks give credence to Havighurst's classification of jobs as being either ego-involving or society-maintaining.

Crites differentiates between job satisfaction and vocational satisfaction.

> The adjective "vocational" has been used rather than "job" to designate the individual's satisfaction with his "life's work," not just the particular position he holds at a given point in time. . . . He may be dissatisfied with his job, because of certain situational factors, such as an incompetent supervisor, but he is satisfied with his vocation—the work for which he has been trained and in which he has gained experience. In other words, he may want to change his job but not his vocation.[14]

Crites defines vocational satisfaction as "an effective state which is a function of the worker's present job, on the one hand, and his frame of reference and his adaptation level on the other."[15] The basic difference between job satisfaction and vocational satisfaction is that the latter is concerned with long-term behavior and the former deals with the current state of affairs.

Crites, after reviewing various measures of vocational satis-

---

[13]H. L. Wilensky, "Varieties of Work Experience," in H. Borow, ed., *Man in the World at Work,* (Boston, Houghton Mifflin Co., 1964), p. 237.

[14]J. O. Crites, *Vocational Psychology* (New York, McGraw-Hill Book Company, 1969), p. 473.

[15]*Ibid.,* p. 472.

faction, concludes that "no one instrument or technique is sufficient to assess an individual's attitudes and feelings about his work. Or, to put it somewhat differently, certain measures are better for some purposes than others."[16] The assessment of vocational satisfaction is a post-choice measure. That is to say, measures of satisfaction tend not to be used to predict occupational choice. Zytowski believes that measures of work values could be used "to explain an individual's level of job satisfaction as the extent to which his job satisfies his needs as well as to forecast his occupational entry."[17] Although there is no universal set of work values, studies have shown "that job satisfaction can be predicted by the degree to which the person's occupation satisfies his needs" and "that persons in a given occupation appear to have value hierarchies more similar than those entering diverse occupations."[18]

When the concepts of job satisfaction, vocational satisfaction, and work values are compared, it would appear that work values have the greatest utility in vocational counseling. If work values are seen as "a set of concepts which mediate between the person's affective orientation and classes of external objects offering similar satisfaction"[19] then specific occupations can be compared as to the degree to which they can satisfy internal dispositions. For example, "those employed in higher level occupations value intrinsic rewards while extrinsic values are held more strongly by lower level workers."[20]

New Managerial Perceptions

Technological progress has changed America from a land of scarcity to one of abundance. In the process, the changing nature and location of work has had an impact on the career patterns of workers. Jobs are calling for new skills and the willingness to learn them and adapt. The shifting fortunes of companies, new

---

[16]*Ibid.,* p. 489.
[17]D. G. Zytowski, "The Concept of Work Values," *Vocational Guidance Quarterly,* 18:176 (1970).
[18]*Ibid.,* p. 178.
[19]*Ibid.,* p. 180.
[20]*Ibid.,* p. 182.

inventories, and new information cause operations to phase out here and spring up there, requiring employees to change jobs.[21]

Gullander suggests that we are living in an age of industrial sophistication. This age not only contains new technology and rapid change but new patterns of management, growing leisure time, and outside-the-plant influences.[22] Generally speaking, management no longer views people merely as tools of productivity, but as individuals "whose job offers them opportunity for growth and a chance to relate to others in a meaningful way so that they can find real fulfillment and satisfaction in their job."[23]

> In the final analysis, the difference between the success and failure of a corporation lies in the way management treats its human resources by encouraging employees to make their maximum contribution by assuring that they are fitted to their task, by recognizing the importance of their work, by requiring supervisors to help employees in their jobs and to be genuinely interested in what they do, by permitting employees a maximum degree of initiative and self-expression.[24]

This focus on the employee could permit every worker to judge his job as being ego-involving. Although many work conditions limit true self-expression, a counselor can help an individual to review his occupational choice to see if his basic needs can be satisfied in the occupation. Information provided by the counselor can help the individual to better understand the demands of the work situation. New patterns of management focus on bringing about a better balance between production, goals, and human values. This improved organizational climate helps the individual to greater self-actualization.

The concept of work, the meaning of work, and job satisfaction are ideas that have played an important role in vocational guidance. As these ideas have changed so have the goals of vocational guidance.

[21]W. P. Gullander, "The Age of Industrial Sophistication," in A. A. McLean, ed., *To Work is Human* (New York, Macmillan Company, 1967), p. 15.

[22]*Ibid.*, p. 18.

[23]*Ibid.*, p. 19.

[24]*Ibid.*, p. 20.

Historical Development of Vocational Guidance[25]

In 1908 Frank Parsons opened the Vocation Bureau of Boston whose purpose was to aid young men and women with their occupational choice. It grew out of his educational activities at the Civil Service House, a settlement house in Boston. The Vocation Bureau is intended to aid young people in choosing an occupation, preparing themselves for it, finding satisfaction in it, and building up a career of efficiency and success.[26]

In his sole report to the Executive Committee of the Vocational Bureau in May, 1908 Parsons stated that "vocational guidance should become a part of the public system in every community, with experts trained as carefully in the art of vocational guidance as men are trained today for medicine or the law and supplied with every facility that science can devise for testing the senses and capacities and the whole physical, intellectual, and emotional make-up of the child."[27] Parsons in his book *Choosing a Vocation* outlined the systematic approach counselors should employ in assisting individuals with their vocational choice:

1. A joint and cooperative analysis of the individual's capabilities, interests, and temperament.
2. The student's study of occupational opportunities, requirements, and employment statistics.
3. A joint and cooperative comparison of these two sets of information.[28]

These three steps, person analysis, job analysis, and synthesis,

[25]See the following for additional development of the topic. H. Borow, "Milestones: A Chronology of Notable Events in the History of Vocational Guidance," in H. Borow, ed., *Man in a World at Work* (Boston, Houghton Mifflin Co., 1964). P. J. Rockwell Jr. and J. W. M. Rothney, "Some Social Ideas of Pioneers in the Guidance Movement," *Personnel and Guidance Journal*, 40:349-354 (1961). J. M. Brewer, *History of Vocational Guidance* (New York, Harper and Brothers, 1942; and R. Barry and B. Wolf, *Epitaph for Vocational Guidance* (New York, Bureau of Publications, Teachers College, Columbia University, 1962).

[26]J. Brewer, *History of Vocational Guidance*, New York, (Harper and Brothers, 1942), p. 61.

[27]H. Borow, "Milestones: A Chronology of Notable Events in the History of Vocational Guidance," in H. Borow, ed., *Man in a World at Work* (Boston, Houghton Mifflin Co., 1964), p. 49.

[28]E. G. Williamson, "An Historical Perspective of the Vocational Guidance Movement," *Personnel and Guidance Journal*, 82:854-859 (1964).

characterized vocational guidance for many years. Diagnosis prior to choice has become a client expectancy; the counselor gives the individual tests and then tells him what job he is best suited for. Unfortunately, this is not what Parsons wanted vocational workers to do. Even Meyer Bloomfield, Parsons' successor, abandoned psychometric procedures in the person diagnosis stage. He substituted self-analysis of capabilities and interests for the objective approach of person assessment. Perhaps the reason that the "test and tell" approach was so accepted by the general public was that the public was not ready to accept the changing concept of work. After centuries of believing that "work is a virtue," the idea that work provides an opportunity for self-development is difficult to assimilate.

There is no doubt that the Parsonian concept of vocational guidance structured the work of the school counselor. In operational terms the scope of vocational guidance had the following features: (1) analysis of the individual; (2) collection of occupational information; (3) community occupational surveys and follow-up studies; (4) group activities; (5) counseling.[29] For a number of years, in many schools, the focal-point of most guidance activities was vocational. In time, the research findings of psychologists, sociologists, and anthropologists were adapted for use in vocational guidance. Among these were the influence of maturational process development of interest, motivational factors in vocational choice, social-class influence on vocational choice, and psychological dimensions of the work situation. The inclusion of these concepts led from emphasis on choice of a vocation to that of vocational development. In addition the notion of choice was supplanted by that of decision making.

Notwithstanding some of the current criticisms of Parson's approach to vocational guidance, Williamson states,

> I conclude that man's recently won freedom of choice of vocation is relatively meaningless, if downright precarious, where he makes his choices without some valid knowledge of his own capabilities and potentialities, and I believe it is true that the method of self-analysis,

[29]L. E. Walton, "The Scope and Function of Vocational Guidance," *Educational Outlook*, 31:119-128 (1957).

while it is simple and thus appealing in its simplicity, is of questionable validity and reliability.[30]

Katz suggests that a high school student has two major choice points: at the beginning of secondary school and near the end.[31] For Katz, decision making is a procedure for acquiring and processing information. The task of the counselor is to help the student to become aware of the range of alternatives open to him, of the social and cultural factors bearing on the situation, and of the function of values in decision making. The goal of the assistance offered the student is to enhance his ability for self-direction. The essential difference between Katz's approach and the Parsonian orientation is that the latter's goal is a choice while the former's is to facilitate the process of choice.

Background Analysis of Theories of Vocational Choice

Crites, in reviewing the historical development of vocational psychology, suggests that the current focus on vocational development grew out of interest in the concepts of matching men and jobs and psychodynamics of vocational behavior.[32] The "matching men and jobs" concept was initiated by Parsons and extended by men such as Yerkes (early developer of intelligence tests), and Edward K. Strong (creator of the *Strong Vocational Interest Blank*). Agencies such as the Minnesota Employment Stabilization Research Institute (occupational ability patterns) and the United States Employment Service (Dictionary of Occupational Titles) provided materials to carry out the matching. After World War II the "matching men and jobs" concept was transformed into the trait and factor theory. Essentially the theory postulates that a person can be understood in terms of his traits, which are external indicators of his individuality. In addition, the theory incorporated the growth aspect from developmental psychology. "When confronted with the necessity of choosing an occupation, an individual proceeds to make an anal-

[30]E. G. Williamson, *op. cit.*, p. 858.

[31]M. Katz, *Decisions and Values: A Rationale for Secondary School Guidance* (New York. College Entrance Examination Board, 1963).

[32]J. O. Crites, *Vocational Psychology* (New York, McGraw-Hill Book Company).

ysis of his vocational assets and liabilities, accumulates information about occupations and arrives at a decision through what Parsons has called 'true reasoning' "[33] This approach places a heavy emphasis on objectivity but minimizes the role of motivation in the choice.

Concern about the psychodynamics of vocational behavior evolved from the work of Elton Mayo at the Hawthorne Plant of the Western Electric Company. This research project studied the relationships between conditions of work, work-groups attitudes, interpersonal relations, and productivity. It culminated in the development of the "human relations" approach to management. Additional concepts from Freudian and neo-analytic writers, need theorists, and phenomenologists were incorporated. The psychodynamics of vocational behavior proposes "that drives and desires rather than attributes, are the salient variables in choosing a vocation."[34] In general, the emphasis is on motivational theory in vocational choice rather than traits and factors.

The vocational development approach evolved as a synthesis of concepts from differential and dynamic psychology. Super, drawing on the works of Charlotte Buhler (life stages) and Havighurst's concept of developmental tasks, formulated the concept that the choice of a vocation is not a one-time event but a process which continues more or less throughout life. Super suggests that vocational choice is the process of implementing one's self concept in the world of work.[35] He is concerned with career patterns rather than occupational choice, with vocational maturity rather than traits, and with the total personality rather than some one aspect of the person.

Occupations Defined

In order to have a better understanding of the various theories of vocational choice the meaning of the term "occupation" should be reviewed. Salz states that "occupation may be

[33]*Ibid.*, p. 119.

[34]*Ibid.*, p. 5.

[35]D. E. Super, *et al.*, *Career Development: Self Concept Theory* (New York, College Entrance Examination Board, 1963).

defined as that specific activity which an individual continually pursues for the purposes of obtaining a steady flow of income. This activity also determines the social position of the individual."[36] Hughes feels that "an occupation in essence is not some particular set of activities, it is part of an individual in any ongoing set of activities."[37]

Shartle has defined an occupation as a group of similar jobs and positions, a position being a group of tasks performed by one person at one point in time.[38]

In general the socioloigst tends to define occupations as a major component of the social structure: "An occupation is the social role performed by adult members of society that directly and/or indirectly yields social and financial consequences and that contributes a major focus in the life of an adult."[39]

Crites suggests that the term "occupation" be used to designate a stimulus variable (i.e., broad aspects of the world of work) while the term "vocational" be used as a response variable (i.e. responses an individual makes in choosing and adjusting to an occupation).[40] He points out that industrial personnel workers are primarily concerned with positions and jobs, vocational psychologists with occupations and counselors with a facilitative process that assists individuals with their choice and adjustment to an occupation.

Vocational Choice Defined

The term "vocational choice" lacks some clarity for it is often used interchangeably with "vocational preference" and "vocational aspiration." Crites points out that "vocational choice has

[36]A. Salz, *Occupations: Theory and History Encyclopedia of the Social Sciences,* Vol. XI (New York, Macmillan Company, 1944), p. 424.

[37]E. Hughes, "The Study of Occupations," in R. K. Merton, L. Broom and L. S. Cottrell, eds., *Sociology Today* (New York, Harper & Row Publishers, 1965), p. 445.

[38]C. L. Shartle, *Occupational Information* (Englewood Cliffs, New Jersey, Prentice-Hall, Inc., 1959).

[39]R. H. Hall, *Occupations and the Social Structure,* Englewood Cliffs, New Jersey, Prentice-Hall, Inc., 1969, p. 5.

[40]J. O. Crites, *op. cit.,* p. 16.

often been defined as what the individual *prefers* to do. Given a number of vocational alternatives, he expressed his preference for one or another and this constitutes his choice."[41] According to Super, the term "choice," when not used to describe training for or entry into an occupation, can have different meanings at different age levels.[42] Super proposes that "preference" be used to delineate unimplemented courses of vocational action. "Vocational aspiration" usually connotes an individual's fantasy choice: under ideal circumstances what would a person wish he could do. Crites states that, when these three terms are compared on a reality continuum, choice is more reality oriented than preference and aspiration. When an individual makes a vocational choice, he considers what his *probable* occupation will be, not what his *possible* (preference) or *fantasy* (aspiration) might be."[43]

Choice implies that an individual is in a position to select from several occupations and that this selection is predicated on an examination of contingencies, personal attributes, work conditions, and worker characteristics. Preference suggests a liking for an occupation and a possible selection if certain personal demands were met. Aspiration represents "wishful thinking."

Crites suggests that a theory of vocational choice should give explicit answers to the following five questions about vocational behavior: "Is it systematic or chance? Is it conscious or unconscious? Is it rational or emotional? Does it represent a compromise or a synthesis of desires and realities? And, is it an event or a process?"

After reviewing the research literature, Crites reached the following generalization about the five questions.

1. If vocational choice is seen as a response, then entry into an occupation or training for an occupation represents deliberate and selective response rather than a random action.
2. Vocational choices of preadolescence tend to be unconscious while those of adolescence are conscious.

[41]*Ibid.*, p. 127.

[42]D. E. Super, "A Theory of Vocational Development," *American Psychologist*, 8:185-190 (1953).

[43]J. O. Crites, *op. cit.*, p. 133.

3. Both emotions and reason enter into choice but the nature of the interaction is not known.

4. Synthesis and compromise are affected by the degree of freedom of choice: As the freedom to choose becomes restricted the amount of compromise between individual needs and reality increases.

5. Although historically vocational choice has been seen as a one-time event, current research evidence suggests that vocational choice tends to be a process because of the continuous nature of the choice.[44]

Theories of Vocational Choice

In 1951 Ginzberg and his associates published the first approach to a general theory of occupational choice.[45] Since that date a large number of theories of vocational choice have been advanced by sociologists, psychologists, economists, and educators. In general the various theories reflect the professional interests and biases of the writers. However, the theories do reflect an organized and systematic approach toward explaining the vocational behavior of individuals.

The various theories of vocational choice have been classified in different ways. Hewer classifies the theories into 3 categories: (1) trait theory, (2) structural theories (i.e. psychoanalytic theory, need theory, and self-concept theory), and (3) developmental theory.[46] Osipow used the following categories: (1) trait-factor theories, (2) sociology and career choice, (3) self-concept theory, and (4) vocational choice and personality theories.[47] Crites uses three major categories to review theories of vocational choice: (1) nonpsychological theories of vocational choice: accident theories, economic theories, cultural and sociological theories; (2) psychological theories of vocational choice (trait and factor theories, psychodynamic theories, psychoanalytic theories, need

[44]*Ibid.*, p. 117.

[45]E. Ginzberg, S. W. Ginsburg, S. Axelrad, and J. L. Herma, *Occupational Choice: An Approach to a General Theory* (New York, Columbia University Press, 1951).

[46]V. H. Hewer, "What Do Theories of Vocational Choice Mean to a Counselor," *Journal of Counseling Psychology,* 10:118-125 (1963).

[47]S. H. Osipow, *Theories of Career Development* (New York, Appleton-Century-Crofts, Inc., 1968).

theories, self-theories, developmental theories, decision theories); and (3) general theories (interdisciplinary conceptions and a typological theory).[48] The purpose of the various classification schemes is to help readers to compare and contrast the various theories so that they can better understand how individuals choose occupations and why they select occupations.

Carkhuff, Alexik, and Anderson have challenged the adequacy of the various theories of vocational choice. "There does not appear to be any theory of vocational choice that meets the inductive-deductive model theory-building."[49] This observation is given support by Osipow:

> In general, the theories have failed to pay serious attention to the satisfaction of the criteria applied to the scientific evaluation of theory. There is a tendency to describe the career development process in very general terms, probably more general than is useful to researcher and practitioner alike. The major exception is Super's revised theory, which has taken on an applied and operational appearance.[50]

Osipow believes that most of the theories are similar in that "they emphasize the same kinds of critical agents and periods in career development."[51] Hoppock supports this observation by stating that "there is no major conflict among carefully formulated theories and the observations of economists, sociologists, psychologists and educators unless one wishes to assert that the influence which he sees is the dominant influence.[52]

The current emphasis on vocational development is an outgrowth of a blend of the "matching men and jobs" concept and the psychodynamics of vocational behavior. It has been also influenced by the changing concepts of work and the nature of man.

Perhaps the greatest contribution that the behaviorial scientists have made during the last half century of research on the industrial scene

---

[48]J. O. Crites, *op. cit.*, p. 79.

[49]R. R. Carkhuff, M. Alexik, and S. Anderson, "Do We Have a 'Theory of' Vocational Choice?," *Personnel and Guidance Journal*, 46:335-345 (1967).

[50]*Op. cit.*, p. 232.

[51]*Ibid.*, p. 233.

[52]R. Hoppock, *Occupational Information* (New York, McGraw-Hill Book Company, 1967), p. 104.

has been to broaden the concept of the needs and nature of man from a solely economic organism to one that encompasses some of the more human aspects — the emotional and social needs.[53]

Vocational development theories are concerned with career patterns rather than with vocational choice. Ivey and Morrill suggest that the term "career process" be substituted for the idea of vocational choice.[54] Career process is defined as "the continuing process through which a person engages in the sequence of developmental tasks necessary for personal growth in occupational life."[55]

In general career process counseling can be integrated within the broad conceptual framework of mental health. Oetting has suggested that mental health be defined as the "ability to engage in and utilize developmental tasks for personal growth."[56] Individuals who undertake to meet the demands of the developmental tasks tend to be ensured of themselves of full development within the context of their environment. Career process counseling is used to correct and facilitate career development. "It is a vehicle for learning to move effectively with the life process of which vocational process is a key element."[57] Vocational guidance focuses on helping individuals to profit from the life experience.

The vocational guidance programs that evolved from vocational development theories are, to a large measure, applied vocational psychology. It is the "process or program of assistance designed to aid the individual in choosing and adjusting to a vocation."[58] It applies knowledge gained from occupational psychology (career patterns, prestige and status of occupations, vocational aspirations, and occupational roles) industrial psychology

[53]F. Herzberg, *Work and the Nature of Man* (Cleveland, The World Publishing Co., 1966), p. 43.

[54]A. E. Ivey and W. H. Morrill, "Career Process: A New Concept for Vocational Behavior," *Personnel and Guidance Journal,* 46:644-649 (1968).

[55]*Ibid.*, p. 645.

[56]E. R. Oetting, "A Developmental Definition of Counseling Psychology," *Journal of Counseling Psychology,* 11:324-333 (1964).

[57]A. E. Ivey and W. H. Morrill, *op. cit.*, p. 646.

[58]J. O. Crites, *op. cit.*, p. 21.

(motivation and incentives, job attitudes and satisfaction, and work adjustment) trait and factor theory (aptitude tests, interest inventories, worker traits), and developmental psychology (life stages, developmental tasks). Economic and social factors although acknowledged as correlates of vocational choice, are not seen as key factors in influencing career decisions. The major goal of the vocational guidance program is not to integrate theories and research findings but to help individuals in choosing and adjusting to a vocation. Vocational choice is not the exclusive province of the economist, or the sociologist or the psychologist, or the educator. It is the province of the person who is doing the choosing and who should be able to command the help of all the related disciplines in learning how best to make his choice.[59]

VOCATIONAL COUNSELING

If vocational choice is seen as an extension of self into the world of work, then vocational counseling is that process which enables the individual to continually compare this changing self-concept to the changing demands of the world of work. It permits self-evaluation and self-exploration to take place simultaneously in the continually developing individual. The counseling process does not match the individual to a job but helps him to discover ways he can relate to himself. "The counseling procedures will involve reciprocating use of personal data and vocational data; interviewing, testing, occupational information and other techniques; of personal appraisals, and of "reality tests" in a progressive restructuring of the client-vocational interrelationships throughout the counseling process."[60]

> The goal of vocational counseling is, thus, not simply finding a job which one can do and in which one can earn a living, but finding a vocation which is consistent with one's self-concept. This means that the individual must view his work, if it is to meet certain basic psychological needs, in terms of his self concept, i.e. is his occupational role compatible with his concept of himself?[61]

[59] R. Hoppock, *op. cit.*, p. 105.

[60] D. H. Pritchard, "The Occupational Process: Some Operational Implications," *Personnel and Guidance Journal*, 1962, 40:674-680.

[61] C. H. Patterson, "Counseling: Self-clarification and the Helping Relationship in H. Borow, *Man in a World of Work* (Boston, Houghton Mifflin Co., 1964), p. 411.

The purpose of vocational counseling is not to restructure personality but to provide the opportunity for self-differentiation. Reality testing, occupational self-categorizing and the formulation of an occupational hypothesis help the individual to put into proper perspective information about himself, and occupational factors so that meaningful exploration or trial can be undertaken. Bell believes that, since vocational decisions are ego-involved, it is difficult for a client to take an objective view of his vocational assets and liabilities.[62] He believes that vocational counseling is a slow process that requires considerable professional skill and active cooperation by the client.

> Self-assimilation and self-acceptance must be achieved by the student and this cannot be hurried. A long time program of consultation, planning, tryout of plans, and self-reflection are needed during which time the student is freeing himself from his old ego-moorings and reaching out to new sources of personal stability and self-acceptance.[63]

Thompson proposes that the counselor not only helps the "client to solve the immediate problem but to become better able to solve future problems."[64] Thus in working with his client, the counselor does not provide the answers but helps the client analyze the problem, formulate the critical questions, obtain the relevant information and draw the wisest conclusions."[65] The counselor helps the client to arrive at functional solutions but only the client has responsibility for arriving at the ultimate solution for only the client knows what is best for him.

> He helps the client acquire understanding, not only of his capacities, interests, and opportunities but also of the emotionalized attitudes which are interfering with rational choices or appropriate behavior. He helps the client to minimize the irrelevancies which so often determine an individual's attitude toward himself and occupations. He structures the counseling process in such a way that it becomes a

[62]H. M. Bell, "Ego-involvement in Vocational Decisions," *Personnel and Guidance Journal,* 38:732-735 (1960).

[63]*Ibid.,* p. 735.

[64]A. S. Thompson, "Personality Dynamics and Vocational Counseling," *Personnel and Guidance Journal,* 38:350-357 (1960).

[65]*Ibid.,* p. 355.

learning experience for the client and that the client grows in the process.[66]

The degree of counselor activity and the content focus of an interview will vary. Counselors who subscribe to the Super orientation will be concerned with providing the clients with information so that they can make decisions appropriate to their stage of development. The interview would be only one way of disseminating information. Both Ginzberg and Super oriented counselors would be concerned with assessing the vocational maturity of the client. The Ginzberg type counselor would use remedial procedures if the client is retarded in his vocational development or in some cases accelerate the individual through a given stage of vocational development. The psychoanalytically oriented counselor may be concerned with the client's impulses and their impact on vocational decisions.

Essentially the counseling process is predicated on the idea that the quality of a vocational choice can be enhanced if the client has a better understanding of himself and has a better knowledge of occupations. This assumption requires that the counselor have a good understanding of assessment strategies and the nature of occupational information. The need for these competencies reflects the historical antecedents of Parsons and the trait-factor theory. During the vocational counseling process the client expects to be tested and be informed about occupational opportunities.

Testing in Vocational Counseling

The role of appraisal in the guidance program has been somewhat controversial. Goldman suggests that factual information (assessment or environmental) tends to interfere with the counseling process because (1) the outside information detracts from the close interaction pattern generated between the client and the counselor during the course of the interview, and (2) there is a tendency for a counselor to be less accepting of the client's own perceptions and values when appraisal data is used.[67] Super

[66]*Ibid.*, p. 355.

[67]L. Goldman, "Information and Counseling: A Dilemma," *Personnel and Guidance Journal,* 46:42-46 (1967).

states that "the role of vocational appraiser has generally been described as that of an objective third person who can assemble, evaluate, and synthesize the facts in a detached manner."[68] This concept of appraisal is somewhat archaic for where vocational choice is considered to be a process, rather than event, appraisal information is used to help the client understand himself. "Tests are used to assist the client in evaluating himself. It is the client who evaluates, not the counselor."[69] Appraisal information helps the client in the formulation of his occupational hypotheses. The large mass of data about the person is reduced so that the client can form inferences about himself. These inferences are used to make predictions about anticipated vocational behavior. Appraisal information is used to formulate "a course of action for which the client is completely willing to take the consequences, leading to a goal which is based on a cooperative realistic appraisal of the factors involved."[70] Information then has a critical role in vocational counseling for it helps the client to form descriptions of himself, to delineate courses of action, and serves as a basis for prediction of future vocational behavior.

Goldman presents a model for the assessment process that can readily be incorporated into the vocational development concept.[71] He suggests that the appraisal process can begin with any one of the following: (1) *predictor variables* (i.e. test data, hobbies, work history, etc.), (2) *avenues* (i.e. ways in which a goal can be reached such as, type of college or specific occupation), or (3) *outcomes* (i.e. some type of specific goal). The generation of an individual trait profile from a set of data, although useful for facilitating client self-understanding, does not facilitate decision making. Most clients lack the skill to project a trait profile into some type of inference about future vocational behavior. Consequently, the counselor must spend time suggesting possible matches between the trait profile and environ-

[68]D. E. Super, "The Preliminary Appraisal in Vocational Counseling," *Personnel and Guidance Journal,* 35:154-161 (1957).

[69]C. H. Patterson, *op. cit.,* p. 448.

[70]D. E. Super, *op. cit.,* p. 156.

[71]L. Goldman, "The Process of Vocational Assessment," in H. Borow, ed., *Man in the World at Work,* (Boston, Houghton Mifflin Co., 1964), pp. 389-409.

mental conditions. There is a tendency for the counselor to rely on set testing procedures and modes of test interpretation. Where the counselor begins with *avenues* he will spend considerable time describing various environmental dimensions (i.e. school or occupation). This type of procedure limits the degree of self-planning a client can undertake. When a client begins with *outcome* (i.e. what is important to me), he becomes an active participant in the counseling process. The client processes the information so that he can compare alternative courses of action and then decide upon a course of action.

The appraisal process places emphasis on the examination of a client's potential. The test data do not yield information about how a person will use his potential or how he will activate it.[72] Since clients formulate inferences about themselves and project them into future on the basis of an occupational hypothesis they are continually evaluating the quality of their predictions. Vocational counseling should not be concerned with the success of predictions but with the personal growth of the individual. The counselor should use the information gathered about the client as a benchmark to evaluate the vocational development of the person. Does the client know more about himself and the world of work? Can he on his own initiative formulate relationships between various types of data? How effective is he when confronted with new dimensions of vocational development?

In a typical school situation most of the students have taken a number of standardized tests whose results are recorded in cumulative folders. These test results usually formulate the basis for initial test interpretation. This type of communication of test results has no specific purpose other than to inform the students of their performance on the test. The students are informed of their relative position on the test continuum. If a student is to make an effective vocational choice he needs information about how he compares to others who are in a given occupation. This type of information permits the student to make inferences about his probable success in the activity. Test data obtained from the

[72]F. Herzberg, *Work and the Nature of Man* (Cleveland, The World Publishing Co., 1966), p. 58.

general school testing program should be supplemented when additional information is required. The counselor's role with reference to information is therefore that of an interpreter of probabilities. Beyond this function, he continues, as with all other counseling matters, to aid his client to express and explore the perceptions, feelings, and values that pertain to the information and to the decision or problem in question.[73]

Occupational Information in Vocational Counseling

Occupational information is used in counseling "to help the client to clarify the goal he wants to reach and to move in the direction in which he wants to go, so long as the goal, and the means for obtaining it are not injurious to others."[74] Occupational information is used to enhance the individual's vocational development. Patterson proposes the following guidelines for the use of occupational information:

1. Occupational information is introduced into the counseling process where there is a recognized need for it on the part of the client.
2. Occupational information is not used to influence or manipulate the client.
3. The most objective way to provide occupational information, and a way which maximizes client initiative and responsibility, is to encourage the client to obtain the information from original sources, that is, publications, employers and persons engaged in the occupations.
4. The client's attitudes and feelings about occupations and jobs must be allowed expression and be dealt with therapeutically.[75]

The concept of vocational development implies that the degree of vocational maturity varies in the population as a consequence of the degree of readiness for certain types of information. In addition not all students wish to participate in the counseling process. Consequently occupational exploration is sometimes a difficult task to undertake in vocational counseling. Hoppock describes some of the more difficult problems that a counselor faces:

[73]L. Goldman, *op. cit.*, p. 46.
[74]R. Hoppock, *op. cit.*, p. 133.
[75]C. H. Patterson, *op. cit.*, pp. 453-455.

1. *The client with no preference.* Usually this type of client has the attitude that since the counselor is an expert he should be in a position to tell him (the client) what to do. In this situation, occupational exploration barely rises above that of identifying and labeling job opportunities.

2. *The impossible choice.* This type of client usually has a limited sense of reality. He selects occupations whose training standards are above his abilities, or enters a training program which does not lead to any type of job. Included in this category is the client whose parents insist on an occupation which the student and counselor agree to be inappropriate.

3. *Changing occupations.* Working with this type of client, the counselor must provide a condition whereby the client has an opportunity to correlate self-exploration with occupation exploration. The counseling process should provide ample opportunity for the client to compare and contrast his present occupation with the one he wishes to enter.

4. *Tentative choice.* This type of client requires assistance in the cognitive substantiation of his choice. Essentially the counselor helps in the reality testing of the choice. In the process the client assesses the wisdom of his choice.[76]

The vocational counseling process in which the assessment function is integrated with the information function has been labeled by Pritchard as *self-at-work exploration.*[77] The outcome of the process at any given moment is not the selection of one occupational category for entry or training but the generation of an occupational hypothesis so that various factors about the individual and the occupation can be put into proper focus. Goldman states that the competencies and skills required of the counselor are demanding: "knowledge of assessment and information resources and their uses; skill interpretation of assessment results and various kinds of information; and the ability and willingness to be neutral about the information, to refrain from urging, and to be nondefensive about interpretations of information. This impressive array of knowledge, skill, and attitudes is then combined with those needed for the relational and other process aspects of counseling."[78]

[76]R. Hoppock, *op. cit.*, pp. 134-140.
[77]D. H. Pritchard, *op. cit.*, p. 680.
[78]L. Goldman, *op. cit.*, 1967, p. 46.

Informational Service in Vocational Guidance

In the above discussion of the role of information in vocational counseling it may have been assumed that these are the only ways through which a student may obtain information. If vocational choice is seen as part of a developmental sequence, the entire school and community must be involved in the informational service. "The goal of the informational service is not only to impart information, but also stimulate the student to critically appraise ideas, conditions, and trends in order to derive personal meanings and implications for the present and the future."[79] The quality of personal growth in any given life stage is affected by the degree of mastery of a previous stage environmental factors and future expectations. The purpose of the information "is that of reducing cultural ambiguity so that the individual can comprehend, to the extent possible, the nature of society of which he will be a contributing member as an adult."[80] The cultural expectations are that by the end of high school, a student should be able to give a reasonable answer to "Who am I?" and "Where am I going?"

The developmental concept assumes that each individual progresses through the various life stages bit by bit rather than by large visible giant steps. In terms of vocational development, Super states that "the essence of development is progressive increase and modification of the individual's behavior repertoire through growth and learning.[81] This suggests that the entire school program be focused on assisting life-stage vocational development. According to Wortz an operational application of the developmental concept would be to have a pupil take a look at himself and then plan for "What's next" on the basis of "What is."[82] The organizational aspects of the school would have to be

[79]B. Shertzer and S. C. Stone, *Fundamentals of Guidance* (Boston, Houghton Mifflin Co., 1965), p. 126.

[80]L. H. Stewart and C. F. Warnath, *The Counselor and Society* (Boston, Houghton Mifflin Co., 1965), p. 126.

[81]D. E. Super, *et al., Vocational Development* (New York, Teachers College Bureau of Publications, 1957).

[82]B. E. Wurtz, "Vocational Development: Theory and Practice," *Vocational Guidance Quarterly*, 15:127-130 (1966).

so structured that a student would be able to see relationships between his daily activity and projected future action. The specific concern would be with such factors as (1) assessment of vocational maturity, (2) information that is personalized, (3) . nature of informational material, and (4) curricular organization.

Assessment of Vocational Maturity

An anomaly created by the use of the vocational developmental concept is that the degrees of freedom an individual has in selecting his course of action are reduced because the demands of the world are envisioned as being static and that a preconceived set of goals is imposed by society on individuals. In normal development the external environmental pressures are restructured through selective perceptions and responses so that an individual has both scope and flexibility for achieving satisfaction in a given stage. The question can be raised whether an individual is going towards something definite or is he going from one thing to another in a random fashion. One possible explanation is offered by Wurtz:

> The individual does not define the next stage and their attempt to evolve into this, although this apparently happens in those cases where the individual's definition of the next step happens to agree with the normal evolutionary pattern for him. Nor can anyone else delineate the desired, or define or describe what the individual should become and then "grow" him into it. This goal-oriented approach may have made us guilty of using "develop" as a transitive verb, i.e. "we will develop him into" rather than the intransive form as in "he will develop from."[83]

Since the vocational counseling process is predicated on the idea of an evolutionary process of development, these efforts to force or manipulate individuals into some preconceived role can be judged as being "bad." However, most individuals do require some type of assistance in choosing a vocation, for in our society the choice of an occupation influences most every other aspect of life. The concept of vocational maturity has value for it provides a framework for evaluating the extent to which an indi-

[83]R. Wurtz, *op. cit.,* p. 127-128.

vidual is performing those vocational developmental tasks expected of his current state of general development and age.[84] Since the individual's current behavior repertoire affects the scope of future action the results of an assessment of vocational maturity could be used to determine the next type of activity that would enhance the student's personal growth. Norton has made a review of the current status of the measurement of vocational maturity.[85]

Orientation to vocational choice:
  a. concern with choice
  b. use of resources in orientation

Information and planning about the preferred occupation
  a. specificity of information about the preferred occupation
  b. specificity of planning for the preferred occupation
  c. extent of planning activity

Consistency of vocational preferences
  a. within fields
  b. within levels
  c. within families (field and levels combined)

Crystallization of traits
  a. degree of patterning of measured interests
  b. interest maturity (Strong Blank Score)
  c. liking for work
  d. patterning of work values
  e. extent of discussion of rewards of work
  f. acceptance of responsibility for choice and planning
  g. vocational independence

Wisdom of vocational preference
  a. agreement between ability and preference
  b. agreement between measured interests and performance

[84]D. E. Super and P. L. Overstreet, *The Vocational Maturity of Ninth Grade Boys* (New York, Bureau of Publications, Teachers College, 1960).
[85]J. L. Norton, "Current Status of the Measurement of Vocational Maturity," *Vocational Guidance Quarterly,* 18:165-170 (1970).

    c. agreement between measured interests and
       fantasy preference

    d. agreement between occupational level of measured
       interests and level of preference

    e. socio-economic accessibility of preference.

The *Vocational Development Inventory* developed by Crites represents a formal attempt to measure vocational maturity.[86] Although this inventory was designed to measure two facets of vocational maturity, its focus is on choice attitudes rather than choice competencies. Listed below is the theoretical framework:

Choice Competencies
    Problem solving
    Planning
    Occupational information
    Self-knowledge
    Goal selection

Vocational Choice Attitudes
    Involvement
    Orientation
    Independence
    Preference
    Conception.

As suggested earlier the concept of vocational maturity has merit for it points to ways by which not only the counselor but the total school could be utilized in assisting students in vocational development. In other words, tactics other than interviewing would be used to facilitate or modify vocational behavior. For example, remediation of past errors of decision making or teaching of new skills for future activity would be incorporated in the modification principle. This principle assumes that not all vocational behavior is executed with maximum efficiency; therefore, individuals need assistance not only in facilitating future action but in correcting past actions. The counselor and the

[86]J. O. Crites, "The Measurement of Vocational Maturity in Adolescence: The Attitude Test of the Vocational Development Inventory," *Psychological Monographs*, 79:1-36 (1965).

Stages	Transitional Procedure	Transitional Concept	Assistance Techniques		Prototype Theorist or School
			Facilitation	Remediation	
Social Amniotic					
↓	Determining program (set)	"me"	Life Style analysis	Environmental manipulation; psychotherapy	Adler
Self-differentiation					
↓	Information input	"go-versus-no-go"	Guidance	Skill Training	Trait-and-factor
Competence					
↓	Information processing	"go-versus-go"	{ Content: Client-centered Process: Training in decision-making		Rogers Tiedeman Krumboltz
Independence					
↓	Information utilization	"application"	{ Intrapsychic: Existential Situational: Job matching		Frankl Beck Herzberg
Commitment					

Figure VIII-1 — Three-dimensional Concept for use of Information in the Developmental Phase of Guidance. From *Personalizing Information Processes*, J. W. Hollis and L. U. Hollis (New York, MacMillan Company, 1969)

school should be concerned not only with the degree of success of a prediction but with the quality of personal growth.

Table VIII-I presents a schematic outline of a set of techniques whose purpose is to assist individuals in their vocational development.[87] Hershenson's formulation incorporates into the developmental vocational sequence, appropriate techniques for facilitating or correcting development. For example, he states that guidance techniques (revealing skills and assets) may facilitate normal transition from one level to another, that client-centered counseling may have to be used to help the client to clearly perceive and symbolize his vocational choice. The competencies and attitude required to answer "Who am I?" are altogether different than "What will I do?" It should be noted that "information" plays an important role in Hershenson's

[87]D. B. Hershenson, "Techniques for Assisting Life-stage Vocational Development," *Personnel and Guidance Journal*, 47:776-780 (1969).

formulation. Essentially, information is a blend of assessment data and environmental information which eventually is synthesized so that it can be applied. How it is applied in vocational behavior is dependent on the degree of vocational maturity a person possesses. Consequently assessment of vocational maturity is central to the concept of vocational development.

Personalizing Information

The title for this section has been taken from the book by Hollis and Hollis.[88] The general theme of the book suggests that all information should be personalized if it is to be assimilated and utilized by an individual. The premises on which the book is based reflect the centrality of the developmental approach. A brief outline of the theoretical orientation is given below.

1. The individual decides his course of action.
2. Every person, regardless of who he is, desires to improve himself.
3. The role of occupational and educational information today is considerably different from its role forty or fifty years ago.
4. Each person is constantly becoming, progressing, changing; and personalized information can facilitate change, can effect direction and pace.
5. An individual gains information from many sources and has experiences with people, things, and ideas.
6. An individual must be able to evaluate, discard, and integrate information continually in order to facilitate his decision-making process as new and varied opportunities arise.
7. Almost every individual will change occupations one or more times during his lifetime.
8. Material should be used as a means rather than an end.
9. The user becomes a major determinant of what information and media are used.
10. The total information processes in all educational, occupational, and personal areas must be considered together rather than separately.
11. Personalized information process must involve the principles of both communication and counseling.
12. Information processes are ongoing and extend over a lifetime.[89]

[88] J. W. Hollis and L. U. Hollis, *Personalizing Information Processes: Educational Occupational, and Personal-Social* (New York, The Macmillan Company, 1969).

[89] *Ibid.*, p. 44.

An informational service based on the above premises not only answers questions but also helps the individual to broaden his horizons. In addition it provides the individual with feedback so that he becomes ego-involved in the task. This is a critical factor if the obtained information is to be implemented.

Figure VIII-1 depicts the three-dimensional concept for use of information in the developmental phase of guidance.[90] Depth refers to the degree of readiness for information. The broadening approach is useful when a student knows little if any about a topic. After a preliminary exploration the student would look at the specifics of a topic. In feedback, the student validates his self-concept and/or verifies his understanding of his topic exploration. "The three depths are a continuum extending from the unknown, to awareness, to comprehension, to applicability or selectivity."[91] Hollis and Hollis suggested the following as a way of understanding the depth continuum:

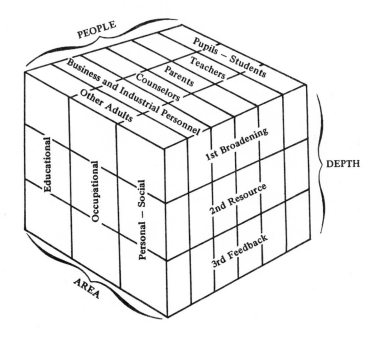

[90] *Ibid.*, p. 37.
[91] *Ibid.*, p. 39.

1. The student takes off his blinders so he can examine the total spectrum.
2. The student identifies the color and detail in the spectrum.
3. The student recognizes the lines of the spectrum with which he can identify.

Hollis and Hollis utilize the concept of vocational maturity to generate framework for structuring a multidimensional relationship between vocational development and understandings, sources and kinds of material meanings and attitudes.[92] From Figure VIII-1 it can be seen that the Super-Crites formulations of vocational maturity have been incorporated into the format. The spectrum aspect of occupational information can also be related to actual work. This relationship can be seen in Figure VIII-2.[93]

Sources and Types of Occupational Information

Informational materials can be obtained from national, regional and local sources. The Department of Labor is the single largest source of information. Divisions within the Department of Labor publish a variety of information. For example the Division of Wage and Industrial Relations provides basic information in the field of wages; the Bureau of Labor Statistics publishes the *Occupational Outlook Handbook* and *Occupational Outlook Quarterly* that describes more than 700 occupations in depth. The Bureau of Employment Security publishes the *Dictionary of Occupational Titles* (D.O.T.) in which jobs are defined and classified. Probably the most widely used references are the *Occupational Outlook Handbook* and the *Dictionary of Occupational Titles*. Every major department of the federal government issues publications on occupation topics that are germane to its area of interest.

Professional organizations and private publishing companies are other national sources of information.[94] Since the material is so extensive and continually changing, a number of bibliographies

[92]*Ibid.*, pp. 46, 47.

[93]A. S. Thompson, Unpublished Report, quoted in K. R. Kunze, "Industry Resources Available to Counselors," *Vocational Guidance Quarterly,* 16:138 (1967).

[94]Books by Hollis and Hollis, Hoppock, Shertzer and Stone (cited previously) and others specifically devoted to occupational information have detailed listings and addresses of where to obtain specific materials.

have been published to help counselors and schools keep current with the latest informational materials. Kroll describes the development of a computer-generated bibliography of occupational information.[95] Although the bibliography is not exhaustive, it is both representative and extensive. He suggests that it has utility because it is coordinated with the D.O.T. Specific suggestions for obtaining the bibliography are given in the article.

State agencies are the principal source of regional information. State employment security division, rehabilitation divisions, and departments of education are among the agencies that publish informational materials. Local sources include material published by fraternal organizations, chambers of commerce, industry and schools. Probably the local source provides the poorest quality of information. This is unfortunate, because the greatest need for reliable information is in job placement in the local job market. To overcome this deficiency, Hoppock gives a detailed account of how a school can conduct its own job survey.[96]

The published occupational material comes in a variety of types. Among them are career fiction, biography, single job description, job family information, jobs in specific business or industry, recruitment literature, wall charts, college catalogs, educational directories, and military service organizations. The National Vocational Guidance Association reviews current occupational literature through its Career Information Service. Each publication is reviewed and classified as to its type, utility, and reading level.

Any informational service has three recurrent problems: (1) obtaining information, (2) maintaining information, and (3) classifying and filing material. The basic resolution of the first two problems are to (1) subscribe to a privately published occupational plan that provides the information material and keeps it current through a subscription service, (2) the staff of the school obtains material on its own initiative in a manner that best services its students, and (3) a combination of these two

[95] A. M. Kroll, "A Computer Generated Bibliography of Occupational Information," *Vocational Guidance Quarterly*, 18:3-9.

[96] R. Hoppock, *op. cit.*, pp. 273-285.

solutions. Each solution has its advantages and disadvantages; which solution is used depends on the amount of money available. No matter what steps are taken to obtain and maintain information budgetary provisions should be made.

Classifying and filing occupational information poses a problem. The two basic methods of classifying material are either alphabetically or according to the Dictionary of Occupational Titles (D.O.T.). Most filing systems sold by publishers are based on the D.O.T. system. Occupational material can be classified by industry employer, geographic locations, academic-subject matter, a level of training, or Bureau of Census data. There are also classification systems that have been developed that combine several schemes (e.g. Bennet Occupations Filing Plan and the Chronicle plan for filing unbound occupational material). Hoppock, after appraising the various filing plans, rated the various plans in this order: (1) a homemade plan, (2) the Chronicle plan, (3) the Bennet plan, and (4) the informational kit published by Science Research Associates.[97]

The following eight characteristics are listed by Hoppock as being essential for a good filing system: (1) information is housed in a safe place; (2) each type of information should be housed in one location; (3) is is easy to use; (4) all like material on any occupation, industry or employer are together; (5) it is possible to identify location of like material in different sources; (6) it expands with increase of material; (7) it provides for filing of related material.

Experts agree that no one location of informational material is best. The information should be so located that not only is it accessible to but it serves the purpose of the user. For example, Hollis and Hollis suggest that the library may be the best place if the students use the material for a broadening experience.[98] On the other hand, if the student wishes to make a specific exploration the location should afford a sense of privacy, plus an opportunity to copy some aspect of the material. The counseling suite should have some occupational material available so that feedback can be facilitated. Since the material may be located

[97]R. Hoppock, *op. cit.,* p. 78.
[98]J. W. Hollis and L. U. Hollis, *op. cit.,* p. 258.

in several places, a card index may be needed to identify its location.

In addition to printed material, the information service should have available audiovisual material. This would include film strips, motion pictures, phonograph records, overhead transparencies, microfilm, audio tapes, and video tapes. Some high schools have provided space in the library where individuals and/or small groups may view visual material. Listening stations, similar to those found in language laboratories may also be located in the library. Audio tapes made by students that describe specific jobs, occupations, or training schools give a sense of credibility to the material. Video taping adds another dimension to the acceptance of the material. The special advantage that student-prepared audiotapes have over the commercially prepared visual material is that it has the most current information on the topic. In general, audiovisual material has greater scope and flexibility than printed material. Its use and development is only limited by the creative mind of the originator.

Curricular Organization for Vocational Development

For many years the objectives of education have been affected by the polarized views that school should be a preparation for life and a preparation for work. Operationally, these views lead to a compartmentalized approach to education. Course sequences were labeled as being vocational, general, and academic. Current curricular designs show a broader approach to education. This change has been affected by an interdisciplinary approach. New conceptions of human development and research evidence led to the modification of various curricular design.

The concept of vocational development has been incorporated into curricular designs. In the idea design the curriculum will feature "both special activities organized and handled by the counselors and activities planned by teachers which might be included in or cut across the various disciplines or subjects."[99] The goals of the integrated program is to enhance vocational de-

[99]L. S. Hansen, "Theory into Practice: A Practitioner Looks at Career Guidance in the School Curriculum," *Vocational Guidance Quarterly*, 16:97-103 (1967).

velopment rather than to select a specific vocation. As such, the experiences in the curriculum should be based on student readiness or need (i.e. vocational maturity). Consequently, the experiences, to be appropriate, must transcend subject matter and the school environment and be projected into the community. Development of vocational maturity cannot be left to happenstance.

Herr suggests that "if Luchin's *Primary Affect* is a valid premise — that the information which is obtained first carries the most weight in the ultimate decision — significantly more attention must be concentrated at the elementary school in terms of attitude development, decision processing, self-awareness, as well as awareness of the broad characteristics and expectations of work."[100] This statement suggests that the guidance program should focus on vocational development as early as kindergarten. The point is that, although vocational choice is usually made during adolescence, attitudes toward work must be developed early. Basically this consists of making pupils aware of the range of opportunities available and the types of satisfaction that can be obtained from them.

The ultimate purpose of exploratory activities is to help the student formulate from his occupational hypotheses a particular specification of what he will do. This specification is usually in the form of an occupational preference. Super believes that this preference is affected by length of training and age of entry into the world of work.[101] To state a preference, requires an awareness of the alternatives. Consequently, the early inclusion in the curriculum of exploratory and broadening activities enable students to learn about occupations. The sifting and winnowing of occupational information is inherent in the vocational developmental process.

[100]E. L. Herr, "Guidance and Vocational Aspects of Education: Some Considerations," *Vocational Guidance Quarterly*, 17:182 (1969), referring to A. S. Luchins, "Influences of Experience with Conflicting Information and Reactions to Subsequent Conflicting Information," *Journal of Social Psychology*, 5:367-385 (1960).

[101]D. E. Super, *et al.*, *Career Development: Self Concept Theory* (New York, College Entrance Examination Board, 1963).

The specification of a vocational preference may be seen as a branching off process. At different ages there is an increase in inclination for certain types of occupations, which combined with external factors, such as age of entry into training programs, determines the model age for decisions to enter these occupations. For certain occupations, such as medicine, this age appears to be early; while for others such as occupations in the social sciences, the future entrants seem to continue without a firm or final specification until they come to an age when changes in interests, values, and personality factors, increase together with the facilities available, helps them to make their vocational decisions.[102]

If the above premise that different occupations are decided upon at different times is accepted, then exploratory and broadening activities can help or hinder vocational development. Because of changes in technology and social conditions, the attractiveness of occupations is variable and as a consequence some types of occupations are more attractive than others. In 1957 junior high school students' vocational aspirations were affected by the birth of the space age. Fifteen years later, many boys who committed themselves to training and entry into space programs are finding that, because of severe budgetary cuts, they are faced with the prospect of radically altering their career pattern. Can the same be said of those who are now planning a lifetime commitment to the resolution of the pollution problem? The combination of anticipated manpower needs and length of training can act as an effective broker to full exploration of the world of work. Some students will make an early choice and thereby precluding any additional vocational exploration. For example, Kaczkowski, George, and Gallagher, found that a year long exploratory shop course had little impact on modifying the shop choice of ninth grade boys.[103] Boys in the exploratory shop course spent six weeks in each of six different shop areas. At the conclusion of the program they selected a shop program for the remaining three years of high school. Most of the boys retained their original choice. Some students may limit their vocational

[102]E. Marr, "Vocational Maturity and Specification of a Preference," *Vocational Guidance Quarterly,* 18:45-48 (1969).

[103]H. R. Kaczkowski, C. George, and P. Gallagher, "The Influence of an Exploratory Shop Course," *Vocational Guidance Quarterly,* 11:202-203 (1963).

exploration because of a lack of an adequate self-concept. They believe that they lack the necessary ability to complete most training programs; therefore, they refuse to make any occupational choice until they graduate from high school.

A curriculum that enhances vocational development is not a panacea for maximizing the vocational choice. Although the program can help students to put psychological and sociological factors into proper perspective, it has little control over training opportunities, economic factors, and manpower needs which ultimately affect the kinds of preferences students make. Consequently, the total school effort in the vocational development process should not only help students in their synthesis of the self but should also help them to affect a meaningful compromise when they enter the world of work.

> Variations in knowledge, in rationality and in discrimination between alternatives constitute, therefore, the limiting conditions within which individuals choose occupations by arriving at a compromise between their preference and expectations. This compromise is continually modified up to the time of actual entry, since each experience in the labor market affects the individual's expectations, and recurrent experiences may also affect his preferences. . . . Occupational choice, then, can be conceptualized as a series of decisions to present oneself to employers or other selectors as a candidate for a number of more or less related occupations. Each decision is governed by the way in which the individual compromises his ideal preference and his actual expectations of being able to enter a given occupation, the latter being conditioned by previous rejections and other experiences.[104]

Blau and others suggest that occupational entry is the result of an interaction between vocational choice and occupational selection. In essence, occupational entry must be a compromise, for vocational choice represents an ideal, while entry represents a compromise between preference and expectation and identity. If this observation is accepted then some aspects of the informational service in the guidance program must be modified.

[104]P. M. Blau, *et al.*, "Occupational Choice: A Conceptual Framework," *Industrial Labor Relations*, 9:531-546 (1956).

Essentially, in high schools the student must have increased opportunity for testing his occupational hypotheses and for feedback regarding his occupational selection. Prior to this stage of vocational development he must have thoroughly learned about occupations and careers. If vocational choice is to be predicated on what is known about the self and the world of work, the student must have acquired the information in some manner. All vocational learning is a function of motivation. The student acts to satisfy his vocational needs. Unless he has a vocational need, he will not pursue a course of action, nor will there be any vocational learning. . . . The vocational responses of the student are determined by the nature of the situation and by the learner's condition of vocational readiness.[105]

O'Hara suggests that the main task in the early years is the creation of goal-directedness.[106] This can be done by making students aware of the consequences of their academic decisions. According to O'Hara, another aspect that can be developed is that of noticing vocational information. "Thus, vocational readiness involves readiness to interpret and respond to available vocational cues. The best vocational learning situation will be one in which the cues are in conformity with the state of readiness.[107] In adolescence, the student will be able to make interpretations of the vocational situation. For O'Hara, the information given to students must be in a form that increases their capacity to understand career development in the world of work. This can be done through the manipulation and study of symbols. Once the student has the ability to symbolize the occupational spectrum he is able to formulate occupational hypotheses and contemplate occupational selection.

The informational services aspect of the guidance program and the curriculum can be potent factors in enhancing vocational development. Activities in these areas must be predicated on the vocational maturity of the students if the students are to notice and respond to vocational information. It is essential that the

---

[105]R. P. O'Hara, A Theoretical Foundation for the Use of Occupational Information in Guidance, *Personnel and Guidance Journal,* 46:636-640 (1968).

[106]*Ibid.,* p. 637.

[107]*Ibid.,* p. 639.

total school recognize that the effort is cognitive and limited in scope and that factors outside the school and inside the individual affect the interpretation of the information. The primary goal of the two facets—guidance and curriculum—is to broaden the occupational horizon of the students so that they may see more alternatives, thereby, maximizing the use of their talents.

Technology in Vocational Guidance

An emerging guidance technology provides opportunities for us to realize in new ways the old goals we strived for, and to accomplish goals previously thought unattainable. We must, however, consider technology within the social context where it will be used.[108]

Wrenn, in commenting on the Walz article, believes that integrating, the hardware, people, and social setting is sound.[109] He cautions that the counselor should not become too comfortable with his computer assistant and rely on it as he once did upon tests. A competent counselor should view the computer as one of the alternative techniques he can use in assisting students. Loughary has proposed a three-level classification for describing computer-assisted counseling systems:

1. *Data-processing tools.* The machine performs the traditional information-processing tasks.
2. *Substitute for counselors.* The machine is not only used as an automated reference system but helps a student to compare his abilities with training opportunities and job opportunities.
3. *Substitute counselor.* The machine is programmed to analyze student remarks and to respond selectively and sensitively. Programs for the first two levels have been developed but not for the third level.[110]

The chief functions of the computer, then, would be to serve as an automated reference system to assist students with

[108]G. R. Walz, "Technology in Guidance: A Conceptual Overview," *Personnel and Guidance Journal,* 49:176-184 (1970). The entire issue is devoted to technology in guidance.

[109]C. G. Wrenn, "Comment: The Dangers Within," *Personnel and Guidance Journal,* 49:183-184 (1970).

[110]J. W. Loughary, "The Computer is In!" *Personnel and Guidance Journal,* 49: 185-191 (1970).

their comparisons of various alternatives and to give students more time with their counselors for higher level decision making.

In a vocational guidance program, whose focus is vocational development, the computer could assist students with their exploration and clarification of vocational choice. Minor, Myers, and Super postulate that a computer system could yield the following benefits for a student:

1. Broaden his knowledge of occupational alternatives and his own multipotentiality by an exploratory process so that he could understand how his alternative tentative goals relate to his personal attributes.
2. Provide the student who is interested in post-high school education with a means of exploring educational or curriculum preferences.
3. Provide the student with a means of narrowing the search for educational or training institutions which satisfy his career or curriculum preferences, his learning abilities, and his personal preferences.[111]

A computer program based on some of the above concepts is being developed by Martin Katz and his associates at Educational Testing Service, and is called SIGI (System of Interactive Guidance and Information).[112] In the program a student can move in four subsystems: Value, Information, Predition, and Planning. The value program helps a student to express and clarify his areas of satisfaction. Within the Information program, the student may *locate, compare,* or *sample* a variety of data. The Prediction program will enable the student to match his self-evaluation with his options and learn his chance of success in each option. The Planning program will assist the student in exploring and evaluating the next steps in career decision making. These programs "will not replace the counselor or his books but will develop the students thinking to the point where he can make intelligent use of these sources."[113]

[111]F. J. Minor, R. A. Myers, and D. E. Super, "An Experimental Computer-based Educational and Career Exploration System, *Personnel and Guidance Journal,* 47:564-569 (1969).

[112] .... "Interactive Computer System Will Help Students Make Career Decisions," *ETS Developments,* Winter 1971, p. 4.

[113]*Ibid.,* p. 4.

Some consider CVIS (Computerized Vocational Information System) of Willowbrook High School (Villa Park, Illinois) as one of the most impressive systems operable in the country. "This system can be described as a high-speed information retrieval system integrated with a student-computer interactive occupational information dialogue capability which facilitates vocational choices."[114]

The objectives of the CVIS system are:

1. To provide a system by which a student may explore (*not choose*) a wide range of occupations with feedback from his own record of ability, achievement and interest.
2. To teach decision-making processes.
3. To accomplish the preceding goals in a way that is innovative enough to capture student interest.
4. To assign to the computer the data retrieval and comparison functions it performs best and to give human counselors more time to perform the counseling functions which require sensitivity and human communication.[115]

Currently there are CVIS programs for the exploration of occupations, educational opportunities (four year colleges, community colleges, specialized and technical schools), apprenticeships, local jobs and military information. (See Figure VIII-2.)

The computer is not the only piece of equipment that can be used to facilitate vocational development. As suggested earlier film projectors, overhead projectors, film strip projectors, rear-screen projectors, tape recorders, and television can be employed in helping students to explore and clarify vocational choice. There has been some reluctance to use a variety of media for these purposes because it tends to be dehumanizing. However, when appropriately used, a multimedia approach can greatly facilitate the vocational development of students.

Multimedia then can be very useful in the hands of guidance workers. It can serve the guidance worker as an effective extension of himself, as a creative device in guidance con-

---

[114]T. L. Roberts, in a book review of *Computer-Assisted Counseling*, by D. E. Super, et al., *Personnel and Guidance Journal*, 49:247-250 (1970).

[115]Computerized Vocational Information System, A project report, Willowbrook High School, Villa Park, Illinois.

Cumulative Rank in Class	Service	Bus. Contact	Organizational	Technology	Outdoor	Science	General Cultural	Arts and Entertainment	Composite Test Battery Score
Top-One Quarter I									Top Quartile 76-99%
1st-2nd Quarter II									1st-2nd Quartile 51-99%
2nd-3rd Quarter III									2nd-3rd Quartile 26-75%
2nd-3rd Quarter IV									2nd-3rd Quartile 26-75%
3rd Quarter V									3rd Quartile 26-50%
4th Quarter VI									4th Quartile 1-25%
Kuder	Social Service	Persuasive	Clerical Computation	Science Mechanical Computational	Outdoor	Scientific	Literary	Artistic Music Literature	

Figure VIII-2 — CVIS Grid Showing Relationship Between Roe's Classification, Kuder Profile, Rank in Class, and Test Composite

sultation and as a means, at last, to significantly help us achieve the noble counseling goals of improving personal satisfaction and effectiveness in human integration.[116]

Placement

In recent years, the appropriateness of placement in the guidance service has been questioned. One factor that has been responsible for this shift in attitude is change in emphasis from vocational choice to vocational development. Traditionally, the placement service has been concerned with assisting students in implementing a decision in the world of work or in a training or school setting. Currently, the emphasis in schools is on educational rather than vocational placement. In many states the function of job placement has been taken over by state employment agencies. These state agencies receive assistance from the United States Employment Service (USES).

Hoppock, among others, has seriously questioned the downgrading of placement in the guidance program. He believes that placement is an integral part of the total guidance program.

> Ultimately every client tests his occupational choice against the realities of occupational life when he tries to make a living. Too often the client cannot get a job in the occupation of his choice. He needs a job. He takes what he can get. It is at this point of placement that much vocational counseling breaks down because neither the client nor his counselor did enough reality testing in anticipation during the process of vocational counseling. Because the client who fails to get a job seldom returns at this point, the counselor seldom learns of these failures.[117]

This harsh indictment has some merit. Essentially, it cautions the counselor not to totally rely on one aspect theory in vocational counseling. The concept that vocational choice as an extension of self into the world of work should be a framework that has utility in explicating career patterns. When the focus is job selection, most individuals compromise between their preferences and expectations. Consequently, Hoppock's remarks have cre-

[116]N. Kagan, "Multimedia in Guidance and Counseling," *Personnel and Guidance Journal*, 49:197-204 (1970).
[117]R. Hoppock, *op. cit.*, p. 106.

dence because the specific job entered can be used as an indicator of the efficacy of vocational counseling. If one of the goals of counseling is to enhance personal growth, then the appraisal of the job entry can be indicative of the quality of that growth.

Ohlsen believes that placement should be an activity for which the school and the community are responsible.[118] The state employment agency should be responsible for the community's contribution to the placement service. In addition to job placement, the state employment agency can provide: (1) information on the labor market; (2) future manpower needs; (3) opportunities for part-time and summer employment; and (4) opportunities for on-the-job training and apprenticeships.[119] Ohlsen suggests that both the school and the state employment agency cooperate in helping students in their vocational development. Part of this cooperation can be in the form of testing students with the *General Aptitude Test Battery*. Performance on this battery can be compared to worker traits in at least 4000 occupations. Those senior students who have no choice can be assisted in formulating a crude occupational hypothesis in this comparison of test profiles. In the process they may have discovered that at least 70 per cent of the occupations "either are repetitive, require work under specific instructions or supervision, have set limitations of performance, or have measurable or verifiable criteria of performance.[120] These occupations tend to be "society maintaining" rather than "ego-involving."

Placement work can be conducted by student personnel specialists other than counselors. The very nature of placement work requires that the specialist assimilate vast amounts of specific information about the world of work. In addition, he must be skilled in interviewing and human relationships. He should be willing to work with the state employment agency in placing

[118]M. M. Ohlsen, *Guidance Services in the Modern School* (New York, Harcourt, Brace and World, 1966), p. 357.

[119]*Ibid.*, p. 359.

[120]C. L. Shartle, "Occupational Analysis, Worker Characteristics, and Occupational Classification Systems," in H. Borow, ed., *Man in a World of Work* (Boston, Houghton Mifflin Co., 1964).

students. Some of the specific functions that the placement service may perform are: (1) assist in the placement of students in the work-experience program; (2) help students with their part-time employment and summer employment; (3) conduct career conferences; (4) teach skills needed in applying for a job; (5) establish relations with business and industry; (6) make referrals to counselors or other agencies; and (7) prepare letters of recommendation.

In some schools educational placement is differentiated from vocational placement. Educational placement is seen as a process that assists students to take successive steps on the educational ladder. Among the tasks undertaken by the placement worker could be, (1) assigning pupils to classes, sections, tracks, or curricula; (2) developing orientation and articulation programs; (3) aiding students in their transfer from one school to another; (4) assisting in completion of application forms; (5) aiding in the procurement of scholarships and loans; (6) providing information concerning entrance requirements to specific schools. Educational placement is concerned with satisfactory adjustment in a school setting. As such, its focus is on learning rather than occupational selection.

Stevens has proposed a concept of placement readiness that can be integrated into that of vocational maturity. "An individual is ready for placement when he is able to identify the job he desires in a geographic location, meets the necessary qualifications to fulfill the job requirements, and is willing and/or able to make the necessary effort of action which will enable him to be effective in obtaining a job."[121] An essential element of placement readiness is goal oriented behavior. An individual must not only mobilize his "personal resources" but he must be in a position to implement his occupational choice. Placement readiness implies well-crystalized job goals. Those who are "vocationally immature" lack direction and purpose.

Stevens postulates that placement readiness is developmental in nature because it is continuous and is differentiable into pat-

[121]N. D. Stevens, "A Concept of Placement Readiness," *Vocational Guidance Quarterly,* 10:143-147 (1962).

terns.[122] It is an expression of self-actualization in that it moves in the direction of greater growth and differentiation. Three levels of placement readiness are suggested. Low placement readiness is indicative of the "inability to balance reality factors in the job market wtih internal factors (interests, abilities, etc.) affecting a choice of job-goal, the developmental process is stunted. Confusion results, and unrealistic job goals are chosen."[123] Moderate placement readiness reflects an attempt to clarify fantasy goals. After the evaluating of both external and internal factors the individual formulates tentative choices. Individuals with high placement readiness compares his tentative choices with the realities of the job market. "A compromise as a result of this evaluation is effected so that the individual is able to crystalize a field choice and finally to specify a job choice."[124]

Hoppock's belief that counselors should see their clients through placement could be expanded to include the school. If the general purpose of the guidance program is to promote personal growth, implementation of a carefully nurtured self-concept into the real world should be of some concern to the school. The school should not be concerned with the "success" the students have but with the quality of life they lead. Consequently, placement should be an integral aspect of the total guidance program.

Follow-Up

To determine the value and effectiveness of the guidance program a systematic analysis of the relationship between the means and ends should be made. Evaluation implies a comparison of goals to some type of standard. It entails judging the value of an experience or a process. These judgments are used to critique the impact the guidance program had on the pupils, school, and community. It can be differentiated from research in that the latter is concerned with obtaining answers to questions through

[122]*Ibid.*, p. 146.
[123]*Ibid.*, p. 145.
[124]*Ibid.*, p. 146.

the application of scientific principles. Some counselors are more concerned with evaluation than they are with research.

Shertzer and Stone suggest that guidance programs can be evaluated according to internal and external characteristics."[125] The external frame of reference is derived from suggestions made by professional organizations, regional accrediting associations, and state departments of public instruction. Among the characteristics evaluated are (1) counselor-student ratio, (2) counselor qualifications, (3) record maintenance, (4) informational materials, (4) physical facilities, (5) financial support, and (6) student appraisal program. The internal characteristics examine the efficiency, effectiveness, and impact of the guidance program. Among the characteristics evaluated are: (1) degree to which pupil needs are met; (2) types of assistance offered to students; (3) quality of organization and program stability; (4) degree of coordination between specialties; and (5) leadership approach. The general purpose of these external and internal characteristics is to serve as guidelines for better understanding of guidance programs and for reference points when modifications are made in existing guidance programs.

The basic problem of evaluation is that of the criterion. Whether a criterion represents the desired outcomes is a matter of opinion. For example, are higher grade point averages indicative of successful educational counseling? Are higher salaries indicative of successful vocational counseling? The time at which the evaluation study is made affects the selection of the criterion. For example, completion of a high school algebra course may be appropriate at one point in time while the level of occupational entry is best at another point in time. Expert opinions do not necessarily generate appropriate criteria. There is nothing magical in the 1 to 300 counselor-student ratio. Complying to this ratio does not necessarily assure a quality guidance program. In some evaluation studies the criterion problem is further complicated by the lack of specificity of guidance objectives. For an evaluation study to be meaningful, the criteria must reflect program objectives so that generalization can be made from the results.

[125]B. Shertzer and S. C. Stone, *op. cit.*, pp. 396-405.

Because of the problems inherent in evaluation studies, counselors tend to conduct follow-up studies. A follow-up study differs from an evaluation study in that the latter is concerned with judgments about outcomes while the former is concerned with descriptions about outcomes. "A well-coordinated follow-up service is needed to obtain from recent graduates a realistic picture of what lies ahead for present students, to help former students reappraise their educational and vocational plans, to appraise the school's program, to obtain ideas for improving the program, and to obtain the information about "the total number of recent school-leavers employed in the local community; number and variety of employment opportunities; means by which former students obtained their jobs; further educational training desired by the school leavers."[126] Follow-up studies provide information that is useful in formulating the direction and intensity of program modifications. In addition follow-up studies provide an opportunity to obtain local occupational and educational information.[127] Follow-up studies provide data that are not only useful in program improvement and in providing supplemental occupational information but which also can be utilized in curriculum reorganization.

Follow-up studies require planning and preparation. A variety of techniques and instruments can be used to obtain information from students, among them are check lists, questionnaires, interviews and group discussions. Ohlsen and Rothney give detailed instructions for conducting follow-up studies.[128] Both suggest that the following procedures enhance a high return of mailed questionnaires: (1) seniors should be informed about purpose of follow-up studies and how they contribute to program modification; (2) appropriate mailing dates should be selected; (3) an all-out effort should be made to obtain the correct address before the mailing of questionnaires. In addition to these prac-

[126]M. M. Ohlsen, *op. cit.,* p. 357.

[127]W. Norris, F. R. Zeran, and R. N. Hatch, *The Information Service in Guidance* (Chicago: Rand McNally & Co., 1966), p. 307.

[128]J. W. M. Rothney, "Follow-up Services in the Small Secondary School," *High School Journal,* 1957, 40:274-279 and M. M. Ohlsen, *op. cit.,* pp. 364-369.

tices, a sufficient amount of money should be allocated in the budget to conduct the follow-up study.

Peters and Farwell suggest that, although follow-up studies and evaluation studies have merit, the counselor should also be concerned with research.[129] The counselor benefits from research because he gains a "better understanding of the human specimen and its development" and a "better delineation of the process of counseling."[130] In studying the counseling process the counselor can place the outcomes of counseling into proper perspective, clarify his role in the guidance program, and substantiate the value of the helping relationship. The focus of research conducted by a counselor will generally be on process and procedures. This could include the appraisal of different modes of test interpretation, impact of writing an autobiography on the self-concept, and role of career conferences in crystalizing vocational choice. Peters and Farwell believe that the longitudinal aspects of the counseling process should be examined. We would take the position that there needs to be greater emphasis on longitudinal study of counseling because this is the unique aspect of what is called guidance, rather than an evaluation of supportive activities to counseling where *counseling per se* receives minimal involvement for either the counselor or counselee.[131]

This suggests that the primary function of a counselor is to counsel and all other activities he undertakes are secondary. In vocational guidance programs, the counselor should devote a major part of his effort to counseling rather than to the ancillary tasks of gathering occupational and educational information, assessing students, placement of students, etc. Since vocational choice takes place within the context of vocational development, the longitudinal approach to research would be very helpful. Data gathered could be used to modify existing theories of vocational development. Peters and Farwell felt that "the practicing school counselor has the responsibility throughout his life time

---

[129]H. J. Peters and G. F. Farwell, *Guidance: A Developmental Approach* (Chicago, Rand McNally & Co., 1967).

[130]*Ibid.*, pp. 549-550.

[131]*Ibid.*, p. 557.

in the study of counselors, counselees, and the totality of the counseling porcess."[132] It is in this way that there is hope for the future in establishing a substantive base for the counseling profession.

[132]*Ibid.,* p. 568.

CHAPTER IX

EDUCATIONAL CONCERNS WITH SPECIAL GROUPS

HAROLD A. MOSES

THERE ARE A NUMBER of groups of individuals who do not have an equal opportunity to live and make a contribution to society. This lack of opportunity may be the result of chance, the fault of the individual, or the fault of society. Regardless of the cause, society does have an obligation to assist those individuals who find themselves at an unfair disadvantage in their struggle to live and compete. Although the school is not the only place where special provisions should be made for these persons, it is one of the major institutions which has the resources or potential resources to develop programs and opportunities to enable them to live a more satisfying and productive life. No segment of society can rightfully deny, either from a humanitarian or economic viewpoint, the desirability of and its obligation for assisting all its citizens to develop their capabilities to the highest degree they might wish. In order to assist members of these groups in overcoming obstacles to their self-actualization, it is essential to have an understanding of the individual and of the problems he faces. In an effort to facilitate this understanding, a representative number, but certainly not all of these groups will be discussed.

The Physically Handicapped Student

The rights of the physically handicapped person to equal services must be obtained and safeguarded while he is in school. He should be provided, insofar as possible, with the same opportunity for effective learning as any other student.

The physically handicapped constitute a sizeable minority segment of most populations. An estimated nearly 45 percent of the population living outside of institutions have some degree of chronic illness or impairment.[1]

Approximately 6.1 million children are in need of some type of special education. About 27 percent of this group receives it in the public schools.[2]

A study conducted by the National Education Association[3] to determine the extent to which special provisions were being made for handicapped children by urban school districts found that 37.8 percent of the districts fully provided for speech therapists, 26.3 percent had limited provisions, and 35.9 percent had no such provisions. Only 11.7 percent of the districts made full provisions for separate classes for hard-of-hearing pupils. Over 7 percent had limited provisions, while 81 percent made no provisions at all for such pupils.

Students with limited vision were fully provided with separate classes in 11 percent of the schools, had limited provisions in 8 percent, and had no provision in 81 percent. For other physically handicapped pupils, 23 percent of the schools had full provisions for separate classes, 16 percent had limited provisions, and 61 percent had no special classes. These data indicate a deplorable lack of provisions for urban handicapped students and rural handicapped students probably have even less favorable conditions.

There is some question as to whether school counselors offer any significant degree of counseling services to the physically handicapped student on problems directly related to his handicap and whether traditional counseling services adequately

[1]J. F. McGowan and T. L. Porter, eds. *An Introduction to the Vocational Rehabilitation Process* (Washington, D. C., U. S. Department of Health, Education, and Welfare, 1967), p. 13.

[2]R. P. Mackie, "Spotlighting Advances in Special Education," *Exceptional Children*, 32:77-81 (1965).

[3]National Education Association Research Division, *Special Provisions for Handicapped Children*, National Education Association Research Division, Research Memo 1961-6 (Washington, D.C., January, 1961).

meet the needs of the handicapped student. The typical school counselor is nevertheless faced with the task of providing counseling for all students placed under his charge. Inappropriate behavior may result from a number of sources, and it is the goal of counseling to help the student discover and correct them.

One of the basic philosophies underlying public education in our democratic society is that schools exist to serve all students. If the school is an institution to develop everyone into self-supporting and contributing members of society, then it must

> not deny the benefit of education to any child who can profit therefrom;
> insist upon an adequate understanding of the disabled child by school personnel;
> adjust its program in order that the disabled child may experience success;
> consider its special program as developmental as well as remedial;
> consider the part that the attitudes of others play in the adjustment of the disabled child; and
> not attempt to shift total responsibility for the disabled child to special teachers and clinical services.[4]

It should be the goal of those who deal with handicapped school children to help them to

> reach the maximum level of effectiveness in tools subjects;
> pursue those curricular matters that strategically determine effective living for specific types of handicapped children;
> consider the mental as well as the physical hygiene of handicapped children;
> develop motivational patterns in the handicapped that will produce achievement in school and out of school;
> produce in the handicapped a desire to participate in the activities of nonhandicapped persons; and
> develop a realistic self-concept in handicapped children.[5]

Although the misguiding of nonhandicapped youth is a serious matter, the misguiding of the handicapped is usually

[4]L. F. Cain, "The Disabled Child in School," *Journal of Social Issues*, 4:90-94 (1948).

[5]T. E. Jordan, *The Exceptional Child* (Columbus, Ohio, Charles E. Merrill Books, 1962).

much more serious due to the restrictions imposed upon him by his physical limitations. The handicapped person should be made aware of these restrictions and their effects upon the many facets of his life, rather than the more narrow interpretation of their effects upon his vocational aspirations.

Some authorities believe the school can and should provide for as many of the handicapped as possible in the regular classroom. They feel this is important, not only for economic reasons, but because it also gives the handicapped student a more realistic outlook on life and experience in competing with the nonhandicapped which will hold him in good stead in later life and eliminates the danger of a secondary handicap brought about by segregation. The lives of both the handicapped and nonhandicapped can be enriched from their contact with each other.

Although the vocationally handicapped student should be identified before he finishes high school, many are not. Many persons never learn about vocational rehabilitation services, for instance, because some school officials don't know about it, aren't in sympathy with the philosophy of public rehabilitation, don't report the handicapped student for fear of embarrassing him, have a lack of interest in the student as a whole person, or don't know the student well enough to know about his impairment—or know him so well and accept his handicap so naturally that they don't think of him as disabled. Further obstacles include opposition of some school administrators to guidance and counseling of any nature, denial of handicaps (even among medical practitioners), and chauvinism.

The handicapped student has not only the same adjustment problems as the nonhandicapped student but also may have additional problems (e.g. greater degree of maladjustment, peer rejection, anxiety) imposed upon him by his handicap. Horrocks states: "Adolescents are particularly prone to ridicule or reject those age mates who have physical anomalies or who deviate in some way from the physical norm. Such ridicule or rejection only accentuates the difficulties of an adolescent who may already be worrying about whether or not he is normal."[6]

However, it is generally agreed that the mere presence of a disability, *per se,* does not automatically make one maladjusted. Shaffer and Shoben state: "Physical and organic inferiorities have some part in the origin of anxieties, not because of any intrinsic characteristics of physical traits as such, but because of the important role that strength plays in the lives of children in our culture."[7]

Kessler[8] says that the most difficult external problem faced by the disabled is adjustment to hostile social forces and that the handicapped are discriminated against by society, employers, government, and labor unions. Standards of what is considered normal are set and those who deviate are to some degree repulsive. They become members of minority groups and suffer the usual disadvantages and discriminations of other minority groups. The physically handicapped person usually has also the additional burden of not having a model, i.e., parents, friends, relatives, or neighbors, which many racial, ethnic, and religious minorities have. He may be the only member of his family, indeed the whole neighborhood, who is so afflicted and may feel that since others have not had similar experiences they cannot understand and accept him.

Counseling with students concerning problems caused by physical disabilities, like all counseling, is a process and not a point in time. Physically disabled students should be identified and, to be as effective as he should be the counselor should work with them as early as possible to help them to obtain necessary experiences at the most advantageous time in their lives. This should enable them to not only profit more from their formal education and to enter the labor force or acquire

[6] J. E. Horrocks, *The Psychology of Adolescence* (Boston, Houghton Mifflin Co., 1969), p. 374.

[7] L. F. Schaffer and E. J. Shoben, *The Psychology of Adjustment* (Boston, Houghton Mifflin Co., 1956), p. 166.

[8] H. H. Kessler, *Rehabilitation of the Physically Handicapped* (New York, Columbia University Press, 1953).

additional training with a minimum of time and energy but act as a safeguard against secondary gains which are frequently greater obstacles to the person than the disability itself.

At its tenth annual convention, the International Society for Crippled Children adopted the following *Crippled Child's Bill of Rights:*

I. Every child has the right to be well born, that is to say, the right to a sound body, complete in its members, physically whole. In the securing of this right we pledge ourselves to use our influence that proper prenatal, intranatal, and postnatal care be provided to the end that congenital deformity, insofar as it is humanly and scientifically possible, be prevented.

II. Every child has the right to develop under clean, wholesome, healthful conditions. In declaring this right, this Society undertakes to use its influence to the end that children everywhere, through proper legislation both local and general, and through proper supervision and protection, may grow to manhood and womanhood free from crippling conditions caused by insufficient nourishment, improper food, or unsanitary environment, and free, so far as possible, from danger of accident, wounding or maiming.

III. Notwithstanding the rights of children to be well born and to be protected throughout childhood, it is recognized that in spite of all human precautions there will be, unfortunately, some crippled children. These we declare to have the right to the earliest possible examination, diagnosis and treatment, recognizing, as we do, the fact that many thousand cases of permanent crippling may be eliminated by early and effective care.

IV. Every crippled child has a right, not only to the earliest possible treatment, but to the most effective continuing care, treatment and nursing, including the use of such appliances as are best calculated to assist in remedying or ameliorating its condition.

V. Every crippled child has the right to an education. Without this, all other provisions, unless for the relief of actual suffering, are vain.

VI. Every crippled child has the right, not only to care, treatment, and education, but to such treatment as will fit him or her for self-support, either wholly or partially, as the conditions may

dictate. Without such practical application education is likewise purposeless.

VII. Every crippled child has the right to vocational placement
for, unless the child—boy or girl—after having been given
physical care and treatment and after being educated and
trained, is actually placed in a proper position in the life of
the world, all that has gone before is of no avail.

VIII. Every crippled child has the right to considerate treatment, not
only from those responsible for its being and for its care,
treatment, education, training and placement, but from those
with whom it is thrown into daily contact, and every possible
influence should be exerted by this and affiliated organizations
to secure this right, in order that, so far as possible, the
crippled child may be spared the stinging jibe or the bitter
taunt, or, worse still, the demoralizing pity of its associates.

IX. Every crippled child has the right to spiritual as well as
bodily development and, without regard to particular religious
or denominational belief, is entitled to have nourishment for
soul growth.

X. In brief, not only for its own sake, but for the benefit of
society as a whole, every crippled child has the right to the
best body which modern science can help it to secure; the
best mind which modern education can provide; the best
training which modern vocational guidance can give; the best
position in life which his physical condition, perfected as best
as it may be, will permit; and the best opportunity for
spirtual development which its environment affords.[9]

These provisions were adopted in 1931 by the Second World
Conference on the problems of crippled persons. We find that
over forty years later the goals are still laudable objectives but
largely unfulfilled.

In spite of efforts to educate the public on how to treat a
disabled person, many individuals, including teachers, feel ill
at ease and uninformed as to how to act when meeting a handicapped person. The National Easter Seal Society[10] has published
a pamphlet containing what they called fifteen hints for reward-

[9]International Society for Crippled Children, *The Crippled Child's Bill of Rights*
(Elyria, Ohio, 1931).

[10]National Easter Seal Society for Crippled Children and Adults, *When You Meet
a Handicapped Person,* National Easter Seal Society for Crippled Children
and Adults (Chicago, no date).

ing relationships. These are reproduced here for the benefit of school personnel and nonhandicapped students and are as follows:

When you met a handicapped person:

1. First of all remember that the person with a handicap is a person. He is like anyone else, except for the special limitations of his handicap.
2. A disability need not be ignored or denied between friends. But until your relationship is that, show friendly interest in him as a person.
3. Be yourself when you meet him.
4. Talk about the same things as you would with anyone else.
5. Help him only when he requests it. When a handicapped person falls, he may wish to get up by himself, just as many blind persons prefer to get along without assistance. So offer help but wait for his request before giving it.
6. Be patient. Let the handicapped person set his own pace in walking or talking.
7. Don't be afraid to laugh with him.
8. Don't stop and stare when you see a handicapped person you do not know. He deserves the same courtesy any person should receive.
9. Don't be overprotective or oversolicitous. Don't shower the handicapped person with kindness.
10. Don't ask embarrassing questions. If the handicapped person wants to tell you about his disability, he will bring up the subject himself.
11. Don't offer pity or charity. The handicapped person wants to be treated as an equal. He wants a chance to prove himself.
12. Don't separate a disabled person from his wheelchair or crutches unless he asks it. He may want them within reach.
13. When dining with a handicapped person, don't offer help in cutting his food. He will ask you or the waiter if he needs it.
14. Don't make up your mind ahead of time about the handicapped person. You may be surprised at how wrong you are in judging his interests and abilities.
15. Enjoy your friendship with the handicapped person. His philosophy and good humor will give you inspiration.

The Emotionally Disturbed Student

The number of emotionally disturbed children attending

regular classes is extremely difficult to determine.[11] After investigating studies dealing with maladjustment, Kaplan[12] estimated that 25 percent of students in our schools and colleges needed professional help or therapy. Dr. Spock states that American children are anxious and that 25 percent to 50 percent are afraid of a nuclear disaster and of separation from their families during disaster and death. The National Association for Mental Health[13] states that one out of every ten persons in the United States has some form of mental or emotional disturbance that needs psychiatric treatment and that there are a half million psychotic or borderline psychotic children in the United States. In spite of varying estimates, one can rest assured that emotional disturbance is one of the major problems facing contemporary society.

Bower[14] concluded from his reading of the literature, attending professional meetings, and studying special programs for educating emotionally handicapped, nonsuccessful children and adolescents that: the problem is a critical and desperate one for most school districts; the school system deals with the problem post facto without a planned program; the problem becomes more severe and unassailable; therapeutic activities are necessary for some children; mental health consultation with school personnel is a necessary part of a preventative program; and the essence of the helping relationship depends upon the quality of the program.

Moses and Delaney[15] found evidence of large numbers of pressures facing students, teachers, and parents. Although the

[11]M. A. White and M. W. Harris, *The School Psychologist* (New York, Harper & Row Publishers, Inc., 1961).

[12]L. Kaplan, *Mental Health and Human Relations in Education* (New York, Harper & Row Publishers, Inc., 1959).

[13]National Association for Mental Health, *Facts about Mental Illness* (New York, National Association for Mental Health, no date).

[14]E. M. Bower, "The Emotionally Handicapped Child and the School," in L. Crow and A. Crow eds., *Mental Hygiene for Teachers* (New York, Macmillan Company, 1963), pp. 162-173.

[15]H. A. Moses and D. J. Delaney, "Dimension of Pressures Faced by Teachers: A Factor Analytic Study, *SPATE Journal*, 8:122-128 (1970).

problem undoubtedly exists and we cannot afford to ignore it, there is an equally dangerous course of overemphasizing the problem and embarking on a witch hunt for maladjusted students, therefore a word of caution seems warranted at this point.

Diagnosis,[16] which to a great many student personnel workers and teachers means the assigning of psychiatric and diagnostic labels to students who enter their offices, is unnecessary and almost invariably detrimental to the goals of education and to the welfare of the student. Nevertheless, there is information that professionals should have when working with students. The word "working" was chosen advisedly to alert us to the fact that, if we are viewed by the student body in the proper perspective, every student who enters our office or classroom does not necessarily want or need counseling or therapy. The fact that many students present pseudo problems to us as their reason for coming in should not lead us to believe that all students are hiding behind a facade which must be penetrated in order to get to the real problem. We must not lose sight of the fact that what we might perceive as trivia may be and often are major concerns for the student.

There are important reasons why we should accept the student's statement as to why he came. First and foremost, we should possess and demonstrate respect for the student. He may be telling the truth and there are a number of ways in which we may assist a student besides counseling with him. If we do an adequate job in helping him with a "mundane" problem or provide him with requested information without probing, he may trust us to help him with other problems, return at a future time when a problem does arise, or refer to us his friends whom he knows to have problems.

When we contact a student who is having difficulty in achieving at a satisfactory level in school, let us not immediately jump to the conclusion that it is the result of an emotional

[16]The following is based upon H. A. Moses, Diagnostic Labeling in Counseling, *ICPA Quarterly*, 26:35-37 (1968).

problem. He very well may have an emotional problem, but it could as easily be the result as the cause of underachieving.

Physical defects are the causal factors in many cases of underachievement and are usually easier to determine and to correct than emotional problems. The law of parsimony would dictate that these more obvious possibilities be ruled out before concluding that the student's lack of academic achievement is the result of an emotional problem. Sight and hearing problems are common in school but certainly do not exhaust the health problems related to underachievement. A recent physical examination does not always insure that a child has no physical defects. Explanation by the parents of the school problems faced by the child may help to provide clues for the physician and alert him to possibilities he had not considered.

Intellectual deficits may result in low-level achievement. If a student does not have the ability to compete successfully with his peers, he may react in a number of ways. He may become so anxious that he cannot achieve as well as he potentially can. He may have found that as he progresses in school, determination and hard work are less effective in compensating for low ability. He may have decided that it is useless to attempt to achieve at the level expected by his parents and teachers and that if he puts forth a reasonable amount of effort and still fails, his deficiency may be discovered. For many students it is much less ego-deflating for them to be known as underachievers, as "clowns," or even as discipline problems than as stupid. Hence, many students are threatened, cajoled, bribed, and begged by parents and teachers to do better school work when they are unable to do so. Think of the anxiety and guilt feelings that these tactics undoubtedly generate and the myriad undesirable reactions the student has due to his predicament. All of this because we are negligent in discovering his "secret" and in helping him resolve his problem.

Poor study habits and/or lack of basic skills, other common reasons for underachievement, are relatively simple to determine and someone on the student personnel team should be able to discover them if they are causing the problem. That many professionals feel that study skill problems are less exciting and prestigious than personal problems does not excuse us from trying to help students with this type of problem. After all, why do we have student personnel workers, for the benefit of the student or for the workers? After determining that the student is in good health, possesses the intellectual ability to compete successfully in school, and has adequate study skills, it may be safe to make the tentative assumption that emotional factors are involved. This does not mean that until this time we should isolate ourselves either physically or psychologically from the student or that we should not attempt to establish a relationship. We should establish as therapeutic a relationship as possible in our contacts with all students because, even if one or any combination of the three discussed problems are present, the student may still need our services. Even though the student neither needs nor wants counseling, establishing a satisfying relationship with an adult is good experience for the student. The advantage of determining the cause of a problem such as academic underachievement is obvious; although no amount of counseling will correct the student's physical defect or raise his intelligence quotient, in many cases it will permit him to perceive his abilities more realistically and utilize them more effectively. A delination of the problem is not synonymous with the assignment of labels.

Even if it has been established that a student has an emotional problem, psychiatric diagnosis and labeling is still dangerous. Diagnosis among psychiatrists is woefully inadequate with very little agreement among them, which should illustrate the unfeasibility of a student personnel worker, trained at a different level with different skills and for different purposes, attempting diagnosis. However, if the label is used, accepted, and placed on the student's record, and subsequently read by others who may possess even less psychological sophistication, the danger that can accrue to the student is multiplied. Even if the student gets through school and later applies for a job, a training program, or admission to a college, he may be rejected because of the label given him. Therefore, we should have a strict rule that we will give serious consideration to any item of information before including it in the student's record. If we accept the basic premise of student personnel work, that individuals can grow and change, we should give the person every opportunity to do so. If we do not accept this premise, we should not be engaged in this type of work.

Most records tend to be negatively oriented; they seem to stress the unhealthy, the abnormal, the pathological. If we are not careful, we may fall into the trap of looking for weakness and completely overlook or ignore the strengths of our students. Records traditionally contain data obtained only from external evaluations. If we are to truly understand other individuals, we must know how they perceive themselves and their environment. To obtain this information, it is mandatory that we view the person from his internal frame of reference. Perhaps one of the greatest dangers of diagnosis is the self-fulfilling prophesy. When we declare that a student is, for example, lazy, a slow-learner, or a schizophrenic, we begin consciously and/or subconsciously to look for evidence to support our prediction and tend to minimize or reject evidence to the contrary. If we exercise enough persistence and ingenuity, we will eventually find sufficient evidence to justify our diagnosis and feel that we have accomplished our objective. We may also use the evidence as an excuse for not spending a lot of time trying to help the student since we know that it is very difficult to help anyone with that particular type of disorder. Perhaps, more tragic is that the student is quite likely to sense our evaluation of him, to accept it as accurate, and to behave accordingly.

Because there are so many possibilities of doing harm and so few, if any, possibilities of helping a student by labeling him, there is no justification under any circumstances for us to enter a psychiatric diagnosis in a student's permanent record or to use psychiatric labels when discussing a student with staff members, administrators, parents, or anyone else. The nonprofessionally trained worker should recognize the limits of his ability and not attempt to use terminology and skills he does not understand or possess. The better-trained worker should recognize the uselessness and futility of psychiatric diagnosis and refrain from engaging in this practice. Therefore, anyone who resorts to this technique to mask his own feelings of inadequacy, to bolster his own self-concept, or for any other reason, should be a client and not a counselor.

How then, are we to communicate significant information to others in order to help them better understand the student and make more adequate provisions for his welfare? The answer is relatively simple. Rather than labels, judgments, and opinions we should provide brief, clear, and concise descriptions of actual behavior along with our suggestions and recommendations. Not only does this provide the receiver with a better basis for understanding the student but it forces us to think through the many implications of a particular type of behavior and reduces the temptation to conceal ignorance by assuming a pseudo-sophisticated attitude and hiding behind ambiguous terminology.

The appropriately trained counselor will be able to work effectively with most emotionally disturbed students attending school. However, he may feel the need for consultation or evaluation by other professionals and in some cases may need to refer to the student. He should feel no qualms in asking for a professional opinion of another and should experience no feeling of inadequacy if a referral is necessary. Indeed, knowing how to utilize consultants and how to make a proper referral are essential activities of all professionals.

The Racial Minority Group Students

A large percentage of students attending the American schools today are from minority groups. However, when we speak of racial minority students we tend to think of Negroes,

American Indians, Mexican-Americans, Puerto Ricans, Orientals, and sometimes Jews.

The Negroes comprise approximately 90 percent of the racial minority students in our schools and it is this group which is currently receiving the most attention. Although all groups have problems peculiar to that particular group, it appears that many writers have gone overboard in trying to accentuate the differences among racial groups. It is the contention of this writer that all races are more alike than different and that the current nit-picking to emphasize differences are detrimental to the eventual integration of the races. All races have their extremists and when we begin to listen to and shape policy on the basis of a vociferous few in any group, we are courting disaster. Conant[17] stated, "Since I believe the evidence indicates that it is the socio-economic situation, not the color of the children, which makes the Negro slum so difficult, the real issue is not racial integration but socioeconomic integration."

Erikson[18] indicates that one of the greatest problems facing the Negro is his search for an identity. The U.S. Department of Labor[19] discusses the matriarchal nature of the Negro community but states that the middle-class Negro American family is more patriarchal than the average.

It would seem that many of the distinctions we make concerning various races are made in the same manner in which the blind men examined the elephant. Many of the differences could be explained by socio-economic conditions, family relationships, geography, background experiences, etc. Student personnel workers must guard against falling into the trap of considering students of the various races as "different" and feel that different

[17]J. B. Conant, *Slums and Suburbs* (New York, McGraw-Hill Book Company, 1961), p. 30.

[18]E. H. Erikson, *Identity: Youth and Crisis* (New York: W. W. Norton & Company, Inc., 1968).

[19]U.S. Department of Labor, "The Tangle of Pathology, in R. C. and N. A. Sprinthall, eds., *Educational Psychology: Selected Readings* (New York: Van Nostrand Reinhold Company, 1969), pp. 345-354.

techniques, practices, perspectives, etc., are essential before they can understand and work with a particular group. Surely the professional worker must understand the possible effects of varying conditions upon students but any attempt to categorize students on the basis of race is untenable. All students are human beings and should be treated as such. They are more alike than different. Special needs of any student or groups of students should be recognized and fulfilled, but to do this on the basis of race is dangerous, usually unwarranted, and may easily lead to the opposite of the effect desired.

Few would question the fact that discrimination against various minority groups has been and continues to be practiced. Student personnel workers are in a unique position and have the opportunity to have some impact upon the integration of all groups within the school. This is a tremendous challenge but a task that American schools can ill-afford to shirk.

Drug Users

Student use of drugs has become a problem of major concern among educators at all levels. Until recently drug usage was confined primarily to adults and individuals from lower socioeconomic areas. Although accurate data are extremely difficult to obtain, reports indicate that drug usage is prevalent in a large number of high schools, infiltrating down to junior high schools and even to an alarming number of elementary schools. The actual number of reported drug users in the American schools varies widely, but one must conclude that the problem warrants the attention and concern of all student personnel workers. The large number of drugs in use and the conflicting reports of the types and severity of reactions among users further complicate the problem.

In spite of the mystery surrounding drug usage and of the unknowns concerning its effects, the school should take a conservative approach and attempt to curb its usage. Even if, as some contend, there are valuable results to some types of drug usage and no negative effects, the fact remains that too little research has been conducted to determine for certain the short-term, let alone the long-term effects of drug usage. Also, most drugs are illegal and, regardless of the wisdom of the law, it is still the law. Scare tactics are largely ineffective and are not being advocated here; nevertheless, many adolescents have a distorted view of the long-term effects that a juvenile or police record may have upon their future. Clarification of this one aspect could have a sobering effect upon some experimenters.

Students tend to have more information (and misinformation) about drugs than do many educators. If we are to put drugs in their proper perspective, we must make a conscientious attempt to learn the facts so we can converse with our students on an intellectual, rather than emotional level. Students are quick to spot phonies and if we attempt to "fake it" on drug usage, we will be discovered and our effectiveness diminished. Good intentions are laudable, but insufficient, in this area as in virtually all areas.

Table IX-I presents an abbreviated chart[20] of some of the more common drugs in use today. It should be understood that the symptoms indicated are usual but may or may not be present in any particular instance. Also, symptoms not indicated may be present due to a number of factors such as the mood of the user, the setting, the dosage, contaminants in the drug, interaction with other drugs already in the body, etc. Although the teacher can hardly be expected to become an expert on drug usage, there are a number of behaviors which may serve as indicators. Radical mood changes, irritability, sleepiness, sloppy dress, and poor work habits are among the various reactions an individual may exhibit due to drug abuse. It is unwise to attribute drug usage to any particular student who displays any of these symptoms, but all may be considered warning signals that something is wrong in the student's life. It is our job as educators to be alert and recognize these symptoms and help the student work through his problems.

The Delinquent Student

Juvenile delinquency refers to crimes committed by indi-

[20]*Drugs and Abuse,* U.S. Department of Justice, Bureau of Narcotics and Dangerous Drugs (Washington, D.C., 1970), pp. 8-9.

Table IX-I

TERMS AND SYMPTOMS OF DRUG ABUSE

SYMPTOMS OF ABUSE O, SYMPTOMS OF WITHDRAWAL X — DANGERS OF ABUSE X

Symptom / Term	MORPHINE	HEROIN	CODEINE	HYDROMORPHONE	MEPERIDINE	METHADONE	EXEMPT PREPARATIONS
SYMPTOMS OF ABUSE O, SYMPTOMS OF WITHDRAWAL X							
DROWSINESS	O	O	O	O	O	O	O
EXCITATION & HYPERACTIVITY							
IRRITABILITY & RESTLESSNESS	X	X	X	X	X	X	X
BELLIGERENCE							
ANXIETY	X O	X O	X O	X O	X O	X O	X O
EUPHORIA	O	O	O	O	O	O	O
DEPRESSION	X	X	X	X	X	X	X
HALLUCINATIONS	O			O			
PANIC	X	X	X	X	X	X	
IRRATIONAL BEHAVIOR							
CONFUSION	X	X	X	X	X	X	X
TALKATIVENESS							
RAMBLING SPEECH							
SLURRED SPEECH	O	O	O	O	O	O	
LAUGHTER							
TREMOR	X	X	X	X	X	X	X
STAGGERING							
IMPAIRMENT OF COORDINATION	O	O	O	O	O	O	O
DIZZINESS							
HYPERACTIVE REFLEXES							
DEPRESSED REFLEXES	O	O	O	O	O	O	O
INCREASED SWEATING	X	X	X	X	X	X	X
CONSTRICTED PUPILS	O	O	O	O	O	O	O
DILATED PUPILS	X	X	X	X	X	X	X
UNUSUALLY BRIGHT SHINY EYES							
INFLAMED EYES							
RUNNY EYES AND NOSE	X	X	X	X	X	X	X
LOSS OF APPETITE	O	O	O	O	O	O	O
INCREASED APPETITE							
INSOMNIA	X	X	X	X	X	X	X
DISTORTION OF SPACE OR TIME							
NAUSEA AND VOMITING	X	X	X	X	X	X	X
ABDOMINAL CRAMPS	X	X	X	X	X	X	X
DIARRHEA	X	X	X	X	X	X	X
CONSTIPATION	O	O	O	O	O	O	O
DANGERS OF ABUSE X							
PHYSICAL DEPENDENCE	X	X	X	X	X	X	X
PSYCHOLOGICAL DEPENDENCE	X	X	X	X	X	X	X
TOLERANCE	X	X	X	X	X	X	X
CONVULSIONS	X	X					
UNCONSCIOUSNESS	X	X		X	X	X	X
HEPATITIS	X	X	X	X	X	X	X
PSYCHOSIS							
DEATH FROM WITHDRAWAL							
DEATH FROM OVERDOSE	X	X	X	X	X	X	
POSSIBLE CHROMOSOME DAMAGE							
HOW TAKEN X							
ORALLY			X	X	X	X	X
INJECTION	X	X	X	X	X	X	
SNIFFED	X	X					
SMOKED		X					

SLANG TERMS

MORPHINE — M, dreamer, white stuff, hard stuff, morpho, unkie, Miss Emma, monkey, cube, morf, tab, emsel, hocus, morfie, melter

HEROIN — Snow, stuff, H, junk, big Harry, caballo, Doojee, boy, horse, white stuff, Harry, hairy, joy powder, salt, dope, Duige, hard stuff, schmeek, shit, skag, thing

CODEINE — Schoolboy

HYDROMORPHONE — Dilaudid®, Lords

MEPERIDINE — Demerol®, Isonipecaine®, Dolantol, Pethidine

METHADONE — Dolophine®, Dollies, dolls, amidone

EXEMPT PREPARATIONS — P.G., P.O., blue velvet (Paregoric with antihistamine), red water, bitter, licorice

TERMS AND SYMPTOMS OF DRUG ABUSE (Cont'd)

	COCAINE	MARIHUANA	AMPHETAMINES
HOW TAKEN (X)			
Smoked		X	
Sniffed	X		
Injection	X		X
Orally		X	X
DANGERS OF ABUSE (X)			
Possible Chromosome Damage			
Death From Overdose	X		X
Death From Withdrawal			
Psychosis			X
Hepatitis	X		X
Unconsciousness			
Convulsions	X		
Tolerance			X
Psychological Dependence	X	X	X
Physical Dependence			
SYMPTOMS OF WITHDRAWAL (X), SYMPTOMS OF ABUSE (O)			
Constipation			
Diarrhea			
Abdominal Cramps			
Nausea and Vomiting			
Distortion of Space or Time		O	
Insomnia	O		O
Increased Appetite		O	
Loss of Appetite	O		O
Runny Eyes and Nose			
Inflamed Eyes		O	
Unusually Bright Shiny Eyes			O
Dilated Pupils	O		O
Constricted Pupils			
Increased Sweating			O
Depressed Reflexes			
Hyperactive Reflexes	O		O
Dizziness			O
Impairment of Coordination		O	
Staggering			
Tremor	O		O
Laughter		O	
Slurred Speech			
Rambling Speech			
Talkativeness	O	O	O
Confusion			
Irrational Behavior			
Panic		O	O
Hallucinations	O	O	O
Depression		O	
Euphoria	O	O	O
Anxiety	O	O	O
Belligerence			
Irritability & Restlessness	O	O	O
Excitation & Hyperactivity	O	O	O
Drowsiness			

SLANG TERMS

COCAINE. The leaf, snow, C, cecil, coke, dynamite, flake, speedball (when mixed with Heroin), girl, happy dust, joy powder, white girl, gold dust, corine, bernies, Burese, gin, Bernice, Star dust, Carrie, Cholly, heaven dust, paradise

MARIHUANA. Smoke, straw, Texas tea, jive, pod, mutah, splim, Acapulco Gold, Bhang, boo, bush, butter flower, Ganja, weed, grass, pot, muggles, tea, has, hemp, griffo, Indian hay, loco weed, hay, herb, J, mu, giggles-smoke, love weed, Mary Warner, Mohasky, Mary Jane, joint, sticks, reefers, sativa, roach

AMPHETAMINES. Pep pills, bennies, wake-ups, eye-openers, lid poppers, co-pilots, truck drivers, peaches, roses, hearts, cart-

TERMS AND SYMPTOMS
OF DRUG ABUSE (Cont'd)

SYMPTOMS OF ABUSE O, SYMPTOMS OF WITHDRAWAL X — DANGERS OF ABUSE X

SLANG TERMS	Amphetamines (cont'd)	Methamphetamines	Other Stimulants	Barbituates	Other Depressants
HOW TAKEN					
ORALLY		X	X	X	X
INJECTION		X	X	X	X
SNIFFED					
SMOKED					
DANGERS OF ABUSE					
POSSIBLE CHROMOSOME DAMAGE					
DEATH FROM OVERDOSE		X	X	X	X
DEATH FROM WITHDRAWAL				X	X
PSYCHOSIS		X			
HEPATITIS		X		X	X
UNCONSCIOUSNESS				X	X
CONVULSIONS				X	X
TOLERANCE		X	X	X	X
PSYCHOLOGICAL DEPENDENCE		X	X	X	X
PHYSICAL DEPENDENCE				X	X
SYMPTOMS					
CONSTIPATION					
DIARRHEA					
ABDOMINAL CRAMPS					
NAUSEA AND VOMITING				X	X
DISTORTION OF SPACE OR TIME					
INSOMNIA				X	X
INCREASED APPETITE					
LOSS OF APPETITE		O			
RUNNY EYES AND NOSE					
INFLAMED EYES					
UNUSUALLY BRIGHT SHINY EYES		O			
DILATED PUPILS		O	O		
CONSTRICTED PUPILS				O	
INCREASED SWEATING		O		O	
DEPRESSED REFLEXES				O	
HYPERACTIVE REFLEXES		O	O		O
DIZZINESS					
IMPAIRMENT OF COORDINATION				O	O
STAGGERING				O	O
TREMOR		O	O	X	X
LAUGHTER				O	
SLURRED SPEECH				O	O
RAMBLING SPEECH					O
TALKATIVENESS		O	O		
CONFUSION				O	
IRRATIONAL BEHAVIOR				O	O
PANIC					
HALLUCINATIONS		O	O	X	X
DEPRESSION				O	O
EUPHORIA		O	O	O	O
ANXIETY					
BELLIGERENCE				X	X
IRRITABILITY & RESTLESSNESS		O	O	X	O X O
EXCITATION & HYPERACTIVITY		O	O		
DROWSINESS				O	O

Slang terms:

Amphetamines (cont'd): wheels, whites, coast to coast, LA turnabouts, browns, footballs, greenies, bombido, oranges, dexies, jolly-beans, A's, jellie babies, sweets, beans, uppers

METHAMPHETAMINES: Speed, meth, splash, crystal, bombita, Methedrine®, Doe

OTHER STIMULANTS: Pep pills, uppers

BARBITUATES: Yellows, yellow jackets, nimby, nimbles, reds, pinks, red birds, red devils, seggy, seccy, pink ladies, blues, blue birds, blue devils, blue heavens, red & blues, double trouble, too-ies, Christmas trees, phennies, barbs

OTHER DEPRESSANTS: Candy, goof-balls, sleeping pills, peanuts

TERMS AND SYMPTOMS OF DRUG ABUSE (Cont'd)

Attribute	LYSERGIC ACID DIETHLAMIDE (LSD)	STP	PHENCYCLIDINE (PCP)	PEYOTE	PSILOCYBIN	DIMETHLTRYPTAMINE (DMT)
HOW TAKEN X						
ORALLY	X	X	X	X	X	X
INJECTION		X	X	X		X
SNIFFED						
SMOKED						X
DANGERS OF ABUSE X						
PHYSICAL DEPENDENCE						
PSYCHOLOGICAL DEPENDENCE	X	X	X	X	X	X
TOLERANCE	X			X	X	X
CONVULSIONS						
UNCONSCIOUSNESS			X	X		
HEPATITIS		X	X	X		X
PSYCHOSIS	X					
DEATH FROM WITHDRAWAL						
DEATH FROM OVERDOSE						
POSSIBLE CHROMOSOME DAMAGE	X					
SYMPTOMS OF ABUSE O, SYMPTOMS OF WITHDRAWAL X						
DROWSINESS			O			
EXCITATION & HYPERACTIVITY	O		O	O	O	O
IRRITABILITY & RESTLESSNESS			O		O	
BELLIGERENCE						
ANXIETY	O		O	O	O	O
EUPHORIA	O	O			O	O
DEPRESSION	O	O			O	O
HALLUCINATIONS	O	O		O	O	O
PANIC			O			
IRRATIONAL BEHAVIOR	O	O			O	O
CONFUSION			O			
TALKATIVENESS	O	O		O	O	O
RAMBLING SPEECH						
SLURRED SPEECH						
LAUGHTER			O			
TREMOR	O	O				
STAGGERING						
IMPAIRMENT OF COORDINATION			O			
DIZZINESS			O			
HYPERACTIVE REFLEXES						
DEPRESSED REFLEXES						
INCREASED SWEATING	O				O	O
CONSTRICTED PUPILS						
DILATED PUPILS	O	O		O	O	O
UNUSUALLY BRIGHT SHINY EYES						
INFLAMED EYES						
RUNNY EYES AND NOSE						
LOSS OF APPETITE						
INCREASED APPETITE						
INSOMNIA						
DISTORTION OF SPACE OR TIME	O	O			O	O
NAUSEA AND VOMITING				O		
ABDOMINAL CRAMPS						
DIARRHEA						
CONSTIPATION						

SLANG TERMS

- **LYSERGIC ACID DIETHLAMIDE (LSD):** Acid, cubes, pearly gates, heavenly blue, royal blue, wedding bells, sugar, Big D, Blue Acid, the Chief, the Hawk, Zen, instant Zen, 25, sugar lump
- **STP:** Serenity, tranquility, peace, DOM, syndicate acid
- **PHENCYCLIDINE (PCP):** PCP, peace pill, synthetic marihuana
- **PEYOTE:** Mescal button, mescal beans, hikori, hikuli, huatari, seni, wokowi, cactus, the button, tops, a moon, half moon, P, the bad seed, Big Chief, Mesc.
- **PSILOCYBIN:** Sacred mushrooms, mushrooms
- **DIMETHLTRYPTAMINE (DMT):** DMT; 45 minute psychosis, business-man's special.

viduals under eighteen years of age. However, in the narrow legal sense before one is considered a delinquent, he must also be caught, have an accuser, and appear in court.[21] The number of delinquents in the United States, as in all industrial nations is on the increase. How much of the increase is actual and how much is due to better police detection is debatable. Jersild[22] states that almost all adolescent boys and a large number of adolescent girls have one time or another committed an act which could be interpreted as delinquent. Estimates of the sex ratio of juvenile delinquency vary from four to one to ten to one; not only do males far outnumber females but the type of act is different. Boys engage in more active forms of delinquency, such as fighting or stealing, while girls are more prone toward passive acts, such as sexual misbehavior, truancy, and incorrigibility. If the present trend continues, according to Kvaraceus, it is likely that one boy in five will have a delinquency record by the time he reaches draft age.[23]

Studies of delinquents tend to show that they are more likely to dislike school, have failed subjects or repeated grades, come from the lower socioeconomic class, feel alienated from society, have below-average intelligence, are behavior problems at home and school, are socially unacceptable and ineffective, and are restless, impulsive, aggressive, destructive, hostile, stubborn, quarrelsome, suspicious, and suggestible. However, most studies have been done on a post hoc basis. Many children who exhibit these symptoms do not become delinquent while some delinquents exhibit few, if any, of them.

Havighurst,[24] *et al.*, lists delinquency in three categories: (1) delinquency due to severe personality disturbance, (2) delinquency that is a normal part of adolescent development, and (3) delinquency that originates in maladjustments in the social structure. They believe that the third category is the most common

---

[21]A. T. Jersild, *The Psychology of Adolescence* (New York, MacMillan Company, 1963).

[22]*Ibid.*, p. 308.

[23]*Ibid.*, p. 309.

[24]R. J. Havighurst, P. H. Bowman, G. P. Liddle, V. B. Matthews, and J. V. Pierce, *Growing Up in River City* (New York, John Wiley & Sons, Inc., 1962).

and includes such things as cultural conflicts, status discontent and lack of legitimate opportunities. Too much attention has been focused on what the delinquent did rather than upon the more productive question of, why did he do it?

The results of traditional psychotherapy, group therapy, and other rehabilitative measures on curbing criminal and delinquent behavior have been discouraging. Delinquents are frequently hostile toward those who are trying to help them and many individuals who are supposed to be trying to help the delinquent are actually hostile toward him.

Havighurst and Neugarten report the following summary of a U.S. Congressional Committee which studied various programs dealing with delinquency and the theories of causation of delinquency:

Programs specifically established to prevent delinquency by treatment of incipient offenders vary widely in plan and underlying theory of causation and cure. Among the favored assumptions as to what will help are the following:

Having an adult friend or sponsor who will stick to the delinquency-prone boy or girl through thick and thin and secure needed services in his behalf will render the child less likely to become delinquent.

Delinquency-prone children can be identified by teachers at an early age (the schools know all the children and their ways, it is said) and referred for treatment to either a particular agency set up for the purpose or to the ongoing service agencies.

Delinquency results largely from disturbances in the parent-child relationship; hence, these disturbances should be recognized by all services (health, schools, day nurseries, police, etc.) that have contact with the families, and prophylactic measures should be taken.

Delinquency frequently results from or is a sign of emotional disturbance, and this disorder can be remedied by individual or group therapy.

Delinquency results largely from a breakdown in the cohesiveness of neighborhoods and in the controls exercised by parents and neighbors. A reduction in delinquency can be secured by restoring these lost or diminished social attributes and functions.

The chief source of delinquent conduct and the chief bearers of the delinquent tradition in slum areas are certain of the established street-corner clubs or gangs. Direct work with these groups is required to carry them fairly peacefully through the tumultuous years of adolescence, to teach them democratic ways of conducting their organization, and—perhaps—to break the chain of transimssion of delinquent customs.

The usual social and mental health services of a community are not effective in delinquency prevention because they do not operate in concert and are inadequately staffed, quantitatively and qualitatively.

Delinquency can be reduced by assuring that all intellectually capable children, even though they are handicapped by language and culturally impoverished homes, should learn to read well and acquire other basic intellectual skills.

Lack of opportunity for paid work is an important factor in juvenile delinquency, partly because denial of a chance to earn money puts an adolescent in a childlike status and does not permit him to progress smoothly toward adulthood (United States, 86th Congress, p. 27).[25]

Student personnel workers are in key positions to identify or help to identify the antisocial and delinquent student. They also are in the unique position to help meet the student's needs through counseling, group counseling, referrals, liaison with home and community agencies, consulting with other professionals both in and out of the school, and the manipulation of certain environmental variables to enable the student to profit more from his school experiences.

Ahlstrom and Havighurst[26] studied delinquent high school boys and made a number of suggestions in working with this problem. They suggested hiring more male teachers who possess flexibility, endless patience, and a determination to help the delinquent make a better adjustment to life. Employers who offer jobs to the delinquent are important, but man-boy relationship with the employer is as important as the job skills learned. They suggested having counselors available in the early grades for preventive counseling and also recommended more tolerance of

[25]R. J. Havighurst and B. L. Neugarten, *Society and Education* (Boston, Allyn & Bacon, Inc., 1962), p. 366.

[26]W. M. Ahlstrom and R. J. Havighurst, *Four Hundred Losers* (San Francisco, Jossey-Bass, Inc., Publishers, 1971).

the school and society for delinquent behavior which is part of normal adolescent development.

The Socially and Culturally Disadvantaged Group

The term socially or culturally disadvantaged or deprived is a euphemism for what was once called poor people. Although poor people have been around at least as far back as the Biblical period, they have only recently been "rediscovered" and renamed. A considerable amount of attention, some sparked by altruistic motives, is currently being given this group. This segment of society has become too large, too vociferous, and too threatening to be ignored. Consequently, many individuals, not the least of whom are educators, have become concerned about this group.

Some of the characteristics of this group typically include: minority ethnic origins, transient families, large families, disorganized families, low income, poor education, low-paying jobs, poor neighborhood, inadequate schools, inadequate public facilities, high divorce rate, and ineffective police protection. Hollis and Hollis in describing them state:

1. Large families with relatives residing with the family unit in inadequate living space and poor sanitary conditions.
2. Unemployment, dependence on welfare, and inadequate education and skills to compete for gainful employment contribute to perpetuating the prevailing conditions of the subpar living.
3. Nonmarital sexual relations, illegitimate children, alcoholism, dope addiction, and violence are marked results of the environment.[27]

In summary form, Reissman characterizes this group as patriarchal (except in certain Negro subcultures) and traditional; is somewhat religious and superstitious; reads ineffectively, is poorly informed in many areas; has rigid opinions; feels alienated; is not individualistic, introspective, self-oriented, or concerned with self-expression; blames the world for his problems; prefers secure jobs; is anticommunist; likes strong leaders; is prejudiced and intolerant; is interested in family and personal comfort; likes

[27]J. W. Hollis and Lucile U. Hollis, *Personalizing Information Processes: Educational, Occupational, and Personal-Social* (Toronto, Ontario, Macmillan Company, 1969), p. 337.

excitement; is pragmatic and anti-intellectual; admires strength and endurance; and emphasizes masculinity.[28]

Although the above descriptions are probably accurate in describing the groups, the student personnel worker should remember that it may or may not appropriately describe any one individual. Also, many students not considered disadvantaged will possess a number of these characteristics.

We may imply from these group descriptions a number of likely traits of students from this type of background. Among these are: low aspiration level, overly dependent or independent, aggressive, practically and vocationally oriented, lower measured I.Q., substandard reading, negative toward school and teachers, undernourished, antisocial, despairing, frustrated, and with low self-esteem.

Working with children like these may be considered a highly challenging or a hopeless task. Conant warned in 1961 that society's failure to provide for this type of student was building up social dynamite.[29] Only after the dynamite began to explode did society become aroused enough to tackle the problem. Commissioner of Health, Education, and Welfare Howe made two salient points in his report to the president. First, minority group children have a serious educational deficiency when they enter school and second, this deficiency increases throughout the child's school career.[30]

It was also determined that: serious cultural deprivation restricted the child's ability to label, discriminate, and generalize; I.Q. tests tend to discriminate against the deprived child; self-esteem is important if the child is to succeed; deprived children have experienced little verbal stimulation and reinforcement at home; deprived children experience more emotional episodes; schools are operated by middle-class attitudes; deprived children perceive school as a threatening place; many teachers neither understand nor accept lower-class attitudes and values; many

[28]F. Reissman, *The Culturally Deprived Child* (New York, Harper & Row, Publishers, Inc., 1962).

[29]J. B. Conant, *Slums and Suburbs* (New York, McGraw-Hill Book Company, 1961).

[30]H. Howe, *Equality of Education Opportunity*, Congressional Report, 1966.

teachers refuse to teach in a lower class neighborhood; few universities adequately prepare teachers of the disadvantaged; teaching in poverty areas should be made more attractive; and discipline is a frustrating experience for many teachers.[31]

If the student personnel worker is to be effective in helping the culturally deprived student, he should encourage remedial instruction in the school, especially in reading. Schools must be made a safe place, both physically and psychologically. Pupil personnel services are essential but they cannot compensate for inadequate instruction.

It has been suggested by Reismann and others that the counselor must be more directive in his approach to lower-class students who have had less experience in talking through their problems and tend to be more action-oriented.[32] Also, they may find it much more difficult to request help so, at times, it may be necessary to seek out these students rather than waiting for them to find the counselor. The counselor must guard against letting his own middle-class value system interfere with his relationships with disadvantaged students.

The School Dropout

The school dropout is usually defined as one who terminates his formal education before graduating from high school. Dropping out of school is a process rather than an event and is as old as school itself, but only in recent years has it been considered a problem and a stigma. This change of attitude results from the high rate of unemployment among dropouts, the decreased earning power of dropouts, society's equating personal worth and assignment of status in proportion to formal education, the large-scale migration from rural to urban areas, the high rate of crime and juvenile delinquency, the increase in number of persons on welfare, the reduction of unskilled jobs through automation and industrial technology, and the high level of social unrest among youth of this country.

[31] W. F. White, *Psychosocial Principles Applied to Classroom Teaching* (New York, McGraw-Hill Book Company, 1969).

[32] *Op. cit.*

If dropping out of school carries such harsh penalties and staying in seems so profitable, why do students drop out? There is no single cause and, although characteristics which correlate highly with the dropout have been identified, pinpointing the real reasons for any individual case may be difficult. Some of the common traits of the dropout are: average or below average intelligence, sixteen years of age, a boy, an academic under-achiever, below grade level in reading, in lowest quarter of his class, overage in grade placement, has repeated a grade in school, has been in trouble for law violations, does not engage in extracurricular activities, has poor attendance record, comes from a transient family, feels rejected by the school, rejects school, is insecure and hostile, receives parental insistence for grades beyond his capacity to earn, is not respected by teachers, has parents or siblings who are school dropouts, comes from broken or "weak home," is resentful of authority, demands immediate gratification, sees curricula as irrelevant, has best friends who do not attend school, is poorly adjusted, is a behavior problem, and feels frustrated in school. The inherent danger in ascribing group characteristics to any one individual is that, when we identify a person who fits our description, there is always the probability that the self-fulfilling prophesy might begin to operate. However, if we are to adequately cope with a problem, we must begin to identify it.

The student may have begun the process of dropping out of school in the first grade and may have dropped out psychologically years before he actually stopped coming to school. As educators, we tend to feel threatened when students drop out of school. Although it sounds sacrilegious for an educator to say so, some individuals may be better off if they drop out. This means, not that we should cease being concerned about dropouts, but that we should make changes in our schools to make them more profitable and palatable to all our students. Merely increasing the compulsory attendance age or telling students how much more money they will earn if they stay in school are ineffective solutions. Conant states:

. . . guidance officers, especially in the large cities, ought to be given the responsibility for following the post-high school careers of youth from the time they leave school until they are twenty-one years of age. Since compulsory attendance usually ends at age sixteen, this means responsibility for the guidance of youth ages sixteen to twenty-one who are out of school and either employed or unemployed.[33]

When Wrenn discussed the problem of dropouts he stated:

School administrators and school counselors up and down the line must move to see: (1) that students capable of high school graduation and beyond are identified early and individually motivated to continue to their optimum educational level; (2) that students easily discouraged in academic work are given as meaningful an educational experience as possible; (3) that potential dropouts for whatever reason in both elementary schools and high schools are prepared for vocational entrance; (4) that continuation education is provided for early school leavers who discover through experience their need for further part-time or full-time school work.[34]

The department of guidance services in the State of Illinois, when discussing the problem of dropout prevention, recommended the identification of the potential dropout and then the implementation of a remedial and preventative program. Included in the proposed program were: individual testing, individual reading instruction, special reading instruction, curriculum modification, group guidance activities, home visitation, more individual conferences, big brother/big sister program, increased parent involvement in the school, business and industry support of the program, job placement, ungraded primary, and a federally subsidized program for dropout-prone and culturally deprived students.[35]

In conclusion, if the dropout problem is to be resolved, all school personnel must strive toward earlier identification and remediation of all types of problems faced by any of its students. Schools must be made more pleasant by: treating all students with respect, providing individual attention as needed, maximizing student success, becoming more flexible in their demands,

[33]J. B. Conant, *op. cit.*, p. 41.
[34]C. G. Wrenn, *The Counselor in a Changing World*, Washington, D.C., American Personnel and Guidance Association, 1962, p. 23.
[35]Department of Guidance Services, *Guidance Services for Illinois Schools*, Department of Guidance Services (Springfield, Illinois, 1966).

improving instructional techniques, providing "specialists" in areas where needed, and developing democratic atmospheres.

The Slow Learner

The slow learner is usually considered to be a student with an I.Q. between 75 and 90 and this group generally constitutes from 15 to 20 percent of the students in the typical classroom. Note that we are not discussing the brain-injured or the retarded student who should probably be in a special classroom with a teacher who has received specific training in how to work most effectively wtih this type of student. Our attention here will be focused on the slower learning 20 percent found in regular classrooms.

The mental age of the slow learner lags behind his chronological age. Research indicates that a mental age of six years and five months is required to learn to read. A child, for example, whose I.Q. is 80 will be past the chronological age of eight years before he reaches the mental age considered necessary for reading and therefore, is likely in the third grade before he is mentally mature enough to read. He may have been given up on by his parents and teachers and suffered irreparable psychological damage to himself, because his teachers and parents did not recognize the simple fact that he is a slow learner. Although reading problems seems to be the outstanding characteristic of the slow learner, there are a number of other characteristics which tend to differentiate them as a group from other students. Karnes lists the following traits: inferior physical size, poor motor coordination, substandard homes, inadequate medical attention, poor manual skills as in reading and arithmetic, mentally immature, poor memory, below-average incidental learning, poor abstract reasoning, poor response to long-range goals and delayed evaluation of their work, poor ability to follow instructions, inadequate self-evaluation, deficiency in creativity, difficulty in transferring learnings, markedly retarded in academic areas, poor adjustment, and poor attendance.[36]

[36]M. B. Karnes, "Teaching the Slow Learner," in E. P. Torrance and R. D. Strom, eds., *Mental Health and Achievement* (New York, John Wiley & Sons, Inc., 1965), pp. 327-337.

The slow learner should not be confused with subcultural retardates, the emotionally disturbed, pseudoretardates, or brain-damaged children. It is frequently difficult to distinguish among these groups and sophisticated medical and/or psychological evaluations beyond the teacher's competency may be required. However, since the etiology and treatment may vary significantly, it is essential that an adequate classification be made of these groups.

Merely grouping students by level of academic achievement is an insufficient procedure to provide for the needs of any group. The Research Division of the National Education Association surveyed the results of studies conducted over the past four decades on the effectiveness of ability grouping. They concluded that:

1. Ability grouping, *per se*, has yet to prove itself as an administrative device to meet both effectively and efficiently the individual needs of all pupils in most areas of educational concern. Teachers, however, tend to prefer ability grouping.
2. More and better research studies which account for or control a larger number of the variables involved are needed.
3. Objectives, materials, curriculum, and teaching methods should also change to fit each of the homogeneous groups at different ability levels.[37]

The most effective practices to be followed in teaching the slow learner listed by Longworthy were:

1. Using substantially more praise than reproof.
2. Extensive use of audio-visual aids.
3. Using student's experiences to stimulate interest.
4. Giving students many chances to apply what they learn.
5. Small-group instruction within the class.
6. Using projects in which students evidence interest.
7. Encouraging cooperation within the class.
8. Keeping students carefully apprised of their progress.
9. Emphasizing the vocational values in materials studied.
10. Emphasizing the social value of the materials studied.
11. Use of school and/or community resource people.
12. Individual work-study contracts.

[37]NEA Research Bulletin, *Ability Grouping*, National Education Association, 46: 75-76 (1968).

13. Doing much planning of the classwork with students.
14. Encouraging competition with the class.[38]

A major problem in providing for the slow learner may be his parents who may resent their child being placed in any curriculum other than college preparatory. The concept of a status hierarchy among certain curricula and courses finds support in a study by Moses and Delaney. They found that teachers perceive a definite hierarchy among school positions and among teachers of various subjects. When their data were further analyzed according to age, sex, training, experience, and teaching majors, they found substantial correlations. Although it is unfortunate that we live in such a status conscious society, if such a condition does actually exist in our schools, recognition is the first step toward change.[39] The faith that some parents put in the value of formal education and the pressure they may apply to their children to succeed in school is sometimes frightening. The fallacy that one must go to college in order to succeed and the Horatio Alger myth that anyone can succeed at anything if he tries hard enough are still prevalent in our society and are causing problems for many students, especially the slow learner.

The Gifted Student

The gifted student is usually defined as having an I.Q. of 120 or above. Some investigators use 140 or higher when identifying gifted students. This variation in definition tends to confuse the reader when the gifted is being discussed. Furthermore, the term gifted has been expanded by some to include other kinds of giftedness, such as, creative, social, mechanical, and leadership.

For our purposes we will restrict our discussion of giftedness to mean the intellectually gifted, i.e. a minimum I.Q. of 120. This group is usually identified via intelligence testing, however, observation by school personnel, student products, and cumulative records may and should be used. The joint NEA-APGA con-

[38]B. S. Longworthy, ed., *The Slow Learner in Secondary Schools* (Trenton, New Jersey Secondary Teachers Association, 1961).

[39]H. A. Moses and D. J. Delaney, "Status of School Personnel," *SPATE Journal,* 9:41-46 (1971).

ference on the academically talented student listed the following characteristics as indications of academic talent: early physical and mental development; curiosity, alertness, observance, interest in many things, and a desire to be informed; interest in books, especially reference books—dictionaries, encyclopedias, atlases—and biographies; pursuit of an interest over a long period of time and with intense concentration; easy and rapid learning; reading, computing, and communicating with ease; enjoyment of abstractions—generalization, making analogies, handling complexities, and using flexible, divergent approaches; and qualities of leadership and responsibility. It should be recognized that all gifted students will not exhibit all of the above characteristics or will exhibit them to varying degrees.[40]

Giftedness and creativity may be found in the same student but the traits are not synonymous and may not even occur together. Although creativity is probably an inherent trait of everyone; parents, peers, and schools seem to extinguish, or at least stifle, this trait in most individuals quite early in life. Student personnel workers may also contribute to the squelching of creativity by failure to recognize, accept, and nurture this characteristic.

Peters and Farwell discuss the prerequisites of what they term the superior student. Among them are native ability, love of surprise learning, ability to concentrate and generalize, spontaneity, originality, self-discipline, favorable environment, and encouragement from others. They must be accorded the right to fail without being made to feel guilty.[41]

A few years ago the stereotype of the gifted student was that he appeared something of an oddity, small in physical size, weak, prone to illnesses, maladjusted, etc. Studies by persons like Terman and Oden,[42] and Gallagher[43] have exposed this as a myth.

[40]Elizabeth M. Drews, ed., *Guidance for the Academically Talented Student* (National Education Association and American Personnel and Guidance Association, Washington, D.C., 1961).

[41]H. J. Peters and G. F. Farwell, *Guidance: A Developmental Approach* (Chicago, Rand McNally, 1967).

[42]L. M. Terman and Melita Oden, "The Standard Studies of the Gifted," in P. Witty, ed., *The Gifted Child* (Boston, D. C. Heath & Company, 1951).

[43]J. J. Gallagher, *Teaching the Gifted Child* (Englewood Cliffs, New Jersey: Allyn & Bacon, Inc., 1964).

Although the gifted child tends to have many advantages over the average, he does have some problems caused by his superior talents. His desire for independence may cause him trouble at home and at school. His superior intellect may be perceived as a threat by his teacher. He has greater latitude in making educational and occupational choices, many of which have the potential to raise his socioeconomic level above that of his parents; this may cause conflict in his family, he may also be hampered in his choices by not having an appropriate adult model in the home.

A number of methods of acceleration have been proposed to help the gifted child. Among these are early admission to school, ungraded classes, skipping grades, taking extra classes above grade level, enrolling in classes for college credit while in high school, early admission to college, and honors programs. Various types of enrichment programs and ability grouping has been tried at all levels. Although no consensus exists, it is probably better if the gifted child is kept with his age mates and provided an enriched school program.

The student personnel worker must make a conscientious effort to insure that all gifted students are identified. He must enlist the aid of all the schools' personnel and systematically guard against biases which may cause some students of superior ability to be overlooked. Once these individuals are identified, he should locate resources, work with teachers and parents and with the student, individually and in groups, to help him realize and actualize his potential.

Counseling Girls

The life expectancy of a baby girl born in 1900 was 48 years, in 1967 it was 74 years.[44] Not only are women living longer, they are marrying earlier and bearing their last child sooner, usually around the age of 30. This means that the typical woman will have almost forty years of life ahead of her after her children enter school. Since most women continue to marry and bear children, they will still need training to provide love and nurture to

[44]The following is based upon H. A. Moses, "Challenges in Counseling Women," *IGPA Quarterly*, 24:39-41, (1967).

their offspring. However, this training is insufficient for women if they are to adequately fulfill the many roles that await them. Women spend more time outside than inside the child-bearing period. Since such a large portion of their lives is spent at study and work, a great deal of time, energy, thought, and careful planning is warranted in mapping out these important aspects of women's lives.

Nearly two out of every five workers are women and about 60 percent of them are married. Recently, there has been a tremendous increase in the number of women in the labor force, a trend which is expected to continue. It is predicted that nine out of ten of today's girls will work at some time during their lives. In 1969 there were 30.5 million gainfully employed women sixteen years of age or over and it is estimated that this number will increase to 36 million by 1980. About half of all women between eighteen and sixty-five years of age are in the labor force. Therefore, women should consider and prepare for the type of work in which they are interested and possess the required aptitude. This means that they may have to transcend the traditional career possibilities open to women.

Why has there been such an increase in the number and percent of working women? There are many reasons for this phenomenon but the basic reason in most cases is economic necessity. Among the many reasons for economic necessity are:

1. A number of girls marry men who are still in college and work to support them until they graduate and sometimes beyond this point until the husband becomes established in his career.
2. Some women (19%), become widows, divorcees, or are separated and are forced to go to work.
3. About 22 percent of the women in the labor force are not married and many of these must work to support themselves.
4. Some students need to work part time to enable them to stay in school.
5. The increasing cost of living and the escalation of living standards may require an extra wage earner in the family.

Additional reasons why women work other than economic necessity are:

1. Some women are childless and work to occupy their time.
2. Labor-saving devices in the home result in household tasks requiring less of the housewife's time and energy.
3. Some women find housework boring and uninteresting and would rather work outside the home and hire someone to help them with their housework.
4. Some women work to feel they are fulfilling themselves and to derive a sense of accomplishment.
5. Some women like the structure which a job provides for their lives.
6. Some women receive pressure from their husbands to bring home a paycheck.
7. Some women in urban centers may not participate in community life and need something to do.

The counseling of girls and women has been called a specialized type of counseling. Professionally trained counselors should be available for all females at all levels of their education. The school dropout (about one-fifth of the women discontinue their education before graduating from high school), the woman entering, reentering or changing jobs within the labor market, the woman who wishes to utilize her leisure time for preparation or advancement within an occupation, and the woman who needs assistance to prevent her skills from becoming obsolete during temporary periods of absence from the labor force, all need and have the right to the services of a professionally trained counselor. Counseling is desirable to help women avoid the common stereotypes and ideas that seem to almost predetermine their lives. Bridging the gap between the type of education and training which women receive and the kind they need is a crucial problem for American educators.

Girls no longer have to choose between marriage or a career. Actually, being a good housewife and mother frequently involves activities outside the home so the distinction is not as clear-cut as it sometimes appears. The typical woman's career pattern consists of working a few years after completion of her formal education until she marries. She may continue working until her first child is born and then drop out of the labor force until her youngest child is in school. At this point she finds herself with time on her hands and most of her life still ahead of her. It is at this point that continuing educational opportunities may be crucial. Education should no longer be considered as the exclusive domain of the young. Women's talents should no longer be necessarily channeled into the narrow and traditional areas of nursing, teaching, social service, and clerical work. Career opportunities for women are more challenging and the range of alternatives is larger and continuously expanding; women should be made aware of these realities.

Institutions of higher learning can help to reduce the obstacles facing women who want to continue their education by becoming more flexible in such areas as: admission policies, academic prerequisites, residence requirements, scheduling, proficiency testing, part-time study, graduation requirements, and transfer of credits. Institutions could work out arrangements whereby credit could be given for life experiences, seminars, correspondence study, and short-term courses. Colleges could use to better advantage such things as taped lectures, programmed learning, refresher courses, televised courses, and independent study. They should offer study habit courses, create special programs when needed, enlarge and improve their extension divisions, provide counseling and guidance services for older women, and provide educational programs of which women can take advantage while confined to the home.

We need additional research on the effects of socioeconomic level, ethnic background, race, and religion on the motivation, aspiration, and learning of women. Sex differences should be noted in research, overlooking this variable may result in obscuring significant differences. Women from deprived groups, bright girls who do not go on to college, and physically handicapped women all contribute to our annual waste of manpower or womanpower. We may need special programs to correct this problem, not only for the benefit of the women concerned but for the betterment of the nation.

Obstacles Facing Women in the Choice and Preparation of a Career

Career choices of girls frequently are not taken seriously by the girl, her parents, her teachers, her peers, and we are sorry to state, her counselor.[45] Lee, *et al.*,[46] states that ". . . the high school senior girls in this study were not well informed about the probable nature and extent of their future vocational participation." The ideal time for career exploration and planning coincides with the time at which sex role identification occurs which may pose a threat to the feminine image the girl wishes to project. Girls are taught not to compete with boys; the games taught to and the toys purchased for girls indicate the way we want them to develop vocationally. Higher education is designed for men, and women are discriminated against in many fields of study, not only in initial selection but in the granting of fellowships, assistantships, scholarships, and research grants. Premature planning and curriculum restrictions in high school may narrow choices in college and preclude entry into certain occupations.

Most girls are marriage-oriented and consider many training periods too expensive in terms of time, energy, and money. They may hesitate to borrow money for college, and who can argue that a debt does anything to help a woman in the marriage market? There seems to be a lack of understanding of how home and outside responsibilities can be integrated. We have to get the point across that a husband and wife can and should compete with the environment and not with each other.

Our cultural attitude that girls should marry while they are young has contributed to the dual role dilemma faced by women. Some countereffects which encourage girls to stay in school are compulsory school attendance laws, child labor laws, increasing family income, greater educational opportunities, and increasing educational requirements for jobs.

What Specifically Can the Counselor Do?

Let us emphasize that in our democratic society all people, including girls, have the right to decide how they will spend their

---

[45]C. G. Wrenn, *op. cit.*

[46]S. L. Lee, *et al.*, *High School Girls and the World of Work: Occupational Knowledge, Attitudes, and Plans* (Columbus, The Ohio State University, 1971), p. 2.

lives. A career of homemaking is an honorable choice and essential to the welfare of the nation; the counselor has no right to put pressure on a girl to seek a career outside the home. However, he does have the obligation to inform her of the additional opportunities which are open to her. The counselor should challenge the rigid, lockstep system of our schools which is found at all educational levels and which narrows and restricts the choices of all our students.

The counselor can initiate group discussion and group counseling in order to break down some of the archaic traditions of what is men's work and what is women's work. This can result in greater opportunities for both sexes by reducing peer pressure and lessening the need for peer approval which assumes such magnitude at the same period that occupational exploration is so important.

The counselor should provide comprehensive, reliable, and up-to-date educational and occupational information to his students. He may need to do some counseling with parents, especially with parents of daughters, who sometimes see little need to be concerned about the education of their daughter. Girls need to realize that they do not have to choose between marriage and a career, that with proper planning they may have both, even if this does mean a discontinuity in the career, referred to as the "split-level" work career. Girls need to be informed of how to keep up-to-date during their temporary absence from the labor force by utilizing such methods as: belonging to professional organizations; attending conventions, lectures, and workshops; taking courses in their areas of interest; doing volunteer work where they can practice their skills; and working at part-time jobs.

Directories of counseling facilities should be available so that a woman can obtain help from professionally trained counselors not only during her academic career but at any other period when it is needed. Assistance with such matters as the use of leisure, solution of marital conflicts, acquisition or retention of job skills, child-rearing problems, and sources of financial aid for continuing education are but a few of the areas in which professional counseling can make a contribution.

Discussion

As indicated previously, there is an inherent danger in separating individuals into groups. Although it was done here for the purposes of discussion, the reader may get the erroneous idea that these persons are much more different than similar to other individuals. Human beings, regardless of the labels we pin on them or how much we emphasize their differences, are still basically the same. They all tend to have similar fears, frustrations, needs, motives, aspirations, and desires.

In any group of students we find a number who are not achieving at the level of their capabilities or of our expectations, a common occurrence among the groups just discussed. Taylor summarizes a number of characteristics or personality traits of lower achievers. Among these are free-floating anxiety, negative self-value, hostility toward authority, negative interpersonal relations, high independence-dependence conflict, unrealistic goal orientation, and a social rather than an academic orientation.[47] It is definitely within the domain of student personnel workers to assist students in the resolution of these kinds of problems. Schools have a threefold obligation in the field of mental hygiene to (1) prevent conditions that contribute to poor mental health, (2) encourage practices which foster mental health, and (3) provide remedial services to students who need them.

In considering the mental health of students, we must remember that all behavior is caused, that the human personality is complex, that problems seldom occur in isolation, that it usually requires considerable time to change attitudes and behavior, and that the way in which the individual perceives the situation is the crucial aspect. Therefore, we should cease searching for simple cause-effect relationships to complex problems. No two individuals are identical in heredity or environment, and even those most similar may react in quite different ways to the same stimuli. One individual reared in an adverse environment may lead a highly constructive life, while another may be overwhelmed by forces he perceives as beyond his control, hence, the confusion in trying to identify the characteristics of any

[47]R. G. Taylor, "Personality Traits and Discrepant Achievement: A Review," *Journal of Counseling Psychology,* 11:76-82 (1964).

subgroup in school. Whether the individual student becomes an academic achiever, a dropout, a neurotic, a psychotic, a delinquent, or a sociopath depends in large measure upon how he perceives himself and his environment. Therefore, if we want students to see themselves as worthwhile, capable, independent, and responsible, we must treat them as such.

In considering the tremendous problems faced by some students it is very easy for the teacher or personnel worker to develop a defeatist attitude. This is especially true with the students who most desperately need our help. "What can I as one person do?" and, "Shouldn't one be realistic?" are frequently posed questions. The answer to the first is that we will never know unless we try and, even though the odds are against us, what alternative do we have? Reality, a nebulous, constantly changing term, is a concept that we should not use to excuse ourselves from accepting our just responsibilities. If we do not exhibit confidence and optimism, we cannot expect our students to develop confidence in themselves, probably the most important thing we can help them to do.

In short, schools must begin to aggressively practice those democratic ideals which they have preached for so long. Some of these are: a belief and demonstrated respect for all individuals; more concern for the physiological needs of students, such as, sleep, food, elimination, and physical activity; more equitable standards of discipline; more flexible curricula to allow all students to experience success; a change in attitude and practice of school personnel to eliminate the sense of frustration and despair among students; the more effective utilization of community facilities and resources; more effective assignment and use of personnel with specialized training; and real student involvement in the accomplishment of these objectives. Schools must begin to pay more attention to the human relations aspect of the total school environment. All school activities should establish this as a major criterion in judging their desirability and effectiveness.

Too many educators have a defensive attitude toward the community they seek to serve. This is unfortunate because the American people have received more than a just return on the size of their investment in public education. This implies, not that schools are doing an exceptionally good job and have little room for improvement, but that for the resources at their disposal, they have done a creditable job.

The defensive attitude of educators interferes with the optimal utilization of a number of nonschool professionals and agencies. The psychiatrist, social worker, physician, clergyman, dentist, law-enforcement officer, etc. are examples of professionals who are generally willing to contribute time and effort to the enhancement of education. Too often these people are called upon only in times of crises; therefore, their talents are only partially used. The United States Employment Service, the Division of Vocational Rehabilitation, Children and Family Services, and numerous agencies designed to deal with specific areas are usually eager to get involved with the schools. The barriers which exist between these agencies and the schools should be broken down and it is the school which should take the initiative.

Many factors have been identified as causing or contributing to the plight that American education finds itself in today. However, merely pinpointing the probable causes, even though they may reside largely outside the domain of the school's sphere of authority, does not absolve educators from corrective responsibility.

Perhaps the following paragraphs written many years ago are still applicable.

I have taught in high school for ten years.
During that time I have given assignments,
among others, to a murderer, an evangelist,
a pugilist, a thief, and an imbecile.

The murderer was a quiet boy who sat on the
front seat and regarded me with pale blue eyes;
the evangelist, easily the most popular boy in
the school, had the lead in the junior play;
the pugilist lounged by the window and let
loose at intervals a raucous laugh that
startled even the geraniums; the thief was a

gay-hearted Lothario with a song on his lips;
and the imbecile a soft-eyed little animal
seeking the shadows.

The murderer awaits death in the state
penitentiary; the evangelist has lain a year
now in the village churchyard; the pugilist
lost an eye in a brawl in Hong Kong; the thief,
by standing on tiptoe, can see the windows of
my room from the county jail; and the once
gentle-eyed moron beats his head against a
padded wall in the state asylum.

All of these pupils once sat in my room, sat
and looked at me gravely across worn brown desks.
I must have been a great help to these pupils—
I taught them the rhyming scheme of the Elizabethan
sonnet and how to diagram a complex sentence.[48]

[48]From "I Taught Them All," *Clearing House* (November, 1937).

SUMMARY

Schools must be made pleasant, enjoyable places of learning
and living for students. Locating scapegoats, making excuses, and
projecting the blame are unacceptable solutions. Educational
problems are at a critical stage and, not only is the future of our
educational system dependent upon a workable solution, our
entire society as we know and envision it will fail or succeed in
direct proportion to the adequacy of our solutions.

A number of groups of students have been shortchanged in
our schools. We can no longer afford to neglect any group of
students and our progress as a nation, perhaps even our survival,
will be determined by the manner in which we resolve the tremendous problems facing our schools.

CHAPTER X

WORKING WITH PARENTS AND COMMUNITY RESOURCES

ROBERT E. BOYD

THE PERSONAL DEVELOPMENT of the student is not limited to the formal activities generated within the school. Education occurs whenever and wherever the student learns. As a result, those persons having impact on the activities and opportunities of the child also affect his development. Zaccaria's concern for the school as a social system highlights the interdependent nature of persons involved in the educative endeavor. The experiences undergone by the child form a unity. He learns, reacts, and learns to react in all the settings in which he finds himself. The methods he adopts to react and his perceptions of himself as a result of these experiences lead to the formation of his self-concept.

The goal of education is to promote the development of a positive self-concept to the end that self-actualizing persons may result. To achieve this result, concern must be evidenced for the members of society that influence the life of the child. Patterson indicated in Chapter 1 that education must produce "free, reasoning, responsible individuals." This is achievable only through effective interpersonal relations; interpersonal relations noted for their understanding, respect, and honesty.

The student's development will be maximized when these relationships occur throughout his environment. Parents and others who have multiple opportunities to influence the life of the child must perform with interpersonal effectiveness if he is to develop appropriately. The experiencing of effective interpersonal relationships serves multiple functions. First, such relationships permit the child to explore himself, test reality, and improve his interpersonal functioning. Second, they provide him with good models to emulate. Third, they provide those with whom he is interacting the possibility to grow as a result of the experience.

Experiencing effective human relations is developmental in that learning about one's self and one's environment is enhanced. These learning opportunities provide reality checks and point the way for continued personal growth. They are preventative in that through the experiencing of such relationships the student learns to interact effectively with others, thus avoiding the misunderstandings which might otherwise occur. One of Pancrazio's opening statements in this volume indicated his concern with this phenomenon: "It appears that many of the problems in our society are related to the ways in which human beings perceive, communicate with, relate to, and behave toward each other."

In a very real sense it is possible to extend the definition of teacher, offered by both Patterson and Pancrazio, to include the other individuals influencing the child's development. Central to this extension are the parents and siblings with whom the child interacts. Fullmer and Bernard state ". . . *the work of the home and the school are inseparable.* Both are concerned with the directed learning processes of the child."[1] The family provides the first organization experienced by the child which is designed as an institution for education. While the learnings achieved in the child's early years are primarily social rather than academic, the family presents a model for social living which affects his behavior. Those aspects of the family which are ineffective and, hence, nonproductive for the child in terms of facilitating his opportunity to develop are legitimate concerns of school personnel.[2]

[1]D. Fullmer and H. W. Bernard, *Family Consultation* (Boston, Houghton Mifflin Co., 1968), p. 20.

[2]C. K. Lipsman, "Revolution and Prophecy: Community Involvement for Counselors," *Personnel and Guidance Journal,* 48:97-100 (1969).

Schools, to accomplish their educational objectives, must be cognizant of the forces acting upon the individual student and prepare methodological procedures for the resolution of those difficulties which impede his development. Implicit in this position is the assumption that school personnel have available the resources necessary to promote sound environments which will promote student development. If the resources are unavailable within the school, knowledge of their availability within the community should be sought. That an active dialogue with the family and other units of the community is necessary for the establishment of a program of this nature goes without saying. Further, if school personnel are to establish and maintain such a program, they must possess the communications skills necessary to carry out such dialogues.

It is the purpose of this chapter to identify general approaches for the resolution of student difficulties expressed as academic, personal, or social issues which appear to be family related. Three general approaches to working with parents have been identified to accomplish this goal: 1) counseling—relationship-based procedures with a member or members of the family unit, 2) consulting—information-based procedures with members of the family unit focusing on the needs of the parents, and 3) coordinating—referral-based procedures, requiring home, school, and agency cooperation, utilized when the needs of the student exceed the skill or assigned responsibility of the available school personnel.

All school personnel are involved in these procedures from time to time. Such personnel may promote their effectiveness by maintaining a continual awareness of the developmental needs of the students with whom they come in contact. They must be alert to both the interpersonal and intrapersonal life of their students. Those persons identified as having major responsibility and expertise for problems of this nature may be termed student personnel specialists. Student personnel specialists are typically either school counselors, social workers, or psychologists. In some cases other professional personnel are assigned some of the functions mentioned above. The important point, however, is not the title of the individual performing the function, but rather, his skills in its execution.

Implicit in this chapter is the indication that the student personnel specialist bears the responsibility for determining the appropriate treatment vehicle for his clientele. While all professionals cannot be expected to perform all potential functions, interprofessional referral within the school unit and in-service training should permit a continued broadening of treatment alternatives. When appropriate capacities are not present, the professional staff has the responsibility for possessing accurate knowledge of those extra-school agencies which are capable of providing the necessary service. It should further be noted that acceptance of this position by both parents and school personnel is based on good public relations, the utilization of which fosters the understandings of others regarding departmental aims and objectives.

Public Relations

The student personnel specialist's communications to the community determine to a large extent the perception the public has of available school services. These communications form the backbone of the student personnel public relations program. Public acceptance of the student personnel specialist as a legitimate school representative possessing the professional skills to perform with educational and therapeutic effectiveness is based in part on the ability of such personnel to accurately and effectively communicate their philosophy and capabilities.

Student personnel specialists represent in their communications not only themselves, but also their profession and their employing organization.[3] Their communications, therefore, should include: 1) statements of philosophy, 2) statements of services available, and 3) statements on operational aspects of the student personnel services organization. Such statements must be made

[3]C. H. Patterson, *An Introduction to Counseling in the School* (New York, Harper & Row, Publishers, Inc., 1971), p. 314.

with due consideration for the proficiencies of the staff and orientation of the employing organization. That the student personnel specialist must have already defined his own role in view of his philosophy and capabilities is imperative if he is to be able to communicate it effectively to others.

Presentations to large audiences, whether through mass media or speaking engagements, are the first line of attack in public relations efforts. However, performance records, built upon being of service to the individuals requesting assistance, is the heart of any public relations program. Performance is the base upon which can be built the trust and recognition necessary for long-term effective professional relationships. Being of service to individuals is of vital importance because it is the "proof of the pudding" in the eyes of the public and because it provides a better opportunity for feedback to occur.

Clarity is an important component of any public relations effort. Because communication requiring a sender and an audience is a two-way process, public relations requires that both participants have an opportunity to respond to the other. Provision for the completion of the communication circuit provides an opportunity for such exchange between participants to occur. This permits (and requires) the active involvement of the recipient. Further, as the recipient of the message provides the sender with a response, the sender is permitted an opportunity to modify his message to the needs and understandings of the recipient. The ultimate result is the reception of more accurately understood communications and increased involvement on the part of the recipient.[4] The continuing exchange between message sender and receiver fosters clarity in the communication process.

Concern for the clarity of the communication also enhances the impact of the message.[5] This issue is of importance whether

[4]H. J. Peters, *Interpreting Guidance Programs to the Public* (Boston, Houghton Mifflin Co., 1968), p. 1.

[5]B. Shertzer and S. C. Stone, "The School Counselor and His Public: A Problem in Role Definition," *Personnel and Guidance Journal,* 41:687-693 (1963).

the communication vehicle is the mass media or an individual message and whether the message is written or verbal. Obviously, the increased propinquity involved when communicating with an individual rather than a group enhances the opportunity for direct, rapid feedback.

Trust is also an important component of any public relations effort. Under the best of circumstances, the recipient of the communication filters it through his own mental set; a mental set influenced by his group of affiliations and the opinions of his associates.[6] He will do so in an attempt to construe the communication as congruent to his own opinions. Should this not be possible, the message will tend to be discredited either because its content is considered unimportant or because the presenter is considered uninformed.[7]

Weiss has shown, however, that it is possible to positively influence receiver reaction to communications.[8] Communications which are begun from a position congruent with audience opinion have greater receiver acceptance. It is then possible to add persuasive comments directed at changing audience perception and attitude. Weiss hypothesized that this technique enhanced the trustworthiness of the sender in the eyes of the receiver. Trustworthiness is also conveyed by the presenter's ability to utilize the idioms which the receiver understands and, hence, feels comfortable with. This is of particular significance when the recipient is of a decidedly different cultural background. Such recipients bring expectations and understandings to interpretation activities divergent from those of the message sender. Trust is also enhanced by the perceived expertness of the presenter, his previously proven reliability, the degree to which his intention is understood, and his personal attractiveness.[9] This strongly indi-

[6]K. Griffin, "The Contribution of Studies of Source of Creditability to a Theory of Interpersonal Trust in the Communications Process," *Psychological Bulletin*, 68:104-120 (1967).

[7]J. S. Adams, "Reduction of Cognitive Dissonance by Seeking Consonant Information," *Journal of Abnormal and Social Psychology*, 62:74-78 (1961).

[8]W. Weiss, "Opinion Congruence," *Journal of Abnormal and Social Psychology*, 54:180-186 (1957).

[9]K. Griffin, *op. cit.,* p. 104-120.

cates that the student personnel specialist must be aware of and concerned with the attitudes and activities of the community regarding the school and its children if communications are to be understood and accepted by the audience.

The history of the department's relationship with the community provides the basis upon which the community reacts to departmental communications. As public relations are built upon this historical base, it is important that programs and presentations are viewed by the public as concerns of the department in terms of that historical perspective. It is also important that the presentations can be viewed by the public as relevant to the purposes of the school and the needs of their children. This calls for continuous effort to provide information which promotes understanding of the mission of the department. However, many of the public relations efforts will not deal with the mission of the department. The presentation of information regarding topics of interest to parents regarding their children, for example, child growth and development, serves the same end by implication. The historical base provides the grounding upon which modifications can be made but they must be seen as logically consistent extensions of prior services.

Student personnel specialists can use as communications vehicles programs and activities which provide information relative to the educational opportunities of the school and the needs of youth. News releases, school reports to parents, school and community survey results, public addresses—both to within-school parent groups and to out-of-school community groups—all permit mass approaches to public relations.[10] Not to be overlooked are the personal associations experienced by professional personnel with individual members of the community. These also provide an opportunity for effective public relations. Topics typically of concern to the audience of the school include services available, areas of professional expertise of the staff, information on child growth and development, patterns of learn-

[10]D. E. Johnson, *Expanding and Modifying Guidance Programs* (Boston, Houghton Mifflin Co., 1968), p. 47.

ing, study skills, career development data, and educational opportunities.

Public relations efforts also provide community agencies an opportunity to coordinate the available social services within their geographic area. The information presented gives the community an opportunity to identify gaps in the services currently available, enabling it to better meet the needs of the citizens. Such coordination of services also lays the groundwork for functional referral policies between the school and other agencies.[11]

Identifying the Client

Extension of student personnel efforts beyond the confines of the student population raises at least two issues regarding client designation. First, who is the client? Second, what is the responsibility or ethics of client designation between self- and other-referred clients?

While Peters intimates that the student is always the client, even when professional contacts to individuals other than students are involved,[12] Krumboltz and Thoreson would tend to deny this position. Their reply to the question, Who is my client?, is in almost all cases, My client is the person who brought me the problem.[13] The implication is that client status cannot be imposed upon those who feel no need for it.[14] As Krumboltz and Thoreson indicate, parents often desire to shift the responsibility for the behavior of their children to someone else whom they can blame if their goals for their child are not met.[15] School personnel have faced this issue particularly in terms of educational achievement and occupational choice.[16] The parent typi-

[11]H. J. Peters, *op cit.,* p. 16.

[12]*Ibid.,* p. 13.

[13]J. D. Krumboltz and C. E. Thoreson, *Behavioral Counseling* (New York, Holt, Rinehart & Winston, Inc., 1969), p. 9.

[14]C. H. Patterson, "The Counselor in the Elementary School," *Personnel and Guidance Journal,* 47:979-986 (1969).

[15]J. D. Krumboltz and C. E. Thoreson, *op cit.,* p. 9.

[16]B. Shertzer and S. C. Stone, *op. cit.,* p. 687-693.

cally appears to request assistance for someone else, his child, and usually such a request is not concerned with why the child behaves as he does, but rather how this behavior can be modified to conform with his parents' wishes.[17] The implication is that the student personnel specialist should act as the agent of the parents in the school. However, the use of persuasion or other manipulative techniques imposed against the will of the student or any individual tends to be nonproductive in terms of behavior change. Client status must be self-assigned if the therapeutic endeavor is to be maximally productive. It is difficult, if not impossible, for a parent to assign client status to a child against his will. A child must be in active agreement if progress is to be made.[18] It should be very clear that, if it is the parents who are seeking assistance, they are the clients of the student personnel specialist. While not all parent-clients are seeking or in need of the same services, the focus of the activities undertaken are still directed toward the client, that individual who has identified himself as possessing a felt need for problem resolution and who is desirous of achieving behavioral or attitudinal change.

The second problem is the method used to identify the client. A self-referred client has, by his presence, expressed a felt need for change, and, hence, a willingness to commit himself to the change process. When referral is suggested by a school representative (other-referred clients), the potential client may feel threatened. While a heightened sense of concern and commitment may serve a facilitative function, extreme anxiety is counter-productive to the changing process. It is, in addition, often the case that suggesters have preconceived notions of what change should occur.[19] This includes those suggestions for referral made to parents by student personnel specialists

---

[17]M. A. Sonstegard, "A Rationale for Interviewing Parents," *School Counselor,* 12:72-76 (1964).

[18]J. D. Krumboltz, "Behavioral Counseling: Rationale and Research," *Personnel and Guidance Journal,* 44:383-387 (1965).

[19]J. F. McGowan and L. D. Schmidt, *Counseling: Readings in Theory and Practice* (New York, Holt, Rinehart & Winston, Inc., 1962), p. 242.

in line with their professional responsibilities to their employing institution and the student population. However, reality dictates that there are occasions upon which school concerns regarding student behavior require indicating to parents that they
might profitably assume client status. Two sets of circumstances
would appear to make such suggestions warranted: 1) for informational purposes, and 2) for counseling purposes. Such
purposes are affected in part by the functional capacity of the
student population. The younger the school population, the
more it is necessary to involve parents in the developmental
processes of their children.[20] Children can and do have some
influence over their environment.[21] However, the amount of
freedom obtained by minor children in our society is functionally
related to their age. That parental responsibility may not be
ignored has been codified through statutory strictures placed
upon parent behavior.

Student personnel specialists can, therefore, offer their services to parents. Acceptance of the offer, however, is the parents'
decision; coerced cooperation is a violation of their personal
integrity. While concern for the attitude which other-referred
individuals bring to the meeting suggests the potential for
nonproductivity, the result may be increased insight and behavior
change. To quote McGowan and Schmidt, "In a sense a client
is often as ready for counseling as we allow him to be."[22] So
while the possibility of receiving unmotivated other-referred
clients is very real, anticipation of client response can be as
counter-productive as the response itself. This means that the
student personnel specialist must provide the opportunity for the
potential client to mobilize his desire for change.[23] The provision

[20]G. R. Mayer, "An Approach for the Elementary School Counselor: Consultant
or Counselor?," *School Counselor,* 14:210-214 (1967).

[21]C. H. Patterson, "Elementary School Counselor or Child Development Consultant?," *Personnel and Guidance Journal,* 46:75-76 (1967).

[22]J. F. McGowan and L. D. Schmidt, *op. cit.,* p. 243.

[23]E. G. Beier, "Client-Centered Therapy and the Involuntary Client," in J. F.
McGowan and L. D. Schmidt, eds., *Counseling: Readings in Theory and Practice* (New York, Holt, Rinehart & Winston, Inc., 1962).

of such opportunity is not, however, designed to force a nonclient to become a client.

Confidentiality

When accepting client status, parents expect their concerns to be treated confidentially. That their expectations can be realized is imperative if a sound association is to be developed. Their right to privacy is limited only insofar as such privacy does not force the professional to violate the statutes governing his practice. Information shared by a client has been called by Schneiders an *"entrusted secret."*[24] The disclosure of an "entrusted secret" would seem to be a direct violation of the ethical standards of the American Personnel and Guidance Association who regard respect for client integrity a primary obligation of the student personnel specialist.[25] While the doctrine of privileged communication, i.e. the legal ability to refuse to release information gained during the treatment process, has not in general been extended to the student personnel specialist,[26] he is not relieved of his responsibility for maintaining his client's integrity, particularly when disclosure is injurious to the treatment relationship.

While the issue would seem to be of formidable proportions in areas such as the one dealt with in this chapter, consideration of the relationships involved will help clarify the issues. The basic question is: Who is the client? In parent counseling and parent consulting, the parent, not the student, is the client. Hence, confidentiality is extended to the parent in his client role. This does not free the therapist from his obligation to his student-client, but rather indicates the focus of the interviewing procedure. While self-referred parent-clients would seem to offer little difficulty, other-referred parents, those initially con-

---

[24]A. A. Schneiders, "The Limits of Confidentiality," *Personnel and Guidance Journal,* 42:252-253 (1963).

[25]American Personnel and Guidance Association Ethical Standards, *Personnel and Guidance Journal,* 40:206-209 (1961).

[26]J. S. Zaccaria, *Approaches to Guidance in Contemporary Education.* Scranton, International Textbooks, 1969), p. 205.

tacted by school personnel, provide additional problems. However, student behavior necessitating other-referrals would, in most instances, be public behavior and, hence, not subject to the dictum of confidentiality. In those instances in which this does not occur, the gaining of student permission for the release of data is recommended.

There are instances in which student requests for confidentiality can be ignored. Some courts have held that the relationship between parent and child requires that parents have controlling rights with respect to their child and, hence, are entitled to the data they consider appropriate from student interviews.[27] Additional instances are those in which the health and well-being of the student requires disclosure. The effect of such disclosure on the professional-client relationship is typically disastrous.

Coordinating (referral) activities, however, provide an alternate problem in that the client may be either the student, his parents, or both. Protection of client welfare usually requires his permission for release of information with the understanding that only such information as is pertinent to the treatment of his case be given to the receiving agency.

The obligation of secrecy lapses, as Schneiders has pointed out, when: 1) the common welfare demands revelation, 2) the secret is invalid, 3) there is unjust aggression, 4) the client gives consent, or 5) there is publication of the secret.[28]

COUNSELING

The counseling of parents and families is based upon the supposition that the development of an affective interpersonal relationship with a therapeutic specialist will assist family members in their achievement of insight into the causes of interpersonal conflict within the family. The establishment of a therapeutic relationship provides an opportunity for the clients

[27]J. J. Marsh and B. C. Kinnick, "Let's Close the Confidentiality Gap. "*Personnel and Guidance Journal,* 48:362-365 (1970).

[28]A. A. Schneiders, *op. cit.,* p. 252-253.

to explore their attitudes, feelings and life style. Such exploration fosters better self-understanding and understanding of others. The therapist's role is to serve as a facilitator of this relationship, assisting parents in their achievement of insight.[29] While provision for information giving activities may be required to promote parent self-exploration, it is the self-exploration, not the information giving, which is the primary focus of this counseling relationship.

Although student personnel specialists are not typically looked upon as persons appropriate for assisting parents in the resolution of their intrapersonal and interpersonal concerns, the impact of noneffective family relationships can have profound effects on children, impeding their academic, personal, and social development. Fullmer and Bernard indicate that since both the home and school are directly concerned with the learning processes of the child, they are both working toward the same objective.[30] Hence, the student personnel specialists may appropriately undertake counseling with family members. Boy and Pine support this opinion: "Many of the problems which pupils experience are rooted in a troubled relationship between student and one parent or both parents. Parents who contact the counselor to discuss pupil problems often become involved in discussing their own personal problems or family relationships. In such situations, the school counselor has an opportunity to help parents express feelings. Through a release of feelings many parents can begin looking at themselves more objectively and see the relationship between pupil and parent behavior."[31] The expression of personal concern helps foster the establishment of a sound parent-child or parent-parent interfamily relationship. In addition to counseling with individual parents, a variety of procedures are available to the student personnel specialist in his efforts to be of assistance to families; among them are marriage coun-

[29]M. Sonstegard, *op. cit.*, p. 72-76.

[30]D. Fullmer and H. W. Bernard, *op. cit.*, p. 20.

[31]A. V. Boy and G. J. Pine. *Client-centered Counseling in the Secondary Schools* (Boston, Houghton-Mifflin Co., 1963), p. 163.

seling, family counseling, group-parent counseling and multiple family counseling.

Marriage Counseling

Parents experiencing conflicts within their marriage may use their children as go-betweens, as levers to increase their power position against their mate, as excuses for remaining married, or in any one of a multitude of ways to solidify their own position within their marriage and to validate their own view of their married world. When the problems of the child can be identified as being related to the interpersonal functionings of the parents, an ideal setting for marriage counseling is attained. Such counseling is designed to resolve the tension-producing difficulties within the marriage. A counseling setting provides an opportunity for them to communicate with the assistance of the therapist, whose job it is to protect the partners and to promote self-exploration. The goal of such counseling is the achievement of a better understanding by marriage partners of themselves and their relationship through the exploring, evaluating, and clarifying of their feelings regarding the issues involved in their discord.

Freeing the partners from their interpersonal conflicts permits them to more adequately utilize their resources in their striving for achieving self-actualization while permitting their mate the same opportunity. As such, increased freedom, self-understanding and understanding of one's mate is tension-reducing and productive of better interpersonal relations within the marriage.[32]

Marriage counseling provides a method of assistance not only to the marriage partners, but also to their children. The resolution of concerns will reflect in their handling of the student identified as a problem, thus leading to improved child rearing practices which will in turn foster their child's learning. It also

[32]A. L. Rutledge, "The Future of Marriage," in B. N. Ard & C. C. Ard, eds., *Handbook of Marriage Counseling* (Palo Alto, Calif., Science and Behavior Books, 1969).

serves as a preventative mental health procedure for other children in the same family as the conflict within that unit is resolved.

Ard lists the following assumptions regarding counseling set when entering into a marriage counseling relationship: 1) anxiety, tension, guilt feelings, or concern over the relationship is the immediate driving force that motivates clients to seek marriage counseling; 2) marital maladjustments and problems can be alleviated or worked through by using certain specific methods, knowledge, and techniques; 3) most, but not all, of the ways of behaving which are adopted by the client are those which are consistent with his concept of self; 4) there is a reality which is different from distorted perceptions as illusions, hallucinations, delusions, projections, fantasies, etc.; 5) it is one of the aims of marriage counseling (or psychotherapy in general) to help the client perceive reality more accurately; 6) the client has the capacity, in most instances, to resolve his own conflicts, given certain circumstances (i. e., in this instance, good therapeutic conditions); 7) through procedures and techniques used in marriage counseling, which establishes a good therapeutic atmosphere, the client is encouraged to communicate (i. e. verbalize) his feelings and experiences, and will thereby gradually bring more and more of his significant feelings and experiences into the realm of awareness; 8) there is a drive or tendency toward psychological health in most clients; 9) the optimal development of the individual's potentialities is the ultimate goal of marriage counseling; 10) marriage counseling is a good (i. e. worthwhile, helpful) thing.[33]

Marriage counseling has been delineated as a subspeciality due to the unique relationship inherent in marriage. It forces the student personnel specialist to work simultaneously with the characteristics of two individuals as well as the relationship they have established with each other. Marriage counseling is

[33]B. N. Ard, *"Assumptions Underlying Marriage Counseling,"* in B. N. Ard and C. C. Ard eds., *Handbook of Marriage Counseling* (Palo Alto, Calif., Science and Behavior Books), 1969.

unique also in that the clients' relationship is their primary
social unit. As such, it continues outside of the therapeutic
session, thereby establishing a decidedly different environment
from counseling with individual parents or with groups of un-
related parents.

Parent Group Counseling

Parent groups have been established along a number of lines
utilizing various models for member selection. They typically
provide for the inclusion of sets of parents who are brought
together initially because of some concern relative to their
school-age youth. However, the focus of the therapeutic efforts,
if the counseling is to become effective, is the parents and not
their children. The goal of such activity includes increased
insights resulting in changed parental behavior toward, attitudes
about, and expectations of their children.[34]

Family Counseling

Family counseling utilizes the family as a group. The term
"family" is used to designate therapy methods in which two or
more generations, usually parents and children, attend sessions
together.[35] Entire families meet together with the therapist as
the facilitator in an attempt to verbalize their thoughts and
feelings to each other. While process goals include self-understanding, the approach readily increases other-member understanding leading to better interpersonal relations as the communications process improves.[36] The result is the creation of a new
way of living for the family.[37] It must be added that this new
way of living cannot be predetermined as there is no idealized

[34]P. B. Mallars, "Thinking About Group Counseling for Parents?" *School Counselor*, 15:374-376 (1968).

[35]M. Bowen, "The Use of Family Theory in Clinical Practice," in B. N. Ard
and C. C. Ard, eds., *Handbook of Marriage Counseling* (Palo Alto, Calif.,
Science and Behavior Books, 1969).

[36]V. Satir, *Conjoint Family Therapy* (Palo Alto, Calif., Science and Behavior
Books, 1967), p. 92.

[37]N. W. Ackerman, *Treating the Troubled Family* (New York, Basic Books,
1966), p. viii.

model of family life. Each family has a certain quality of uniqueness in its behavior patterns.[38] These unique patterns have resulted from the interchange of emotion between family members. The healthy family is the one that can respond adequately to the specific conditions of living it faces while offering opportunities for its members to strive for self-fulfillment. In these terms, there is an assumption that the family is a learning model for socialization.

The term "familial-organism" has been used to denote the family's functional unity.[39] To operate effectively as an organism, the family develops the kinds of persons it needs to carry out its function. Thus the members of the family influence each other to behave in a manner enabling each to achieve some degree of reward in the family unit. Homeostasis results with the achievement of a mutually rewarding family.

Satir has noted that family communications patterns are the vehicle used to balance the relationships within the organism.[40] Modification of the communications pattern without additional interpersonal understanding disrupts family equilibrium.

Sometimes disruption occurs because the messages sent between family members carry multiple meanings. The reading of multiple meaning messages leaves the receiver either 1) uncomfortable in that he cannot respond to all meanings adequately, or 2) free to respond to whichever meaning seems appropriate to him, usually at the expense of the message sender.[41] At other times, disruption occurs as a result of conflicting efforts to shape the behaviors of other family members. While parents are attempting to influence their children, each child is, in turn, attempting to influence his parents' behavior in an effort to fulfill his needs. Hence, the emotional climate of the family is constantly evolving.[42]

Disruption also occurs when parental self-esteem is the

[38]*Ibid.,* p. 51.
[39]*Ibid.,* p. 58.
[40]V. Satir, *op. cit.,* p. 1.
[41]*Ibid.,* p. 35.
[42]N. W. Ackerman, *op. cit.,* p. 61.

issue. This is the case when the child is perceived by his parents to be operating as an extension of them in the community. As their representative, they equate his behavior with theirs. This condition makes it difficult for the parents to discipline the child because they are, from their view, punishing themselves. The punishment is an acknowledgement of their imperfect state thus causing them to suffer a loss in self-esteem.[43] In this case, the child may not only be the victim of his parents, but also victimize them by requiring extra attention, secondary rewards, or release from responsibility.

When change produces a state of disequilibrium within the family, all the family members feel pain.[44] The result is distorted family relationships. The more distortion that occurs, the more rigidity is introduced into the family unit.[45] Spontaneity further decreases as the efforts of the family are directed toward trying to reestablish some degree of equilibrium. The disequilibrium experienced within the family results in the singling out of a family member who becomes the *identified patient*, the individual who, in the eyes of the others, needs to change.[46]

Scapegoating is another term used to identify a family member whom others see as not fulfilling his role. The identification of a scapegoat provides a focus for family members in their attempt to regain homeostasis. He is available as an object to be used as an anxiety reduction vehicle.[47] In these terms, scapegoating provides an opportunity for other members of the family to rid themselves of the responsibility for their actions toward that member. By so doing, family members rid themselves of felt threat. The identification of a scapegoat, however, also generates fear among the other family members. The fear is based on the realization that if it can happen to one member of the family, it can happen to any of them.

While scapegoating patterns are highly idiosyncratic to the

43V. Satir, *op. cit.,* p. 28.

44V. Satir, *ibid.,* p. 1.

45N. W. Ackerman, *op. cit.*

46V. Satir, *op. cit.,* p. 1.

47N. W. Ackerman, *op. cit.,* p. 77.

family involved, one common cause is the developmental progress of the child. Rigid families who must struggle to retain the equilibrium between their members have difficulty accepting change in the child. The passage from one stage to another in his striving toward adulthood constantly results in disequilibrium within the family unit, bringing forth adult reaction in an attempt to maintain the child's prior behavior.[48] Such families cause the child to act in a deviant manner to satisfy their own needs even though they verbalize their concern about his behavior. As a result, the child is in conflict with the larger society outside of the family.

An outgrowth of the conflict may be expressed as somewhat atypical school behavior, resulting in numerous home-school contacts. The parents of these students usually report being unable to help them act in a more appropriate manner. However, not all students who appear to be acting inappropriately to school personnel are, in fact, candidates for family counseling. Key conditions include not only the parents' desire for behavior change and willingness to participate actively in family counseling, but also strong expressed needs to reestablish harmonious parent-child relationships. Without parental desire, such counseling procedure would tend to be inappropriate. Further, some students who appear to be acting inappropriately to school personnel are accurately reflecting and actively participating in a harmonious family relationship. This may be the result of the differing cultural expectations of home and school. To summarize, healthy family relationships depend upon the complementary fulfilling of five areas: 1) the support of self-esteem; 2) cooperation in the quest for solutions to conflict; 3) the satisfaction of needs; 4) the support of needed defenses against anxiety; and 5) support for the development and creative fulfillment of the individual family member.[49]

Multiple Family Group Counseling

In addition to offering the advantages of family counseling,

[48]*Ibid.,* p. 165.
[49]*Ibid.,* p. 72.

multiple family group counseling provides an opportunity for cross-cultural influences from family to family. By grouping families together, the experiential base of each family unit is enriched. It allows both children and adults an opportunity to find additional sources of information and support within the counseling setting. Providing a facilitative environment for each discourse should lead to improved interpersonal communications within the family unit. As the sessions are large and primarily informational, the impact for change is minimal.[50]

CONSULTING

The goals of counseling and consulting with parents are similar in that the ultimate aim of both is to assist the student in his development. There is, however, a decided difference in the methodology used and the focus adopted by the student personnel specialist. The activities engaged in are often severely circumscribed and topic specific. This differs from counseling which tends to be more global in nature, is long term, and deals with more pervasive aspects of the client's behavior.

There is a decided difference in the nature of the relationship that is established in counseling and consulting. The parent's concerns are typically directed toward his relationship with or responsibilities toward a third party, in this case his child, a unit external to the setting in which consulting takes place. While an emotional content is obvious, there is a definite emphasis on the cognitive aspects of the relationship. Action rather than causation is the issue.[51] The expectation is that the activity will be brief and direct. Thus, the recipient has some expectation that the help he is receiving will translate directly into action or permit him to make decisions upon which to act.

The student personnel specialist is viewed as an expert; a purveyor of knowledge or information, the receipt of which will allow the client to resolve the issues of concern to him. In this

[50]S. R. Sauber, "Multiple-family Group Counseling," *Personnel and Guidance Journal,* 49:459-465 (1971).

[51]M. M. Lawrence, *The Mental Health Team in the Schools* (New York, Behavioral Publications, 1971), p. 17.

sense, the consultant becomes a teacher.[52] It is his responsibility to 1) reinforce, corroborate, or validate; 2) clarify, analyze, or interpret; 3) inform, supplement, or advise; 4) motivate, facilitate, or change.[53]

The presenter hopes that the information will assist in the development of improved interpersonal relationships within the family unit which in turn will result in a more personally satisfying, self-fulfilling life for the child. The giving of information to parents fosters an environment which allows the child to more fully profit from his learning experiences and to achieve more mature, independent behavior.

In 1969, Ronald Lippitt offered a highly useful definition of consulting. He wrote:

1. The consultation relationship is a voluntary relationship between
2. a professional helper (consultant) and a help-needing system (client)
3. in which the consultant is attempting to give some help to the client in solving some current or potential problems,
4. and the relationship is perceived as temporary by both parties.
5. Also, the consultant is an "outsider," i.e. is not part of any hierarchical power system in which the client is located.[54]

This definition generally satisfies the conditions found in the consultant activities of school personnel. Consultation is typically the result of a voluntary relationship initiated by the client. There are times, however, when some form of suggestion for entering into the relationship comes from the consultant. He is seen as an expert problem solver. In the sense that he is not a member of the family, he is an outsider involved in its internal affairs. Definitionally, when the consulting role requires that the con-

[52]H. R. Kaczkowski, *The Consultation Process: A Comparison of Practice.* Unpublished paper, University of Illinois. 1972.

[53]M. H. Gilmore, "Consultation as a Social Work Activity," in L. Rapoport, ed., *Consultation in Social Work* (New York, National Association of Social Work, 1963).

[54]R. Lippitt, "Dimensions of a Consultant's Job," *Journal of Social Issues,* 14:5-12 (1969).

sultant actively participate in the change process, his role changes to that of a collaborator.[55]

While information recipients bear the responsibility of determining uses to be made of the information, the student personnel specialist is responsible for the accuracy of the data and the establishment of a set designed to accomplish the purposes for which the information is provided. Since effective consultation can proceed only with the consent of the client, the student personnel specialist is responsible for determining the willingness of the information-recipient to act upon the information received. Although the consultant bears responsibility for supporting the parent in his attempts to act on the received information, he does not bear responsibility for its use in the family unit. Typically, parents require continued support throughout the period of change if the information is to be utilized effectively.

Consulting procedures are undertaken in an attempt to resolve concerns in one or more of the following areas:

1. Preventative—procedures undertaken to avoid future problems. Concerns classified in this area include general information regarding human growth and development, including the social and emotional factors in interpersonal relationships, particularly as they relate to anticipated changes in the student. Learning and achievement styles, educational opportunities within the school, and general guidelines for increased interpersonal satisfaction with social units, whether school, friends, or family, are also topics of interest. Information regarding the cultural environment of the school and community is included under this heading.

2. Developmental—procedures undertaken to resolve current concerns. Information of this nature might be directed toward specific information relative to human growth and development as it relates to an individual child. This may include information about the social, sexual, or emotional forces at work in the child along with procedures to implement changing interpersonal relations as a function of his development. Also included are topics which cover educational attainment, educational decision making

[55] J. F. Gorman, "Some Characteristics of Consultation," in L. Rapoport, ed., *Consultation in Social Work* (New York, National Association of Social Work, 1963).

and changing interpersonal relationships both in and out of the home as the child develops.

3. Remedial—procedures undertaken to alleviate long standing difficulties. These include "emotional re-education"[56] for the parents. It also considers resolution of friction areas with the child through the inclusion of training programs regarding specific procedures such as contingency management. Information to assist parents in reassessing their previous decision regarding their relationship with their child, whether educational, social, or familial, is also considered under this heading.

These activities relate generally to the normal difficulties experienced within family units. The focus of such endeavors is based upon the premise that family consultation is a form of family education.[57]

According to Haylett and Rapoport, criteria used to classify activities in mental health consultations are: 1) method used (such as, group work or group consultation); 2) the content of the work problems presented by the consultee (such as, case material, program considerations, or administrative matters); 3) the problem area on which the consultant focuses (such as, problems of the client, problems of the consultee in dealing with his client or with other professional tasks or the problems of the organization in relation to policies and procedures as they affect the mental health of the client).[58] The following major categories will be derived from the Haylett and Rapoport classification with emphasis on the method used.

Mass Consulting

Parents need and often want information relative to the academic expectations of the school, the social climate of the school community, and the general life style of the students at various developmental stages, much of which is in a state of flux as a result of the current cultural evolution. Wrenn recognized this dimension in regard to parent needs when he acknowledged

[56]M. M. Lawrence, *op. cit.*, p. 15.
[57]D. Fullmer and H. W. Bernard, *op. cit.*, p. 68.
[58]C. H. Haylett and L. Rapoport, "Mental Health Consultation," in L. Bellak, ed., *Handbook of Community Psychiatry and Community Mental Health*. (New York, Grune and Stratton, 1964).

that while a child can be attuned to the social environment, it is difficult for the parent to stay informed and knowledgeable about the world the child is experiencing.[59] Various methods for the provision of such information have been utilized by school personnel dependent upon the needs of the parent and the capacities and concerns of the professionals involved. Student personnel specialists have tended to avoid activities of this nature, either because they felt information giving was non-therapeutic or because they lacked the time or capacities to deal with these concerns. However, the introduction of such data is therapeutic when it provides new understandings for parents, assisting them in their effort to modify current behavior patterns. The activities can lead to the attainment of more positive attitudes toward the child and more compatible family relations.

Large scale informational activities may be handled through the mass media or large group meetings. While such activities may be termed a "shotgun approach" toward providing information, they do present data of value to some segments of the attending audience. The job of the student personnel specialist is to determine those global needs of the parent population which are amenable to these procedures and select a usable form for their presentation. The impact of such general programs is increased by topic specificity.

Provision for small group sessions as a part of large audience presentations increases parent involvement through their participation, increasing the impact of the received information. Brakel adopted this procedure, holding four weekly meetings designed to provide juniors and seniors and their parents with information relative to post-high school planning. The meetings not only gave them information, but also proved to be anxiety reducing and increased parent cooperation.[60]

The indication from the literature is that increasing parent involvement with the school and increasing parent understanding of student needs is conducive to student achievement and re-

[59]C. G. Wrenn, *Counselor in a Changing World,* (Washington, American Personnel and Guidance Association, 1962), p. 62.

[60]E. Brakel, "Parents: The Neglected Party in Pre-college Counseling," *School Counselor,* 16:216-217 (1969).

duction of interpersonal friction between parent and child. Further results include increased 1) parent acceptance of the child; 2) understanding of the problems inherent in child-parent relations; 3) parent understanding of the potentialities of the child; and 4) understanding of the culture experienced by the child. Such information may also enhance consistency in the family environment and promote the independence of the child.[61]

Group Consulting

Group consulting as an approach to the development of family understanding has involved many diverse activities. One is parent effectiveness training aimed at improving the communications within the family and teaching parents problem solving skills. This technique has been utilized with classroom instructional sized units.[62] Another is the use of programs from four to six weeks in duration which focus on specific aspects of child growth and development.[63] A third is small group consultation. While the family unit itself proves a primary group, Zwetscke presents a description and rationale for dealing with groups of families for the purpose of consulting with one another and the professional staff. They reported joining together three or four families who met weekly with multiple counselors. The group orientation provided the participants with an opportunity to discuss common problems. The sessions included children as well as parents.[64] While it is difficult to separate this activity from counseling, the intent is to focus on information acquisition by the members of the group and not directly on attempts to develop strong within-session interpersonal relationships.

Individualized Consulting

In addition to providing general information, conferences

[61]J. M. Lee and N. J. Pallone, *Guidance and Counseling in the Schools: Foundations and Processes* (New York, McGraw-Hill Book Company, 1966), p. 365.

[62]B. G. Peterson, "Parent Effectiveness Training," *School Counselor,* 16:367-369 (1969).

[63]L. D. Crow and A. Crow, *An Introduction to Guidance: Basic Principles and Practices* (New York, American Books, 1960), p. 159.

[64]E. T. Zwetscke and J. E. Grenfell, "Family Group Consultation: A Description and a Rationale," *Personnel and Guidance Journal,* 43:974-980 (1965).

with individual parents are also considered consulting procedures. These conferences can be used to share information relative to the child, his behavior at home and at school, and to discuss procedures for the modification of behavior seen as undesirable by the family. Luckey reports that parent-counselor conferences can provide an effective vehicle for information sharing relative to parent goals and expectations as well as school expectations and available educational opportunities.[65] Wooton used this procedure in a summer orientation program held for the parents of new students in grades 9 through 12. It reduced parent misunderstandings relative to student needs, providing a ventilating device for parents, and increased parent-school cooperation.[66] The affective content of such procedures is generally of minimal import, but the meeting does offer an opportunity for the sharing of information. The therapeutic portion of the meeting is centered around the planning for behavior change which the information suggests.

The content of the sessions includes as varied concerns as manipulation of the student's daily behavior patterns and suggestions for change in the interactional activities of the family. Procedures for realizing these goals include conferences with individual parents, family units, parent groups, and groups of families.

While teaching behavioral procedures is highly manipulative, the specialist in human relations can and should be able to impart this information effectively. The parent retains the ability to accept and act upon or reject the suggestions. Such information should help promote parental feelings of independence, self-assurance, and control within their immediate family environment.

The effectiveness of such procedures is enhanced by specific knowledge of the child and his family. It is further enhanced when a school representative has the ability to make specific suggestions to the parents.

[65]E. B. Luckey, "The Elementary School Counselor: Counselor for Parents," *School Counselor*, 14:204-209 (1969).

[66]R. R. Wooton, "Parents Evaluate Pre-school Conferences," *School Counselor*, 12:77-79 (1964).

Consulting interviews can be either remedial or developmental. While some parents want information regarding a future stage of their child's educational development, others are primarily concerned with the resolution of current concerns which are impeding his educational progress. The difference in intent between the two approaches is primarily the degree of specificity of the recommendation, training provided for parents, and follow-up generally necessary for behavior changing procedures. Consulting conferences may run from one to many interviews depending upon the nature and severity of the presented problems. While students tend to be excluded from such conferences, their inclusion is considered helpful and potentially productive for behavior change.

COORDINATING

Student personnel specialists becomes the "connecting link" between the school and those community agencies whose function it is to provide specialized services for the client.[67] As this connecting link they bear responsibility for coordinating the services within the school with those available in the community to maximize client opportunities. While the implication in the foregoing statement is that referrals are flowing from the school to other agencies, the fulfilling of the coordinating function indicates that the student personnel specialist may also be the recipient of referrals from other community services. This point has been, and continues to be, overlooked by student personnel specialists in their referral procedures. The goal is the establishment of a cooperative two-way effort for the provision of services to the community. Bowman and Zimpfer reported a study indicating that while almost all of the counselors in their survey said they wanted to work in a cooperative manner with community agencies, only approximately half of them were doing so. Some of the counselors in the study did not know which referral sources were available. Bowman and Zimpfer drew the following conclusions: 1) school personnel need to know the community referral sources available and to establish working relationships

[67]R. K. Bowman and D. G. Zimpfer, "The Community-team Approach to Referral in the Secondary School, *School Counselor,* 14:110-115 (1966).

with them, and 2) the potential for school-agency cooperation was marked.

Referral does not imply release from responsibility. The student personnel specialist continues to maintain involvement with, not necessarily treatment of, his client to the end that the value of the referral may be enhanced. Such an approach has been called a "community team approach" to referral indicating the coordinated effort necessary to maximize client opportunities.

A student personnel specialist's decision to refer is based upon his knowledge of his own professional adequacies, those of other available school personnel and community resources. Patterson states, "It is a mark of the responsible professional that he recognizes when a problem is beyond his competence, and that he make an appropriate referral."[68] Professional competence is not the only relevant issue; an additional reason for referral is client willingness to work with the available professional. Williamson states that the client may accept other professionals within human relations specialties more readily than he does those available in the school.[69] Referrals are also made so that clients may receive the benefit of specialized services, not necessarily within the realm of the school.[70] Examples of the latter include needed physical health services, employment services, or services for the handicapped. There are, therefore, three primary reasons for referral: 1) client concerns which lay beyond the skills possessed by school personnel; 2) instances in which clients are more willing to accept assistance from non-school personnel, and 3) instances in which client needs for specialized services fall beyond the bounds of the professional role played by the student personnel specialist.

While requests for referral may originate with either the client or the professional, Shertzer and Stone state that the professional bears the responsibility for the referral decision. This

---

[68]C. H. Patterson, *Counseling and Guidance in Schools: A First Course* (New York, Harper and Row Publishers, Inc., 1962), p. 327.

[69]E. Williamson, "Value Orientation in Counseling," in J. F. McGowan and L. D. Schmidt, eds., *Counseling: Readings in Theory and Practice* (New York, Holt, Rinehart & Winston, Inc., 1962).

[70]B. Shertzer and S. C. Stone, *Fundamentals of Counseling* (Boston, Houghton Mifflin Co., 1968), p. 433.

is true only in a limited sense. The professional determines which of the possible alternatives seems the most feasible in light of client needs. The client, however, determines his willingness to accept the available services. As a result, referral becomes a cooperative effort. When clients do accept referral decisions they need support from school personnel if the referral is to be effectively completed.[71]

Four stages of such support can be identified. The first stage is client consideration of referral. Whether the suggestion was first offered by the counselor or the client, the client will need time to "work through" the meaning of referral. It is the professional's responsibility to provide the client with information relative to the necessity for referral and the availability of referral sources.

The second stage, discussion of referral with significant others, is potentially necessary whether the client is parent or child. While adult clients and those minors, who are considering agencies which do not require parental permission to attend, may not be faced with the issue of discussing referral alternatives with a third party, it is not unusual to find a child or adolescent who must first come to terms with the problems involved in referral through a discussion with his parents. School personnel must be attuned to this additional ramification of referral procedures if the referral is to be carried out effectively. While the individual being referred must maintain as much responsibility as possible for the referral activity, he may need the active involvement of the student personnel specialist to explain the referral to his parents. Parents considering referral for themselves may find it necessary to discuss the implications of such action with their children or other family members and, in this case, require as much support as children faced with the same problem.

The third stage, initiation of the referral, may require the services of the student personnel specialist to help gather data, assist in appointment making, and see the client through the potential trauma of a first interview.

While some referral services are relatively similar from com-

[71]C. H. Patterson, *op. cit.*, p. 329.

munity to community, others are highly idiosyncratic, based upon felt needs of the individual community. Knowledge of community resources helps validate the student personnel specialist as a psychologically sophisticated practitioner. The accuracy and availability of such knowledge promotes client and parent acceptance of the referral decision. In an often quoted study of Iowa counselors, it was noted that on the average the counselors had knowledge of 58 percent of the agencies available to them and utilized only 12 percent of them.[72]

Referral agencies, in addition to being known, should be correctly used. The student personnel specialist's knowledge should include the parameters of the services offered, primary theoretical approach of the service, and available professionals within the agency. It is important for the client to know the waiting period, data required by the agency, and the individual responsible for his treatment. Data such as cost, hours of operation, and physical facilities are also of concern to the client when considering the acceptability of various referral alternatives.

The fourth stage, follow-up, requires the maintaining of continual awareness of client involvement with the referral agency. Fear of the unknown and potential financial drain make referral difficult. These two factors tend to discourage the completion of the referral process. The more knowledge the student personnel specialist can bring to the sessions prior to initiation of the referral, the more comfort the client will feel in carrying through on the referral decision. Greater comfort increases the potentiality of his actively completing the process. Support for the client during the transitional phase will assist him in feeling the concern and awareness of the student personnel specialist for his position. It may be necessary to maintain routine contact until such a referral is well established. There are cases in which the referral agency may be providing suggestions or making requests of school personnel in an attempt to promote client treat-

[72]K. B. Hoyt and J. W. Loughary, "Acquaintance With the Use of Referral Sources by Iowa Secondary School Counselors," in J. F. McGowan and L. D. Schmidt, ed., *Counseling: Readings in Theory and Practice,* (New York, Holt, Rinehart & Winston, Inc., 1962).

ment. In this instance, the continued involvement of the student personnel worker with the client is solicited by the agency.

The student personnel specialist maintains one responsibility which is occasionally overlooked in the referral process. Should the needs of the client fall beyond his capabilities, whether professional or organizational, and the client refuses or is unmotivated to participate in a referral activity, the professional is faced with determining whether or not he should continue treatment of the client. Should the professional-client relationship be maintained? McGowan and Schmidt take the position supported here that one of the rights retained by the professional is the right to determine when client problems are appropriate for his capacities. If they are not, and the client refuses referral, his only ethical alternative is termination.[73]

Referral Sources

Referral sources within most communities can usually be identified in a number of areas. The following are typically considered nonresidential treatment services:

1. PUBLIC AGENCIES. Public agencies are normally of three types, those supported through federal funding, those funded jointly by the federal government and state or local efforts, and those supported entirely by the state or local government. These agencies provide services within the statutory limits placed upon their operation. The Veterans' Administration program for qualified veterans and their dependents is an example of the first category. An example of the second are the state agencies of the United States Employment Service. Examples of the third category include locally supported public health programs.

2. PRIVATE BENEVOLENT AGENCIES. Private benevolent agencies may provide services on either a free or ability-to-pay basis. Such agencies may be either single or multiple service agencies, usually operating from some unified or underlying philosophy. The rehabilitation and education programs of the Salvation Army are examples of the multiple service, unified philosophy approach. The Planned Parenthood organization provides a variety of services, but with a single focus. The pastor of the local church might also be considered an available benevolent resource.

[73] J. F. McGowan and L. D. Schmidt, *op. cit.,* p. 244.

3. Private Agencies. Most private agencies are designed to service a single category client. Some family counseling clinics and child guidance agencies would fall into this category. Many of these agencies are simply a number of professionals in group practice. Others are coordinated attempts to provide multifaceted treatment opportunities for clients. These are user-supported agencies and must charge at a rate commensurate with their costs.

4. Private Individuals. This includes the services of private professional practitioners and some individual volunteers. The physicians, psychologists, or other practitioners in private practice charge on a fee basis. The services of individual volunteers are available for some kinds of help, usually to discuss occupational areas or commercial organizations of interest to students. These individuals are often provided as a public service by their employer or professional organization.

5. Local Colleges and Universities. Local colleges and universities occasionally accept clients for therapeutic functions related to their operation or their educational programs. Speech and hearing clinics, counseling services, and health services are all examples of potential aid which might be available from these institutions.

Residential referral services can also be identified. They are typically divided into two groups, public and private.

1. Public Institutions. Public institutions are those organized by units of government for: a) the physical control of individuals considered by the state to be in need of such control; e.g. juvenile detention centers and state hospitals; and b) the provision of treatment, whether physical or mental, assumed to be unavailable in the private sector.

2. Private Institutions. Private institutions are those organized by corporations or other groups for the provision of in-patient service to patients in need of care more intensive than that afforded by outpatient agencies. Attendance may be mandatory or voluntary, depending upon the nature of the problem and the involvement of statutory requirements. Occasionally, attendance may be required by law enforcement agencies or court assignments as a function of medical or parental request.

CONCLUSION

The emotional development of the child as a legitimate goal of education was offered by Patterson in Chapter 1. To help realize this goal, procedures are necessary which facilitate working with individuals other than the child himself. The focus of this chapter has been directed toward those non-school people who have major influence in the life of the child—his family. Helping parents to achieve a healthy self-concept permits them an opportunity to foster a healthy self-concept in their child. Sub goals designed to assist in their achievement include: 1) helping significant others in the life of the student develop some understanding of human growth and development, 2) assisting others to understand the learning environment experienced by the child both in and out of school, 3) assisting others to understand the capacities of the child and his method of performance in school and in other significant areas of his life, 4) reducing student intrapersonal conflict and improving interpersonal communications between the student and his family, 5) assisting in the development of an environment conducive to the acceptance of information and the resolution of conflict between the family and the child.[74]

This chapter has attempted to identify three general approaches toward the achievement of the above goals: 1) counseling with members of the family or family unit, 2) consulting with members of the family through a variety of means ranging from the mass media to individual informational sessions, and 3) coordinating referral activities between the school, family, and agency when the specialized needs of the student exceed the skills or organizational parameters available to the school personnel. It has also indicated that on a larger scale the public relations program of the school can influence the community at large, thus further promoting the opportunities for personal development available to children and youth.

[74]M. A. Ciavarella, "The Counselor as a Mental Health Consultant," *School Counselor*, 18:121-125 (1970).

CHAPTER XI

THE INTEGRATION OF THE FUNCTIONS OF SPECIALISTS

Henry R. Kaczkowski

A LTHOUGH THE ROLE of the counselor has been emphasized to this point, the entire school staff is involved in helping all pupils. The renewed interest in all pupils stems from the fact that the federal government has expanded its involvement in pupil personnel services to include programs other than guidance services. Traditionally, the school social worker and the school psychologist have worked with children who have social and emotional problems. Since these professional workers were not specifically oriented toward education, the staff of most schools did not accept them professionally. However, the new focus on all students requires an integrated interdisciplinary program whose goal is to help pupils in their development as self-actualized persons.

The Nature and Goals of Pupil Personnel Programs

"The primary purpose of a program of pupil personnel services is to facilitate the maximum development of each individual through education."[1] Since pupil personnel services is considered as one of the essential components in a school district's educational program, care must be taken in developing a set of services that help all students. The development of a meaningful program is complicated by the complexity of pupil personnel functions. The program should be so designed that it provides a balanced and coordinated set of services rather than fragmentized help. "While a coordinated program can contribute

[1]*Responsibilities of State Departments of Education for Pupil Personnel,* (Washington, D.C., Council of Chief State School Officers, 1960), p. 2.

330

in a significant and effective way, a distorted and unbalanced program cannot be effective and may be rejected by education."[2]

Administrative Orientations

The school administrator in his design of an educational program for a school district must place into proper perspective the different roles that personnel specialists undertake in discharging their particular functions. Two major administrative orientations can be used to organize pupil personnel programs. The first administrative orientation reflects the traditional approach in that the personnel functions are seen as an adjunct to the teaching process. The program provides a series of technically oriented professional activities concentrated on problem children. The chief task of the specialist is to diagnose problems and to prescribe treatments. Usually, the treatment process is undertaken by some staff member. The program must be so designed that the effort of the various specialists and workers is coordinated so as to insure that all the phases of the helping relationship are carried out. Without coordination the various personnel functions become fragmented or disorganized to the point of being virtually useless.

The second administrative orientation approaches pupil personnel work from the standpoint of direct assistance to the individual student so that his needs can be met. Since its focus is on all children rather than just the problem cases, the functions of this program are more broadly defined. It requires the specialists to function as generalists because they do more than just diagnose and prescribe treatment. At times, the work of the specialist requires a team effort because a specific activity transcends any given specialty. A staff, whose professional functioning is integrated, provides different alternatives of helping pupils rather than being restricted to one basic method.

The key function of a school administrator is to provide the necessary leadership in helping the staff to put the divergent views about pupil personnel work into proper perspective. The

[2]Dean L. Hummel and S. J. Bonham, Jr., *Pupil Personnel Services in Schools,* (Chicago, Rand McNally & Co., 1968), p. 39.

school administrator provides the staff with an opportunity to exchange views about the program so that a plan of operation acceptable to all can be generated. This approach is especially necessary when a program that has been operational for some time is being modified. The staff input should not only dwell on the structural aspects of the program but on attitudes that are needed for acceptance of the change. Of particular importance, is the examination of norms and expectations of the staff.

In addition to providing the staff with an opportunity to exchange views, the school administrator must also be aware of the influence of community attitudes, the state school code that regulates educational programs, and policy statements of professional organizations. Because of the complexity of interactions, many school districts adopt a "wait and see" posture rather than implementing innovations. School districts have learned that there is usually a substantial difference between suggested guidelines of professional organizations and those required by state statute. The differences arise because professional organizations tend to be idealistic while state departments of education are more realistic about its feasibility. School districts are careful about implementing new ideas for they have learned that, unfortunately, schools are judged more by their failures than successes.

It is rather difficult to delineate the characteristics of a balanced pupil personnel program because each administrative unit has a different perspective of the educative process. What is a balanced program to a building principal may be seen as "chaos" by the state department of education. The key to a successful program is to blend the work of the personnel workers with that of the larger educative process. The local school district administrator very often is excluded from providing the necessary leadership function because he is required to monitor federally and state imposed programs. Time taken for this function may force the administrator to rely on outside resources for the development of the program. If the consultants fail to identify the local school district needs, their suggested program very often fails. It is better to take additional time to develop an adequate program rather than to implement one that is doomed to failure.

Professional associations have a direct impact on the structure of the pupil personnel program in that they define the work domain of the professional specialists and the skills and competencies required to function in the setting. In some instances specialists have refused to seek employment because the local school district failed to provide adequate support in terms of staff and facilities. Professional associations use a variety of criteria to define the work setting. For example, in the health field, the work domain is defined in terms of (1) disease covered, (2) population served, (3) services rendered.[3] This classification system can be applied to pupil personnel work. For example, the school psychologist may restrict his activities to appraising elementary school children who are suspected of being mentally retarded while the school social worker may restrict her activities to visiting homes of children who have manifested severe social maladjustment. Levine and White state that "the goals of the organization constitute in effect the organization's claim to future functions, whereas the present or actual functions carried out by the organization constitute de facto claims to these elements."[4] There is a reluctance to restructure professional activities because of the fear that a position can be either eliminated in the future or so drastically altered that currently employed personnel workers cannot carry out the new tasks because of a lack of appropriate competencies. It is for this reason that many revisions of license requirements carry a "grandfather clause" which enables the current personnel workers to meet the new certification requirements. In some states licenses are issued for a limited time period, thereby forcing those who are presently qualified to keep their professional preparation current if they wish to have their licenses renewed. This procedure does not automatically guarantee quality but it does force personnel workers to become aware of changes in the field.

The formal delineation of the work domain is usually done by means of a state school code which specifies the certification

---

[3]S. Levine and P. E. White, "Exchange as a Conceptual Framework for the Study of Interorganizational Relationships," *Administrative Quarterly*, 5:584-601 (1961).

[4]*Ibid.*, p. 590.

requirements for various pupil personnel workers, the tasks they may do, and the outcomes that should be obtained. In some instances the statutes may prescribe the type of personnel workers that must be employed in a school district. The basic limitation of this type of legislation is that its focus is on the specialist rather than on the student. In attempting to restrict the practice of certain activities to qualified specialists, the legislators have only minimally considered the relationship between competencies and outcomes. It assumed that individuals who take a series of courses will have a set of competencies which will meet the needs of the students. The piecemeal development of pupil personnel services can in part be attributed to the school's providing help for specific problems rather than for the total concerns of its pupils. This piecemeal approach, in part, grew out of certification requirements. The basic attitude is that only qualified personnel can undertake a specific activity.

School Social Worker[5]

The school social worker undertakes a number of roles in discharging his functions. He must be able to do many different things because his work takes him to the school, home, and community.

> The *school social worker* is a *caseworker* who counsels with students and their parents. He is a *collaborator* who works cooperatively with other members of the school staff. He is a *coordinator* who serves as an agent to bring school and home, school and community into better working relationships. He is a *consultant* who is available to confer with other school staff members even though he may not be directly involved with students or the problems immediately in question.[6]

[5]This section represents a synthesis of the historical development of social work found in the writings of L. B. Costin, *An Analysis of the Tasks of School Social Work as a Basis for Improved Use of Staff: A Final Report,* Washington, D.C., U.S. Department of Health, Education and Welfare, 1968; V. Faust, *Establishing Guidance Programs in the Elementary School* (Boston, Houghton Mifflin Co., 1968); D. L. Hummel and S. J. Bonham, Jr., *Pupil Personnel Services* (Chicago, Rand McNally & Co., 1968); G. A. Salzman and H. J. Peters, *Pupil Personnel Services: Selected Readings* (Itasca, Illinois, E. A. Peacock, Publishers, 1967).

[6]J. L. Kelley, "Children With Problems: What Does the School Social Worker Do?" *National Education Association Bulletin,* 51:54 (1962).

When social work was introduced into the school setting, its functions were rather limited. The need for this type of service developed when compulsory education laws were introduced into this country at the turn of the century. In 1906 a visiting teacher program was introduced in the Boston and New York areas in order to help parents and schools have a better understanding of one another so that by working together they could give the child a more meaningful educational experience. Almost from its inception, the home-school-community liaison function was modified to include work with truants and delinquents. Through the 1920's the principal focus of the school social worker was on factors outside the school setting that affected the students. The manner in which this function was carried out was influenced by concepts from the mental hygiene movement and from differential psychology.

The depression of the 1930's modified the work of the school social worker in that caring for the needs of children became the principal function. This change in focus gave impetus to casework service whose activities are clinically oriented. Work with parents of emotionally disturbed children was emphasized. Teachers were consulted in order to assist them in the identification of emotional difficulties of children and to interpret the child's problem to them. In complex problems the school social worker collaborated with other pupil personnel workers in developing the treatment procedures.

The social problems of the 1960's precipitated another modification in the work of the school social worker. The school was seen as a social system within which the different subgroups did not have equal access to educational opportunities. Some social workers were of the opinion that their main function was to modify conditions and policies that blocked these subgroups from having a meaningful educational experience. Working with community action groups, the school social worker reverted back to his old function of home-school-community liaison. The basic difference was that the school social worker relied more on group work than conferences with parents.

The school social worker continues to focus his attention on problems that are generated from the interaction between the student and social forces. As social policies change, new problems confront the students and their parents. In the past, the school social worker has relied on a number of tactics to ameliorate or prevent difficulties or rehabilitate those who could not cope with societal forces. Most school administrators continue to see the school social worker's function as that of helping with the social adjustment of students in order that they have a meaningful school experience. In some school districts, the social workers are beginning to work with parents of preschool and primary level children in order to influence child rearing practices and to help parents understand how to cope with some of the problems they are having in bringing up their children. This is done by forming parent education groups and counseling groups for parents and by providing consultation services to individual parents. There is some evidence that suggests that these tactics are more beneficial to the students than some of the more traditional activities that have been performed by the school social worker.

School Psychologist

What a school psychologist does in a particular school district is a function of his level of training, the type of pupil personnel services provided by the district, and the organizational structure of the district. Generally speaking, the school psychologist has undertaken the following functions: (1) individual testing and case studies; (2) interviewing students and parents; (3) assisting in special education; (4) assisting in in-service education.[7] Interest in these functions reflects the emphasis on clinical-diagnostic-remedial orientations that the early school psychologist received in his training.

The Chicago Public Schools established the first psychological services department in the United States in 1899. The Bureau of Child Study, as it was called, investigated the physical and mental development of children. Based on its studies the Bureau of Child Study initiated classes for mentally handicapped

[7]N. Cutts, ed., *School Psychologist at Mid-Century* (Washington, D.C., American Psychological Association, 1955), p. 32.

and exceptional children. This initial program reflects the diagnostic-remedial orientation that has characterized the work of psychological services. The clinical aspect was introduced when the school psychologist began to work with juvenile delinquents and emotionally disturbed children. In some school districts responsibility for the instruction of the exceptional child has been transferred from psychological services departments to departments of instruction.

It is rather difficult for the school psychologist to escape his diagnostic function, because in many states placement in classes for exceptional children can be done only upon the recommendation of the school psychologist. Testing children and writing reports make it necessary for the school psychologist to work directly with those who require remediation or rehabilitation. Change in the role and function of the school psychologist can be brought about only by changing some of the statutes that govern their activities.

In recent years there have been a number of suggestions on the future course of school psychology. In reviewing the literature on the future role and function of the school psychologist, Magary identified the following suggestions: data oriented problem solver, consultant to teachers, educational programmer, facilitator of adjustment, facilitator of learning, coordinator of prescriptive teaching, specialist in preventative mental health, master teacher.[8] He also observed that some writers saw the school psychologist as "a clinical psychologist functioning in the schools while others see him as a general educational psychologist in the schools."[9] A role and function that appeals to many doctoral-trained school psychologists, since it would make maximum use of their skills and understandings, is that of consultant to the school district. This activity has come to be recognized as essential in large school districts because of the complexity of problems that have to be resolved.

Although there have been many suggestions made as to the

[8]J. F. Magary, ed., *School Psychological Services* (Englewood Cliffs, N.J., Prentice-Hall, In., 1967), pp. 686-705.
[9]*Ibid.*, p. 686.

direction that the school psychologist should take in the future, tradition will probably minimize the total reconstruction of the role. Faust suggests that the school psychologist will probably remain child crisis oriented but will be able to give an added dimension to those facets of his role with which he has success.[10] This broadening of the role of the psychologist can be brought about by means of a team approach to pupil personnel work. The team approach will enable the school psychologist to become more directly involved in the treatment process than he has in the past.

Other Pupil Personnel Workers

The counselor, school psychologist, and social worker are but part of the pupil personnel services. If the pupil personnel services program is to serve all students, additional staff is needed. Some of the additional staff that is required include attendance worker, nurse, physician, dental hygienist, psychiatrist, speech therapist, hearing therapist, and specialists associated with pupil appraisal services, remedial services, and special education services. The degree to which these staff members are employed in a school district depends on the size of the school district, its organizational structure, and statutory requirements. For example, attendance workers may not only be responsible for compulsory attendance in a district but may work with federal legislation as it applies to minority groups. In some school districts medical personnel are used to provide instruction in such areas as sex education and drug abuse programs.

Data processing specialists can help a school district by facilitating the work of pupil personnel workers. In addition to keeping track of students, the specialist can make data about students readily available so that the staff can better understand them. Computers can be used to make diagnoses, prescribe treatment, and in many instances monitor the remedial program. The computer can be used to help a student plan his career possibilities by helping him analyze his test scores in relationship

[10]V. Faust, *The Counselor-consultant in the Elementary School* (Boston, Houghton-Mifflin Co., 1968), p. 177.

to profiles of individuals employed in specific occupational groups. Some computer programs enable an individual to study college entrance requirements and course offerings. This search enables a student to gain greater insight into the educational opportunities that are available to him. In the near future most schools will be in a position to have access to computer programs because of such innovations as data phones and low cost terminals. In many respects, the work of the staff will have more depth because many of the time-consuming tasks will be eliminated.

A careful analysis of the work activities of counselors, social workers, and psychologists would indicate that there is a considerable amount of overlap in the functions performed by each. Not only is there an overlap in what is done but also in how it is done. Arbuckle, in reviewing the work of these specialists, makes this observation:

> It is obvious from these definitions, which I think are fairly representative and are at least "semi-official," that all three groups view themselves as working in the same milieu, namely the school and its immediate environment, and with the same basic population — the children and those who most immediately affect them — teachers, parents, and community. To varying degrees, all three see their functions as involvement in counseling, appraisal, and consultation with children, teachers, parents, other school personnel, and various members of the community.[11]

Arbuckle suggests that schools examine the functions of these specialists and reconstruct the pupil personnel program so that each student may derive greater benefits from the combined skills of its workers.

Hill presents a four-fold classification system that provides a frame of reference for considering the roles and functions of pupil personnel workers. These roles are:[12]

1. THE SUPPORTIVE ROLE. The worker is in one way or another

[11]D. S. Arbuckle, "Counselor, Social Worker, Psychologist: Let's 'Ecumenicalize,'" *Personnel and Guidance Journal,* p. 335 (1967).

[12]G. E. Hill, *Management and Improvement of Guidance* (New York, Appleton-Century-Croft, Inc., 1965), pp. 102-104.

able to provide material or moral support to those primarily responsible for the achievement of the purpose in question.

2. THE CONSULTATIVE ROLE. The school worker makes himself available to discuss with his colleague in guidance the needs and problems of a child who the counselor has had come to him for assistance.

3. THE REFERRAL ROLE. With specialization of function and competence of those in both the school and the community, referral of children to those best able to assist them is essential if the whole team is to function effectively.

4. THE SERVICE ROLE. Service is provided by all members of a school's staff to each other, service to community groups, and agencies, and service to children.

The above classification scheme helps put into perspective the relationship among the various specialists. It suggests that all those who are associated with the schools should see themselves as educators rather than specialists. In this way they can closer identify themselves with the schools rather than with their specialties and thereby increase the scope and depth of the help they give to the students.

Development of a Balanced Pupil Personnel Program

The superintendent of the school district must provide the necessary leadership needed to develop a balanced pupil personnel program. The design of the program "reflects how the school district accommodates to the expectations of society while assisting the individual pupil to optimum development."[13] In order to enhance the relationship among the various specialists, school districts evolve a complex description of tasks and job functions. The interrelationship among the specialists is formalized by rules and regulations that stipulate "who is seen by whom." The purpose of the rules is to insure uniformity and coordination.

In many instances the rules and regulations distract rather than facilitate the working relationships because they reflect bureaucratic expectations.[14] These expectations include standardi-

[13]D. L. Hummel and S. J. Bonham, *op. cit.,* p. 64.

[14]R. Corwin, "Professional Persons in Public Organizations," *Educational Administrative Quarterly,* pp. 1-22 (1965).

zation of work, division of labor, efficiency of technique, task orientation, uniformity of clients' problems, and loyalty to the school. It should also be noted that the expectations of the specialists may not necessarily be congruent with the expectations of administrators. It is this difference in expectations that very often prevents the development of a balanced pupil personnel program.

Another factor that hinders the development of a balanced pupil personnel program is the difference in expectations among the different specialists. It has been suggested that these different expectations developed because of the manner in which the different specialties were introduced into the school. In many instances it is difficult to restructure programs because it upsets tradition. "We have always done it this way" is the typical defense against innovation. Perhaps Hill's four-fold classification of roles can be used as a tactic to clarify role definitions and expectations among the staff. It would demonstrate to them that there is a range of appropriate behaviors for the specialists rather than a definite set of tasks that each should perform. The first step in the development of a balanced program is to obtain some agreement as to the possible range of appropriate behavior so that the consumers of the program would know how to cope with restructuring. For example, the teachers may take some time to comprehend the idea that the counselor, social worker, and psychologist may all engage in counseling and consulting. The distinct advantage of the range concept is that it helps the workers escape the stereotyped way of helping students.

It has been suggested by some authorities that the team approach to pupil personnel work would reduce some of the difficulties cited above. The team approach implies that all students are helped, not just those with problems. The team approach has the distinct advantage of having a greater latitude in helping a student than any one specialist. The distinct disadvantage of the team approach is the lack of designated responsibility for the team's actions. Most school administrators like to have a clearly identifiable leader so that, when they measure the team's efficiency and effectiveness, there is some specific person whom they can praise or blame for the consequences of the team's actions.

Most descriptions of a pupil personnel team fail to describe how a team functions in actions. Usually the description consists of roles, functions, and goals. Teams have been based either on the coordination or collaboration orientation. A team organized on the coordination principle functions on the idea that the resolution of a student's problem can be obtained by a systematic application of the various specialists' skills. The key to successful treatment is the appropriate ordering of the skills. This approach has some of the following weaknesses: (1) serialization of treatment negates the "whole" child concept; (2) treatment tends to be impersonal; (3) responsibility for case management is difficult to locate.

A team organized on the collaboration principle functions as though each problem confronted by the team is the team's problem. Attention is given to the whole child rather than to some part of him. Skills and competencies are used spontaneously rather than in some predetermined manner. It requires that each member of the team be concerned with the welfare of the child rather than with tenets of his professional association.

The first step in planning for a balanced pupil personnel program is to set into proper perspective the relationship between the goals of education and the goals of the pupil personnel services. Just as schools do not focus solely on the 3 R's, the pupil personnel program cannot be just problem oriented. The functions of the program must be stated in proactive rather than reactive terms.

A balanced program of pupil personnel services has as its focus the educational environment, mental health of the students, and social forces of the community. The staff of the program may be directly or indirectly involved in prevention, diagnosis, remediation, and rehabilitation of the problems associated with the three major areas. The basic purpose of the pupil personnel services program is to provide an environment which enhances the student's quest for self-actualization. The program should be balanced in terms of meeting the needs of all the students rather than permitting the specialists to exercise their skills and competencies.

SUMMARY

A balanced pupil personnel services program is one in which all students are helped to meet their needs rather than being restricted to those students who have particular problems with the school. Its focus is the total environment in which the students interact. Although it is basically interested in the educational elements of the environment, the staff is also concerned with the students' mental health and the social forces that impinge on them. The structure of the program is affected by state and federal legislation and by prescriptions of professional associations. The superintendent of schools provides the leadership for designing the program. He does this by primarily allowing the staff to interact in a manner that permits them to explore their professional expectations in terms of role behaviors and outcomes. This type of interaction permits the staff to reach a consensus as to who does what, for what purpose. Although the basic mode of operating the program may be in terms of coordination of effort or collaboration of skills and understanding, the guiding theme should be the needs of the students rather than the professional interests of the staff.

CHAPTER XII

TRENDS AND ISSUES IN EDUCATION

Harold A. Moses

A CCOUNTABILITY AND RELEVANCY, two concepts which have come into recent prominence in education, will continue to exert a powerful influence upon pupil personnel work, as well as upon all aspects of education. By accountability, we mean that the value of education will no longer be accepted on faith but will have to demonstrate its usefulness to the individual and to society. Any institution which depends upon public support for its existence can ill afford to ignore or neglect that public. The current financial status of many school systems and institutions of higher learning offer agonizing proof of this.

With the vast explosion of knowledge, it becomes more and more apparent that everything which might be considered important cannot be taught by the schools. Since only a small percentage of the worthwhile information can be exposed, what is to be taught becomes a crucial issue. The question of what should be included is debatable, but that there must be a realignment of priorities cannot be denied. Even a superficial appraisal of the conditions existing in society should convince the most conservative educator that, not only should it be possible to improve the situation, but that our very survival depends on it.

Professional Ethics

The question of ethics, confidentiality, and legality pertaining to student personnel specialists continues to constitute an area of concern and debate. Most professional organizations have attempted to clarify these issues by developing codes of ethics.

However, codes by necessity must be general and brief and cannot possibly cover all situations. Therefore, the personnel worker frequently finds himself confronted by issues which require that he make individual decisions. It is relatively rare, however, that, if the worker has exercised the foresight to anticipate and think through possible problems, he will get caught in ethical dilemmas. Many so-called ethical problems are not due to ethics per se, but are caused, among other reasons, by our own ineptness, fear of offending others, or great need for acceptance. The code of ethics of the American Personnel and Guidance Association, the American Psychological Association, the National Association of Social Workers, and the National Education Association, organizations to which most student personnel workers belong or should belong, are presented in Appendixes A, B, C, and D of this volume. A careful reading and consideration of these Codes, plus discussion of the issues with professional colleagues, should help resolve most ethical problems which the typical student personnel worker will encounter. This statement is meant, not to deny the importance of ethical issues, but to emphasize that, as professionals, we are capable of doing more than wringing our hands and bemoaning our fate. Indeed, it is one of the characteristics of a profession that the individual is required to make independent decisions and is held responsible for them.

Labor Unions

For the past quarter of a century, union membership has constituted from one-fourth to one-fifth of the total labor force in our nation. One's attitude toward unions doesn't alter this basic fact. That labor unions are a powerful force in society today is indisputable and, whether or not one joins or approves of a labor union, his life is influenced by them.

Personnel workers, especially when dealing with vocational planning, must consider unions. For all practical purposes some union membership, like admission to some professional schools, is restricted to a select few. Although every personnel worker should abhor and fight discrimination wherever it is exercised, he should neither underestimate the strength of his foe nor use his students as vehicles to breaking down barriers without the students' knowledge and approval. Crusaders are needed and encouraged, but the crusader who uses others to do the dirty work or suffer the consequences of an unsuccessful crusade are to be condemned. This holds true regardless of the righteousness or aim of the crusade, whether to benefit minority groups, the physically disabled, or the socially handicapped.

Changes in Education

Wrenn[1] notes a number of changes in the education system as a whole within the school and within the curriculum, of which the counselor should be aware. He states that school districts are combining at a rapid rate, school buildings are becoming more functional in design and more flexible in operation, schools will be utilized for more than the traditional thirty-six to thirty-eight weeks a year, and adult education will increase.

Wrenn predicts that within the school there will be a more widespread use of audio visual aids, programmed instruction, better utilization of teaching talent, and flexible ability grouping to provide for individual differences.[2]

The National Education Association reported on a survey study of ability grouping.[3] One argument in favor of homogenous grouping is that it challenges pupils and allows them to advance at their own rate. Proponents maintain that, since pupils are together in other school activities, homogenous grouping is not undemocratic. Teaching methods and materials, more directly applicable, saves time so that the teacher can provide individual attention and raise educational standards.

Opponents of ability grouping point out that true homogenous grouping is impossible and question the validity of the

---

[1]C. G. Wrenn, *The Counselor in a Changing World* (Washington, D.C., American Personnel and Guidance Association, 1962).

[2]*Ibid.*

[3]"Ability Grouping," *NEA Research Bulletin*, 1968, 74-76.

data used for grouping. They argue that stigma and snobbishness are encouraged by grouping and that students are denied the opportunity to learn to live and work with others of different abilities.

The survey concluded from fifty research studies conducted since 1960 that, although extensive research results were available, they were indefinite and inconclusive. There seems to be no consensus as to what ability grouping means, therefore, the results of various studies are noncomparable and uninterpretative. They point out that positive results may be due to other factors such as modification of materials, methods, objectives, or curricula. They also question the use of standardized tests of academic achievement as the criterion of success and emphasize the difficulty of determining the ability of students, especially during the early years.

Wrenn, in discussing curriculum changes, says that more attention either is being given or should be given to understanding of other cultures, making wise economic and family choices, developing a sense of values, and providing for the educational needs of girls.[4]

Counselor Certification

A study of certification procedures of school counselors in all fifty states plus the District of Columbia was reported in the American School Counselor Association (ASCA) Newsletter. Highlights of the report were:[5]

> By 1971, every state in the United States will have specific requirements for certifying school counselors.
>
> Most states now grant separate certificates, rather than by endorsement of teaching certificates.
>
> The majority of states provide a provisional or temporary license and period of review before issuing life-time certification (the most common permanent certification).
>
> The Master's Degree is the educational level at which permanent certification is most commonly granted.

[4]Wrenn, *op. cit.*

[5]*ASCA Newsletter,* January 23, 1970.

Nine states will certify school counselors without the teaching requirement, while over one-half of the states require other-than-teaching vocational experience.

Reciprocity of certification is now available in five states while fifteen states will certify fully certified counselors from all other states.

Certification refusal normally occurs from a lack of specific course work, required work experiences, training institution recommendation, practicum experience, college accreditation, or recent academic course work.

When asked about the ways in which ASCA might be most helpful in bringing about improvement in the certification of school counselors, the following suggestions were offered:

Nationwide certification of counselors through program and institution accreditation efforts.

Bring about or publish information of reciprocal agreements between states involving the ACES Standards for Counselor Preparation.

Develop closer working relationships between state guidance personnel, counselor educators, and ASCA. This would hopefully help equate course content and training experiences.

Evaluation of Pupil Personnel Services

A question frequently asked by administrators is, How do I know that student personnel workers are doing an effective job? This is a legitimate question but a difficult one to answer.

Froehlich[6] reported on his intensive review of a large number of approaches, studies, surveys, and commentaries on evaluation of guidance procedures. The seven basic approaches or methods of evaluation he identified were external criteria, follow-up, client opinion, expert opinion, specific techniques, within-the-group-changes, and between-the-group-changes.

Although each of these methods has the potential to yield valuable information, each has its shortcomings and may fail to answer the question of effectiveness if a more basic question has not previously been asked.

The basic question that must be raised is, What are the purposes or goals of a student personnel program? Only after

[6]C. P. Froehlich, *Evaluating Guidance Procedures,* Washington, D. C., Office of Education, 1949.

this question has been analyzed and clarified can one approach the issue of effectiveness. Many workers have been derelict in developing a position paper or a detailed explanation of the goals of student personnel services. Goals such as the development of the whole child, while laudable and worthwhile, are too generic to be of much value in the evaluation of student personnel programs. Jenson, Coles, and Nestor[7] have described the characteristics of a useful criterion variable as one that is definable, stable, relevant, shows variability in the general population, and its ultimate-immediate nature is known. Unless the personnel worker can describe what he is trying to do, demonstrate that conditions under investigation have some degree of constancy, show that what he did has relationship to the measured outcome, indicate that variability was possible, and provide evidence that there is a known or logical relationship between measures of immediate performance with ultimate objectives, his study of effectiveness will be of little benefit.

Frequently, student personnel workers have found that their duties have been prescribed by others who do not understand or appreciate the appropriate role and function of personnel workers. Their reaction to such a situation may be anger, defensiveness, or apathy. A more positive course of action is recommended.

Ground rules are extremely important in any endeavor and personnel services is no exception. These rules must be spelled out and areas of disagreement resolved before issues and personalities become involved. If the game is played by ear it is much more difficult, if not impossible, to obtain consensus or even a workable arrangement during crisis periods.

Most educators tend to be reasonable individuals and, if the student personnel worker knows his role and function and can articulate his position, it is highly probable that he can convince significant others as to the feasibility of his reasoning. If

[7]B. T. Jenson, G. Coles, and B. Nestor. "The Criterion Problem in Guidance Research," in C. H. Patterson ed., *The Counselor in the School* (New York, McGraw-Hill Book Company, 1967), p. 425-431.

the worker is hazy as to what he should be doing or fails to communicate his position to others, it is primarily his own neglect that causes his problems.

Student personnel services take a considerable amount of a school's budget, and administrators, teachers, parents, and taxpayers have the right, even the responsibility, to ask, Of what value is student personnel work? Rather than giving workers reason to become vague or defensive, this inquiry should be welcomed and viewed as an opportunity to educate the public about the values of personnel services. If the worker has developed a professional attitude toward his work, he should, on the whole, find that answering questions is a challenging and gratifying task, though he may at times find it difficult to convince some individuals of the value of his work.

Rights and Obligations of Student Personnel Workers

There is some evidence that student personnel workers have fallen victim to the currently popular national pastime of bemoaning their lack of rights and criticizing others for their dilemma. This form of projection is probably a universal defense mechanism, perhaps sometimes beneficial when not overused, but it may become self-defeating and inhibit constructive effort.

Why, we may ask, have student personnel workers failed to receive the rights, respect, and prestige which they feel is rightfully theirs? For illustrative purposes, let's consider the school counselor. Admittedly, many counselors have gone into or have been caught in situations where they have little if anything to say about the definition of their role. This is indeed unfortunate, but again many have been assigned unacceptable roles by default. Everyone who works in a school system must have a role to perform; if he doesn't define this role, he may rest assured that someone else define it for him. It is much simpler to work out one's role and obtain approval of it than to change a role, that has been defined by someone else. The counselor, who accepts a job without inquiring about what is expected of him, should blame only himself if he is assigned duties which he feels are uncomplimentary to his training or contradictory to the role he feels he should perform.

The counselor who oversells himself and his function is asking for future problems. Counseling is not a panacea for all of a school's ills and any counselor, who so advertises it or who sits silently by while others do so, is laying the groundwork for future dissatisfaction and disillusionment of the counseling program. Although schools have no rock piles to assign to their personnel, they do have myriad clerical tasks and flunky chores which are almost as monotonous and nonrewarding.

Teachers who see counseling as an escape from the classroom are a detriment to the counseling movement. They usually seek to fulfill only the minimum requirements for certification and are usually not really qualified to function as counselors. Consequently, they often welcome or even seek routine chores from the administration to occupy their time. Since their time is then occupied, they can say with righteous indignation, "How can you expect me to do counseling when I have all these other duties to perform?"

The person, who becomes a "counselor' 'and then is afraid to establish a close interpersonal relationship with another person, will do little if any counseling. He, too, will seek out and find other excuses for not performing his rightful duties.

These persons are not only guilty of unethical practice but actually prostitute themselves and the counseling profession. They fail to do counseling and make it very difficult for a new member of the staff to counsel, since the new member will, in all probability, be expected to do as many routine noncounseling duties as they. They are detrimental to the recruitment of desirable candidates into the counseling profession; a person, who is interested in counseling but observes what "counselors" do or hears criticism from school staff members because counselors submerge themselves in minutiae and are unavailable for help which they are supposedly capable of giving, may change his mind.

Any person who calls himself a counselor should spend a

minimum of fifty percent of his time in direct contact with students in a counseling situation. If he does not, he should not be called a counselor. The person who does not desire to spend time with students should leave the field, thereby allowing someone who is interested in counseling to fill his position and fulfill this important function.

Counseling should not be considered a reward for long years of faithful service to a school. The fact that one is a good teacher does not guarantee that he will be a good counselor and vice versa. The skills required of each are probably equal but not necessarily identical. Having good teachers is as important to a school as having good counselors; we should be alert to the fallacy of believing that the positions of counselor and teacher are interchangeable. Therefore, the use of effective teaching as the sole criterion for encouraging good teachers to become counselors may be an injustice to teaching, counseling, the individual, the students, and society.

The counselor who has arrived, who knows all he needs to know about counseling, is a drawback to the profession. No one knows all he should know about this field and, even if he did, new developments would soon put him back in the Dark Ages as far as counseling is concerned. Therefore, the professional counselor must constantly strive to keep his skills and knowledge from becoming obsolete. He can do this in many ways but a conscious, determined effort on his part is essential.

Before we as individual counselors and as a profession begin to scream for our rights, we should take a glance at our obligations. We, as do all other persons in our society, do have rights, but we should never lose sight of the fact that for every right any individual or professional person has, he has a corresponding responsibility.

We have the right to help define our functions as counselors, but we have the obligation to make our ideas known to the proper authorities. We have the right to be treated as professionals, which carries the responsibility of being professionally trained and performing our duties in a professional manner.

We have the right to counsel students, but we must be qualified, ready, and willing to do so. We should be consulted on all issues pertaining to our specialty, but we must be prepared to make positive contributions. Therefore, counselors, as members of an emerging but healthy profession, should be as equally conscious of their responsibilities as they are of their rights. If they make a serious attempt to fulfill their obligations, they will have less need to worry about their rights.

The Student Personnel Worker of the Future

The complexity of modern society has contributed to feelings of loneliness and alienation of its citizens, and students are no exception. The large modern schools make it easy for one to feel lost and insignificant, a number instead of a person. Students feel "caught up" in the system with no recourse, a feeling that nobody really cares and that their lives are other-directed instead of self-directed. Often this feeling has too much basis in fact.

Student personnel workers of the future should serve as student advocates, a kind of ombudsmen, to whom the student may come to air his gripes and concerns. A two-way communication process in which both parties can understand each other better is needed. Many problems are caused by a breakdown in communication or interpretation. Lines of communication, kept open and used routinely, should go a long way toward preventing crisis situations. If the two-way communication is to be effective, the student personnel worker must be perceived by the student as a confidant, not as a quasi-administrator or disciplinarian. He must be the person to whom the student can talk, without fear of recrimination or a violation of confidence. If this concept sounds too radical for many administrators and teachers, it is the responsibility of the personnel worker to inform them of the necessity for it.

The student personnel worker will increasingly find that he is a team member. Since no one discipline has all the answers to the problems faced by students, teamwork is not only desirable but essential if students are to be served in a humanistic manner. A high degree of cooperation among large numbers of individuals will be required, and integration of ideas and compromise will become important. It will become of greater importance that the personnel worker become more actively involved with parents and community agencies. The perspective of the school must be enlarged to encompass all aspects of the student's life. The school should not be expected to attend to all the needs of the student, but it must at least be aware of the various forces and pressures which influence his life.

SUMMARY

Prediction for education, as in any area is a hazardous activity. However, it does seem safe to state unequivocally that change is currently the "in" thing in education and will probably continue to be for some time. A climate of change and innovations should be welcomed by educators because it affords them the opportunity to try out new ideas and methods. Certainly few would maintain that we have reached the optimum or ultimate in education. However, one should avoid the two extremes which are omnipresent in most settings. One extreme is to resist any suggestions of change and to maintain that the way things have been done in the past is the only way. Equally dangerous is to want change merely for the sake of change. Because something is new does not necessarily mean that it is better; it may be grossly inferior.

Many changes, espoused as new, are actually quite old. Two reasons for this are possible. The individual may actually think that he has a new idea and hasn't bothered to investigate the issue; or, since innovations are held in such high esteem, he may be tempted to dress up old ideas in an attempt to palm them off as original. While he should not demand high level research results or empirical evidence before he is willing to try or let others try new ideas, the innovator should be able to at least furnish a logical rationale for making changes if he expects others to embrace his ideas.

ETHICAL STANDARDS

APPENDIX A

American Personnel and Guidance Association

PREAMBLE

The American Personnel and Guidance Association is an educational, scientific, and professional organization dedicated to service to society. This service is committed to profound faith in the worth, dignity, and great potentiality of the individual human being.

The marks of a profession, and therefore of a professional organization, can be stated as follows:

1. Possession of a body of specialized knowledge, skills, and attitudes known and practiced by its members.

2. This body of specialized knowledge, skills, and attitudes is derived through scientific inquiry and scholarly learning.

3. This body of specialized knowledge, skills, and attitudes is acquired through professional preparation, preferably on the graduate level, in a college or university as well as through continuous in-service training and personal growth after completion of formal education.

4. This body of specialized knowledge, skills, and attitudes, is constantly tested and extended through research and scholarly inquiry.

5. A profession has a literature of its own, even though it may, and indeed must, draw portions of its content from other areas of knowledge.

6. A profession exalts service to the individual and society above personal gain. It possesses a philosophy and a code of ethics.

7. A profession through the voluntary association of its

Reprinted with permission of the American Personnel and Guidance Association, Washington, D.C., 1961.

members constantly examines and improves the quality of its professional preparation and services to the individual and society.

8. Membership in the professional organization and the practice of the profession must be limited to persons meeting stated standards of preparation and competencies.

9. The profession affords a life career and permanent membership as long as services meet professional standards.

10. The public recognizes, has confidence in, and is willing to compensate the members of the profession for their services.

The Association recognizes that the vocational roles and settings of its members are identified with a wide variety of academic disciplines and levels of academic preparation. This diversity reflects the pervasiveness of the Association's interest and influence. It also poses challenging complexities in efforts to conceptualize:

a. the characteristics of members;

b. desired or requisite preparation or practice; and

c. supporting social, legal and/or ethical controls.

The specification of ethical standards enables the Association to clarify to members, future members, and to those served by members the nature of ethical responsibilities held in common by its members.

The introduction of such standards will inevitably stimulate greater concern by members for practice and preparation for practice. It will also stimulate a general growth and identification with and appreciation for both the common and diverse characteristics of the definable roles within the world of work of Association members.

There are six major areas of professional activity which encompass the work of members of APGA. For each of these areas certain general principles are listed below to serve as guide lines for ethical practice. These are preceded by a general section which includes certain principles germane to the six areas and common to the entire work of the Association members.

Section A

GENERAL

1. The member exerts what influence he can to foster the development and improvement of the profession and continues his professional growth throughout his career.

2. The member has a responsibility to the institution within which he serves. His acceptance of employment by the institution implies that he is in substantial agreement with the general policies and principles of the institution. Therefore, his professional activities are also in accord with the objectives of the institution. Within the member's own work setting, if, despite his efforts, he cannot reach agreement as to acceptable ethical standards of conduct with his superiors, he should end his affiliation with them.

3. The member must expect ethical behavior among his professional associates in APGA at all times. He is obligated, in situations where he possesses information raising serious doubt as to the ethical behavior of other members, to attempt to rectify such conditions.

4. The member is obligated to concern himself with the degree to which the personnel functions of non-members with whose work he is acquainted represent competent and ethical performance. Where his information raises serious doubt as to the ethical behavior of such persons, it is his responsibility to attempt to rectify such conditions.

5. The member must not seek self-enhancement through expressing evaluations or comparisons damaging to other ethical professional workers.

6. The member should not claim or imply professional qualifications exceeding those possessed and is responsible for correcting any misrepresentations of his qualifications by others.

7. The member providing services for personal remuneration shall, in establishing fees for such services, take careful account of the charges made for comparable services by other professional persons.

8. The member who provides information to the public

or to his subordinates, peers, or superiors has a clear responsibility to see that both the content and the manner of presentation are accurate and appropriate to the situation.

9. The member has an obligation to ensure that evaluative information about such persons as clients, students, and applicants shall be shared only with those persons who will use such information for professional purposes.

10. The member shall offer professional services only, through the context of a professional relationship. Thus testing, counseling, and other services are not to be provided through the mail by means of newspaper or magazine articles, radio or television programs, or public performances.

Section B

COUNSELING

This section refers to practices involving a counseling relationship with a counselee or client and is not intended to be applicable to practices involving administrative relationships with the persons being helped. A counseling relationship denotes that the person seeking help retain full freedom of choice and decision and that the helping person has no authority or responsibility to approve or disapprove of the choice of decisions of the counselee or client. "Counselee" or "client" is used here to indicate the person (or persons) for whom the member has assumed a professional responsibility. Typically the counselee or client is the individual with whom the member has direct and primary contact. However, at times, "client" may include another person(s) when the other person(s) exercise significant control and direction over the individual being helped in connection with the decisions and plans being considered in counseling.

1. The member's *primary* obligation is to respect the integrity and promote the welfare of the counselee or client with whom he is working.

2. The counseling relationship and information resulting

therefrom must be kept confidential consistent with the obligations of the member as a professional person.

3. Records of the counseling relationship including interview notes, test data, correspondence, tape recordings and other documents are to be considered professional information for use in counseling, research, and teaching of counselors but always with full protection of the identity of the client and with precaution so that no harm will come to him.

4. The counselee or client should be informed of the conditions under which he may receive counseling assistance at or before the time he enters the counseling relationship. This is particularly true in the event that there exist conditions of which the counselee or client would not likely be aware.

5. The member reserves the right to consult with any other professionally competent person about his counselee client. In choosing his professional consultant the member must avoid placing the consultant in a conflict of interest situation, i.e., the consultant must be free of any other obligatory relation to the member's client that would preclude the consultant being a proper party to the member's efforts to help the counselee or client.

6. The member shall decline to initiate or shall terminate a counseling relationship when he cannot be of professional assistance to the counselee or client either because of lack of competence or personal limitation. In such instances the member shall refer his counselee or client to an appropriate specialist. In the event the counselee or client declines the suggested referral, the member is not obligated to continue the counseling relationship.

7. When the member learns from counseling relationships of conditions which are likely to harm others over whom his institution or agency has responsibility, he is expected to report *the condition* to the appropriate responsible authority, but in such a manner as not to reveal the identity of his counselee or clients.

8. In the event that the counselee or client's condition is such as to require others to assume responsibility for him, or when

there is clear and imminent danger to the counselee or client or to others, the member is expected to report this fact to an appropriate responsible authority, and/or take such other emergency measures as the situation demands.

9. Should the member be engaged in a work setting which calls for any variation from the above statements, the member is obligated to ascertain that such variations are justifiable under the conditions and that such variations are clearly specified and made known to all concerned with such counseling services.

Section C

TESTING

1. The primary purpose of psychological testing is to provide objective and comparative measures for use in self-evaluation or evaluation by others of general or specific attributes.

2. Generally, test results constitute only one of a variety of pertinent data for personnel and guidance decisions. It is the member's responsibility to provide adequate orientation or information to the examinee(s) so that the results of testing may be placed in proper perspective with other relevant factors.

3. When making any statements to the public about tests and testing care must be taken to give accurate information and to avoid any false claims or misconceptions.

4. Different tests demand different levels of competence for administration, scoring, and interpretation. It is therefore the responsibility of the member to recognize the limits of his competence and to perform only those functions which fall within his preparation and competence.

5. In selecting tests for use in a given situation or with a particular client the member must consider not only general but also specific validity, reliability, and appropriateness of the test(s).

6. Tests should be administered under the same conditions which were established in their standardization. Except for research purposes explicitly stated, any departures from these

conditions, as well as unusual behavior or irregularities during the testing-session which may affect the interpretation of the test results, must be fully noted and reported. In this connection, unsupervised test-taking or the use of tests through the mails are of questionable value.

7. The value of psychological tests depends in part on the novelty to persons taking them. Any prior information, coaching, or reproduction of test materials tends to invalidate test results. Therefore, test security is one of the professional obligations to the member.

8. The member has the responsibility to inform the examinee(s) as to the purpose of testing. The criteria of examinee's welfare and/or explicit prior understanding with him should determine who the recipients of the test results may be.

9. The member should guard against the appropriation, reproduction, or modifications of published tests or parts thereof without express permission and adequate recognition of the original author or publisher.

Regarding the preparation, publication, and distribution of tests reference should be made to:

"Tests and Diagnostic Techniques"—Report of the Joint Committee on the American Psychological Association, American Educational Research Association, and National Council of Measurements used in Education. Supplement to *Psychological Bulletin*, 1954, 2, 1-38.

Section D

RESEARCH AND PUBLICATION

1. In the performance of any research on human subjects, the member must avoid causing any injurious effects or aftereffects of the experiment upon his subjects.

2. The member may withhold information or provide misinformation to subjects only when it is essential to the investigation and where he assumes responsibility for corrective action following the investigation.

3. In reporting research results, explicit mention must be made of all variables and conditions known to the investigator which might affect interpretation of the data.

4. The member is responsible for conducting and reporting his investigations so as to minimize the possibility that his findings will be misleading.

5. The member has an obligation to make available original research data to qualified others who may wish to replicate or verify the study.

6. In reporting research results or in making original data available, due care must be taken to disguise the identity of the subjects, in the absence of specific permission from such subjects to do otherwise.

7. In conducting and reporting research, the member should be familiar with, and give recognition to, previous work on the topic.

8. The member has the obligation to give due credit to those who have contributed significantly to his research, in accordance with their contributions.

9. The member has the obligation to honor commitments made to subjects of research in return for their cooperation.

10. The member is expected to communicate to other members the results of any research he judges to be of professional or scientific value.

Section E

CONSULTING AND PRIVATE PRACTICE

Consulting refers to a voluntary relationship between a professional helper and help-needing social unit (industry, business, school, college, etc.) in which the consultant is attempting to give help to the client in the solving of some current or potential problem.

1. The member acting as a consultant must have a high degree of self-awareness of his own values and needs in entering a helping relationship which involves change in a social unit.

2. There should be understanding and agreement between

consultant and client as to directions or goals of the attempted change.

3. The consultant must be reasonably certain that he or his organization have the necessary skills and resources for giving the kind of help which is needed now or that may develop later.

4. The consulting relationship must be one in which client adaptability and growth toward self-direction are encouraged and cultivated. The consultant must consistently maintain his role as a consultant and not become a decision maker for the client.

5. The consultant in announcing his availability for service as a consultant follows professional rather than commercial standards in describing his services with accuracy, dignity, and caution.

6. For private practice in testing, counseling, or consulting the ethical principles stated in all previous sections of this document are pertinent. In addition, any individual, agency, or institution offering educational and vocational counseling to the public should meet the standards of the American Board on Professional Standards in Vocational Counseling, Inc.

Section F

PERSONNEL ADMINISTRATION

1. The member is responsible for establishing working agreements with supervisors and with subordinates especially regarding counseling or clinical relationships, confidentiality, distinction between public and private material, and a mutual respect for the positions of parties involved in such issues.

2. Such working agreements may vary from one institutional setting to another. What should be the case in each instance, however, is that agreements have been specified, made known to those concerned, and whenever possible the agreements reflect institutional policy rather than personal judgment.

3. The member's responsibility to his superiors requires that he keep them aware of conditions affecting the institution, particularly those which may be potentially disrupting or damaging to the institution.

4. The member has a responsibility to select competent

2. Shall not deliberately suppress or distort subject matter for which he bears responsibility.
3. Shall make reasonable effort to protect the student from conditions harmful to learning or to health and safety.
4. Shall conduct professional business in such a way that he does not expose the student to unnecessary embarrassment or disparagement.
5. Shall not on the ground of race, color, creed, or national origin exclude any student from participation in or deny him benefits under any program, nor grant any discriminatory consideration or advantage.
6. Shall not use professional relationships with students for private advantage.
7. Shall keep in confidence information that has been obtained in the course of professional service, unless disclosure serves professional purposes or is required by law.
8. Shall not tutor for remuneration students assigned to his classes, unless no other qualified teacher is reasonably available.

Principle II

Commitment to the Public

The educator believes that patriotism in its highest form requires dedication to the principles of our democratic heritage. He shares with all other citizens the responsibility for the development of sound public policy and assumes full political and citizenship responsibilities. The educator bears particular responsibility for the development of policy relating to the extension of educational opportunities for all and for interpreting educational programs and policies to the public.

In fulfilling his obligation to the public, the educator:

1. Shall not misrepresent an institution or organization with which he is affiliated, and shall take adequate precautions to distinguish between his personal and institutional or organizational views.

2. Shall not knowingly distort or misrepresent the facts concerning educational matters in direct and indirect public expressions.
3. Shall not interfere with a colleague's exercise of political and citizenship rights and responsibilities.
4. Shall not use institutional privileges for private gain or to promote political candidates or partisan political activities.
5. Shall accept no gratuities, gifts, or favors that might impair or appear to impair professional judgment, nor offer any favor, service, or thing of value to obtain special advantage.

Principle III

Commitment to the Profession

The educator believes that the quality of the services of the education profession directly influences the nation and its citizens. He therefore exerts every effort to raise professional standards, to improve his service, to promote a climate in which the exercise of professional judgment is encouraged, and to achieve conditions which attract persons worthy of the trust to careers in education. Aware of the value of united effort, he contributes actively to the support, planning, and programs of professional organizations.

In fulfilling his obligation to the profession, the educator:

1. Shall not discriminate on the ground of race, color, creed, or national origin for membership in professional organizations, nor interfere with the free participation of colleagues in the affairs of their association.
2. Shall accord just and equitable treatment to all members of the profession in the exercise of their professional rights and responsibilities.
3. Shall not knowingly withhold information regarding a position from an applicant or misrepresent an assignment or conditions of employment.
4. Shall give prompt notice to the employing agency of any

change in availability of service, and the employing agent shall give prompt notice of change in availability or nature of a position.

5. Shall not refuse to participate in a professional inquiry when requested by an appropriate professional association.
6. Shall provide upon the request of the aggrieved party a written statement of specific reason for recommendations that lead to the denial of increments, significant changes in employment, or termination of employment.
7. Shall not misrepresent his professional qualifications.
8. Shall not knowingly distort evaluations of colleagues.

Principle IV

Commitment to Professional Employment Practices

The educator regards the employment agreement as a pledge to be executed both in spirit and in fact in a manner consistent with the highest ideals of professional service. He believes that sound professional personnel relationships with governing boards are built upon personal integrity, dignity, and mutual respect. The educator discourages the practice of his profession by unqualified persons.

In fulfilling his obligation to professional employment practices, the educator:

1. Shall apply for, accept, offer, or assign a position or responsibility on the basis of professional preparation and legal qualifications.
2. Shall apply for a specific position only when it is known to be vacant, and shall refrain from underbidding or commenting adversely about other candidates.
3. Shall not knowingly withhold information regarding a position from an applicant or misrepresent an assignment or conditions of employment.
4. Shall give prompt notice to the employing agency of any change in availability of service, and the employing agent shall give prompt notice of change in availability or nature of a position.

5. Shall adhere to the terms of a contract or appointment, unless these terms have been legally terminated, falsely represented, or substantially altered by unilateral action of the employing agency.
6. Shall conduct professional business through channels, when available, that have been jointly approved by the professional organization and the employing agency.
7. Shall not delegate assigned tasks to unqualified personnel.
8. Shall permit no commercial exploitation of his professional position.
9. Shall use time granted for the purpose for which it is intended.

Bylaws, National Education Association

Article I, Section 12. Adherence to the Code of Ethics adopted by the Association shall be a condition of membership. The Committee on Professional Ethics shall after due notice and hearing have power to censure, suspend, or expel any member for violation of the Code subject to review by the Executive Committee. A member may within sixty days after a decision by the Ethics Committee file an appeal of the decision with the Executive Secretary.

Provisions for National Enforcement

Code Development—It shall be the duty of the Committee to maintain a continuous review of the Code of Ethics of the Education Profession. Amendments or revision of the Code shall be presented for approval to the Representative Assembly.

Interpretations of the Code of Ethics of the Education Profession—A request for interpretation of the Code shall be in writing and shall describe the matter to be interpreted in sufficient detail to enable the members of the Committee on Professional Ethics to evaluate the request in all its aspects.

Disciplinary Action—In addition to the provisions of Article I, Section 12, the Committee on Professional Ethics will consider disciplinary action against a member when written charges are preferred by the official governing body of the NEA affiliated state or local education association or NEA Department of which the person in question is a member.

If charges are based on a hearing held by any of the groups authorized to prefer charges, a record of the hearing shall be submitted to the Committee on Professional Ethics. Disciplinary action will only be considered as resulting from a fair hearing or a proper hearing record. A member will have an opportunity to show cause why such action should not be taken.

Reprinted with permission of the National Education Association.

CODE OF ETHICS

(Adopted by the Delegate Assembly of the National Association
of Social Workers, October 13, 1960, and
amended April 11, 1967)

Social work is based on humanitarian, democratic ideals. Professional social workers are dedicated to service for the welfare of mankind; to the disciplined use of a recognized body of knowledge about human beings and their interactions and to the marshaling of community resources to promote the well-being of all without discrimination.

Social work practice is a public trust that requires of its practitioners integrity, compassion, belief in the dignity and worth of human beings, respect for individual differences, a commitment to service, and a dedication to truth. It requires mastery of a body of knowledge and skill gained through professional education and experience. It requires also recognition of the limitations of present knowledge and skill and of the services we are now equipped to give. The end sought is the performance of a service with integrity and competence.

Each member of the profession carries responsibility to maintain and improve social work service; constantly to examine, use, and increase the knowledge upon which practice and social policy are based; and to develop further the philosophy and skills of the profession.

This Code of Ethics embodies certain standards of behavior for the social worker in his professional relationships with those he serves, with his colleagues, with his employing agency, with other professions, and with the community. In abiding by it, the social worker views his obligations in as wide a context as the situation requires, takes all of the principles into consideration, and chooses a course of action consistent with the code's spirit and intent.

As a member of the National Association of Social Workers I commit myself to conduct my professional relationships in accord with the code and subscribe to the following statements:

—I regard as my primary obligation the welfare of the individual or group served, which includes action for improving social conditions.

—I will not discriminate because of race, color, religion, age, sex, or national ancestry, and in my job capacity will work to prevent and eliminate such discrimination in rendering service, in work assignments, and in employment practices.

—I give precedence to my professional responsibility over my personal interests.

—I hold myself responsible for the quality and extent of the service I perform.

—I respect the privacy of the people I serve.

—I use in a responsible manner information gained in professional relationships.

—I treat with respect the findings, views, and actions of colleagues, and use appropriate channels to express judgment on these matters.

—I practice social work within the recognized knowledge and competence of the profession.

—I recognize my professional responsibility to add my ideas and findings to the body of social work knowledge and practice.

—I accept responsibility to help protect the community against unethical practice by any individuals or organizations engaged in social welfare activities.

—I stand ready to give appropriate professional service in public emergencies.

—I distinguish clearly, in public, between my statements and actions as an individual and as a representative of an organization.

—I support the principle that professional practice requires professional education.

—I accept responsibility for working toward the creation and maintenance of conditions within agencies which enable social workers to conduct themselves in keeping with this code.

—I contribute my knowledge, skills, and support to programs of human welfare.

Reprinted with permission from NASW Policy Statement I: Code of Ethics (New York, National Association of Social Workers, 1967).

ETHICAL STANDARDS OF PSYCHOLOGISTS[1]

The psychologist believes in the dignity and worth of the individual human being. He is committed to increasing man's understanding of himself and others. While pursuing this endeavor, he protects the welfare of any person who may seek his service or of any subject, human or animal, that may be the object of his study. He does not use his professional position or relationships, nor does he knowingly permit his own service to be used by others, for purposes inconsistent with these values. While demanding for himself freedom of inquiry and communication, he accepts the responsibility this freedom confers: for competence where he claims it, for objectivity in the report of his findings, and for consideration of the best interests of his colleagues and of society.

Specific Principles

Principle 1. Responsibility. The psychologist,[2] committed to increasing man's understanding of man, places high value on objectivity and integrity, and maintains the highest standards in the services he offers.

   a. As a scientist, the psychologist believes that society will be best served when he investigates where his judgment indicates investigation is needed; he plans his research in such a way to minimize the possibility that his findings will be misleading; and he publishes full reports of his work, never discarding without explanation data which

---

[1]Reprinted from *Casebook on Ethical Standards of Psychologists.* Washington, D.C.: American Psychological Association, 1967.

[2]A student of psychology who assumes the role of psychologist shall be considered a psychologist for the purpose of this code of ethics.

may modify the interpretation of results.

b. As a teacher, the psychologist recognizes his primary obligation to help others acquire knowledge and skill, and to maintain high standards of scholarship.

c. As a practitioner, the psychologist knows that he bears a heavy social responsibility because his work may touch intimately the lives of others.

Principle 2. Competence. The maintenance of high standards of professional competence is a responsibility shared by all psychologists, in the interest of the public and of the profession as a whole.

a. Psychologists discourage the practice of psychology by unqualified persons and assist the public in identifying psychologists competent to give dependable professional services. When a psychologist or a person identifying himself as a psychologist violates ethical standards, psychologists who know firsthand of such activities attempt to rectify the situation. When such a situation cannot be dealt with informally, it is called to the attention of the appropriate local, state, or national committee on professional ethics, standards, and practices.

b. The psychologist recognizes the boundaries of his competence and the limitations of his techniques and does not offer services or use techniques that fail to meet professional standards established in particular fields. The psychologist who engages in practice assists his client in obtaining professional help for all important aspects of his problem that fall outside the boundaries of his own competence. This principle requires, for example, that provision be made for the diagnosis and treatment of relevant medical problems and for referral to or consultation with other specialists.

c. The psychologist in clinical work recognizes that his effectiveness depends in good part upon his ability to maintain sound interpersonal relations, that temporary or more enduring aberrations in his own personality may interfere with this ability or distort his appraisals of others. There he refrains from undertaking any activity in which his personal problems are likely to result in inferior professional services or harm to a client; or, if he is already engaged in such an activity when he becomes aware of his personal problems, he seeks competent professional assistance to determine whether he should continue or terminate his services to his client.

Principle 3. Moral and Legal Standards. The psychologist in the practice of his profession shows sensible regard for the social codes and moral expectations of the community in which he works, recognizing that violations of accepted moral and legal standards on his part may involve his clients, students, or colleagues in damaging personal conflicts and impugn his own name and the reputation of his profession.

Principle 4. Misrepresentation. The psychologist avoids misrepresentation of his own professional qualifications, affiliations, and purposes, and those of the institutions and organizations with which he is associated.

    a. A psychologist does not claim either directly or by implication professional qualifications that differ from his actual qualifications, nor does he misrepresent his affiliation with any institution, organization, or individual, nor lead others to assume he has affiliations that he does not have. The psychologist is responsible for correcting others who misrepresent his professional qualifications or affiliations.

    b. The psychologist does not misrepresent an institution or organization with which he is affiliated by ascribing to it characteristics that it does not have.

    c. A psychologist does not use his affiliation with the American Psychological Association or its divisions for purposes that are not consonant with the stated purpose of the Association.

    d. A psychologist does not associate himself with or permit his name to be used in connection with any services or products in such a way as to misrepresent them, the degree of his responsibility for them, or the nature of his affiliation.

Principle 5. Public Statements. Modesty, scientific caution, and due regard for the limits of present knowledge characterize all statements of psychologists who supply information to the public, either directly or indirectly.

    a. Psychologists who interpret the science of psychology or the services of psychologists to clients or to the general public have an obligation to report fairly and accurately. Exaggeration, sensationalism, superficiality, and other kinds of misrepresentation are avoided.

    b. When information about psychological procedures and techniques is given, care is taken to indicate that they should be used only by persons adequately trained in their use.

    c. A psychologist who engages in radio or television activities does not participate in commercial announcements recommending purchase or use of a product.

Principle 6. Confidentiality. Safeguarding information about an individual that has been obtained by the psychologist in the course of his teaching, practice, or investigation is a primary obligation of the psychologist. Such information is not communicated to others unless certain important conditions are met.

    a. Information received in confidence is revealed only after most careful deliberation and when there is clear and imminent danger to an individual or to society, and then only to appropriate professional workers or public authorities.

    b. Information obtained in clinical or consulting relationships, or evaluative data concerning children, students, employees, and others are discussed only for professional purposes and only with persons clearly concerned with the case. Written and oral reports should present only data germane to the purposes of the evaluation; every effort should be made to avoid undue invasion of privacy.

    c. Clinical and other materials are used in classroom teaching and writing only when identity of the persons involved is adequately disguised.

    d. The confidentiality of professional communications about

individuals is maintained. Only when the originator and other persons involved give their express permission is a confidential professional communication shown to the individual concerned. The psychologist is responsible for informing the client of the limits of the confidentiality.

e. Only after explicit permission has been granted is the identity of research subjects published. When data have been published without permission for identification, the psychologist assumes responsibility for adequately disguising their sources.

f. The psychologist makes provisions for the maintenance of confidentiality in the preservation and ultimate disposition of confidential records.

Principle 7. Client Welfare. The psychologist respects the integrity and protects the welfare of the person or group with whom he is working.

a. The psychologist in industry, education, and other situations in which conflicts of interest may arise among various parties, as between management and labor, or between the client and employer of the psychologist, defines for himself the nature and direction of his loyalties and responsibilities and keeps all parties concerned informed of these commitments.

b. When there is a conflict among professional workers, the psychologist is concerned primarily with the welfare of any client involved and only secondarily with the interest of his own professional group.

c. The psychologist attempts to terminate a clinical or consulting relationship when it is reasonably clear to the psychologist that the client is not benefiting from it.

d. The psychologist who asks that an individual reveal personal information in the course of interviewing, testing, or evaluation, or who allows such information to be divulged to him, does so only after making certain that the responsible person is fully aware of the purposes of the interview, testing, or evaluation and of the ways in which the information may be used.

e. In cases involving referral, the responsibility of the psychologist for the welfare of the client continues until this responsibility is assumed by the professional person to whom the client is referred or until the relationship with the psychologist making the referral has been terminated by mutual agreement. In situations where referral, consultation, or other changes in the conditions of the treatment are indicated and the client refuses referral, the psychologist carefully weighs the possible harm to the client, to himself, and to his profession that might ensue from continuing the relationship.

f. The psychologist who requires the taking of psychological tests for didactic, classification, or research purposes protects the examinees by ensuring that the tests and test results are used in a professional manner.

g. When potentially disturbing subject matter is presented to students, it is discussed objectively, and efforts are made to handle constructively any difficulties that arise.

h. Care must be taken to ensure an appropriate setting for clinical work to protect both client and psychologist from actual or imputed harm and the profession from censure.

i. In the use of accepted drugs for therapeutic purposes special care needs to be exercised by the psychologist to assure himself that the collaborating physician provides suitable safeguards for the client.

Principle 8. Client Relationship. The psychologist informs his prospective client of the important aspects of the potential relationship that might affect the client's decision to enter the relationship.

a. Aspects of the relationship likely to affect the client's decision include the recording of an interview, the use of interview material for training purposes, and observation of an interview by other persons.

b. When the client is not competent to evaluate the situation (as in the case of a child), the person responsible for the client is informed of the circumstances which may influence the relationship.

c. The psychologist does not normally enter into a professional relationship with members of his own family, intimate friends, close associates, or others whose welfare might be jeopardized by such a dual relationship.

Principle 9. Impersonal Services. Psychological services for the purpose of diagnosis, treatment, or personalized advice are provided only in the context of a professional relationship and are not given by means of public lectures or demonstrations, newspaper or magazine articles, radio or television programs, mail, or similar media.

a. The preparation of personnel reports and recommendations based on test data secured solely by mail is unethical unless such appraisals are an integral part of a continuing client relationship with a company, as a result of which the consulting psychologist has intimate knowledge of the client's personnel situation and can be assured thereby that his written appraisals will be adequate to the purpose and will be properly interpreted by the client. These reports must not be embellished with such detailed analyses of the subject's personality traits as would be appropriate only after intensive interviews with the subject. The reports must not make specific recommendations as to employment or placement of the subject which go beyond the psychologist's knowledge of the job required of the company. The reports must not purport to eliminate the company's need to carry on such other regular employment or personnel practices as appraisal of the work history, checking of references, past performance in the company.

Principle 10. Announcement of Services. A psychologist adheres to professional rather than commercial standards in making known his availability for professional services.

a. A psychologist does not directly solicit clients for individual diagnosis or therapy.

b. Individual listing in telephone directories are limited to name, highest relevant degree, certification status, address, and telephone number. They may also include identification in a few words of the psychologist's major areas of practice; for example, child therapy, personnel selection, industrial psychology. Agency listings are equally modest.

c. Announcements of individual private practice are limited to a simple statement of the name, highest relevant degree, certification or diplomate status, address, telephone number, office hours, and a brief explanation of the types of services rendered. Announcements of agencies may list names of staff members with their qualifications. They conform in other particulars with the same standards as individual announcements, making certain that the true nature of the organization is apparent.

d. A psychologist or agency announcing nonclinical professional services may use brochures that are descriptive of services rendered but not evaluative. They may be sent to professional persons, schools, business firms, government agencies, and other similar organizations.

e. The use in a brochure of "testimonials from satisfied users" is unacceptable. The offer of a free trial of services is unacceptable if it operates to misrepresent in any way the nature or the efficacy of the services rendered by the psychologist. Claims that a psychologist has unique skills or unique devices not available to others in the profession are made only if the special efficacy of these unique skills or devices has been demonstrated by scientifically acceptable evidence.

f. The psychologist must not encourage (nor, within his power, even allow) a client to have exaggerated ideas as to the efficacy of services rendered. Claims made to clients about the efficacy of his services must not go beyond those which the psychologist would be willing to subject to professional scrutiny through publishing his results and his claims in a professional journal.

Principle 11. Interprofessional Relations. A psychologist acts with integrity in regard to colleagues in psychology and in other professions.

a. A psychologist does not normally offer professional

services to a person receiving psychological assistance from another professional worker except by agreement with the other worker or after the termination of the client's relationship with the other professional worker.

b. The welfare of clients and colleagues requires that psychologists in joint practice or corporate activities make an orderly and explicit arrangement regarding the conditions of their association and its possible termination. Psychologists who serve as employers of other psychologists have an obligation to make similar appropriate arrangements.

Principle 12. Remuneration. Financial arrangements in professional practice are in accord with professional standards that safeguard the best interest of the client and the profession.

a. In establishing rates for professional services, the psychologist considers carefully both the ability of the client to meet the financial burden and the charges made by other professional persons engaged in comparable work. He is willing to contribute a portion of his services to work for which he receives little or no financial return.

b. No commission or rebate or any other form of remuneration is given or received for referral of clients for professional services.

c. The psychologist in clinical or counseling practice does not use his relationships with clients to promote, for personal gain or the profit of an agency, commercial enterprises of any kind.

d. A psychologist does not accept a private fee or any other form of remuneration for professional work with a person who is entitled to his services through an institution or agency. The policies of a particular agency may make explicit provision for private work with its clients by members of its staff, and in such instances the client must be fully apprised of all policies affecting him.

Principle 13. Test Security. Psychological tests and other assessment devices, the value of which depends in part on the naïveté of the subject, are not reproduced or described in popular publications in ways that might invalidate the techniques. Access to such devices is limited to persons with professional interests who will safeguard their use.

    a. Sample items made up to resemble those of tests being discussed may be reproduced in popular articles and elsewhere, but scorable tests and actual test items are not reproduced except in professional publications.

    b. The psychologist is responsible for the control of psychological tests and other devices and procedures used for instruction when their value might be damaged by revealing to the general public their specific contents or underlying principles.

Principle 14. Test Interpretation. Test scores, like test materials, are released only to persons who are qualified to interpret and use them properly.

    a. Materials for reporting test scores to parents, or which are designed for self-appraisal purposes in schools, social agencies, or industry are closely supervised by qualified psychologists or counselors with provisions for referring and counseling individuals when needed.

    b. Test results or other assessment data used for evaluation or classification are communicated to employers, relatives, or other appropriate persons in such a manner as to guard against misinterpretation or misuse. In the usual case, an interpretation of the test result rather than the score is communicated.

    c. When test results are communicated directly to parents and students, they are accompanied by adequate interpretive aids or advice.

Principle 15. Test Publication. Psychological tests are offered for commercial publication only to publishers who present their tests in a professional way and distribute them only to qualified users.

    a. A test manual, technical handbook, or other suitable report on the test is provided which describes the method of constructing and standardizing the test and summarizes the validation research.

    b. The populations for which the test has been developed

and the purposes for which it is recommended are stated in the manual. Limitations upon the test's dependability, and aspects of its validity on which research is lacking or incomplete, are clearly stated. In particular, the manual contains a warning regarding interpretations likely to be made which have not yet been substantiated by research.

c. The catalog and manual indicate the training or professional qualifications required for sound interpretation of the test.

d. The test manual and supporting documents take into account the principles enunciated in the *Standards for Educational and Psychological Tests and Manuals.*

e. Test advertisements are factual and descriptive rather than emotional and persuasive.

Principle 16. Research Precautions. The psychologist assumes obligations for the welfare of his research subjects, both animal and human.

a. Only when a problem is of scientific significance and is not practicable to investigate it in any other way is the psychologist justified in exposing research subjects, whether children or adults, to physical or emotional stress as part of an investigation.

b. When a reasonable possibility of injurious aftereffects exists, research is conducted only when the subjects or their responsible agents are fully informed of this possibility and agree to participate nevertheless.

c. The psychologist seriously considers the possibility of harmful aftereffects and avoids them, or removes them as soon as permitted by the design of the experiment.

d. A psychologist using animals in research adheres to the provisions of the Rules Regarding Animals, drawn up by the Committee on Precautions and Standards in Animal Experimentation and adopted by the American Psychological Association.

e. Investigations of human subjects using experimental drugs (for example, hallucinogenic, psychotomimetic, psychedelic, or similar substances) should be conducted only in such settings as clinics, hospitals, or research facilities maintaining appropriate safeguards for the subjects.

Principle 17. Publication Credit. Credit is assigned to those who have contributed to a publication, in proportion to their contribution, and only to these.

  a. Major contributions of a professional character, made by several persons to a common project, are recognized by joint authorship. The experimenter or author who has made the principal contribution to a publication is identified as the first listed.

  b. Minor contributions of a professional character, extensive clerical or similar nonprofessional assistance, and other minor contributions are acknowledged in footnotes or in an introductory statement.

  c. Acknowledgment through specific citations is made for unpublished as well as published material that has directly influenced the research or writing.

  d. A psychologist who compiles and edits for publication the contributions of others publishes the symposium or report under the title of the committee or symposium, with his own name appearing as chairman or editor among those of the other contributors or committee members.

Principle 18. Responsibility toward Organization. A psychologist respects the rights and reputation of the institute or organization with which his is associated.

  a. Materials prepared by a psychologist as a part of his regular work under specific direction of his organization are the property of that organization. Such materials are released for use or publication by a psychologist in accordance with policies of authorization, assignment of credit, and related matters which have been established by his organization.

  b. Other material resulting incidentally from activity supported by any agency, and for which the psychologist rightly assumes individual responsibility, is published with disclaimer for any responsibility on the part of the supporting agency.

Principle 19. Promotional Activities. The psychologist associated with the development or promotion of psychological devices, books, or other products offered for commercial sale is responsible for ensuring that such devices, books, or products are presented in a professional and factual way.

a. Claims regarding performance, benefits, or results are supported by scientifically accepted evidence.

b. The psychologist does not use professional journals for the commercial exploitation of psychological products, and the psychologist-editor guards against such misuse.

c. The psychologist with a financial interest in the sale or use of a psychological product is sensitive to possible conflict of interest in his promotion of such products and avoids compromise of his professional responsibilities and objectives.

INDEX OF SUBJECTS

INDEX OF NAMES